Ford Escort Owners Workshop Manual

D0996993

J H Haynes
Member of the Guild of Motoring Writers

Models covered
All models of Escort and Escort Popular in Saloon and Estate car forms, including Linnet, Harrier and Goldcrest versions, with 1100, 1300 and 1600 ohv engines.

ISBN 0 85696 553 7

Printed in England   *(280 - 1K3)*

HAYNES PUBLISHING GROUP
SPARKFORD YEOVIL SOMERSET BA22 7JJ ENGLAND
distributed in the USA by
HAYNES PUBLICATIONS INC
861 LAWRENCE DRIVE
NEWBURY PARK
CALIFORNIA 91320
USA

Acknowledgements

Thanks are due to the Ford Motor Company Limited for the supply of certain illustrations and technical material, to Castrol Limited who provided lubrication data and to the Champion Sparking Plug Company Limited who provided the colour illustrations showing the various spark plug conditions. The bodywork repair photographs used in this manual were provided by Holt Lloyd Limited who supply 'Turtle Wax', 'Dupli-Color Holts', and other Holts range products.

Two Ford dealerships were also very helpful, these being Douglas Seaton Limited of Yeovil, and White Brothers Limited of Taunton.

Last, but not least, thanks are due to all those people at Sparkford who assisted in the production of this manual.

About this manual

Its aim

The aim of this manual is to help you get the best value from your car. It can do so in several ways. It can help you decide what work must be done (even should you choose to get it done by a garage), provide information on routine maintenance and servicing, and give a logical course of action and diagnosis when random faults occur. However, it is hoped that you will use the manual by tackling the work yourself. On simpler jobs it may even be quicker than booking the car into a garage and going there twice to leave and collect it. Perhaps most important, a lot of money can be saved by avoiding the costs the garage must charge to cover its labour and overheads.

The manual has drawings and descriptions to show the function of the various components so that their layout can be understood. Then the tasks are described and photographed in a step-by-step sequence so that even a novice can do the work.

Its arrangement

The manual is divided into thirteen Chapters, each covering a logical sub-division of the vehicle. The Chapters are each divided into Sections, numbered with single figures, eg 5; and the Sections into paragraphs (or sub-sections), with decimal numbers following on from the Section they are in, eg 5.1, 5.2, 5.3 etc.

It is freely illustrated, especially in those parts where there is a detailed sequence of operations to be carried out. There are two forms of illustration: figures and photographs. The figures are numbered in sequence with decimal numbers, according to their position in the Chapter — eg Fig. 6.4 is the fourth drawing/illustration in Chapter 6. Photographs carry the same number (either individually or in related groups) as the Section or sub-section to which they relate.

There is an alphabetical index at the back of the manual as well as a contents list at the front. Each Chapter is also preceded by its own individual contents list.

References to the 'left' or 'right' of the vehicle are in the sense of a person in the driver's seat facing forwards.

Unless otherwise stated, nuts and bolts are removed by turning anti-clockwise, and tightened by turning clockwise.

Whilst every care is taken to ensure that the information in this manual is correct, no liability can be accepted by the authors or publishers for loss, damage or injury caused by any errors in, or omissions from, the information given.

Introduction to the Escort

The range of cars covered by this manual was introduced in January 1975 as front engine/rear drive models, and finished in the autumn of 1980 when the new front wheel drive version was announced.

All models are powered by the well-proven Kent ohv engine in 1100, 1300 and 1600cc forms and the range embraces a wide range of options in performance, body style and trim levels.

In virtually all respects the car can be described as conventional. It has independent Macpherson strut front suspension, and a live axle with leaf springs at the rear. Drum brakes are fitted at the rear but, according to the particular model, disc or drum brakes may be fitted at the front. Automatic transmission is available on certain 1300 and 1600cc models.

Contents

Escort 1.3 GL 4 - door saloon

Escort Popular Plus

Escort Ghia 1600 Automatic 2-door saloon

Escort L Estate

General dimensions and weights

Dimensions

Wheel base, mm (in)	2407 (94.7)
Track, mm (in):	
Front (12 in wheels)	1258 (49.5)
Front (13 in wheels)	1270 (50.0)
Rear (12 in wheels)	1284 (50.6)
Rear (13 in wheels)	1296 (51.0)
Overall width, mm (in):	
Saloon	1596 (62.8)
Estate	1564 (61.6)
Overall height, mm (in):	
Saloon	1398 (55.1)
Estate	1414 (55.7)
Overall length, with bumper overrider, mm (in):	
Saloon	3978 (156.6)
Estate	4056 (159.7)
Van	3994 (157.2)
Turning circle, m (ft):	
Between kerbs	8.9 (29.2)
Between walls	9.8 (32.1)

Nominal kerb weights kg (lb)

Model	2dr Saloon	4dr Saloon	Estate Car
1.1	875 (1930)	905 (1995)	910 (2005)
1.3	880 (1940)	915 (2006)	920 (2030)
1.3 Sport	885 (1950)	—	—
1.3 Ghia	910 (2005)	940 (2070)	—
1.6 Sport	900 (1985)	—	—
1.6 Ghia	—	955 (2105)	—

Maximum roof rack load kg (lb) 75 (165)

Buying spare parts
and vehicle identification numbers

Buying spare parts

Spare parts are available from many sources, for example: Ford garages, other garages and accessory shops, and motor factors. Our advice regarding spare part sources is as follows:

Officially appointed Ford garages - This is the best source of parts which are peculiar to your car and are otherwise not generally available (eg; complete cylinder heads, internal gearbox components, badges, interior trim etc). It is also the only place at which you should buy parts if your car is still under warranty - non-Ford components may invalidate the warranty. To be sure of obtaining the correct parts it will always be necessary to give the storeman your car's vehicle identification number, and if possible, to take the 'old' part along for positive identification. Remember that many parts are available on a factory exchange scheme - any parts returned should always be clean! It obviously makes good sense to go straight to the specialists on your car for this type of part for they are best equipped to supply you.

Other garages and accessory shops - These are often very good places to buy materials and components needed for the maintenance of your car (eg; oil filters, spark plugs, bulbs, fan belts, oils and greases, touch-up paint, filler paste etc). They also sell general accessories, usually have convenient opening hours, charge lower prices and can often be found not far from home.

Motor factors - Good factors will stock all of the more important components which wear out relatively quickly (eg; clutch components, pistons, valves, exhaust systems, brake cylinders/pipes/hoses/seals/shoes and pads etc). Motor factors will often provide new or reconditioned components on a part exchange basis - this can save a considerable amount of money.

Vehicle identification numbers

Although many individual parts, and in some cases sub-assemblies, fit a number of different models it is dangerous to assume that just because they look the same, they are the same. Differences are not always easy to detect except by serial numbers. Make sure therefore, that the appropriate identity number for the model or sub-assembly is known and quoted when a spare part is ordered.

The vehicle identification plate is mounted on the right-hand side of the front body panel and may be seen once the bonnet is open. Record the numbers from your car on the blank spaces of the accompanying illustration. You can then take the manual with you when buying parts ; also the exploded drawings throughout the manual can be used to point out and identify the components required.

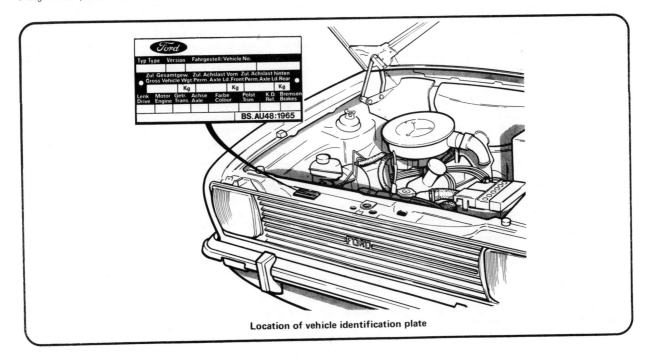

Location of vehicle identification plate

Tools and working facilities

Introduction

A selection of good tools is a fundamental requirement for anyone contemplating the maintenance and repair of a motor vehicle. For the owner who does not possess any, their purchase will prove a considerable expense, offsetting some of the savings made by doing-it-yourself. However, provided that the tools purchased are of good quality, they will last for many years and prove an extremely worthwhile investment.

To help the average owner to decide which tools are needed to carry out the various tasks detailed in this manual, we have compiled three lists of tools under the following headings: Maintenance and minor repair; Repair and overhaul; and Special. The newcomer to practical mechanics should start off with the 'Maintenance and minor repair' tool kit and confine himself to the simpler jobs around the vehicle. Then , as his confidence and experience grows, he can undertake more difficult tasks, buying extra tools as, and when, they are needed. In this way a 'Maintenance and minor repair' tool kit can be built-up into a 'Repair and overhaul' tool kit over a considerable period of time without any major cash outlays. The experienced do-it-yourselfer will have a tool kit good enough for most repair and overhaul procedures and will add tools from the 'Special' category when he feels the expense is justified by the amount of use these tools will be put to.

It is obviously not possible to cover the subject of tools fully here. For those who wish to learn more about tools and their use there is a book entitled 'How to Choose and Use Car Tools' available from the publishers of this manual.

Maintenance and minor repair tool kit

The tools given in this list should be considered as a minimum requirement if routine maintenance, servicing and minor repair operations are to be undertaken. We recommend the purchase of combination spanners (ring one end, open-ended the other); although more expensive than open-ended ones, they do give the advantages of both types of spanner.

Combination spanners - 7/16, 1/2, 9/16, 5/8, 11/16, 3/4 AF
Combination spanners - 10, 11, 13, 14, 17 mm
Adjustable spanner - 9 inch
Engine sump/gearbox/rear axle drain plug key (where applicable)
Spark plug spanner (with rubber insert)
Spark plug gap adjustment tool
Set of feeler gauges
Brake adjuster spanner (where applicable)
Brake bleed nipple spanner
Screwdriver - 4 in. long x ¼ in. dia. (plain)
Screwdriver - 4 in. long x ¼ in. dia. (crosshead)
Combination pliers - 6 in.
Hacksaw, junior
Tyre pump
Tyre pressure gauge
Grease gun (where applicable)
Oil can
Fine emery cloth (1 sheet)
Wire brush (small)
Funnel (medium size)

Repair and overhaul tool kit

These tools are virtually essential for anyone undertaking any major repairs to a motor vehicle, and are additional to those given in the Basic list. Included in this list is a comprehensive set of sockets. Although these are expensive they will be found invaluable as they are so versatile - particularly if various drives are included in the set. We recommend the ½ in. square-drive type, as this can be used with most proprietary torque wrenches. If you cannot afford a socket set, even bought piecemeal, then inexpensive tubular box spanners are a useful alternative.

The tools in this list will occasionally need to be supplemented by tools from the Special list.

Sockets (or box spanners) to cover range 6 to 27 mm
Reversible ratchet drive (for use with sockets)
Extension piece, 10 inch (for use with sockets)
Universal joint (for use with sockets)
Torque wrench (for use with sockets)
'Mole' wrench - 8 inch
Ball pein hammer
Soft-faced hammer, plastic or rubber
Screwdriver - 6 in. long x 5/16 in. dia. (plain)
Screwdriver - 2 in. long x 5/16 in. square (plain)
Screwdriver - 1½ in. long x ¼ in. dia. (crosshead)
Screwdriver - 3 in. long x 1/8 in. dia. (electricians)
Pliers - electricians side cutters
Pliers - needle nosed
Pliers - circlip (internal and external)
Cold chisel - ½ inch
Scriber (this can be made by grinding the end of a broken hacksaw blade)
Scraper (this can be made by flattening and sharpening one end of a piece of copper pipe)
Centre punch
Pin punch
Hacksaw
Valve grinding tool
Steel rule/straight edge
Allen keys
Selection of files
Wire brush (large)
Axle stands
Jack (strong scissor or hydraulic type)

Special tools

The tools in this list are those which are not used regularly, are expensive to buy, or which need to be used in accordance with their manufacturers instructions. Unless relatively difficult mechanical jobs are undertaken frequently, it will not be economic to buy many of these tools. Where this is the case, you could consider clubbing together with friends (or a motorists club) to make a joint purchase, or borrowing the tools against a deposit from a local garage or tool hire specialist.

The following list contains only those tools and instruments freely available to the public, and not those special tools produced by the vehicle manufacturer specifically for its dealer network. You will find occasional references to these manufacturers special tools in the text of this manual. Generally, an alternative method of doing the job without the vehicle manufacturers special tool is given. However, sometimes there is no alternative to using them. Where this is the case and the relevant tool cannot be bought or borrowed you will have to entrust the work to a franchised garage.

Valve spring compressor
Piston ring compressor
Ball joint separator
Universal hub/bearing puller
Impact screwdriver
Micrometer and/or vernier gauge
Carburettor flow balancing device (where applicable)
Dial gauge
Stroboscopic timing light
Dwell angle meter/tachometer
Universal electrical multi-meter
Cylinder compression gauge
Lifting tackle
Trolley jack
Light with extension lead

Buying tools

For practically all tools, a tool factor is the best source since he will have a very comprehensive range compared with the average garage or accessory shop. Having said that, accessory shops often offer excellent quality tools at discount prices, so it pays to shop around.

Remember, you don't have to buy the most expensive items on the shelf, but it is always advisable to steer clear of the very cheap tools. There are plenty of good tools around, at reasonable prices, so ask the proprietor or manager of the shop for advice before making a purchase.

Care and maintenance of tools

Having purchased a reasonable tool kit, it is necessary to keep the tools in a clean and serviceable condition. After use, always wipe off any dirt, grease and metal particles using a clean, dry cloth, before putting the tools away. Never leave them lying around after they have been used. A simple tool rack on the garage or workshop wall, for items such as screwdrivers and pliers is a good idea. Store all normal spanners and sockets in a metal box. Any measuring instruments, gauges, meters etc., must be carefully stored where they cannot be damaged or become rusty.

Take a little care when the tools are used. Hammer heads inevitably become marked and screwdrivers lose the keen edge on their blades from time-to-time. A little timely attention with emery cloth or a file will soon restore items like this to a good serviceable finish.

Working Facilities

Not to be forgotten when discussing tools, is the workshop itself; if anything more than routine maintenance is to be carried out, some form of suitable working area becomes essential.

It is appreciated that many an owner mechanic is forced by circumstance to remove an engine or similar item, without the benefit of a garage or workshop. Having done this, any repairs should always be done under the cover of a roof.

Wherever possible, any dismantling should be done on a clean flat workbench or table at a suitable working height.

Any workbench needs a vice; one with a jaw opening of 4 in (100 mm) is suitable for most jobs. As mentioned previously, some clean dry storage space is also required for tools, as well as the lubricants, cleaning fluids, touch-up paints and so on which soon become necessary.

Another item which may be required, and which has a much more general usage, is an electric drill with a chuck capacity of at least 5/16 in. (8 mm). This, together with a good range of twist drills, is virtually essential for fitting accessories such as wing mirrors and reversing lights.

Last, but not least, always keep a supply of old newspapers and clean, lint-free rags available, and try to keep any working area as clean as possible.

Spanner jaw gap comparison table

Jaw gap (in)	Spanner size
0.250	1/4 in. AF
0.276	7 mm
0.313	5/16 in. AF
0.315	8 mm
0.344	11/32 in AF 1/8 in Whitworth
0.354	9 mm
0.375	3/8 in. AF
0.394	10 mm
0.433	11 mm
0.438	7/16 in. AF
0.445	3/16 in. Whitworth 1/4 in. BSF
0.472	12 mm
0.500	1/2 in. AF
0.512	13 mm
0.525	1/4 in. Whitworth 5/16 in. BSF
0.551	14 mm
0.563	9/16 in. AF
0.591	15 mm
0.600	5/16 in. Whitworth 3/8 in. BSF
0.625	5/8 in. AF
0.630	16 mm
0.669	17 mm
0.686	11/16 in. AF
0.709	18 mm
0.710	3/8 in. Whitworth 7/16 in. BSF
0.748	19 mm
0.750	3/4 in. AF
0.813	13/16 in. AF
0.820	7/16 in. Whitworth 1/2 in. BSF
0.866	22 mm
0.875	7/8 in. AF
0.920	1/2 in. Whitworth 9/16 in. BSF
0.938	15/16 in. AF
0.945	24 mm
1.000	1 in. AF
1.010	9/16 in. Whitworth 5/8 in. BSF
1.024	26 mm
1.063	1 1/16 in. AF 27 mm
1.100	5/8 in. Whitworth 11/16 in. BSF
1.125	1 1/18 in. AF
1.181	30 mm
1.200	11/16 in. Whitworth 3/4 in. BSF
1.250	1 1/4 in. AF
1.260	32 mm
1.300	3/4 in. Whitworth 7/8 in. BSF
1.313	1 5/16 in. AF
1.390	13/16 in. Whitworth 15/16 in. BSF
1.417	36 mm
1.438	1 7/16 in AF
1.480	7/8 in Whitworth 1 in. BSF
1.500	1 1/2 in. AF
1.575	40 mm 15/16 in. Whitworth
1.614	41 mm
1.625	1 5/8 in. AF
1.670	1 in. Whitworth 1 1/8 in. BSF
1.688	1 11/16 in. AF
1.811	46 mm
1.813	1 13/16 in. AF
1.860	1 1/8 in. Whitworth 1 1/4 in. BSF
1.875	1 7/8 in. AF
1.969	50 mm
2.000	2 in. AF
2.050	1 1/4 in. Whitworth 1 3/8 in. BSF
2.165	55 mm
2.362	60 mm

A Haltrac hoist and gantry in use during a typical engine removal sequence

Jacking and Towing

Jacking points

To change a wheel in an emergency, use the jack supplied with the vehicle, standing it on firm level ground. Fully apply the handbrake and chock the diagonally opposite wheel. Loosen the roadwheel nuts then push the jack arm into the sleeve below the side sill panel. On saloon models one sleeve is provided on each side, whereas on estate and van models two are provided, one for each wheel. Position the jack vertically and turn the handle to raise the wheel off the ground.

Where maintenance or repairs are being carried out, use a hydraulic or screw-type jack located beneath the front cross-member, bodyframe side-members or rear axle casing. Always supplement the jack with axle stands or blocks before crawling beneath the car.

Towing points

If your vehicle is being towed, attach the tow-rope to the front crossmember or towing eye (where fitted). If you are towing another vehicle, attach the tow-rope to the left-hand side spring seat or towing eye (where fitted). Note that the ignition key must be in position II when being towed so that the steering lock is released.

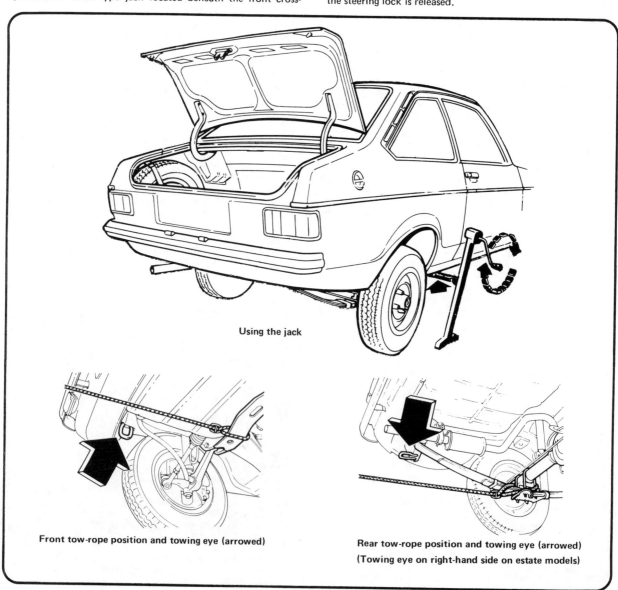

Using the jack

Front tow-rope position and towing eye (arrowed)

Rear tow-rope position and towing eye (arrowed)
(Towing eye on right-hand side on estate models)

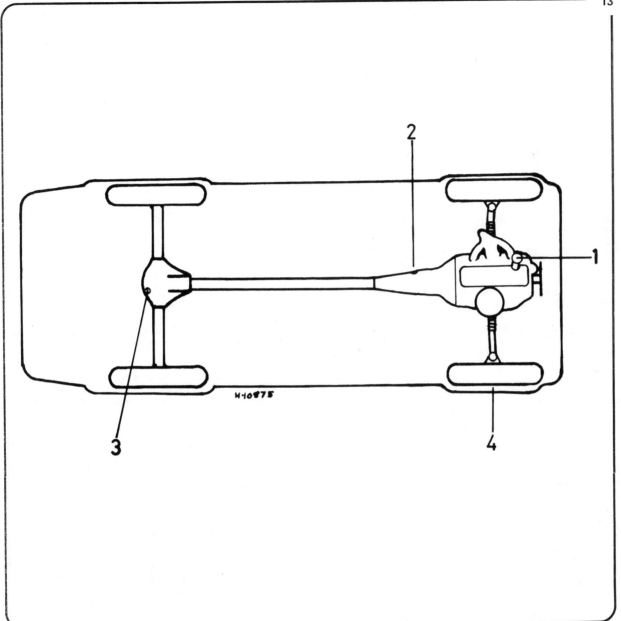

H·10875

Recommended lubricants

Component or System	Lubricant Type or Specification	Castrol Product
Engine (1)	Multigrade engine oil	Castrol GTX
Gearbox (2)		
Manual	SAE 80EP hypoid gear oil	Castrol Hypoy Light
Automatic	Automatic transmission fluid	Castrol TQF
Rear axle (3)	SAE 90EP hypoid gear oil	Castrol Hypoy B
Front wheel bearings (4)	Multi-purpose lithium based grease ...	Castrol LM Grease

Note: *The above recommendations are general and are intended for guidance only. Lubrication requirements vary from territory-to-territory and depend upon vehicle useage. If in doubt, consult the operators handbook supplied with the vehicle.*

Routine maintenance

The maintenance instructions listed below are basically those recommended by the manufacturer. They are supplemented by additional maintenance tasks which, through practical experience, the author recommends should be carried out at the intervals suggested. Figure numbers correspond with paragraph numbers. Where no illustration is show, refer to Chapter indicated.

Weekly or every 250 miles (400 km)

1 Check the level of the engine oil: With the vehicle standing on level ground, withdraw the dipstick, wipe it with a piece of non-fluffy cloth, re-insert it and then withdraw it again - read off the oil level. Keep the oil level between the 'MIN' and 'MAX' marks.

2 Check the battery electrolyte level: This should be maintained at a level just above the tops of the plates by the addition of distilled water only.

3 Check the coolant level in the radiator: Add soft water if necessary to bring the level to within not more than ½ inch (12.7 mm) of the bottom of the filler neck.

4 Check the fluid level in the automatic transmission unit (where fitted): This must be checked with the oil hot after at least five miles (8 km) road running. Refer to Chapter 6, Section 19.

5 Check the brake reservoir fluid level: Wipe any dirt from mark with recommended fluid taken from a sealed tin. With dual circuit braking systems, keep reservoir level above dividing baffle.

6 Top-up windscreen washer fluid container: Add a recommended quantity of washer cleaning fluid to the water as a grease solvent and to prevent freezing.

7 Check tyre pressures (including the spare): Check when tyres are cold and inflate as necessary to pressures given in Specifications, Chapter 11.

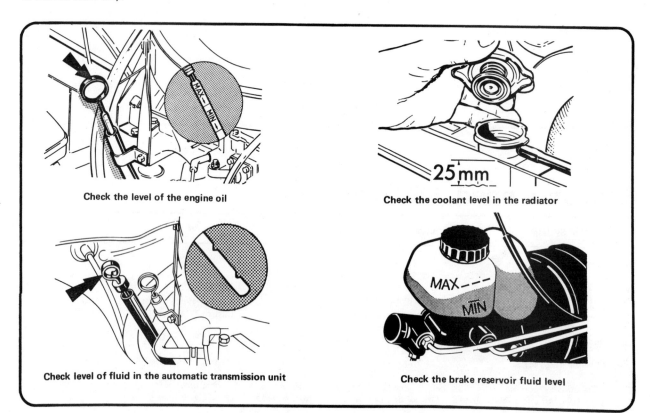

Check the level of the engine oil

Check the coolant level in the radiator

Check level of fluid in the automatic transmission unit

Check the brake reservoir fluid level

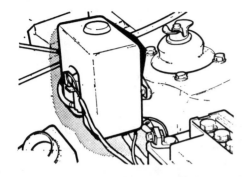

Top up the windscreen washer fluid reservoir

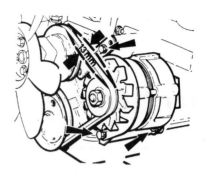

Check fan belt tension and adjust if necessary

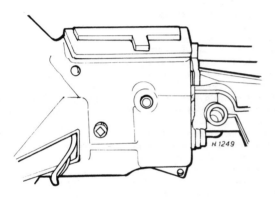

Check manual gearbox oil level

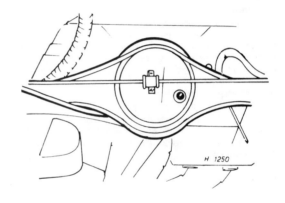

Check rear axle oil level

Six monthly or every 6000 miles (10,000 km)
Twelve monthly or every 12,000 miles (20,000 km)
from 1979

8   Drain engine oil and renew filter (Chapter 1).
9   Check ignition timing, adjust if necessary, check operation of advance/retard mechanism.
10 Clean spark plugs and set gap (Chapter 4).
11 Clean and adjust (or renew) distributor contact points.
12 Check and adjust if necessary carburettor idling and mixture (Chapter 3).
13 Check battery terminals for tightness. Grease terminals.
14 Check and adjust valve clearances (cold).
15 Check fan belt tension and adjust if necessary.
16 Check tightness of alternator mounting bolts.
17 Check manual gearbox oil level: Remove the plug on the side of the casing and inject oil of the recommended grade until it begins to run out. Refit the plug. Draining of the gearbox is not specified by Ford and no drain plug is provided.
18 Check rear axle oil level: Remove the plug from the rear of the casing and inject oil until it begins to run out. Refit the plug. Draining of the rear axle is not specified by Ford and no drain plug is provided.
19 Lubricate accelerator linkage, adjust cable.
20 Adjust drum brakes and check linings for wear.
21 Check front disc brakes for pad wear.
22 Check brake flexible hoses for deterioration (Chapter 9).
23 Check all cooling system hoses for deterioration (Chapter 2).

24 Check exhaust system for damage or leaks (Chapter 3).
25 Check steering ball joints for wear or damaged rubber dust excluders (Chapter 11).
26 Check steering gear rubber bellows for deterioration.
27 Check clutch free-movement and adjust if necessary (Chapter 5).
28 Check tightness of exhaust manifold and downpipe bolts.
29 Oil all engine controls, door hinges and locks etc.
30 Check condition of steering shaft flexible coupling and renew if necessary.
31 Clean HT leads, check for security.
32 Check operation of all lights.
33 Check condition/operation of seat belts.

Eighteen monthly or every 18,000 miles (29,000 km)

34 Clean crankcase emission valve and oil filler cap.
35 Renew air cleaner element.
36 Check torque of rear spring 'U' bolts.

Every two years or 36,000 miles (60,000 km)

37 Clean, repack with grease and adjust front wheel bearings.
38 Renew all flexible brake hoses, cylinder seals and hydraulic fluid within the system (Chapter 9).
39 Renew coolant antifreeze.

Chapter 1 Engine

For modifications, and information applicable to later models, see Supplement at end of manual

Contents

Specifications

1100 Engine

Engine

Camshaft position	In crankcase on right			
Valve control	By rockers and pushrods			
Firing order	1 - 2 - 4 - 3			
Bore	80,98 mm (3.188 in.)			
Stroke	53,29 mm (2.098 in.)			
Swept volume	1097 cc			
Idling speed	800 ± 25 rpm			
Maximum continuous speed	5800 rpm			
	1,1 lc	**1,1 hc**	**1,1 2v**	
Engine coding	G1B	G2C	G3A	
Compression ratio	8.0 : 1	9.0 : 1	9.0 : 1	
Compression at starter speed	9 to 11 kp.cm^2	10 to 12 kp.cm^2	10 to 12 kp.cm^2	
	(128 to 156 lbf.in^2)	(142 to 170 lbf.in^2)	(142 to 170 lbf.in^2)	
Mean working pressure	8,23 kp.cm^2	8.58 kp.cm^2	8,58 kp.cm^2	
	(117 lbf.in^2)	(122 lbf.in^2)	(122 lbf.in^2)	
Engine output (DIN)	32 kW (44 HP)	35 kW (48 HP)	42 kW (57 HP)	
	at 5500 rpm	at 5500 rpm	at 5500 rpm	
Torque (DIN)	71 Nm (7,2 m.kp)	74 Nm (7,5 m.kp)	77 Nm (7,7 m.kp)	
	at 3000 rpm	at 3000 rpm	at 4000 rpm	

Cylinder Block

Cast cylinder block marking	711M-6015-A-A
Number of main bearings	5
Cylinder liner bore	84,112 to 84,175 mm (3.311 to 3.314 in.)
Cylinder bore diameter	
A (standard)	80,947 to 80,957 mm (3.1869 to 3.1873 in.)
B	80,957 to 80,967 mm (3.1873 to 3.1877 in.)
C	80,967 to 80,977 mm (3.1877 to 3.1880 in.)
D	80,977 to 80,987 mm (3.1880 to 3.1885 in.)
E	80,987 to 80,997 mm (3.1885 to 3.1889 in.)
F	80,997 to 81,007 mm (3.1889 to 3.1893 in.)
Bearing width	26,822 to 26,873 mm (1.056 to 1.058 in.)
Fitted main bearing shells, vertical interior diameter	54,013 to 54,044 mm (2.126 to 2.128 in.)
Undersize - 0,254 mm (0.010 in.)	53,759 to 53,790 mm (2.116 to 2.118 in.)
Undersize - 0,508 mm (0.020 in.)	53,505 to 53,536 mm (2.106 to 2.108 in.)
Undersize - 0,762 mm (0.030 in.)	53,251 to 53,282 mm (2.096 to 2.098 in.)
Main bearing bore (in block):	
Standard	57,683 to 57,696 mm (2.271 to 2.272 in.)
Oversize	58,064 to 58,077 mm (2.286 to 2.287 in.)
Camshaft bearing bore (in block):	
Standard	42,888 to 42,913 mm (1.689 to 1.690 in.)
Oversize	+0,508 mm (+0.020 in.)

Crankshaft

Main journal diameter - Standard	53,983 to 54,003 mm (2.125 to 2.126 in.)
Undersize - 0,254 mm (0.010 in.)	53,729 to 53,749 mm (2.115 to 2.116 in.)
Undersize - 0,508 mm (0.020 in.)	53,475 to 53,495 mm (2.105 to 2.106 in.)
Undersize - 0.762 mm (0.030 in.)	53,221 to 53,241 mm (2.095 to 2.096 in.)
Crankshaft endfloat	0,075 to 0,280 mm (0.003 to 0.011 in.)
Length of main bearing shell	25,273 to 25,527 mm (0.995 to 1.005 in.)
Play in main journal bearing shell	0,010 to 0,061 mm (0.0004 to 0.0024 in.)
Crank pin diameter - Standard	49,195 to 49,215 mm (1.937 to 1.938 in.)
Undersize - 0,05 mm (0.002 in.)	49,144 to 49,164 mm (1.935 to 1.936 in.)
Undersize - 0,25 mm (0.010 in.)	48,941 to 48,961 mm (1.927 to 1.928 in.)
Undersize - 0,51 mm (0.020 in.)	48,687 to 48,707 mm (1.917 to 1.918 in.)
Undersize - 0,76 mm (0.030 in.)	48,433 to 48,453 mm (1.907 to 1.908 in.)
Undersize - 1.02 mm (0.040 in.)	48,179 to 48,199 mm (1.897 to 1.898 in.)

Camshaft

Coding (paint ring):	
1,1 LC	Yellow
1,1 HC	Yellow
1,1 2V	Red/white
Drive	By chain with tensioner
Thickness of camshaft retaining plate	4,470 to 4,520 mm (0.176 to 0.178 in.)
Cam lift:	
Inlet	5,985 to 5,866 mm (0.236 to 0.231 in.)
Exhaust	5,894 mm (0.232 in.)
Length of cams (between heel and tip):	
Inlet	33,417 to 33,298 mm (1.316 to 1.311 in.)
Exhaust	33,326 mm (1.312 in.)
Camshaft bearing diameter - Front, centre, rear	39,616 to 39,637 mm (1.560 to 1.561 in.)
Bearing bush internal diameter - Front, centre, rear	39,662 to 39,675 mm (1.561 to 1.562 in.)
Camshaft endfloat	0,06 to 0,2 mm (0.002 to 0.008 in.)

Pistons

Piston diameter (Standard):	
Grade E	80,954 to 80,964 mm (3.187 to 3.1875 in.)
Grade F	80,964 to 80,974 mm (3.1875 to 3.188 in.)
Piston diameter (Oversize):	0.064 mm (0.0025 in.)
Grade E	81,018 to 81,028 mm (3.1896 to 3.190 in.)
Grade F	81,028 to 81,038 mm (3.190 to 3.1904 in.)
Piston to bore clearance	0,023 to 0,043 mm (0.0009 to 0.0016 in.)
Ring gap (fitted in bore):	
Top	0,23 to 0,36 mm (0.009 to 0.014 in.)
Centre	0,23 to 0,36 mm (0.009 to 0.0014 in.)
Bottom	0,23 to 0,36 mm (0.009 to 0.014 in.)

Gudgeon Pins

Length of gudgeon pin	70,99 to 71,37 mm (2.795 to 2.810 in.)
Pin diameter:	
1	20,622 to 20,625 mm (0.8119 to 0.8120 in.)
2	20,625 to 20,627 mm (0.8120 to 0.8121 in.)
3	20,627 to 20,630 mm (0.8121 to 0.8122 in.)
4	20,630 to 20,632 mm (0.8122 to 0.8123 in.)
Pin interference in piston at 21°C (70°F)	0,003 to 0,008 mm (0.0001 to 0.0003 in.)
Clearance in connecting rod at 21°C (70°F)	0,004 to 0,010 mm (0.0002 to 0.0004 in.)

Connecting Rods

Bore diameter of big-end	52,89 to 52,91 mm (2.082 to 2.083 in.)
Bore diameter of small end:	
White	20,629 to 20,632 mm (0.8122 to 0.8123 in.)
Red	20,632 to 20,634 mm (0.8123 to 0.8124 in.)
Yellow	20,634 to 20,637 mm (0.8124 to 0.8125 in.)
Blue	20,637 to 20,640 mm (0.8125 to 0.8126 in.)
Vertical internal diameter - Standard	49,221 to 49,260 mm (1.938 to 1.939 in.)
Undersize - 0,051 mm (0.002 in.)	49,170 to 49,208 mm (1.936 to 1.937 in.)
Undersize - 0,254 mm (0.010 in.)	48,967 to 49,005 mm (1.928 to 1.929 in.)
Undersize - 0,508 mm (0.020 in.)	48,713 to 48,751 mm (1.918 to 1.919 in.)
Undersize - 0,762 mm (0.030 in.)	48,491 to 48,592 mm (1.909 to 1.913 in.)
Undersize - 1,016 mm (0.040 in.)	48,205 to 48,243 mm (1.889 to 1.999 in.)
Clearance - Big-end journal to bearing	0,006 to 0,064 mm (0.0002 to 0.0025 in.)

Cylinder Head

Cast marking on cylinder head	33
Valve seat angle in head	44° 30' to 45°
Stem bore, inlet and exhaust valve	7,907 to 7,937 mm (0.311 to 0.312 in.)
Bore for bushes	11.133 to 11.153 mm (0.438 to 0.439 in.)

Valves

	1,1 lc	1,1 hc	1,1 2v
Valve play (cold):-			
Inlet	0,20 mm (0.008 in.)	0,20 mm (0.008 in.)	0.25 mm (0.010 in.)
Exhaust	0,55 mm (0.022 in.)	0,55 mm (0.022 in.)	0,55 mm (0.022 in.)
Inlet valve:-			
Opens	21° BTDC	21° BTDC	29° BTDC
Closes	55° ABDC	55° ABDC	63° ABDC
Exhaust valve:-			
Opens	70° BBDC	70° BBDC	71° BBDC
Closes	22° ATDC	22° ATDC	21° ATDC
Valve springs (Number of turns)	3.75 or 5.75		
Cam follower diameter	13,081 to 13,094 mm (0.515 to 0.516 in.)		
Clearance (Cam follower to block)	0,013 to 0,05 mm (0.0005 to 0.002 in.)		

Inlet Valves

Length	110,668 to 111,176 mm (4.357 to 4.377 in.)
Valve head diameter	35,94 to 36,19 mm (1.415 to 1.425 in.)
Valve stem diameter - Standard	7,868 to 7,886 mm (0.3098 to 0.3105 in.)
Oversize - 0,076 mm (0.003 in.)	7,945 to 7,962 mm (0.3127 to 0.3135 in.)
Oversize - 0,381 mm (0.015 in.)	8,249 to 8,267 mm (0.3247 to 0.3255 in.)
Valve stem play in guide	0,02 to 0,068 mm (0.0008 to 0.0027 in.)
Valve stroke:-	
1,1LC	8,81 mm (0.347 in.)
1,1HC	8,81 mm (0.347 in.)
1,12V	8,63 mm (0.340 in.)

Exhaust valves

Length	110,363 to 110,871 mm (4.345 to 4.365 in.)
Valve cup diameter	31,34 to 31,59 mm (1.234 to 1.244 in.)
Valve stem diameter - Standard	7,846 to 7,863 mm (0.3089 to 0.3096 in.)
Oversize - 0,076 mm (0.003 in.)	7,922 to 7,939 mm (0.3119 to 0.3126 in.)
Oversize - 0,381 mm (0.015 in.)	8,227 to 8,243 mm (0.3239 to 0.3245 in.)
Valve stem play in guide	0,043 to 0,091 mm (0.0017 to 0.0036 in.)
Valve stroke	8,67 mm (0.341 in.)

Engine Lubrication

Oil type	HD oil
Viscosity:	
under -12°C	SAE 5W/20
under 0°C	SAE 5W/30
−23° to +32°C	SAE 10W/30, SAE 10W/40 or SAE 10W/50
Over −12°C	SAE 20W/40 or SAE 20W/50
Ford specification	SS-M2C-9001AA
Initial capacity with filter	3,67 litres (6.5 pints)
Oil change without filter change	2,75 litres (4.8 pints)
Oil change with filter change	3,25 litres (5.7 pints)
Minimum oil pressure at:	
700 rpm and 80°C	0,6 kp/cm^2 (8.5 lbf/in^2)
2000 rpm and 80°C	1,5 kp/cm^2 (21 lbf/in^2)
Oil pressure warning light come on at	0,4 $\pm$ 0,1 kp/cm^2 (6 $\pm$ 1.5 lbf/in^2)
Excess pressure valve opens at	2,46 to 2,81 kp/cm^2 (35 to 40 lbf/in^2)
Oil pump play in outer rotor casing	0,1397 to 0,2667 mm (0.0055 to 0.0105 in.)
Gap between internal and outer rotor	0,0508 to 0,1270 mm (0.002 to 0.005 in.)
Axial play of outer and internal rotor in relation to oil pump cover	0,0254 to 0,0635 mm (0.001 to 0.0025 in.)

Torque wrench settings (1100 engines)

	lb f ft	kg f m
Main bearing cover	55 to 60	7,5 to 8,2
Connecting rod bolts	31 to 35	4,2 to 4,8
Crankshaft belt pulley	24 to 28	3,3 to 3,8
Camshaft chain sprocket	13 to 15	1,7 to 2,1
Rear sealing ring carrier	13 to 15	1,7 to 2,1
Flywheel	50 to 56	6,8 to 7,6
Clutch thrust plate to flywheel	13 to 15	1,7 to 2,1
Front crankcase cover	5 to 7	0,7 to 1,0
Oil pump	13 to 15	1,7 to 2,1
Inlet line	13 to 15	1,7 to 2,1
Oil pump cover	5 to 7	0,7 to 1,0
Rocker shaft	18 to 22	2,4 to 3,0
Cylinder head:		
(1)	5	0,7
(2)	21 to 31	2,8 to 4,2
(3)	52 to 56	7,0 to 7,6
(4) After 10 to 20 minutes wait	66 to 71	9,0 to 9,7
(5) After engine has warmed up (15 minutes at 1000 rpm) tighten up.	66 to 71	9,0 to 9,7
Cylinder head cover	3 to 4	0,35 to 0,5
Sump:		
(1)	3 to 5	0,4 to 0,7
(2)	6 to 8	0,8 to 1,1
Oil drain screw	20 to 25	2,7 to 3,4
Oil pressure switch	10 to 11	1,3 to 1,5
Spark plugs	22 to 29	3,0 to 3,9
Inlet manifold	13 to 15	1,7 to 2,1
Exhaust manifold	15 to 18	2,1 to 2,5
Fuel pump	12 to 15	1,63 to 2,03
Water pump	5 to 7	0,7 to 1,0
Thermostat housing	13 to 15	1,7 to 2,1
Fan to water pump flange	5 to 7	0,7 to 1,0
Timing chain tensioner	5 to 7	0,7 to 1,0

1300/1600 Engines

Engine

Position of camshaft	In crankcase on right-hand side
Valve control	By pushrods and rocker levers
Firing order	1 - 2 - 4 - 3
Bore	80,98 mm (3,188 in.)

	1,3 lc	1,3 hc	1,3 2v	1,6 2v
Engine coding	J1F	J2H	J3D	L3A
Stroke	62,99 mm (2,478 in.)	62,99 mm (2,478 in.)	62,99 mm (2,478 in.)	77,62 mm (3.056 in.)
Swept volume..	1297 cc	1297 cc	1297 cc	1598 cc
Compression ratio ...	8.0 : 1	9.0 : 1	9.0 : 1	9.0 : 1
Pressure at starter speed	9 to 11 kp.cm^2 (128 to 156 lbf.in^2)	10 to 12 kp.cm^2 (142 to 170 lbf.in^2)	10 to 12 kp.cm^2 (142 to 170 lbf.in^2)	11 to 13 kp.cm^2 (156 to 184 lbf.in^2)

	1,3 lc	1.3 hc	1,3 2v	1,6 2v
Mean working pressure	8,43 kp.cm^2 (120 lbf.in^2)	9,0 kp.cm^2 (128 lbf.in^2)	9,0 kp.cm^2 (128 lbf.in^2)	10,0 kp.cm^2 (142 lbf.in^2)
Idling speed	800 $\pm$ 25 rpm	800 $\pm$ 25 rpm	800 $\pm$ 25 rpm	800 $\pm$ 25 rpm
Maximum continuous speed	5800 rpm	5800 rpm	5800 rpm	6000 rpm
Engine output (DIN)	40 kW (54 HP)	42 kW (57 HP)	51 kW (70 HP)	62 kW (84 HP)
	at 5500 rpm	at 5500 rpm	at 5500 rpm	at 5500 rpm
Torque (DIN)	85 Nm (8,7 m.kp)	91 Nm (9,3 m.kp)	92 Nm (9,4 m.kp)	125 Nm (12,7 m.kp)
	at 3000 rpm	at 3000 rpm	at 4000 rpm	at 4000 rpm

Cylinder Block

Cast marking on cylinder block:-

1,3 litre	711M-6015—A-A
1,6 litre	711M-6015-B-A
Number of main bearings	5
Cylinder liner bore	84,112 to 84,175 mm (3.311 to 3.314 in.)

Cylinder bore diameter:

A (standard)	80,947 to 80,957 mm (3,1869 to 3.1873 in.)
B	80,957 to 80,967 mm (3.1873 to 3.1877 in.)
C	80,967 to 80,977 mm (3,1877 to 3,1881 in.)
D	80,977 to 80,987 mm (3,1881 to 3,1885 in.)
E	80,987 to 80,997 mm (3.1885 to 3.1889 in.)
F	80,997 to 81,007 mm (3,1889 to 3,1893 in.)
Bearing width	26,822 to 26,873 mm (1.056 to 1.058 in.)
Fitted main bearing shells, vertical internal diameter	54,013 to 54,044 mm (2.126 to 2.128 in.)
Undersize - 0,254 mm (0.010 in.)	53,759 to 53,790 mm (2.116 to 2.118 in.)
Undersize - 0,508 mm (0.020 in.)	53,505 to 53,536 mm (2.106 to 2.108 in.)
Undersize - 0,762 mm (0.030 in.)	53,251 to 53,282 mm (2.096 to 2.098 in.)

Main bearing bore (in block):

Standard	57,683 to 57,696 mm (2.271 to 2.2715 in.)
Oversize	58,064 to 58,077 mm (2.286 to 2.2865 in.)

Camshaft bearing bore (in block):

Standard	42,888 to 42,913 mm (1.6885 to 1.6894 in.)
Oversize	+0,508 mm (+0.020 in.)

Crankshaft

Main bearing journal diameter - Standard	53,983 to 54,003 mm (2.125 to 2.126 in.)
Undersize - 0,254 mm (0.010 in.)	53,729 to 53,749 mm (2.115 to 2.116 in.)
Undersize - 0.508 mm (0.020 in.)	53,475 to 53,495 mm (2.105 to 2.106 in.)
Undersize - 0,762 mm (0.030 in.)	53,221 to 53,241 mm (2.095 to 2.096 in.)
Crankshaft endfloat	0,075 to 0,280 mm (0.003 to 0.011 in.)
Length of main bearing shell	25,273 to 25,527 mm (0.995 to 1.005 in.)
Play in main journal bearing shell	0,010 to 0,061 mm (0.0004 to 0.0024 in.)
Crank pin diameter - Standard	49,195 to 49,215 mm (1.937 to 1.938 in.)
Undersize - 0,05 mm (0.002 in.)	49,144 to 49,164 mm (1.935 to 1.936 in.)
Undersize - 0,25 mm (0.010 in.)	48,941 to 48,961 mm (1.927 to 1.928 in.)
Undersize - 0,51 mm (0.020 in.)	48,687 to 48,707 mm (1.917 to 1.918 in.)
Undersize - 0,76 mm (0.030 in.)	48,433 to 48,453 mm (1.907 to 1.908 in.)
Undersize - 1,02 mm (0.040 in.)	48,179 to 48,199 mm (1.897 to 1.898 in.)

Camshaft

Coding (paint ring):

1,3 LC	Yellow
1,3 HC	Yellow
1,3 2V	Red/white
1,6 2V	Red

	1,3 litre	1,6 litre
Thickness of camshaft retaining plate	4,470 mm (0.1760 in.)	4,520 mm (0.178 in.)
Cam lift:		
Inlet	5,985 mm (0.236 in.)	5,865 mm (0.231 in.)
Exhaust	5,894 mm (0.232 in.)	5.895 mm (0.2321 in.)
Length of cams (between heel and tip):		
Inlet	33,087 mm (1.303 in.)	33,357 mm (1.313 in.)
Exhaust	33,326 mm (1.312 in.)	33,267 mm (1.310 in.)
Drive	By chain with tensioning device	
Camshaft bearing diameter - Front, centre, rear	39,616 to 39,637 mm (1.560 to 1.561 in.)	
Internal diameter of bearing bush - Front, centre rear	39,662 to 39,675 mm (1.561 to 1.562 in.)	
Camshaft endfloat	0,06 to 0,2 mm (0.002 to 0.008 in.)	

Pistons

Piston diameter:	
Grade E - Standard	80,954 to 80,964 mm (3.1872 to 3.1876 in.)
Grade F	80,964 to 80,974 mm (3.1876 to 3.1880 in.)
Piston diameter (Oversize):	0,064 mm (0.003 in.)
Grade E	81,018 to 81,028 mm (3,1890 to 3.1901 in.)
Grade F	81,028 to 81,038 mm (3.1901 to 3.1904 in.)
Piston to bore clearance	0,023 to 0,043 mm (0.0009 to 0.0010 in.)
Ring gap (fitted in block):	
Top	0,23 to 0,36 mm (0.009 to 0.014 in.)
Centre	0,23 to 0,36 mm (0.009 to 0.014 in.)
Bottom	0,23 to 0,36 mm (0.009 to 0.014 in.)

Gudgeon Pins

Length of gudgeon pin	70,99 to 71,37 mm (2.795 to 2.810 in.)
Pin diameter:	
1	20,622 to 20,625 mm (0.8119 to 0.8120 in.)
2	20,625 to 20,627 mm (0.8120 to 0.8121 in.)
3	20,627 to 20,630 mm (0.8121 to 0.8122 in.)
4	20,630 to 20,632 mm (0.8122 to 0.8123 in.)
Pin interference in piston at 21°C (70°F)	0,003 to 0,008 mm (0.0001 to 0.0003 in.)
Clearance in connecting rod at 21°C (70°F)	0,004 to 0,010 mm (0.00015 to 0.0004 in.)

Connecting rods

Bore diameter of big-end	52,89 to 52,91 mm (2,0823 to 2,0831 in.)
Bore diameter of small end:	
White	20,629 to 20,632 mm (0.8122 to 0.8123 in.)
Red	20,632 to 20,634 mm (0.8123 to 0.8124 in.)
Yellow	20,634 to 20,637 mm (0.8124 to 0.8125 in.)
Blue	20,637 to 20,640 mm (0.8125 to 0.8126 in.)
Vertical internal diameter - Standard	49,221 to 49,260 mm (1.938 to 1.939 in.)
Undersize - 0,051 mm (0.002 in.)	49,170 to 49,208 mm (1.936 to 1.937 in.)
Undersize - 0,254 mm (0.010 in.)	48,967 to 49,005 mm (1.928 to 1.929 in.)
Undersize - 0,508 mm (0.020 in.)	48,713 to 48,751 mm (1.918 to 1.919 in.)
Undersize - 0,762 mm (0.030 in.)	48,491 to 48,592 mm (1.909 to 1.913 in.)
Undersize - 1,016 mm (0.040 in.)	48,205 to 48,243 mm (1.898 to 1.899 in)
Clearance - Big-end journal to bearing	0,006 to 0,064 mm (0.0002 to 0.003 in.)

Cylinder Head

Cast marking on cylinder head:	
1,3 litre	33
1,6 litre	37
Valve seat angle in head	44° 30' to 45°
Stem bore, inlet and exhaust valves	7,907 to 7,937 mm (0.311 to 0.312 in.)
Bore for bushes	11.133 to 11.153 mm (0.438 to 0.439 in.)

Valves

	1,3 lc and 1,3 hc	1,3 2v and 1,6 2v
Valve play (cold):		
Inlet	0,20 mm (0.008 in.)	0,25 mm (0.010 in.)
Exhaust	0,55 mm (0.022 in.)	0,55 mm (0.022 in.)
Inlet valve:		
Opens	21° BTDC	27° BTDC
Closes	55° ABDC	65° ABDC
Exhaust valve:		
Opens	70° BBDC	65° BBDC
Closes	22° ATDC	27° ATDC
Valve springs (Number of turns)	3,75 to 5.75	
Cam follower diameter	13,081 to 13,094 mm (0.515 to 0.516 in.)	
Clearance (cam follower to block)	0,013 to 0,05 mm (0.0005 to 0.0019 in.)	

Inlet Valves

Length	110,67 to 111,67 mm (4.357 to 4.396 in.)
Valve head diameter:	
1,3 litre	38,02 to 38,28 mm (1.497 to 1.507 in.)
1,6 litre	39,2 to 39,6 mm (1.543 to 1.559 in.)
Valve stem diameter - Standard	7,868 to 7,886 mm (0.3097 to 0.3104 in.)
Oversize - 0,076 mm (0.003 in.)	7,945 to 7,962 mm (0.3128 to 0.3135 in.)
Oversize - 0,381 mm (0.015 in.)	8,249 to 8,267 mm (0.3248 to 0.3255 in.)
Valve stem play in guide	0,02 to 0,068 mm (0.0008 to 0.0027 in.)
Valve stroke	8,81 mm (0.347 in.)

Exhaust Valves

Length	110,36 to 110,87 mm (4.345 to 4.365 in.)
Valve cup diameter:	
1,3 litre	31,34 to 31,59 mm (1.234 to 1.244 in.)
1,6 litre	33,8 to 34,0 mm (1.331 to 1.339 in.)
Valve stem diameter - Standard	7,846 to 7,863 mm (0.3089 to 0.3096 in.)
Oversize - 0,076 mm (0.003 in.)	7,922 to 7,939 mm (0.3119 to 0.3126 in.)
Oversize - 0,381 mm (0.015 in.)	8,227 to 8,243 mm (0.3239 to 0.3245 in.)
Valve stem play in guide	0,043 to 0,091 mm (0.0017 to 0.0036 in.)
Valve stroke	8,67 mm (0.341 in.)

Engine Lubrication

Oil type	HD oil
Viscosity:	
under -12°C	SAE 5W/20
under 0°C	SAE 5W/30
-23°C to $+32^{\circ}$C	SAE 10W/30, SAE 10W/40 or SAE 10W/50
over -12°C	SAE 20W/40 or SAE 20W/50
Ford specification	SS-M2C-9001AA
Initial capacity with filter	3,67 litres (6.5 pints)
Oil change without filter change	2,75 litres (4.8 pints)
Oil change with filter change	3,25 litres (5.7 pints)
Minimum oil pressure at:	
700 rpm and 80°C	0,6 kp/cm^2 (8.5 lbf/in^2)
2000 rpm and 80°C	1,5 kp/cm^2 (21 lbf/in^2)
Oil pressure warning light glows at	0,4 $\pm$ 0,1 kp/cm^2 (6 $\pm$ 1.5 lb f/in^2)
Excess pressure valve opens at	2,46 to 2,81 kp/cm^2 (35 to 40 lb f/in^2)
Oil pump play with external rotor casing	0,1397 to 0,2667 mm (0.0055 to 0.0105 in.)
Gap internal/external rotor	0,0508 to 0,1270 mm (0.002 to 0.005 in.)
Axial play of external and internal rotor in relation to oil pump cover	0,0254 to 0,0635 mm (0.001 to 0.0025 in.)

Torque wrench settings

	lb f ft	kg f m
Main bearing cover	55 to 60	7,5 to 8,2
Connecting rod bolts	31 to 35	4,2 to 4,8
Crankshaft belt pulley	24 to 28	3,3 to 3,8
Camshaft chain sprocket	13 to 15	1,7 to 2,1
Rear sealing ring carrier	13 to 15	1,7 to 2,1
Flywheel	50 to 56	6,8 to 7,6
Clutch thrust plate to flywheel	13 to 15	1,7 to 2,1
Front crankcase cover	5 to 7	0,7 to 1,0
Oil pump	13 to 15	1,7 to 2,1
Oil pump inlet pipe	13 to 15	1,7 to 2,1
Oil pump cover	5 to 7	0,7 to 1,0
Rocker shaft	18 to 22	2,4 to 3,0
Cylinder head:		
(1)	5	0.7
(2)	20 to 31	2,8 to 4,2
(3)	52 to 56	7,0 to 7,6
(4) After 10 to 20 minutes wait	66 to 71	9,0 to 9,7
(5) After engine has warmed up (15 minutes at 1000 rpm)		
tighten up.	66 to 71	9.0 to 9.7
Cylinder head cover	3 to 4	0,35 to 0,5
Sump:		
(1)	3 to 5	0,4 to 0,7
(2)	6 to 8	0,8 to 1,1
Oil drain screw	20 to 25	2,7 to 3,4
Oil pressure switch	10 to 11	1,3 to 1,5
Spark plugs	22 to 29	3,0 to 3,9
Inlet manifold	13 to 15	1,7 to 2,1
Exhaust manifold	15 to 18	2,1 to 2,5
Fuel pump	12 to 15	1,63 to 2,03
Water pump	5 to 7	0,7 to 1,0
Thermostat housing	13 to 15	1,7 to 2,1
Fan to water pump flange	5 to 7	0,7 to 1,0
Timing chain tensioner	5 to 7	0,7 to 1,0

1 General description

The basic power unit for the Escort range is the four cylinder, OHV, in-line engine available in capacities of 1097 cc, 1297cc and 1598cc. In its smallest capacity the engine develops 48 bhp at 5500 rpm, while for the same revolutions on the 1598cc engine the rated output is 84 bhp.

Automatic transmission is optionally available but only in conjunction with the 1300cc and 1600cc engines.

The bore on all engines is identical, the variations in capacity being achieved by different crankshaft strokes. All units are identical in design and differ only in the size of some of the components used (eg; block, connection rods and pistons).

Two valves per cylinder are mounted vertically in the cast iron cylinder head and run in integral valve guides. They are operated by rocker arms, pushrods and tappets from the camshaft which is located at the base of the cylinder bores in the right-hand side of the engine. The correct valve stem to rocker arm pad clearance can be obtained by the adjusting screws in the ends of the rocker arms. Valve size varies engine capacity in the interests of improved performance.

A crossflow cylinder head is used with four inlet ports on the right-hand side and four exhaust on the left. High or low compression ratios may be used.

The cylinder block and the upper half of the crankcase are cast together. The open half of the crankcase is closed by a pressed steel sump.

The pistons are made from anodised aluminium alloy with solid skirts. Two compression rings and a slotted oil control ring are fitted. The gudgeon pin is retained in the little end of the connecting rod by circlips. The combustion chamber is machined in the piston crown and a different piston is used for each engine capacity and compression ratio. The connecting rod bearings are all steel backed and may be of copper/lead, lead/bronze, or aluminium/tin.

At the front of the engine a single chain drives the camshaft via the camshaft and crankshaft chain wheels which are enclosed in a pressed steel cover.

The chain is tensioned automatically by a snail cam which bears against a pivoted tensioner arm. This presses against the non-driving side of the chain so avoiding any lash or rattle.

The camshaft is supported by three renewable bearings located directly in the cylinder block. Endfloat is controlled by a plate bolted to the front bearing journal and the chain wheel flange.

The statically and dynamically balanced cast iron crankshaft is supported by five renewable thin wall shell main bearings which are in turn supported by substantial webs which form part of the crankcase. Crankshaft endfloat is controlled by semi-circular thrust washers located on each side of the centre main bearings.

The centrifugal water pump and radiator cooling fan are driven, together with the generator, from the crankshaft pulley wheel by a flexible belt. The distributor is mounted toward the front of the right-hand side of the cylinder block and advances and retards the ignition timing by mechanical and vacuum means. The distributor is driven at half crankshaft speed from a skew gear on the camshaft.

The oil pump is mounted externally on the right-hand side of the engine under the distributor and is driven by a short shaft from the same skew gear on the camshaft as for the distributor and may be of eccentric bi-rotor of sliding vane type.

Bolted to the flange on the end of the crankshaft is the flywheel to which is bolted in turn the clutch. Attached to the rear of the engine is the gearbox bellhousing.

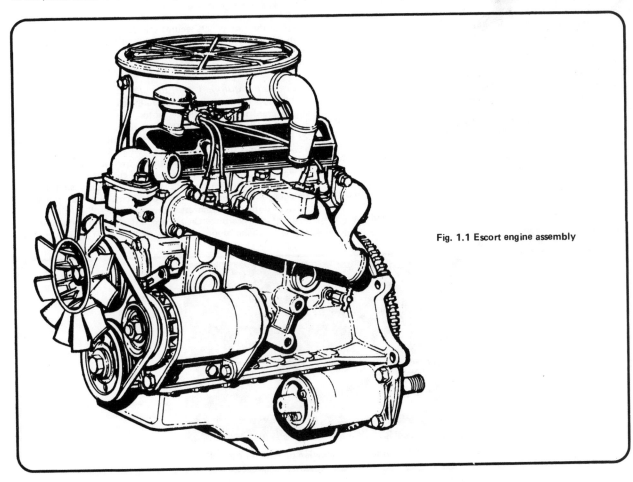

Fig. 1.1 Escort engine assembly

2 Major operations possible with engine in vehicle

The following major operations can be carried out to the engine with it in place in the bodyframe. Removal and replacement of the:

1 *Cylinder head assembly*
2 *Oil pump*
3 *Engine front mountings*
4 *Engine/gearbox rear mounting*

3 Major operations requiring engine removal

The following major operations can be carried out with the engine out of the bodyframe and on the bench or floor. Removal and replacement of the:

1 *Main bearings*
2 *Crankshaft*
3 *Flywheel*
4 *Crankshaft rear bearing oil seal*
5 *Camshaft*
6 *Sump*
7 *Big-end bearings*
8 *Pistons and connecting rods*
9 *Timing chain and gears*

4 Method of engine removal

The engine complete with gearbox can be lifted as a unit from the engine compartment. Alternatively, the engine and gearbox can be split at the front of the bellhousing, a stand or jack placed under the gearbox to provide additional support, and the engine lifted out. The easiest method of engine removal is to remove the engine leaving the gearbox in place in the car. If the engine and gearbox are removed as a unit they have to be lifted out at a very steep angle which can be difficult.

5 Engine - removal (without gearbox or automatic transmission unit)

1 Before commencing operations, it is essential to have a good hoist, and two strong axle stands if an inspection pit is not available. Engine removal will be much easier if you have a friend to help you.
2 Open the bonnet. Undo the two bolts and washers from the bonnet side of each of the two hinges.
3 Remove the radiator cap and if the cooling system contains antifreeze, place two trays under the engine to catch the coolant.
4 Remove the radiator bottom hose at the radiator and allow the coolant to drain into one of the trays. Unscrew and remove the cylinder block drain plug (left-hand side of block) and let the engine coolant drain into the second tray (Fig. 1.2).

5 Prise the air cleaner lugs out of their respective stays and lift the cleaner off the carburettor. (photo)
6 Disconnect the battery.
7 Disconnect the radiator top hose from the thermostat housing outlet and from the radiator. Remove the hose. (photo) Then, remove the radiator side securing bolts and lift it out of the engine compartment. Remove the bottom hose from the engine (Fig. 1.3).
8 Remove the bolts securing the accelerator cable bracket to the inlet manifold (photo) disengage the throttle shaft from the carburettor linkage (photo) and position the cable and bracket to one side in the engine compartment.
9 Detach the inner and outer choke control cables (manually operated choke) (photo)
10 Unscrew the two nuts which connect the exhaust manifold to the downpipe.
11 From the rear of the alternator detach the leads by pulling off the spring clip and the plug connector.
12 Disconnect the lead from the oil pressure switch which is located just below, and forward of the distributor.
13 Disconnect the lead from the water temperature transmitter unit. (photo)
14 Pull the centre HT lead from the coil tower and disconnect the LT lead from the '−' terminal of the coil.
15 Disconnect the heater hoses from the engine.
16 Similarly, disconnect the vacuum servo hose from its outlet stub on the inlet manifold.
17 Disconnect the earth strap from the left-hand side of the cylinder block. (photo 5.13).
18 Disconnect the fuel inlet pipe at the fuel pump. Unless the level in the fuel tank is very low, plug the pipe to prevent loss
19 Slacken the alternator mountings (Fig. 1.4) tilt the alternator towards the engine and remove the fan belt. Then remove the fan and fan pulley. (photo)
20 On vehicles equipped with inertia type starter motors, unscrew the nut which secures the lead to the solenoid switch. With pre-engaged type starter motors, disconnect the lead from the terminal on the motor end plate. (photo)
21 Unscrew and remove the sump shield (where fitted). (Fig. 1.5)

On vehicles equipped with manual gearboxes

22 Unscrew the bolts which secure the clutch bellhousing to the engine crankcase. The starter motor is retained by these bolts and it should be removed at the same time.
23 Remove the nuts from the engine mountings. Using slings and a suitable hoist, take the weight of the engine so that the studs can be drawn through the two engine front mountings. (photos)
24 Position a jack under the gearbox and then raise both the hoist and jack together until the top of the bellhousing is almost touching the underside of the body floor. Now pull the engine forward until the clutch assembly clears the splined first motion shaft of the gearbox. On no account allow the weight of the engine to hang upon the first motion shaft while it is still

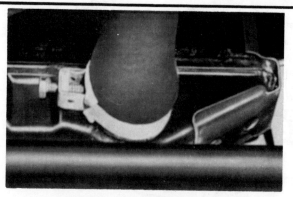

Fig. 1.2 Bottom hose location on radiator (Sec 5)

Fig. 1.3 Removing radiator assembly (Sec 5)

5.5 Lifting away the air cleaner

5.7 Disconnecting the radiator top hose

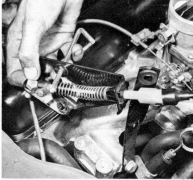

5.8A Detach the throttle cable bracket and ...

5.8B ... unclip the throttle shaft from the carburettor

5.9 Detach the choke inner and outer cables from the carburettor

5.13 Upper left: water temperature sender removal. Centre: engine earth strap

Fig. 1.4 Slacken bolts (arrowed) to enable removal of fan belt (Sec 5)

Fig. 1.5 Sump shield retaining bolts (arrowed) (Sec 5)

5.19 Removing the fan and fan pulley

5.20 Unscrew the nut and detach the cable from the starter motor

5.23 Lift the engine sufficiently to release the engine mountings

6.2A Mark the relative positions of the two flanges, then remove the bolts ...

6.2B ... next, detach the centre bearing from the floorpan. Note exactly the positions of any jacking shims

6.2C Withdraw the propeller shaft from the gearbox extension

engaged with the clutch mechanism. Once clear, tilt the engine at an angle of 45° and lift it from the engine compartment.

25 Check that no loose nuts and bolts have been left in the empty engine compartment. Lightly screw any nuts or bolts back from where they were removed or place them where they will not become lost.

On vehicles equipped with automatic transmission
26 Disconnect the downshift cable from its rocker cover support bracket and from the throttle linkage. Disconnect the water hoses from the automatic choke.
27 Remove the upper four bolts securing the torque converter housing to the engine crankcase.
28 Using slings and a suitable hoist, take the weight of the engine so that the bolts can be removed from the two engine front mountings.
29 Position a jack under the automatic transmission oil pan (use a block of wood to prevent distortion of the oil pan) and raise both hoist and jack together until the top of the converter housing is almost touching the body floor.
30 Unscrew each of the crankshaft drive plate to torque converter securing bolts. These are accessible, one at a time, through either the starter motor aperture or the lower semi-circular cover plate on the torque converter housing. The crankshaft will have to be rotated to bring each bolt in to view.
31 Pull the engine forward and lift it out of the engine compartment in a similar manner to that already described for vehicles with manually operated gearboxes.

---

6 Engine - removal (with gearbox or automatic transmission unit)

1 Carry out operations 1 to 25 in the preceding Section.
2 Mark the edges of the propeller shaft rear driving flange and the rear axle pinion flange and remove the four connecting bolts.

(photo) Remove the bolts securing the shaft centre beam (if fitted) to the floor pan. (photo) Note the exact position of any packing shims. Pull the propeller shaft slightly forward and then downward and pull it from engagement with the gearbox mainshaft rear end. (photo)
3 Jack-up the front of the car and fit stands. It is now necessary to remove the gearlever. From inside the car lift up the gearlever gaiter and then remove the circlip in the spring.
4 Bend back the lock tab and with a pair of mole grips or similar across the flats, undo the plastic dome nut and lift out the gearlever from the car. (photo)
5 From under the car disconnect the clutch cable from the clutch release arm. To do this it is necessary to loosen the clutch cable at the adjuster on the rear bulkhead or at the clutch bellhousing dependent upon its location, so that with the cable loose it can be pushed ½ inch (12.7 mm) backward from the release arm. This brings the narrow portion of the cable into line with the slot in the end of the release arm from which it can be detached. (photo)
6 Free the speedometer cable from the gearbox extension housing by extracting the circlip which holds the cable in place. (photo) Detach the reversing light leads.
7 From under the car, detach the crossmember which supports the gearbox. To do this first place a jack (preferably of the trolley type) under the gearbox; undo the two bolts at each end of the gearbox crossmember. (photo)
8 Lower and remove the jack, and then remove the stands from the front of the car and lower the front to its normal height.
9 Attach a lifting chain or a strong rope round the engine, and take the weight on suitable lifting tackle. Place the rope as far forward as practicable as the engine will have to come out at a fairly steep angle.
10 Undo the nut on each side which holds the front engine mounting in place. (photo)
11 If a trolley jack is available it is helpful to position it under the gearbox so the gearbox rolls forward with the jack. (photo)

6.4 Lift out the gearlever

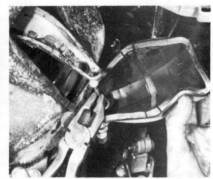
6.5 Disconnect the clutch cable from the release arm

6.6 Remove the circlip and withdraw the speedometer cable from the gearbox

6.7 The gearbox crossmember. Remove the four outer bolts

6.10 Remove the nuts securing the two front engine mountings

6.11A If available a trolley jack will facilitate engine/gearbox removal

Pull the power unit forward at the same time lifting it on the hoist. As the gearbox tilts oil will run out of the rear of the gearbox extension. When the gearbox is clear of the gearbox tunnel lift the power unit out of the car with the hoist at an angle of approximately 30° to the horizontal. (photo)

On vehicles equipped with automatic transmission
12 The procedure is similar to that already described but the following additional operations must be carried out.
13 Drain the automatic transmission fluid and retain for refilling the unit.
14 Disconnect the leads from the starter inhibitor switch. The switch is located on the left-hand side of the transmission housing and the two larger terminals are the reversing light terminals.
15 Disconnect the speed selector linkage by removing the split pin and clevis pin at the selector arm on the side of the transmission unit and the support bracket.

6.11B The engine/gearbox unit should be hoisted out at an angle of approximately 30° to the horizontal

7 Dismantling the engine - general

1 It is best to mount the engine on a dismantling stand but if one is not available, then stand the engine on a strong bench so as to be at a comfortable working height.
2 During the dismantling process the greatest care should be taken to keep the exposed parts free from dirt. As an aid to achieving this, it is a sound scheme to thoroughly clean down the outside of the engine, removing all traces of oil and congealed dirt.
3 Use paraffin or a good grease solvent such as Gunk. The latter compound will make the job much easier, as, after the solvent has been applied and allowed to stand for a time, a vigorous jet of water will wash off the solvent and all the grease and filth. If the dirt is thick and deeply embedded, work the solvent into it with a stiff paintbrush.
4 Finally wipe down the exterior of the engine with a rag and only then, when it is quite clean, should the dismantling process begin. As the engine is stripped, clean each part in a bath of paraffin or petrol.
5 Never immerse parts with oilways in paraffin, ie the crankshaft, but to clean wipe down carefully with a petrol dampened rag. Oilways can be cleaned out with wire. If an air line is present all parts can be blown dry and the oilways blown through as an added precaution.
6 Re-use of old engine gaskets is a false economy and can give rise to oil and water leaks, if nothing worse. To avoid the possibility of trouble after the engine has been reassembled **always** use new gaskets throughout.
7 Do not throw away the old gaskets as it sometimes happens that an immediate replacement cannot be found and the old gasket is then very useful as a template. Hang up the old gaskets as they are removed on a suitable hook or nail.
8 To strip the engine it is best to work from the top down. The sump provides a firm base on which the engine can be supported in an upright position. When the stage where the sump must be removed is reached, the engine can be turned on its side and all other work carried out with it in this position.
9 Wherever possible, replace nuts, bolts and washers fingertight from wherever they were removed. This helps avoid later loss and muddle. If they cannot be replaced then lay them out in such a fashion that it is clear from where they came.
10 If the engine was removed in unit with the gearbox separate them by undoing the nuts and bolts which hold the bellhousing to the engine endplate.
11 Also undo the bolts holding the starter motor in place and lift off the motor.
12 Carefully pull the gearbox and bellhousing from the engine to separate them.

8 Removing ancillary engine components

1 Before basic engine dismantling begins the engine should be stipped of all its ancillary components. These items should also be removed if a factory exchange reconditioned unit is being purchased. The items comprise:
Alternator and brackets
Water pump and thermostat housing
Starter motor
Distributor and spark plugs
Inlet and exhaust manifold and carburettor
Fuel pump and fuel pipes
Oil filter and dipstick
Oil filler cap
Clutch assembly (Chapter 5)
Engine mountings
Oil pressure sender unit
Oil separator unit
2 Without exception all these items can be removed with the engine in the car if it is merely an individual item which requires attention. (It is necessary to remove the gearbox if the clutch is to be renewed with the engine in position).
3 Remove the alternator after undoing the nuts and bolts which secure it in place. Remove the alternator mounting bracket. (photos)
4 Remove the distributor by disconnecting the vacuum pipe, unscrew the single bolt at the clamp plate and lift out the distributor. (photos)
5 Remove the oil pump assembly by unscrewing the three securing bolts with their lockwashers. (photo)
6 Unscrew the two bolts securing the fuel pump. (photo)
7 Unscrew the oil pressure gauge unit or the oil pressure sender unit, depending on models. (photo)
8 Remove the inlet and exhaust manifolds together with the carburettor by undoing the bolts and nuts which hold the units in place. (photo)
9 Unbolt the securing bolts of the water elbow and lift out the thermostat. (photos)
10 Bend back the tab lockwashers where fitted and undo the bolts which hold the water pump and engine mountings in place.
11 Undo the bolts holding the clutch cover flange to the flywheel a third of a turn each in a diagonal sequence repeating until the clutch and driven plate can be lifted off. (photo)
12 Loosen the clamp securing the rubber tube from the oil separator unit to the inlet manifold and pull off the tube (where a positive crankcase ventilation system is fitted). Remove the oil

8.3A Removing the alternator from the engine - the adjusting arm bolt

8.3B The lower mounting bolts

8.3C The adjusting arm

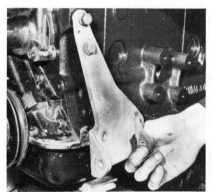

8.3D Removing the alternator mounting bracket

8.4A Removing the distributor vacuum pipe from the carburettor

8.4B Removing the distributor from the engine

8.5 Oil pump retaining bolts (arrowed) on cylinder block. Note: the oil filter is shown removed

8.6 Removing the fuel pump from the cylinder block

8.7 Unscrewing the oil pressure sender unit from the cylinder block after first disconnecting the sender unit lead

8.8 The exhaust manifold shown ready for removal from the cylinder head

8.9A Removing the water elbow to expose the thermostat ...

8.9B ... which can then be lifted from its location in the cylinder head

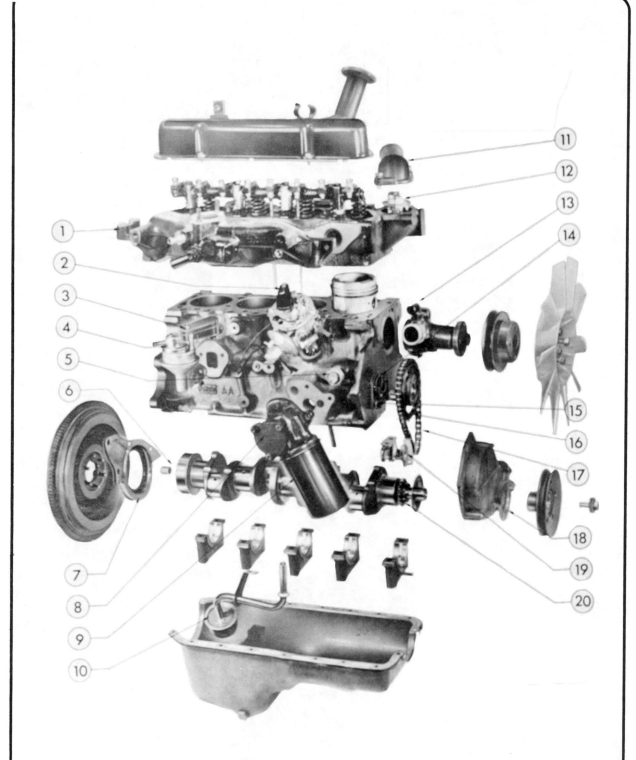

Fig. 1.6 Cylinder head, crankcase and sump components

1 Cylinder head	6 Spigot bearing	11 Water outlet elbow	16 Camshaft timing gear
2 Distributor	7 Rear oil seal carrier	12 Thermostat	17 Timing chain
3 Oil separator (ventilation system)	8 Oil pump	13 Water pump	18 Front cover and oil seal
4 Fuel pump	9 Oil filter	14 Camshaft	19 Timing chain tensioner
5 Oil pressure switch	10 Pick up pipe	15 Thrust plate	20 Crankshaft

separator location on the fuel pump mounting pad by carefully prising it off, after first unscrewing the bolt retaining the separator to the block. (photo)

13 The engine is now stripped of ancillary components and ready for major dismantling to begin.

9 Cylinder head - removal

1 Undo the four screw headed bolts and flat washers which hold the flange of the rocker cover to the cylinder head and lift off the rocker cover and gasket. (photo)

2 Unscrew the four rocker shaft pedestal bolts evenly and remove together with their washers.

3 Lift off the rocker assembly as one unit. (photo)

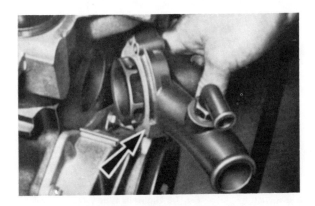

Fig. 1.7 Removing water pump (arrowed) (Sec 8)

4 Remove the pushrods, keeping them in the relative order in which they were removed. The easiest way to do this is to push them through a sheet of thick paper or thin card in the correct sequence. (photo)

5 Undo the cylinder head bolts half a turn at a time in the reverse order to that shown in Fig. 1.41 on page 51. When all the bolts are no longer under tension they may be unscrewed from the cylinder head one at a time. (photo)

6 The cylinder head can now be removed by lifting upward. If the head is jammed, try to rock it to break the seal. Under no circumstances try to prise it apart from the block with a screwdriver or cold chisel as damage may be done to the faces of the head or block. If the head will not readily free, turn the engine over by the flywheel as the compression in the cylinders will often break the cylinder head joint. If this fails to work, strike the head sharply with a plastic headed hammer, or with a wooden hammer, or with a metal hammer with an interposed piece of wood to cushion the blows. Under no circumstances hit the head directly with a metal hammer as this may cause the iron casting to fracture. Several sharp taps with the hammer at the same time pulling upward should free the head. (photo)

7 Do not lay the cylinder head face downward unless the plugs have been removed as they protrude and can be easily damaged.

8 The operations described in this Section can equally well be carried out with the engine in or out of the vehicle but with the latter, the cooling system must be drained, the battery disconnected and all attachments to the cylinder head removed as described in the appropriate paragraphs of Section 5.

10 Valves - removal

1 The valves can be removed from the cylinder head by compressing each spring in turn with a valve spring compressor

8.11 Lifting the clutch pressure plate and disc off the flywheel after first removing the pressure plate bolts. Note the dowel pegs in the flywheel to ensure correct location of the plate

8.12 Lifting the crankcase emission oil separator unit from the cylinder block. Note the rubber 'O' ring on the separator stub and the steady bracket and bolt location on the cylinder block

9.1 Removing the rocker cover to expose the valve train. Note the 'dovetails' in the rocker cover and gasket to assist in gasket location

9.3 Lifting the rocker shaft assembly off the cylinder head

9.4 Removing the valve pushrods. Pushrods MUST be replaced in the order that they were removed from the cylinder head

9.5 Removing the cylinder head bolts. All bolts must be slackened off before any bolt is removed

9.6 Lifting the cylinder head off the cylinder block

10.1A Valve spring partially compressed showing collets (arrowed) ready for removal

10.1B Valve spring retaining cap being lifted off after the removal of the valve collets

10.1C Valve spring ready for removal

10.4 Valve stem seal: seal is removed by sliding up valve stem. Note collet retaining grooves at top of valve stem

Fig. 1.8 Umbrella type valve stem oil seal (Sec 10)

12.2A Crankshaft centre bolt (arrowed)

12.2B ... must be removed before crankshaft pulley can be detached from crankshaft

Fig. 1.9 Removing crankshaft pulley using two leg puller (Sec 12)

12.4 Removing timing cover. Note that sump is shown already removed

12.6 Oil thrower location on crankshaft

Fig. 1.10 Bending back camshaft timing gear retaining bolt locktabs (Sec 12)

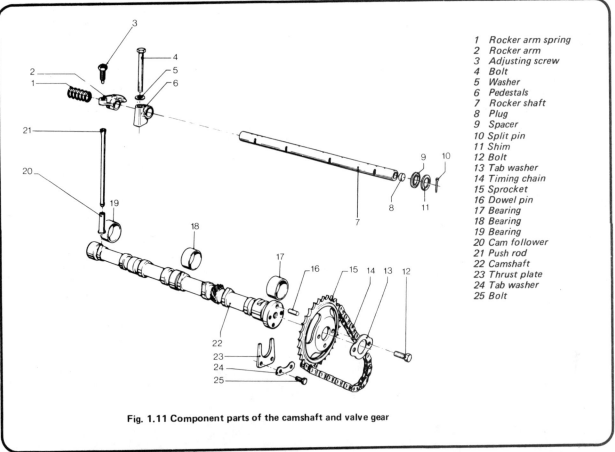

1   Rocker arm spring
2   Rocker arm
3   Adjusting screw
4   Bolt
5   Washer
6   Pedestals
7   Rocker shaft
8   Plug
9   Spacer
10 Split pin
11 Shim
12 Bolt
13 Tab washer
14 Timing chain
15 Sprocket
16 Dowel pin
17 Bearing
18 Bearing
19 Bearing
20 Cam follower
21 Push rod
22 Camshaft
23 Thrust plate
24 Tab washer
25 Bolt

Fig. 1.11 Component parts of the camshaft and valve gear

until the two halves of the collets can be removed. Release the compressor and remove the spring and spring retainer. (photos)

2   If, when the valve spring compressor is screwed down, the valve spring retaining cap refuses to free to expose the split collet, do not continue to screw down on the compressor as there is a likelihood of damaging it.

3   Gently tap the top of the tool directly over the cap with a light hammer. This will free the cap. To avoid the compressor jumping off the valve spring retaining cap when it is tapped, hold the compressor firmly in position with one hand.

4   Slide the rubber oil control seal off the top of each inlet valve stem and then drop out each valve through the combustion chamber. (photo)

5   It is essential that the valves are kept in their correct sequence unless they are so badly worn that they are to be renewed. If they are going to be kept and used again, place them in a sheet of card having eight holes numbered 1 to 8 corresponding with the relative positions the valves were in when originally installed. Alsp keep the valve springs, washers and collets in their original sequence.

11 Dismantling the rocker assembly

1   Pull out the split pin from each end of the rocker shaft and remove the flat washer, crimped spring washer and the remaining flat washer.

2   The rocker arms, rocker pedestals, and distance springs can now be slid off the end of the shaft.

12 Timing cover, gearwheels and chain - removal

1   The timing cover cannot be removed until the sump has also been removed, which necessitates removal of the engine from the car (See Section 14).

2   Unscrew the bolt from the centre of the crankshaft pulley. The best way to do this is to fit a ring spanner and then to give it a sharp blow with a club hammer in an anticlockwise direction. Alternatively, with manual gearbox vehicles, engage a gear and apply the handbrake fully to prevent the engine turning when the spanner is turned. On vehicles equipped with automatic transmission, remove the starter motor and jam the ring gear with a large screwdriver or cold chisel. (photos)

3   The crankshaft pulley wheel may pull off quite easily. If not, place two large screwdrivers behind the wheel at 180° to each other, and carefully lever off the wheel. It is preferable to use a proper pulley extractor if this is available, but large screwdrivers or tyre levers are quite suitable, providing care is taken not to damage the pulley flange. (Fig. 1.9)

4   Undo the bolts which hold the timing cover in place, noting that four sump bolts must also be removed before the cover can be taken off. (photo)

5   Check the chain for wear by measuring how much it can be depressed. More than ½ inch (12.5 mm) means a new chain must be fitted on reassembly.

6   With the timing cover off, take off the oil thrower. Note that the concave side faces outward. (photo)

7   With a drift or screwdriver tap back the tabs on the lock-washer under the two camshaft gearwheel retaining bolts and undo the bolts. (Fig. 1.10)

8   To remove the camshaft and crankshaft timing wheels complete with chain, ease each wheel forward a little at a time levering behind each gear wheel in turn with two large screw-drivers at 180° to each other. If the gearwheels are locked solid then it will be necessary to use a proper pulley extractor, and if one is available this should be used in preference to screwdrivers (Fig. 1.12). With both gearwheels safely off, remove the Woodruff key from the crankshaft with a pair of pliers. (photo)

13 Camshaft - removal

1   The camshaft can only be removed from the engine when the engine is removed from the vehicle.

2   With the engine inverted and sump rocker gear, pushrods, timing cover, oil pump, gearwheels and timing chain removed, take off the chain tensioner and arm.

3   Knock back the lockwasher tabs from the two bolts which hold the 'U' shaped camshaft retainer in place behind the camshaft flange and slide out the retainer.

4   Rotate the camshaft so that the tappets are fully home and then withdraw the camshaft from the cylinder block. Take great care that the cam lobe peaks do not damage the camshaft bearings as the shaft is pulled forward.

14 Sump - removal

1   The procedure described assumes that the engine has been removed and the gearbox and starter motor detached.

2   Unscrew the sump securing bolts and remove the sump. If it is stuck, cut round the joint with a sharp knife.

3   Remove the cork strips from the timing cover and rear oil seal carrier, and then thoroughly clean all the mating surfaces of the sump flange and cylinder block.

15 Pistons, connecting rods and big-end bearings - removal

1   The pistons and connecting rods can be removed with the engine on the bench.

2   With the cylinder head and sump removed, undo the big-end retaining bolts. (photo)

3   The connecting rods and pistons are lifted out through the top of the cylinder block.

4   Remove the big-end caps, one at a time, noting that they are numbered 1 to 4 with matched cap numbers, so that exact refitting will be facilitated (Fig. 1.15/photo)

5   Keep the original shell bearings with each connecting rod. Should the big-end caps be difficult to remove, then they may be tapped gently using a plastic faced mallet.

6   The shell bearings may be removed from the big-end caps and the connecting rods by pressing them at a point opposite to their grooves.

Fig. 1.12 Removing crankshaft timing gear using two leg puller (Sec. 12)

Fig. 1.13 Track control arm to front crossmember retaining bolt (arrowed) (Sec 14)

12.8 Easing the crankshaft and camshaft sprockets off their respective stubs

14.1A Removing sump bolts and ...

14.1B ... detaching sump from underside of block

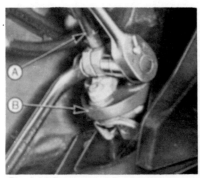

Fig. 1.14 Removing clamp bolts from steering shaft (A) and flexible coupling (B) (Sec 14)

15.2 Big-end bearing cap retaining bolts (arrowed)

15.4 Detaching big-end cap from rod and crankshaft journal

Fig. 1.15 Method of numbering connecting rods (arrowed) and main bearing caps (Sec 15)

7   As each piston/connecting rod assembly is withdrawn, mark it so that it will be returned to its original bore. Temporarily refit the big-end caps to the connecting rods to reduce the risk of mixing them up.

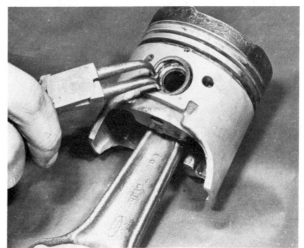

16.1 Removing the gudgeon pin circlip

16 Gudgeon pins - removal

1   To remove the gudgeon pin to free the piston from the connecting rod, remove one of the circlips at either end of the pin with a pair of circlip pliers. (photo)
2   Press out the pin from the rod and piston.
3   If the pin shows reluctance to move, then on no account force it out, as this could damage the piston. Immerse the piston in a pan of boiling water for three minutes. On removal the expansion of the aluminium should allow the gudgeon pin to slide out easily.
4   Ensure that each gudgeon pin is kept with the piston from which it was removed for exact refitting.

17 Piston rings - removal

1   To remove the piston rings, slide them carefully over the top of the piston, taking care not to scratch the aluminium alloy. Never slide them off the bottom of the piston skirt. It is very easy to break the iron piston rings if they are pulled off roughly

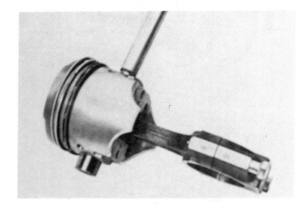

Fig. 1.16 Removing gudgeon pin (Sec 16)

so this operation should be done with extreme caution. It is useful to employ three strips of thin metal or feeler gauges to act as guides to assist the rings to pass over the empty grooves and to prevent them from dropping in.
2   Lift one end of the piston ring to be removed out of its groove and insert the end of the feeler gauge under it.
3   Turn the feeler gauges slowly round the piston and as the ring comes out of its groove apply slight upward pressure so that it rests on the land above. It can then be eased off the piston.

18 Flywheel - manual gearbox - removal

1   Remove the clutch (Chapter 5).
2   No lock tabs are fitted under the six bolts which hold the flywheel to the flywheel flange on the rear of the crankshaft.
3   Unscrew the bolts and remove them. (photo)
4   Lift the flywheel away from the crankshaft flange.
Note: Some difficulty may be experienced in removing the bolts through the rotation of the crankshaft every time pressure is put on the spanner. To lock the crankshaft in position while the bolts are removed, wedge a block of wood between the crankshaft and the side of the block inside the crankcase.

19 Drive plate - automatic transmission - removal

1   The drive plate is attached to the crankshaft rear flange by six bolts and a locking plate.

2   When removing it, note the reinforcing plate and spacer.

20 Main bearings and crankshaft - removal

1   Unscrew each of the ten bolts securing the five crankshaft main bearing caps and remove them. (photo)
2   Remove each main bearing cap in turn noting that they are marked so that there can be no confusion when refitting regarding sequence or orientation. (photo)
3   Remove the semicircular thrust washers fitted each side of the centre main bearing. (photo)
4   Lift the crankshaft from the crankcase and then withdraw the shell bearing halves from the crankcase.

21 Timing chain tensioner - removal

1   Undo the two bolts and washers which hold the timing chain

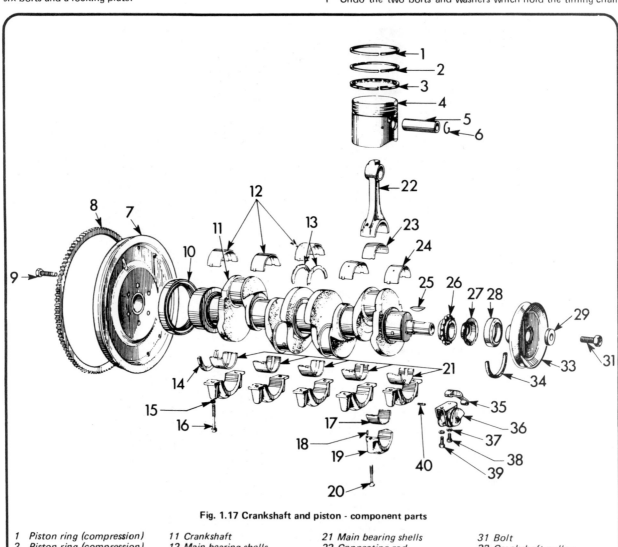

Fig. 1.17 Crankshaft and piston - component parts

1 Piston ring (compression)	11 Crankshaft	21 Main bearing shells	31 Bolt
2 Piston ring (compression)	12 Main bearing shells	22 Connecting rod	33 Crankshaft pulley
3 Piston ring (oil control)	13 Thrust washers	23 Big-end shell	34 Seal
4 Piston	14 Seal	24 Main bearing shell	35 Timing chain tensioner
5 Gudgeon pin	15 Spring washer	25 Woodruff key	36 Tensioner ratchet assembly
6 Circlip	16 Set screw	26 Timing chain sprocket	37 Spring washer
7 Flywheel	17 Big-end bearing shell	27 Oil thrower	38 Screw
8 Starter - ring gear	18 Dowel	28 Oil seal	39 Screw
9 Bolt	19 Big-end bearing cap	29 Spacer	40 Swivel pin

18.3 Flywheel bolt location

20.1 Removing a main bearing cap

20.2 Main bearing caps. Note markings i.e. 'F', 'R2', 'C', 'R4' and 'R'

20.3 Removing the main bearing thrust washers from their location on each side of the centre main bearing

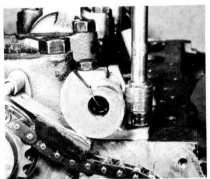

21.1 Removing the two bolts retaining the timing chain tensioner to the underside of the block

21.2 Timing chain tensioner arm on tensioner hinge pin

tensioner in place. Lift off the tensioner. (photo)

2　Pull the timing chain tensioner arm off its hinge pin on the front of the block. (photo)

22 Lubrication system - description

1　A forced feed system of lubrication is fitted, with oil circulated round the engine by a pump drawing oil from the sump below the block.

2　The full flow filter and oil pump assembly is mounted externally on the right-hand side of the cylinder block. The pump is driven by means of a short shaft and skew gear off the camshaft.

3　Oil reaches the pump via a tube pressed into the cylinder block sump face. Initial filtration is provided by a spring loaded gauze on the end of the tube. Drillings in the block carry the oil under pressure to the main and big-end bearings. Oil at a reduced pressure is fed to the valve and rocker gear and the timing chain and gearwheels.

4　One of two types of oil pump may be fitted. The eccentric bi-rotor type can be identified by four recesses cast in the cover whereas the vane type cover is flat. The pumps are directly interchangeable.

23 Oil filter - removal and refitting

1　A full-flow type oil filter is located adjacent to the oil pump on the right-hand side of the engine block.

2　This is a cartridge type filter which screws directly into the underside of the pump assembly.

3　Before unscrewing the filter from the pump remember to position a drain tray to catch any oil spillage.

4　Smear the sealing ring of the new filter with clean oil, then

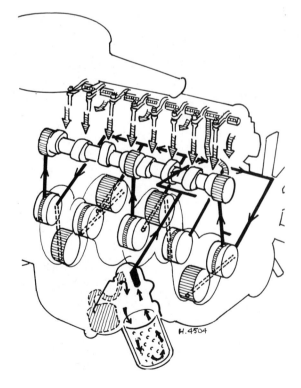

Fig. 1.18 Escort engine: lubrication circuit (Sec 22)

Fig. 1.19 Removing oil filter using strap wrench (Sec 23)

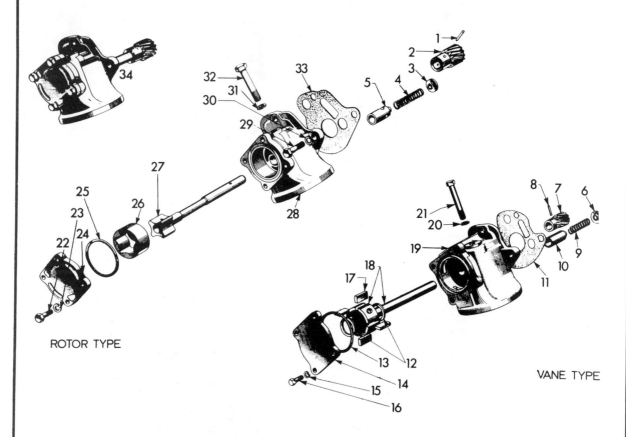

ROTOR TYPE

VANE TYPE

Fig. 1.20 Types of oil pump - component parts

1 Locking pin	8 Locking pin	17 Rotor blade	26 Rotor
2 Oil pump drive gear	9 Relief valve spring	18 Rotor and shaft assembly	27 Rotor shaft
3 Oil pressure relief valve retainer	10 Relief valve plunger	19 Pump assembly	28 Pump body
4 Relief valve spring	11 Gasket	20 Spring washer	29 Bolt
5 Relief valve plunger	12 Spacer	21 Bolt	30 Spring washer
6 Oil pressure relief valve retainer	13 Oil pump cover sealing ring	22 Bolt	31 Spring washer
7 Oil pump drive gear	14 Cover	23 Spring washer	32 Securing bolt
	15 Spring washer	24 Cover	33 Gasket
	16 Bolt	25 Sealing ring	34 Complete pump assembly

screw the filter on to the pump until hand tight. Then tighten the filter by hand a further ½ turn.

---

24 Oil pump - servicing

---

1 If the pump is worn it is best to purchase an exchange reconditioned unit as a good oil pump is at the very heart of long engine life. Generally speaking, an exchange or overhauled pump should be fitted at a major engine reconditioning. If it is wished

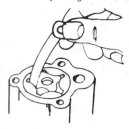

Fig. 1.21 Measuring clearance between inner and outer oil pump rotors (Sec 24)

Fig. 1.22 Measuring clearance between outer rotor and oil pump body (Sec 24)

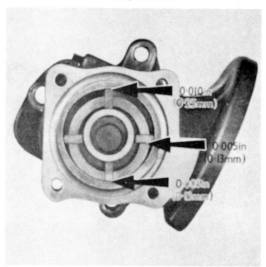

Fig. 1.23 Measuring clearance between rotor and rotary valve type oil pump body (Sec 24)

Fig. 1.24 Measuring oil pump endfloat (Sec 24)

to overhaul the oil pump, detach the pump and filter unit from the cylinder block, and remove the filter body and element or cartridge, according to type.

2 Unscrew and remove the four bolts and lockwashers which secure the oil pump cover and remove the cover. Lift out the 'O' ring seal from the groove in the pump body.

Eccentric bi-rotor type pumps

3 Check the clearance between the inner and outer rotors with a feeler gauge (Fig. 1.21). This should not exceed 0.006 inch (0.15 mm).

4 Check the clearance between the outer rotor and the pump body (Fig. 1.22). This should not exceed 0.010 inch (0.25 mm).

Rotary vane type pump

5 Check the clearances as indicated (Fig. 1.23).

All pumps

6 Check the endfloat of both types of pump by placing a straight-edge across the open face of the pump casing and measuring the gap between its lower edge and the face of the rotor. This should not exceed 0.005 inch (0.1270 mm) (Fig. 1.24).

7 Replacement rotors are only supplied as a matched pair so that if the clearance is excessive, a new rotor assembly must be fitted. When it is necessary to renew the rotors, drive out the pin securing the skew gear and pull the gear from the shaft. Remove the inner rotor and drive shaft and withdraw the outer rotor. Install the outer rotor with the chamfered end towards the pump body.

8 Fit the inner rotor and drive shaft assembly, position the skew gear and install the pin. Tap over each end of the pin to prevent it loosening in service. Position a new 'O' ring in the groove in the pump body, fit the end plate in position and secure with the four bolts and lockwashers.

9 Refit the oil pump assembly together with a new gasket and secure in place with three bolts and lockwashers.

---

25 Crankcase ventilation systems - description and servicing

---

1 On all engines a semi-closed positive ventilation system is

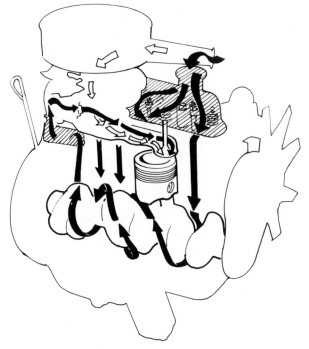

Fig. 1.25 Escort engine: ventilation system (Sec 25)

fitted. A breather valve in the oil filler cap allows air to enter as required. Crankcase fumes travel out through an oil separator and emission control valve, and then via a connecting tube back into the inlet manifold. In this way the majority of crankcase fumes are burnt during the combustion process in the cylinder.

2 With the simple fume outlet draught tube, no regular maintenance is required but is is a good idea to remove it from the crankcase once a year and to wash it thoroughly with paraffin to ensure that the gauze filter is not blocked.

3 With the emission control type system, clean the valve and rocker box cover breather cap every 18,000 miles (29,000 km). To remove the valve, disconnect the hose and then pull it from its grommet in the oil separator box.

4 Dismantle the valve by removing the circlip (1) and extracting the seal, valve and spring (2) from the valve body (3) (Fig. 1.27)

5 Wash and clean all components in petrol to remove sludge or deposits, and renew the rubber components if they have deteriorated.

6 Reassembly and refitting are reversals of removal and dismantling procedures.

26 Engine front mountings - removal and installation

1 With time the bonded rubber insulators, one on each of the front mountings, will perish causing undue vibration and noise from the engine. Severe juddering when reversing or when moving off from rest is also likely and is a further sign of worn mounting rubbers.

2 The front mounting rubber insulators can be changed with the engine in the car.

3 Apply the handbrake firmly, jack up the front of the car, and place stands under the front of the car.

4 Lower the jack, take off the engine sump shield where fitted, and place the jack under the sump to take the weight of the engine.

5 Undo the large bolt which holds each of the engine mountings to the body crossmember. Then knock back the locking tabs and undo the four bolts holding each of the engine mountings in place.

6 Fit new mountings using new tab washers and tighten the four bolts down and bend up the locking tabs.

7 Screw in the bolts which connect the mountings to each side of the crossmember.

8 Lower the vehicle.

27 Examination and renovation - general

With the engine stripped down and all parts thoroughly cleaned, it is now time to examine everything for wear. The following items should be checked and where necessary renewed or renovated as described in the following Sections.

28 Crankshaft - examination and renovation

1 Examine the crankpin and main journal surfaces for signs of scoring or scratches. Check the ovality of the crankpins at different positions with a micrometer. If more than 0.001 inch (0.0254 mm) out of round, the crankpins will have to be reground. They will also have to be reground if there are any scores or scratches present. Also check the journals in the same fashion.

2 If it is necessary to regrind the crankshaft and fit new bearings, your local Ford garage or engineering works will be able to decide how much metal to grind off and the size of new bearing shells.

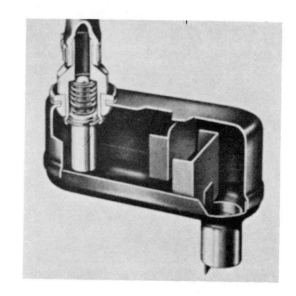

Fig. 1.26 Oil separator and emission control valve (later 1100 and all 1300 models) (Sec 25)

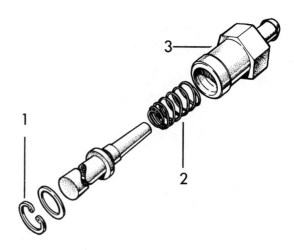

Fig. 1.27 Crankcase emission control valve - component parts (Sec 25)

1 Circlip   2 Return spring   3 Body

Fig. 1.28 Engine front mountings (Sec 26)

29 Big-end and main bearings - examination and renovation

1 Big-end bearing failure is accompanied by a knocking from the crankcase, and a slight drop in oil pressure. Main bearing failure is accompanied by vibration which can be quite severe as the engine speed rises. Inspect the big-end, main bearings, and thrust washers for signs of general wear, scoring, pitting and scratches. The bearings should be matt grey in colour. With lead-indium bearings, should a trace of copper colour be noticed, the bearings are badly worn as the lead bearing material has worn away to expose the indium underlay. Renew the bearings if they are in this condition or if there is any sign of scoring or pitting

2 The undersizes available are designed to correspond with the regrind sizes, ie. −0.010 inch (0.2540 mm) bearings are correct for a crankshaft reground −0.010 inch (0.2540 mm) undersize. The bearings are in fact slightly more than the stated undersize as running clearances have been allowed for during their manufacture.

3 Very long engine life can be achieved by changing big-end bearings at intervals of 30,000 miles (48,000 km) and main bearings at intervals of 50,000 miles (80,000 km), irrespective of bearing wear. Normally, crankshaft wear is infinitesimal and a change of bearings will ensure mileages of between 80,000 to 100,000 miles (128,000 to 161, 000 km) before crankshaft regrinding becomes necessary. Crankshafts normally have to be reground because of scoring due to bearing failure.

30 Cylinder bores - examination and renovation

1 The cylinder bores must be examined for taper, ovality, scoring and scratches. Start by carefully examining the top of the cylinder bores. If they are at all worn a very slight ridge will be found on the thrust side. This marks the top of the piston ring travel. The owner will have a good indication of the bore wear prior to dismantling the engine, or removing the cylinder head. Excessive oil consumption accompanied by blue smoke from the exhaust is a sure sign of worn cylinder bores and piston rings.

2 Measure the bore diameter just under the ridge with a micrometer and compare it with the diameter at the bottom of the bore which is not subject to wear. If the difference between the two measurements is more than 0.006 inch (0.1524 mm) it will be necessary to fit special pistons and rings or to have the cylinders rebored and fit oversize pistons. If a micrometer is not available, remove the rings from each piston in turn (do not mix the rings from piston to piston) and place each piston in its respective bore about ¾ inch (19.05 mm) below the top surface of the cylinder block. If an 0.010 inch (0.2540 mm) thick feeler gauge can be slid between the piston and the cylinder wall on the thrust side of the bore, then the following action must be taken. Oversize pistons are available in the following sizes: +0.010 inch (0.2540 mm), +0.020 inch (0.508 mm), +0.030 inch (0.762 mm).

3 These are accurately machined to just below these measurements so as to provide correct running clearances in bores of the exact oversize dimensions.

4 If the bores are slightly worn but not so badly worn as to justify reboring them, then special oil control rings and pistons can be fitted which will restore compression and stop the engine burning oil. Several different types are available and the manufacturers' instructions concerning their fitting must be followed closely.

5 If new pistons are being fitted and the bores have not been reground, it is essential to slightly roughen the hard glaze on the sides of the bores with fine glass paper so the new piston rings will have a chance to bed in properly.

6 Newly fitted pistons should be tested for clearance using a feeler gauge and spring balance. Place the feeler gauge between the piston and cylinder wall and having attached the spring balance to it, check the pull required to remove it in accordance with the following data.:

1100cc and 1600cc engines

7 to 11 lb (3.2 to 4.5 kg) pull using an 0.002 inch (0.05 mm) thick feeler 0.5 inch (12.7 mm) wide.

1300cc engines

7 to 11 lb (3.2 to 4.5 kg) pull using an 0.0025 inch (0.064 mm) thick feeler 0.5 inch (12.7 mm) wide.

31 Pistons and piston rings - examination and renovation

1 If the old pistons are to be refitted, carefully remove the piston rings and then thoroughly clean them. Take particular care to clean out the piston ring grooves. At the same time do not scratch the aluminium in any way. If new rings are to be fitted to the old pistons then the top ring should be stepped so as to clear the ridge left above the previous top ring. If a normal but oversize new ring is fitted, it will hit the ridge and break because the new ring will not have worn in the same way as the old. This will have worn in unison with the ridge.

2 Before fitting the rings on the pistons, each should be inserted approximately 2 inch (50.8 mm) down the cylinder bore and the gap measured with a feeler gauge. This should be between 0.009 inch (0.2286 mm) and 0.014 inch 90.3556 mm). It is essential that the gap is also measured at the bottom of the worn bore, as even if the gap is correct at the top, the ring could easily seize at the bottom. If the ring gap is too small rub down the ends of the ring with a very fine file until the gap, when fitted, is correct. To keep the rings square in the bore for measurement, line each up in turn by inserting an old piston in the bore upside down, and use the piston to push the ring down about 2 inches (50.8 mm). Remove the piston and measure the piston ring gap.

3 When fitting new pistons and rings to a rebored engine, the piston ring gap can be measured at the top of the bore as the bore will not now taper. It is not necessary to measure the side clearance in the piston ring grooves with the rings fitted as the groove dimensions are accurately machined during manufacture. When fitting new oil control rings to old pistons, it may be necessary to have the grooves widened by machining to accept the new wider rings. In this instance the manufacturer's fitting instructions will indicate the procedure.

32 Camshaft and camshaft bearings - examination and renovation

1 Carefully examine the camshaft bearings for wear. If the bearings are obviously worn or pitted, then they must be renewed. This is an operation for your local Ford dealer or the

local engineering works as it demands the use of specialised equipment. The bearings are removed with a special drift after which new bearings are pressed in, care being taken to ensure the oil holes in the bearing line up with those in the block.

2   The camshaft itself should show no signs of wear. If scoring on the cams is noticed, the only permanently satisfactory cure is to fit a new camshaft.

3   Examine the skew gear for wear, chipped teeth or other damage.

4   Carefully examine the camshaft thrust plate. Excessive wear will be visually self-evident and will require the fitting of a new plate.

33   Valve and valve seats - examination and renovation

1   Examine the heads of the valves for pitting and burning, especially the heads of the exhaust valves. The valve seatings should be examined at the same time. If the pitting on valve and seat is very slight, the marks can be removed by grinding the exhaust seats and valves together with coarse, and then fine, valve grinding paste. **The inlet valves are aluminised and must not be ground in.**

2   Where bad pitting has occurred to the valve seats, it will be necessary to recut them and fit new valves. If the valve seats are so worn that they cannot be recut, then it will be necessary to fit new valve seat inserts. These latter two jobs should be entrusted to the local Ford agent or engineering works. In practice it is very seldom that the seats are so badly worn that they require renewal. Normally, it is the valve that is too badly worn for replacement, and the owner can easily purchase a new set of valves and match them to the seats by valve grinding.

3   Valve grinding is carried out as follows: Smear a trace of coarse carborundum paste on the seat face and apply a suction grinder tool to the valve head. With a semi-rotary motion, grind the valve head to its seat, lifting the valve occasionally to re-distribute the grinding paste. When a dull matt even surface finish is produced on both the valve seat and the valve, then wipe off the paste and repeat the process with fine carborundum paste, lifting and turning the valve to redistribute the paste as before. **A light spring placed under the valve head will greatly** ease this operation. When a smooth, unbroken ring of light grey matt finish is produced, on both valve and valve seat faces, the grinding operation is complete.

4   Scrape away all carbon from the valve head and the valve stem. Carefully clean away every trace of grinding compound, taking great care to leave none in the ports or in the valve guides. Clean the valves and valve seats with a paraffin soaked rag then with a clean rag, and finally, if an air line is available, blow the valves, valve guides and valve ports clean.

34   Timing gears and chain - examination and renovation

1   Examine the teeth on both the crankshaft gearwheel and the camshaft gear wheel for wear. Each tooth forms an inverted V with the gearwheel periphery, and if worn the side of each tooth under tension will be slightly concave in shape when compared with the other side of the tooth, ie one side of the inverted V will be concave when compared with the other. If any sign of wear is present the gearwheels must be renewed.

2   Examine the links of the chain for side slackness and renew the chain if any slackness is noticeable when compared with a new chain. It is a sensible precaution to renew the chain at about 30,000 mile (48,000 km) and at a less mileage if the engine is stripped down for a major overhaul. The rollers on a very badly worn chain may be slightly grooved.

Fig. 1.29 Using suction tool to hold valve head while grinding-in (Sec 33)

35   Rockers and rocker shaft - examination and renovation

1   Thoroughly clean the rocker shaft and then check it for distortion by rolling it on a piece of plate glass. If it is out of true, renew it. The surface of the shaft should be free from wear ridges and score marks.

2   Check the rocker arms for wear of the rocker bushes, for wear at the rocker arm face which bears on the valve stem, and for wear of the adjusting ball ended screws. Wear in the rocker arm bush can be checked by gripping the rocker arm tip and holding the rocker arm in place on the shaft, noting if there is any lateral rocker arm shake. If shake is present, and the arm is very loose on the shaft, a new bush or rocker arm must be fitted.

3   Check the top of the rocker arm where it bears on the valve head for cracking or serious wear on the case hardening. If none is present re-use the rocker arm. Check the lower half of the ball on the end of the rocker arm. Check the lower half of the ball on the end of the rocker arm adjusting screw. Check the pushrods for straightness by rolling them on a piece of plate glass. Renew any that are bent.

36   Tappets (cam followers) - examination and renovation

Examine the bearing surface of the mushroom tappets which lie on the camshaft. Any indentation in this surface or any cracks indicate serious wear and the tappets should be renewed. Thoroughly clean them out, removing all traces of sludge. It is most unlikely that the sides of the tappets will prove worn, but if they are a very loose fit in their bores and can readily be rocked, they should be exchanged for new units. It is very unusual to find any wear in the tappets, and any wear is likely to occur only at very high mileages.

37   Connecting rods - examination and renovation

1   Examine the mating faces of the big-end caps to see if they have ever been filed in a mistaken attempt to take up wear. If so, the offending rods must be renewed.

2   Insert the gudgeon pin into the little end of the connecting rod. It should go in fairly easily, but if any slackness is present then take the rod to your local Ford dealer and exchange it for a rod of identical weight.

38   Starter ring gear - examination and renovation

1   If the teeth on the converter (automatic transmission) are worn then the converter must be renewed as an assembly.

2 If the flywheel ring gear teeth are worn then the ring gear can be renewed without the need to replace the flywheel.

3 To remove a starter ring either split it with a cold chisel after making a cut with a hacksaw blade between two teeth, or heat the ring, and use a soft headed hammer (not steel) to knock the ring off, striking it evenly and alternately, at equally spaced points. Take great care not to damage the flywheel during this process.

4 Clean and polish with emery cloth four evenly spaced areas on the outside face of the new starter ring.

5 Heat the ring evenly with an oxyacetylene flame until the polished portions turn dark blue (600°F/316°C). Hold the ring as this temperature for five minutes and then quickly fit it to the flywheel so the chamfered portion of the teeth faces the gearbox side of the flywheel.

6 The ring should be tapped gently down onto its register and left to cool naturally when the contraction of the metal on cooling will ensure that it is a secure and permanent fit. Great care must be taken not to overheat the ring, indicated by it turning light metallic blue, as if this happens the temper of the ring will be lost.

7 It does not matter which way round the ring for pre-engaged starters is fitted as it has no chamfers on its teeth. This also makes for quick identification between the two rings.

---

39 Cylinder head - decarbonising

1 This can be carried out with the engine either in or out of the car. With the cylinder head off, carefully remove with a wire brush mounted in an electric drill and blunt scraper, all traces of carbon deposits from the combustion spaces and the ports. The valve head stems and valve guides should also be freed from any carbon deposits. Wash the combustion spaces and ports down with petrol and scrape the cylinder head surface free of any foreign matter with the side of steel rule, or a similar article.

2 Clean the pistons and top of the cylinder bores. If the pistons are still in the block then it is essential that great care is taken to ensure that no carbon gets into the cylinder bores as this could scratch the cylinder walls or cause damage to the piston and rings. To ensure that this does not happen, first turn the crankshaft so that two of the pistons are at the top of their bores. Stuff rag into the other two bores or seal them off with paper and masking tape. The waterways should also be covered with small pieces of masking tape to prevent particles of carbon entering the cooling system and damaging the water pump.

3 There are two schools of thought as to how much carbon should be removed from the piston crown. One school recommends that a ring of carbon should be left round the edge of the piston and on the cylinder bore wall as an aid to low oil consumption. Although this is probably true for early engines with worn bores, on modern engines it is preferable to remove all traces of carbon deposits.

4 If all traces of carbon are to be removed, press a little grease into the gap between the cylinder walls and the two pistons which are to be worked on. With a blunt scraper carefully scrape all the carbon from the piston crown, taking great care not to scratch the aluminium. Also scrape away the carbon from the surrounding lip of the cylinder wall. When all carbon has been removed, scrape away the grease which will now be contaminated with carbon particles, taking care not to press any into the bores. To assist prevention of carbon build-up the piston crown can be polished with a metal polish. Remove the rags or masking tape from the other two cylinders and turn the crankshaft so that the two pistons which were at the bottom are now at the top. Place rag or masking tape in the cylinders which have been decarbonised and proceed as already described.

5 Thoroughly clean out the cylinder head bolt holes in the top face of the block. If these are filled with carbon, oil or water it is possible for the block to crack when the bolts are screwed in due to the hydraulic pressure created by the trapped fluid.

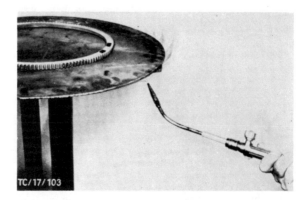

TC/17/103

Fig. 1.30 Heating the flywheel ring gear prior to assembly on flywheel (Sec 38)

---

40 Valve guides - examination and renovation

1 Examine the valve guides internally for scoring and other signs of wear. If a new valve is a very loose fit in a guide and there is a trace of lateral rocking then new guides will have to be fitted.

2 The fitting of new guides is a job which should be done by your local Ford dealer.

---

41 Engine reassembly - general

1 To ensure maximum life with minimum trouble from a rebuilt engine, not only must everything be correctly assembled, but everything must be spotlessly clean, all the oilways must be clear, locking washers and spring washers must always be fitted where indicated and all bearing and other working surfaces must be thoroughly lubricated during assembly.

2 Before assembly begins renew any bolts or studs, the threads of which are in any way damaged, and whenever possible use new spring washers.

3 Apart from your normal tools, a supply of clean rag, an oil can filled with engine oil, a new supply of assorted spring washers, a set of new gaskets, and a torque wrench, should be collected together.

42 Assembling the engine

1   Thoroughly clean the block and ensure that all traces of old gaskets etc are removed.

2   Position the upper halves of the shell bearings in their correct positions so that the tabs of the shells engage in the machined keyways in the sides of the bearing locations. (photo)

3   Oil the main bearing shells after they have been fitted in position. (photo)

4   Thoroughly clean out the oilways in the crankshaft with the aid of a thin wire.

5   To check for the possibility of an error in the grinding of the crankshaft journal (presuming the crankshaft has been reground) smear engineers blue evenly over each big end journal in turn with the crankshaft end flange held firmly in position in a vice.

6   With new shell bearings fitted to the connecting rods fit the correct rod to each journal in turn, fully tightening down the securing bolts.

7   Spin the rod on the crankshaft a few times and then remove the big-end cap. A fine unbroken layer of engineers blue should cover the whole of the journal. If the blue is much darker on one side than the other or if the blue has disappeared from a certain area (ignore the very edges of the journal) then something is wrong and the journal will have to be checked with a micrometer.

8   The main journals should also be checked in similar fashion with the crankshaft in the crankcase. On completion of these tests remove all traces of the engineers blue.

9   The crankshaft can now be lowered carefully into place. (photo)

10 Fit new endfloat thrust washers. These locate in recesses on each side of the centre main bearing in the cylinder block and must be fitted with the oil grooves facing the crankshaft flange.

With the crankshaft in position check for endfloat which should be between 0.008 and 0.011 inch (0.203 to 0.279 mm). If the endfloat is correct, remove the thrust washer and select suitable washers to give the correct endfloat.

11 Place the lower halves of the main bearing shells in their caps, making sure that the locking tabs fit into the machined grooves. Refit the main bearing caps ensuring that they are the correct way round and that the correct cap is on the correct journal. The front cap is marked 'F' the second 'R2', the centre cap 'C', the fifth cap 'RA' and the rear cap 'R'. Tighten the cap bolts to a torque of 55 to 60 lbf ft (7.5 to 8.2 Kgf m) (photo). Spin the crankshaft to make certain it is turning freely.

12 Fit a new rear main oil seal bearing retainer gasket to the rear of the cylinder block. (photo)

13 Then fit the rear main oil seal bearing retainer housing (photo). Note that the oil seal is also circular and is simply prised out when removed, a new one being pressed in (Fig. 1.33).

14 Lightly tighten the four retaining bolts with spring washers under their heads noting that two bolts are dowelled to ensure correct alignment and should be tightened first.

15 Torque the bolts to 13 to 15 lbf ft (1.7 to 2.1 Kgf m) check that the housing is centralised.

16 Check that the piston ring grooves and oilways are thoroughly clean and unblocked. Piston rings must always be fitted over the head of the piston and never from the bottom. Fit the rings by the same method used for removing them (Section 17).

17 When assembling the rings note that the compression rings are marked 'top', and that the upper ring is chromium plated. The ring gaps should be spaced at 120° angles round the piston. (photos)

18 If the same pistons are being re-used, then they must be mated to the same connecting rod with the same gudgeon pin. If new pistons are being fitted it does not matter which connecting

42.2 Upper half of main bearing shell in place on cylinder block. Note shell tab engaged in block keyway (arrowed)

42.3 Oiling main bearing shells

42.9 Replacing crankshaft

Fig. 1.31 Position of crankshaft thrust washer half on centre main bearing cap (Sec 42)

Fig. 1.32 Main bearing cap markings: "——" indicates front of engine (Sec 42)

42.11 Tighten the main bearing cap bolts to the correct torque

42.12 Fit the oil seal housing gasket to the rear of the cylinder block ...

42.13 ... then fit the housing

42.17A 'Top' markings on piston compression rings

42.17B Piston rings in place on piston with gaps set at 120° angles around the piston

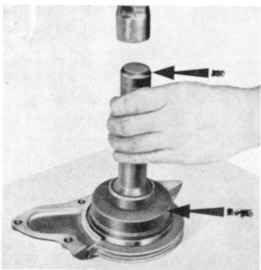

Fig. 1.33 Installing an oil seal to a circular crankshaft rear retainer (Sec 42)

Fig. 1.34 Relationship between piston (arrow) and con-rod (front) assembly (Sec 42)

rod they are used with. Note that the word 'FRONT' is stamped on one side of each of the rods. On reassembly the side marked 'FRONT' must be towards the front of the engine. (photo)
19 Fit a gudgeon pin circlip in position at one end of the gudgeon pin hole in the piston and fit the piston to the connecting rod by sliding in the gudgeon pin. The arrow on the crown of each piston must be on the same side as the word 'FRONT' on the connecting rod. (photos)
20 Fit the second circlip in position. Repeat this procedure for

the remaining three pistons and connecting rods.
21 Fit the connecting rod in position and check that the oil hole in the upper half of each bearing aligns with the oil squirt hole in the connecting rod. (photo)
22 With a wad of clean rag wipe the cylinder bores clean, and then oil them generously. The pistons complete with connecting rods, are fitted to their bores from above. As each piston is inserted into its bore, ensure that it is the correct piston/connecting rod assembly for that particular bore and that the connecting rod is the right way round, and that the front of the piston is towards the front of the bore, ie; towards the front of the engine.
23 The piston will only slide into the bore as far as the oil control ring. It is then necessary to compress the piston rings in a clamp. (photos)
24 Gently tap the piston into the cylinder bore with a wooden or plastic hammer. (photo) If a proper piston ring clamp is not available then a suitable jubilee clip does the job very well.
25 Note the directional arrow on the piston crown (Fig. 1.35).

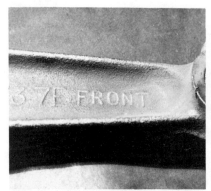

42.18 The word 'front' on the connecting rod must be towards the front of the engine on re-assembly

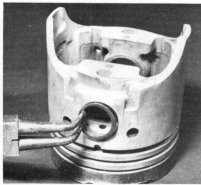

42.19A Replacing the gudgeon pin circlip prior to inserting gudgeon pin and conrod

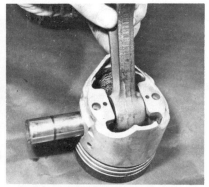

42.19B Inserting gudgeon pin through piston and conrod

42.21 Fitting connecting rod upper shell in conrod. Note alignment of shell and conrod oil holes

42.23A Using a piston ring clamp to compress rings ...

42.23B ... prior to inserting piston in bore

42.24 Using the shaft of a hammer to tap the piston down the bore

42.27 Torquing connecting rod bearing caps

42.28 Semi-rebuilt engine ready to receive camshaft and tappets

42.29A Inserting the cam followers into their bores

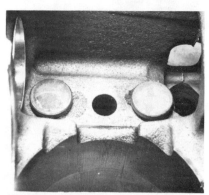

42.29B Inserting the cam followers into their bores

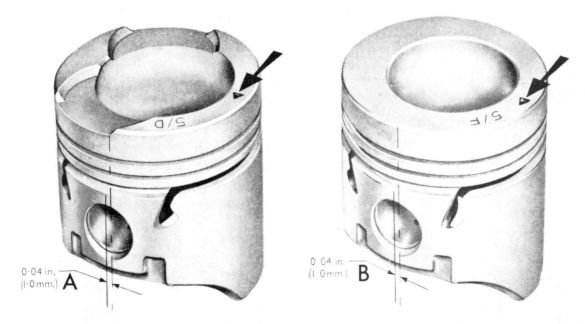

Fig. 1.35 Piston identification, gudgeon pin offset and front facing directional arrow (Sec 42)

A 1100 and 1300 models   *B GT/Sport/1300E*

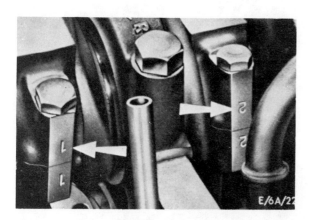

Fig. 1.36 Connecting rod and cap markings: always keep the caps and rods in their correct pairs (Sec 42)

26 Fit the shell bearings to the big-end caps so the tongue on the back of each bearing lies in the machined recess.

27 Generously oil the crankshaft connecting rod journals and then replace each big-end cap on the same connecting rod from which it was removed. Fit the locking plates under the heads of

the big-end bolts, tap the caps right home on the dowels and then tighten the bolts to a torque of 31 to 35 lbf ft (4.2 to 4.8 Kgf m). To facilitate reassembly the rod and cap are marked (ie; 1 - 2 - 3 - 4) these numbers should be together and on the camshaft side of the engine (photo). (Fig. 1.36).

28 The semi-rebuilt engine will now look as in the photograph and is ready for the cam followers and cam to be fitted. (photo)

29 Fit the eight cam followers into the same holes in the block from which each was removed. The cam followers can only be fitted with the block upside down. (photos)

30 Fit the Woodruff key in its slot on the front of the crankshaft and then press the timing sprocket into place so the timing mark faces forward. Oil the camshaft shell bearings and insert the camshaft into the block (which should still be upside down). (photo)

31 Make sure the camshaft turns freely and then fit the thrust plate behind the camshaft flange as shown in the photograph. Torque the thrust plate bolts to 2.5 to 3.5 lb ft (0.35 to 0.48 kg m). Measure the endfloat with a feeler gauge - it should b between 0.002 and 0.008 inch (0.06 and 0.2 mm). If this is not so, then renew the plate. (photo).

32 Turn up the tab under the head of each bolt to lock it in place.

33 Refit the camshaft timing gear and loosely retain with its two retaining bolts. Use a **new** tab washer.

34 When refitting the timing chain round the gearwheels and to

42.30 Carefully insert camshaft

42.31A Inserting camshaft thrust plate behind camshaft

42.31B Plate bolted in position with tab washers turned up to lock bolt. Note timing gear locating peg (arrowed)

42.34 Crankshaft and camshaft timing sprocket marks aligned with peg fully inserted in camshaft sprocket (arrows)

42.36 Bending up tabs of lock washer to retain camshaft sprocket bolts

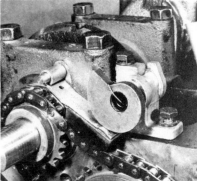
42.40 Timing chain tensioner in place on underside of cylinder block

42.41 Replacing front cover oil seal

42.42 Front cover gasket in position on block ready to receive timing cover

42.44 Oil pick-up pipe bracket location on underside of cylinder block

42.45A Sump gasket in place on cylinder block sump flange

42.45B Gaskets being fitted to the rear oil seal carrier ...

the engine, the two timing lines (arrowed) must be adjacent to each other on an imaginary line passing through each gearwheel centre. (photo)

35 With the timing marks correctly aligned turn the camshaft until the protruding dowel locates in the hole (arrowed) in the camshaft sprocket wheel. (photo 42.34)

36 Tighten the two retaining bolts and bend up the tabs on the lockwasher. (photo)

37 Fit the oil slinger to the nose of the crankshaft, concave side facing outwards. The cut-out locates over the Woodruff key.

38 Then slide the timing chain tensioner arm over its hinge pin on the front of the block.

39 Turn the tensioner back from its free position so that it will apply pressure to the tensioner arm and replace the tensioner on the block sump flange.

40 Bolt the tensioner to the block using spring washers under the heads of the two bolts. (photo)

41 Remove the front oil seal from the timing chain cover and carefully press a new seal into position (photo). Lightly lubricate the face of the seal which will bear against the crankshaft.

42 Using jointing compound, fit a new timing cover gasket in place.

43 Fit the timing chain cover, replacing and tightening the two dowel bolts first. These fit in the holes nearest the sump flange and serve to align the timing cover correctly. Ensure spring washers are used and then tighten the bolts evenly.

44 Refit the tube or crankcase emission device to its recess adjacent to the top of the petrol pump, tapping it gently into place Replace the oil pump suction pipe using a new tab washer and position the gauze head so that it clears the crankshaft throw and the oil return pipe (where fitted). Tighten the

nut and bend back the tab of the lockwasher.

45 Clean the flanges of the sump and fit new gaskets in place. Fit a new oil seal to the flange at the rear of the crankcase and at the front. (photos)

46 Locate the flywheel or drive plate (automatic transmission) onto the crankshaft flange and tighten the securing bolts to a torque of between 50 and 56 lbf ft (6.8 and 7.6 Kgf m). (photo)

47 Locate the sump in position on the crankcase and tighten the securing bolts evenly in diagonal sequence. Where the sump is being refitted with the engine in position in the vehicle, stick the gaskets in position on the face of the crankcase with jointing compound. Reconnect the dismantled steering and tighten the crossmember bolts to a torque of between 29 and 37 lbf ft (4.1 and 5.1 Kgf m).

48 The engine can now be turned over so that it is the right way up. Coat the oil pump flanges with jointing compound.

49 Fit a new gasket in place on the oil pump

50 Position the oil pump against the block ensuring that the skew gear teeth on the driveshaft mate with those on the camshaft. (photo)

51 Replace the three securing bolts and spring washers and tighten them down evenly.

52 Moving to the front of the engine align the slot in the crankshaft pulley wheel with the key on the crankshaft and gently tap the pulley wheel home.

53 Secure the pulley wheel by fitting the large flat washer, the spring washer and then the bolt which should be tightened securely. (photo)

54 The next step is to thoroughly clean the faces of the block and cylinder head. Then fit a new cylinder head gasket. In order to correctly position the gasket it is a good idea to temporarily screw in two lengths of studding (one in each extreme diagonal

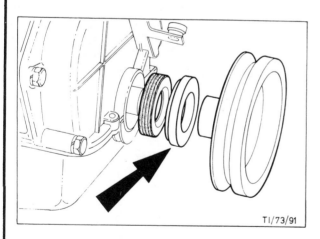

Fig. 1.37 Special tool (arrowed) available from Ford dealers to assist in accurate alignment of front cover oil seal during replacement (Sec 42)

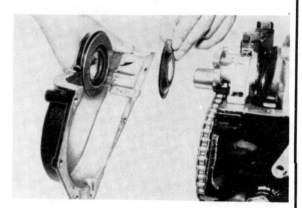

Fig. 1.38 Replacing oil slinger and timing cover complete with oil seal (Sec 42)

42.45C ... and front timing cover

42.46 Torquing flywheel retaining bolts

42.50 Oil pump in place on cylinder
block   prior to receiving retaining bolts

42.53 Tightening the crankshaft pulley
bolt

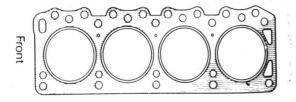

Fig. 1.39 Upward facing side of cylinder head gasket (Sec 42)

hole) to act as locating dowels. These should be removed once
two of the cylinder head bolts have been screwed into position.
55 With the cylinder head on its side lubricate the valve stems
and refit the valves to their correct guides. The valves should
previously have been ground in (see Section 33).
56 Then fit the valve stem umbrella oil seals open ends down.
(photo)

57 Next slide the valve spring into place. Use new ones if the old
set has covered 20,000 miles (32,000 km).
58 Slide the valve spring retainer over the valve stem.
59 Compress the valve spring with a compressor.
60 Then refit the split collets. (photo) A trace of grease will help
to hold them to the valve stem recess until the spring compressor
is slackened off and the collets are wedged in place by the spring.
61 Carefully lower the cylinder head onto the block. (Fig. 1.40)
62 Replace the cylinder head bolts and screw them down finger
tight. Note that two of the bolts are of a different length.
63 With a torque wrench tighten the bolts to 66 to 71 lbf ft
(9.0 to 9.7 Kgf m) in the order shown in Fig. 1.41.
64 Fit the pushrods into the same holes in the block from which
they were removed. Make sure the pushrods seat properly in the
cam followers.
65 Reassemble the rocker gear into the rocker shaft and fit the

42.56 Valve stem oil seal correctly fitted

42.60 Compress the spring and fit the collets

Fig. 1.40 Replacing cylinder head: replacement is made easier if two old bolts are ground down and placed as at 'A'. (Sec 42)

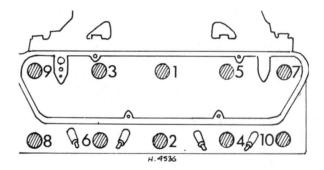

Fig. 1.41 Cylinder head bolt tightening sequence: torque bolts in order shown to 66 to 71 lbf ft (9.0 to 9.7 Kgf m) by following the procedure given in the specification (Sec 42)

shaft to the cylinder head (photo). Ensure that the oil holes are clear and that the cut-outs for the securing bolts lie facing the holes in the brackets.

66 Tighten down the four rocker bracket washers and bolts to a torque of 18 to 22 lbf ft (2.4 to 3.0 Kgf m). (photo)

67 The valve adjustments should be made with the engine cold. The importance of correct rocker arm/valve stem clearances cannot be overstressed as they vitally affect the performance of the engine. If the clearances are set too open, the efficiency of the engine is reduced as the valves open late and

close earlier than was intended. If, on the other hand, the clearances are set too close there is a danger that the stems will expand upon heating and not allow the valves to close properly which will cause burning of the valve head and seat and possible warping. if the engine is in the car access to the rockers is by removing the four holding down screws from the rocker cover, and then lifting the rocker cover and gasket away.

68 It is important that the clearance is set when the tappet of the valve being adjusted is on the heel of the cam (ie; opposite the peak). This can be ensured by carrying out the adjustments

in the following order (which also avoids turning the crankshaft more than necessary):

Valves open		Valves to adjust	
1 ex	6 in	3 in	8 ex
2 in	4 ex	5 ex	7 in
3 in	8 ex	1 ex	6 in
5 ex	7 in	2 in	4 ex

The valve positions are numbered from the front of the engine.

Valve clearance for all 1100, 1300, 1600 2V engines

Inlet 0.010 in (0.25 mm) exhaust 0.022 in (0.55 mm)

Valve clearance for all other 1100 and 1300 engines

Inlet 0.008 in (0.20 mm) exhaust 0.022 in (0.55 mm)

69 Working from the front of the engine (No 1 valve), the correct clearance is obtained by rotating the hexagon adjuster with a spanner whilst the appropriate size feeler gauge is installed between the valve stem and the rocker arm. The feeler gauge should be a firm sliding fit; take care that it is not pinched by over-tightening the adjuster. (photo).

70 Do not refit the rocker cover before replacing the distributor and setting the ignition timing. It is important to set the distributor drive correctly as otherwise the ignition timing will be totally incorrect. It is possible to set the distributor drive in apparently the right position, but, in fact, 180° out by omitting to select the correct cylinder which must not only be at TDC but must also be on its firing stroke with both valves closed. The distributor drive should therefore not be fitted until the cylinder head is in position and the valves can be observed. Alternatively, if the timing cover has not been replaced, the distributor drive can be replaced when the lines on the timing wheels are adjacent to each other.

71 Rotate the crankshaft so that No 1 piston is at TDC and on its firing stroke (the lines in the timing gears will be adjacent to each other). When No 1 piston is at TDC both valves will be closed and both rocker arms will 'rock' slightly because of the stem to arm pad clearance.

72 Note the timing marks on the timing case and the notch on the crankshaft wheel periphery (photo). Set the crankshaft so the cut-out is in the right position of initial advance which varies, depending on the model. For further information see Chapter 4 Specifications.

73 Hold the distributor in place so that the vacuum unit is towards the rear of the engine and at an angle of about 30° to the block. Do not yet engage the distributor drive gear with the skew gear on the camshaft.

74 Turn the rotor arm so that it points toward No 2 inlet port. (photo)

75 Push the distributor shaft into its bore and note, as the distributor drive gear and skew gear on the camshaft mate, that the rotor arm turns so that it assumes a position of approximately 90° to the engine (photo). Fit the bolt and washer which holds the distributor clamp plate to the block.

76 Loosen the clamp on the base of the distributor and slightly turn the distributor body until the points just start to open while holding the rotor arm against the direction of rotation so no lost motion is present. Tighten the clamp. For a full description of how to do this accurately see Chapter 4.

77 Fit a new gasket to the water pump and attach the pump to the front of the cylinder block. (photo)

78 Note that the generator adjustment strap fits under the head of the lower bolt on the water pump.

79 Replace the fuel pump using a new gasket and tighten up the two securing bolts.

80 Fit the thermostat and thermostat gasket to the cylinder head and then replace the thermostat outlet pipe. Replace the spark plugs and refit the rocker cover using a new gasket.

81 Refit the generator and adjust it so there is ½ inch (12.7 mm) play in the fan belt between the water pump and generator pulley. Refit the vacuum advance pipe to the distributor and refit the sender units.

43 Final assembly

1 Reconnect the ancillary components to the engine in the reverse order to which they were removed.

2 It should be noted that in all cases it is best to reassemble the engine as far as possible before refitting it to the car. This means that the inlet and exhaust manifolds, carburettor, generator, water thermostat, oil filter, distributor and engine mounting brackets, should all be in position.

44 Engine installation - general

1 Although the engine can be installed with one man and a suitable winch, it is easier if two are present; one to lower the engine into the engine compartment and the other to guide the engine into position and to ensure that it does not foul anything.

2 At this stage one or two tips may come in useful. Ensure all the loose leads, cables, etc are tucked out of the way. If not, it is easy to trap one and so cause much additional work after the engine is replaced. Smear grease on the top of the gearbox input shaft before fitting the gearbox.

3 Always fit a new fan belt and new cooling hoses and jubilee clips as this will help eliminate the possibility of failure while on the road.

45 Engine - installation (without gearbox or automatic transmission)

1 Position a sling round the engine and secure it to the hoist.

2 Lower the engine into the engine compartment, ensuring that nothing is fouling. Align the height of the engine with the gearbox or automatic transmission unit, which will still be supported on the jack which was located prior to removal of the engine.

On vehicles equipped with manual gearbox

3 Move the engine rearward until the splines of the gearbox first motion shaft enter the splined hub of the clutch driven plate (friction disc). The clutch driven plate will have already been aligned as described in Chapter 5. The engine may need turning fractionally to obtain engagement. If so, turn the crankshaft pulley using a spanner applied to its centre bolt.

4 Move the engine fully to the rear to mate the faces of the clutch bellhousing and the engine crankcase. Insert and tighten the securing bolts; fit the starter.

On vehicles equipped with automatic transmission

5 Check that the front pump drive tangs are fully engaged with the slots on the inner gear and that the torque converter is pushed fully rearwards (see Chapter 6).

6 Move the engine fully to the rear to mate the faces of the torque converter housing and the engine crankcase. Insert and tighten the lower two engine to converter housing bolts.

7 Rotate the crankshaft or torque converter until the holes in the drive plate are in alignment with those in the torque converter. It will only be possible to screw in and tighten one drive plate to converter bolt at a time through the converter housing lower aperture, the crankshaft will then have to be turned

42.65 Ensure that the rocker shaft adjusting nuts engage their respective pushrods before tightening the rocker shaft bolts.

42.66 Torquing the rocker shaft bolts

42.69 Using feeler gauge and ring spanner to adjust the valve clearances

42.72 Timing marks cast into front cover and cut into crankshaft pulley flange (arrowed)

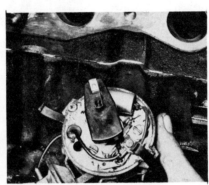

42.74 Position of rotor arm before installing distributor

42.75 Position of rotor arm after installing distributor

42.77 Refitting water pump

through 90° to obtain access to the next bolt hole. When all four bolts are screwed in, tighten them finally to a torque of between 26 and 30 lbf ft (3.6 and 4.1 Kgf m)

8 Reconnect the oil filler tube bracket, fill the unit with specified transmission fluid, fit the starter motor, then insert the remaining engine to torque converter housing bolts and tighten to a torque of 22 and 27 lbf ft (3.0 and 3.7 Kgf m). Refit the semicircular dust cover to the torque converter housing.

On all vehicles

9 Reconnect the engine front mountings and bolt them to the body sideframe members (it will be easier if the weight of the engine is still taken by the hoist so that it can be moved slightly to align the mounting bolt holes).

10 Connect the starter motor cable and the engine earth strap.

11 Reconnect the servo vacuum pipe to the inlet manifold.

12 Unplug the fuel line and connect it to the fuel pump.

13 Reconnect coil, distributor and spark plug leads (Fig. 1.42).

14 Connect the exhaust downpipe and connect the accelerator cable bracket and choke controls.

15 Connect the oil pressure switch and temperature gauge transmitter unit leads.

16 Fit the radiator together with radiator and heater hoses, followed by the engine shield and the air cleaner (do not overtighten the air cleaner bolts or the carburettor may fracture).

17 Connect the leads to the rear of the alternator and then connect the battery negative terminal.

18 Refill the cooling system (Chapter 2).

19 Refill the engine with the correct grade and quantity of oil (an extra pint will be required for absorption by the new filter element).

20 Refit the bonnet and check its alignment before tightening the hinge bolts fully. This operation will be easier to perform if the help of an assistant is obtained.

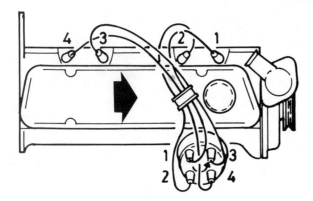

Fig. 1.42 Plug lead arrangement. Exact orientation of distributor cap may vary between models (Sec 45)

46 Engine - installation (with gearbox or automatic transmission unit attached)

1   Position a sling round the engine/gearbox unit and support its weight on suitable lifting tackle. If using a fixed hoist raise the power unit and roll the car under it so the power unit will easily drop into the engine compartment.

2   Lower the power unit into position moving the car forward at the same time. When the engine is three-quarters in it will be found helpful to place a trolley jack under the gearbox.

3   Connect the engine front mountings and the rear one with its supporting crossmember.

4   Fit the propeller shaft, aligning the drive flange mating marks made before removal. If the shaft has a centre bearing refit any packing shims in exactly the same position that they were taken from (photo). Connect the speedometer cable.

On vehicles equipped with manual gearbox

5   Connect the clutch operating cable and adjust the clutch, as described in Chapter 5.

6   Refit the gearlever and gaiter.

On vehicles equipped with automatic transmission

7   Reconnect the speed selector linkage and test for correct operation (Chapter 6).

8   Reconnect the leads to the combined starter-inhibitor/ reversing light switch.

9   Refill the unit with the correct grade and quantity of transmission fluid.

On all vehicles

10 Carry out operations 9 to 20, as described in the preceding Section.

46.4 Refit any packing shims in their exact original positions

47 Engine - initial start-up after major overhaul

1   There is no reason why the reassembled engine should not fire at the first operation of the starter switch.

2   If it fails to do so, make two or three more attempts as it may be that the carburettor bowl is empty and requires filling by a few revolutions of the camshaft operated fuel pump.

3   If the engine still does not fire, check the following points:
   a)   There is fuel in the tank
   b)   Ignition and battery leads are correctly and securely connected. (Check particularly the spark plug HT lead sequence - Chapter 4).
   c)   The choke is correctly connected
   d)   The distributor has been correctly installed and not fitted 180° out (paragraphs 70 to 76, Section 42)
   e)   Work systematically through the fault diagnosis chart at the end of this Chapter.

4   Run the engine until normal operating temperature is reached and check the torque setting of all nuts and bolts, particularly the cylinder head bolts. This is done by slackening the bolts slightly and retightening to the correct torque.

5   Adjust the slow-running and carburettor mixture control screws (Chapter 3).

6   Check for any oil or water leaks and when the engine has cooled, check the levels of the radiator and sump and top-up as necessary.

48 Fault diagnosis - engine

Symptom	Reason/s	Remedy
Engine fails to turn over when starter operated		
No current at starter motor	Flat or defective battery	Charge or replace battery. Push-start car.
	Loose battery leads	Tighten both terminals and earth ends of earth lead.
	Defective starter solenoid or switch or broken wiring	Run a wire direct from the battery to the starter motor or by-pass the solenoid.
	Engine earth strap disconnected	Check and retighten strap.
Current at starter motor	Jammed starter motor drive pinion	Place car in gear and rock to and fro. Alternatively, free exposed square end of shaft with spanner.
	Defective starter motor	Remove and recondition.
Engine turns over but will not start		
No spark at spark plug	Ignition damp or wet	Wipe dry the distributor cap and ignition leads.
	Ignition leads to spark plugs loose	Check and tighten at both spark plug and distributor cap ends.
	Shorted or disconnected low tension leads	Check the wiring on the CB and SW terminals of the coil and to the distributor.
	Dirty, incorrectly set, or pitted contact breaker points	Clean, file smooth, and adjust.
	Fault condenser	Check contact breaker points for arcing, remove and fit new.
	Defective ignition switch	By-pass switch with wire.
	Ignition leads connected wrong way round	Remove and replace leads to spark plugs in correct order.
	Faulty coil	Remove and fit new coil.
	Contact breaker point spring earthed or broken	Check spring is not touching metal part of distributor. Check insulator washers are correctly placed. Renew points if the spring is broken.
Excess of petrol in cylinder or carburettor flooding	Too much choke allowing too rich a mixture to wet plugs	Remove and dry spark plugs or with wide open throttle, push-start the car.
	Float damaged or leaking or needle not seating	Remove, examine, clean and replace float and needle valve as necessary.
	Float lever incorrectly adjusted	Remove and adjust correctly.
Engine stalls and will not start		
No spark at spark plug	Ignition failure - sudden	Check over low and high tension circuits for breaks in wiring.
	Ignition failure - misfiring precludes total stoppage	Check contact breaker points, clean and adjust. Renew condenser if faulty.
	Ignition failure - in severe rain or after traversing water splash	Dry out ignition leads and distributor cap.
No fuel at jets	No petrol in petrol tank	Refill tank.
	Petrol tank breather choked	Remove petrol cap and clean out breather hole or pipe.
	Sudden obstruction in carburettor(s)	Check jets, filter, and needle valve in float chamber for blockage.
	Water in fuel system	Drain tank and blow out fuel lines.
Engine misfires or idles unevenly		
Intermittent spark at spark plug	Ignition leads loose	Check and tighten as necessary at spark plug and distributor cap ends.
	Battery leads loose on terminals	Check and tighten terminal leads.
	Battery earth strap loose on body attachment point	Check and tighten earth lead to body attachment point.
	Engine earth lead loose	Tighten lead.
	Low tension leads to SW and CB terminals on coil loose	Check and tighten leads if found loose.
	Low tension lead from CB terminal side to distributor loose	Check and tighten if found loose.
	Dirty, or incorrectly gapped plugs	Remove, clean, and regap.
	Dirty, incorrectly set, or pitted contact breaker points	Clean, file smooth, and adjust.

Symptom	Reason/s	Remedy
	Tracking across inside of distributor cover	Remove and fit new cover.
	Ignition too retarded	Check and adjust ignition timing.
	Faulty coil	Remove and fit new coil.
No fuel at carburettor float chamber or at jets	No petrol in petrol tank	Refill tank!
	Vapour lock in fuel line (In hot conditions or at high altitude)	Blow into petrol tank, allow engine to cool or apply a cold wet rag to the fuel line.
	Blocked float chamber needle valve	Remove, clean, and replace.
	Fuel pump filter blocked	Remove, clean, and replace.
	Choked or blocked carburettor jets	Dismantle and clean.
	Faulty fuel pump	Remove, overhaul and replace.
Fuel shortage at engine	Mixture too weak	Check jets, float chamber needle valve, and filters for obstruction. Clean as necessary. Carburettor incorrectly adjusted.
	Air leak in carburettor	Remove and overhaul carburettor.
	Air leak at inlet manifold to cylinder head, or inlet manifold to carburettor	Test by pouring oil along joints. Bubbles indicate leak. Renew manifold gasket as appropriate.
Mechanical wear	Incorrect valve clearances	Adjust rocker arms to take up wear.
	Burnt out exhaust valves	Remove cylinder head and renew defective valves.
	Sticking or leaking valves	Remove cylinder head, clean, check and renew valves as necessary.
	Weak or broken valve springs	Check and renew as necessary.
	Worn valve guides or stems	Renew valve guides and valves.
	Worn pistons and piston rings	Dismantle engine, renew pistons and rings.
Lack of power and poor compression Fuel/air mixture leaking from cylinder	Burnt out exhaust valves	Remove cylinder head, renew defective valves.
	Sticking or leaking valves	Remove cylinder head, clean, check, and renew valves as necessary.
	Worn valve guides and stems	Remove cylinder head and renew valves and valve guides.
	Weak or broken valve springs	Remove cylinder head, renew defective springs.
	Blown cylinder head gasket (accompanied by increase in noise)	Remove cylinder head and fit new gasket.
	Worn pistons and piston rings	Dismantle engine, renew pistons and rings.
	Worn or scored cylinder bores	Dismantle engine, rebore, renew pistons and rings.
Incorrect adjustments	Ignition timing wrongly set. Too advanced or retarded	Check and reset ignition timing.
	Contact breaker points incorrectly gapped	Check and reset contact breaker points.
	Incorrect valve clearances	Check and reset rocker arm to valve stem gap.
	Incorrectly set spark plugs	Remove, clean and regap.
	Carburation too rich or too weak	Tune carburettor for optimum performance.
Carburation and ignition faults	Dirty contact breaker points	Remove, clean, and replace.
	Distributor automatic balance weights or vacuum advance and retard mechanisms not functioning correctly	Overhaul distributor.
	Faulty fuel pump giving top end fuel starvation	Remove, overhaul, or fit exchange reconditioned fuel pump.
Excessive oil consumption Oil being burnt by engine	Badly worn, perished or missing valve stem oil seals	Remove, fit new oil seals to valve stems.
	Excessively worn valve stems and valve guides	Remove cylinder head and fit new valves and valve guides.
	Worn piston rings	Fit oil control rings to existing pistons or purchase new pistons.
	Worn pistons and cylinder bores	Fit new pistons and rings, rebore cylinders.
	Excessive piston ring gap allowing blow-by	Fit new piston rings and set gap correctly.
	Piston oil return holes choked	Decarbonise engine and pistons.

Symptom	Reason/s	Remedy
Oil being lost due to leaks	Leaking oil filter gasket	Inspect and fit new gasket as necessary.
	Leaking timing case gasket	Inspect and fit new gasket as necessary.
	Leaking timing case gasket	Inspect and fit new gasket as necessary.
	Leaking sump gasket	Inspect and fit new gasket as necessary.
	Loose sump plug	Tighten, fit new gasket if necessary.
Unusual noises from engine Excessive clearances due to mechanical wear	Worn valve gear (noisy tapping from rocker box)	Inspect and renew rocker shaft, rocker arms, and ball pins as necessary.
	Worn big-end bearing (regular heavy knocking)	Drop sump, if bearings broken up clean out oil pump and oilways, fit new bearings. If bearings not broken but worn fit bearing shells.
	Worn timing chain and gears (rattling from front of engine)	Remove timing cover, fit new timing wheels and timing chain.
	Worn main bearings (rumbling and vibration)	Drop sump, remove crankshaft; if bearings worn but not broken up, renew. If broken up strip oil pump and clean out oilways.
	Worn crankshaft (knocking, rumbling and vibration	Regrind crankshaft, fit new main and big-end bearings.

Chapter 2 Cooling system

For modifications, and information applicable to later models, see Supplement at end of manual

Contents

Specifications

Type of system ... ... Pressurised fluid circulation

Coolant
Type ... ... Ford long life cooling fluid
Coolant mixture 45%

Coolant capacity
Without heater ... ... 4.4 litres
With heater ... ... 5.0 litres

Radiator
Type ... ... Tube + fin
Frontal area ... ... 1180 sq/cm (1100 cc), 1310 sq/cm (1300 cc), 1520 sq/cm (1600 cc)
Radiator cap type ... ... Bayonet catch
Pressure relief valve opens ... ... 0.9 to 1.1 kg cm^2

Thermostat
Type ... ... Wax capsule
Minimum lift at 102°C ... ... 9.5 mm
Opening commences ... ... 85 to 89°C
Fully open ... ... 99 to 102°C

Water pump
Type ... ... Centrifugal
Delivery at 5000 rpm engine speed ... ... 136 litres min
Drive ... ... 'V' belt

Fan
Type ... ... Asymmetrical
No of blades 7
Diameter ... ... 305 mm
Fan hub O/D ... ... 31 mm
Colour code ... ... Ivory (1300 cc 1600 cc), Orange (1100 cc)
Drive belt:
    Nominal width ... ... 9.7 mm
    Nominal length ... ... 736.6 mm
    Angle of 'V' ... ... 36°

Torque wrench settings

	lb f ft	Kg f m
Fan bolts	5.0 to 7.0	0.7 to 1.0
Thermostat housing	13.0 to 15.0	1.7 to 2.1
Water pump	5.0 to 7.0	0.7 to 1.0

1 General description

The engine cooling water is circulated by a thermo-syphon, water pump assisted system, and the whole system is pressurised. This is both to prevent the loss of water down the overflow pipe with the radiator cap in position and to prevent premature boiling in adverse conditions. The radiator cap is pressurised to 13 lb sq in. This has the effect of considerably increasing the boiling point of the coolant. If the water temperature goes above this increased boiling point the extra pressure in the system forces the internal part of the cap off its seat, thus exposing the overflow pipe down which the steam from the boiling water escapes thereby relieving the pressure. It is therefore, important to check that the radiator cap is in good condition and that the spring behind the sealing washer has not weakened. Most garages have a special machine in which radiator caps can be tested. The cooling system comprises the radiator, top and bottom water hoses, heater hoses, the impeller water pump (mounted on the front of the engine, it carries the fan blades, and is driven by the fan belt), the thermostat and the cylinder block drain plug. The inlet manifold is water heated, also the automatic choke.

The system functions in the following fashion. Cold water in the bottom of the radiator circulates up the lower radiator hose to the water pump where it is pushed round the water passages in the cylinder block, helping to keep the cylinder bores and pistons cool.

The water then travels up into the cylinder head and circulates round the combustion spaces and valve seats absorbing more heat, and then, when the engine is at its proper operating temperature, travels out of the cylinder head, past the open thermostat into the upper radiator hose so into the radiator header tank.

The water travels down the radiator where it is rapidly cooled by the in-rush of cold air through the radiator core, which is created by both the fan and the motion of the car. The water, now cold, reaches the bottom of the radiator, when the cycle is repeated.

When the engine is cold the thermostat (which is a valve which opens and closes according to the temperature of the water) maintains the circulation of the same water in the engine.

Only when the correct minimum operating temperature has been reached, as shown in the Specifications, does the thermostat begin to open, allowing water to return to the radiator.

2 Cooling system - draining

1 With the car on level ground drain the system as follows:
2 If the engine is cold remove the filler cap from the radiator by turning the cap anticlockwise. If the engine is hot, having just been run, then turn the filler cap very slightly until the pressure in the system has had time to disperse. Use a rag over the cap to protect your hand from escaping steam. If, with the engine very hot, the cap is released suddenly, the drop in pressure can result in the water boiling. With the pressure released the cap can be removed.
3 If antifreeze is in the radiator drain it into a clean bucket or bowl for re-use.
4 Remove the cylinder block drain plug, located on the rear left-hand side of the block, using a suitably sized spanner.
5 As there is no radiator drain plug fitted to the Escort radiator the system must be further drained by slackening the radiator bottom hose clip and pulling the hose off the radiator outlet.

3 Cooling system - flushing

1 Provided the coolant is kept to its recommended concentration with antifreeze and it is renewed at the recommended intervals, flushing will not usually be required. However, due to neglect or gas or oil entering the system because of a faulty gasket the radiator may become choked with rust scales, deposits from the water and other sediment.
2 To flush the radiator it must first be removed, as described in Section 5.
3 Ensure that the radiator cap is in place, then turn the radiator upsidedown and, using a high pressure supply, insert a hose in the lower hose stub and force water through the radiator and out of the upper hose stub.
4 Similarly insert the hose in the thermostat housing (after first removing the thermostat) and force water through the engine and out of the lower hose (Fig. 2.1).
5 Continue flushing both radiator and engine until the emerging water runs clean.

4 Cooling system - filling

1 Ensure that the cylinder block drain plug is securely tightened and that the radiator bottom hose is connected.
2 Fill the system slowly to ensure that no airlocks develop. If a heater is fitted, check that the valve to the heater unit (where fitted) is open, otherwise an airlock may form in the heater. The best type of water to use in the cooling system is rainwater, so use this whenever possible.
3 Do not fill the system higher than within 1 in (25 mm) of the filler orifice. Overfilling will merely result in wastage, which is especially to be avoided when antifreeze is in use.
4 Only use antifreeze mixture with a glycol or ethylene base (Section 13).
5 Replace the filler cap and turn it firmly clockwise to lock it in position.

5 Radiator - removal, inspection, cleaning and refitting

1 To remove the radiator first drain the cooling system, as described in Section 2.
2 Slacken the clip securing the radiator top hose to the radiator and pull the hose off the radiator stub. On automatic transmission variants slacken the union nuts and pull the automatic transmission oil cooler pipes from their locations in the radiator.
3 At the rear of the radiator there is a cowling, designed to channel the airflow through the vehicle on to the fan and engine. This cowling is secured to the radiator with four bolts and washers. There must now be removed and the cowling detached and placed to one side (over the fan blades) (Figs. 2.3 and 2.4).
4 Undo and remove the two bolts and washers on each side of the radiator which hold it in place then lift the radiator out of the engine compartment.
5 With the radiator out of the car any leaks can be soldered or repaired. Clean out the inside of the radiator by flushing as detailed in Section 3. When the radiator is out of the

Fig. 2.1 Back flushing engine using high pressure hose (arrowed) in thermostat outlet (Sec 3)

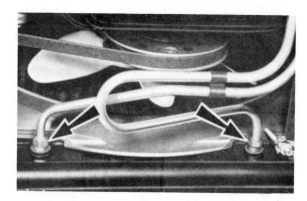

Fig. 2.2 Automatic transmission oil cooler pipe location in the bottom of the radiator (Automatic transmission variants only) (Sec 5)

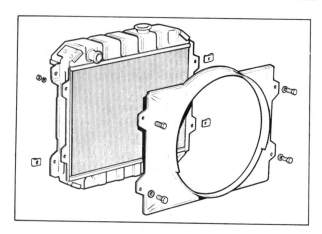

Fig. 2.3 Radiator cowl fixing to radiator (Sec 5)

Fig. 2.4 Hanging the radiator cowl (arrowed) over the fan blades (Sec 5)

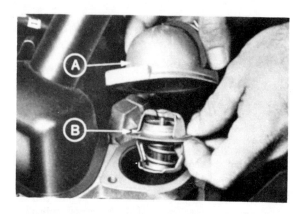

Fig. 2.5 Lifting the thermostat housing and top hose (A) off the cylinder head and removing the thermostat (B) (Sec 6)

Fig. 2.6 Testing the thermostat (Sec 6)

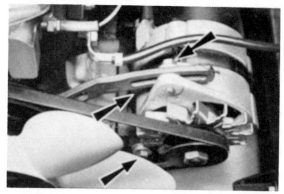

Fig. 2.7 Alternator mounting bolt location: these bolts must be slackened before the alternator can be moved and the fan belt adjusted (Sec 7)

car, it is advantageous to turn it upside down for reverse flushing. Clean the exterior of the radiator by hosing down the radiator matrix with a strong jet of water to clear away road dirt, dead flies etc.

6 Inspect the radiator hoses for cracks, internal or external perishing, and damage caused by overtightening of the securing clips. Replace the hoses as necessary. Examine the radiator hose securing clips and renew them if they are rusted or distorted.

7 Replacement is a straightforward reversal of removal procedure.

6 Thermostat - removal, testing and refitting

1 To remove the thermostat partially drain the cooling system (four pints is enough) then loosen the wire clip retaining the top radiator hose to the outlet elbow and pull the hose off the elbow.

2 Undo the two bolts holding the elbow to the cylinder head and remove the elbow and gasket.

3 The thermostat can now be lifted out. Should the

thermostat be stuck in its seat, do not lever it upwards but cut through the corrosion all round the edge of the seat with a sharp pointed knife. This will usually release the thermostat without causing any damage. (Fig. 2.5)

4 Test the thermostat for correct functioning by suspending it by a length of string in a saucepan of cold water together with a thermometer. (Fig. 2.6)

5 Heat the water and note when the thermostat begins to open. The correct opening temperature is stamped on the flange of the thermostat, and is also given in the Specifications.

6 Discard the thermostat if it opens too early. Continue heating the water until the thermostat is fully open. Then let it cool down naturally. If the thermostat will not open fully in boiling water, or does not close down as the water cools, then it must be renewed.

7 If the thermostat is stuck open when cold this will be apparent when removing it from the housing.

8 Replacing the thermostat is a reversal of the removal procedure. Remember to use a new gasket between the elbow and the cylinder head. If any pitting or corrosion is apparent, it is advisable to apply a layer of sealing compound such as Hermatite to the metal surfaces of the housing before reassembly. If the elbow is badly eaten away it must be replaced with a new component.

7 Water pump - removal and refitting

1 Drain the cooling system, as described in Section 2, then undo the clip on the small heater hose and pull the hose off the pump.

2 Undo and remove the alternator adjustment arm bolt, slacken the two bolts securing the alternator to the mounting bracket and push the alternator towards the engine. Prise the fan belt from the alternator and water pump pulleys and then from around the crankshaft pulley. (Fig. 2.7)

3 Remove the radiator, as described in Section 5.

4 Undo the four bolts and washers which hold the fan and the pulley wheel in place. (Fig. 2.8)

5 Remove the fan and the pulley wheel and then undo the three bolts holding the water pump in place and withdraw the pump together with its gasket. (Fig. 2.9)

6 Replacement is a reversal of the above procedure but always remember to use a new gasket. When adjusting the fan belt ensure that there is 0.5 in (13 mm) total movement at the centre of the span between the alternator and water pump pulleys before finally tightening the alternator mounting bolts. (Fig. 2.10)

8 Water pump - dismantling and reassembly

Note: All numbers used in this Section refer to Fig. 2.11.

1 Remove the hub (15) from the water pump shaft (3) by using a suitable hub puller.

2 Carefully pull out the bearing retainer wire (7) and then with the aid of two blocks (a small mandrel and a large vice, if the proper tools are not available) press out the shaft and bearing assembly (3) together with the impeller (1) and seal from the water pump body (5).

3 The impeller vane is removed from the spindle with an extractor.

4 Remove the seal (19) and the slinger (18) by splitting the latter with the aid of a sharp cold chisel.

5 The repair kit available comprises a new shaft and bearing assembly, a slinger, seal, bush, clip and gasket.

6 To reassemble the water pump, press the shaft and bearing assembly (3) into the housing with the short end of the shaft to the front, until the groove in the shaft is in line with the groove in the housing. The bearing retainer wire (7) can then be inserted.

7 Press the pulley hub (15) onto the front end of the shaft (3) until the end of the shaft is half an inch from the outer face of the hub.

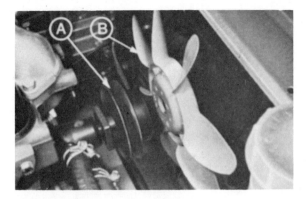

Fig. 2.8 Fan (B) and pulley (A) assembly on water pump hub (Sec 7)

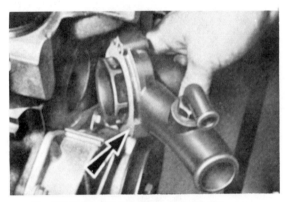

Fig. 2.9 Removing the water pump (Sec 7)

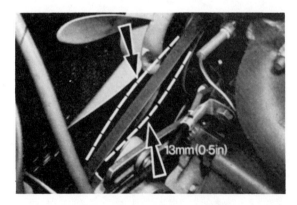

Fig. 2.10 Fan belt adjustment showing a total free-movement of 13 mm (0.5 in) at the mid-point of the longest span of the belt (Sec 7)

8 Fit the new slinger bush (18) with the flanged end first onto the rear of the shaft (3) and refit the pump seal (19) with the thrust face towards the impeller (1).

9 Press the impeller (1) onto the shaft (3) until a clearance of 0.030 inch (0.76 mm) is obtained between the impeller blades and the housing face as shown in Fig. 2.12.

10 It is important to check at this stage that the pump turns freely and smoothly before replacement onto the block. After replacement check carefully for leaks.

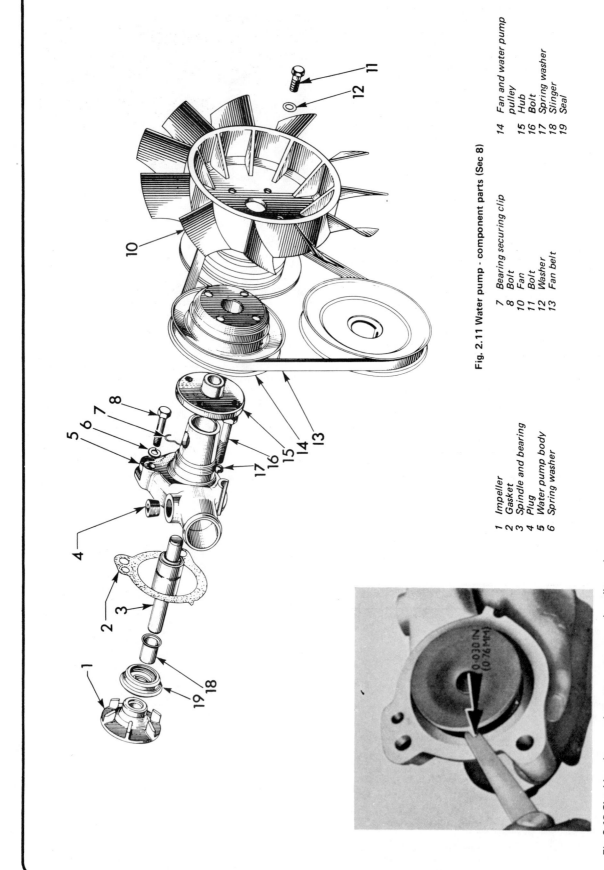

Fig. 2.11 Water pump - component parts (Sec 8)

1 Impeller
2 Gasket
3 Spindle and bearing
4 Plug
5 Water pump body
6 Spring washer
7 Bearing securing clip
8 Bolt
10 Fan
11 Bolt
12 Washer
13 Fan belt
14 Fan and water pump pulley
15 Hub
16 Bolt
17 Spring washer
18 Slinger
19 Seal

Fig. 2.12 Checking clearance between water pump impeller and body (Sec 8)

0·030 IN
(0.76 MM)

9 Fan belt - adjustment

1 The fan belt tension is correct when there is ½ inch (13 mm) of lateral movement at the midpoint position of the belt between the alternator pulley wheel and the water pump pulley wheel.

2 To adjust the fan belt, slacken the alternator securing bolts and move the alternator either in or out until the correct tension is obtained. It is easier if the alternator securing bolts are only slackened slightly so it requires some force to move the alternator. In this way the tension of the belt can be arrived at more quickly than by making frequent adjustments.

3 If difficulty is experienced in moving the alternator away from the engine, a long spanner or screwdriver placed behind the alternator and resting against the cylinder block serves as a very good lever and can be held in this position while the alternator securing bolts are tightened down.

10 Fan belt - removal and refitting

1 If the fan belt is worn or has stretched unduly it should be renewed. The most usual reason for renewal is that the belt has broken in service. It is therefore recommended that a spare belt is always carried. Replacement is a reversal of the removal sequence, but as renewal due to breakage is the most usual operation, it is described below.

2 To remove the belt loosen the alternator securing bolts and push the alternator in towards the engine.

3 Slip the old belt over the crankshaft, alternator and water pump pulley wheels and lift it off over the fan blades. (Fig. 2.13)

4 Put on a new belt in the same way and adjust it as described in the previous Section. Note: after fitting a new belt it will require adjustment due to its initial stretch after about 250 miles (400 km).

11 Temperature gauge - fault finding

1 If the temperature gauge fails to work either the gauge, the sender unit, the wiring or the connections are at fault.

2 It is not possible to repair the gauge or the sender unit and they must be replaced by new units if at fault.

3 First check the wiring for breaks using an ohmmeter or continuity tester. The sender unit and gauge should be tested by substitution.

12 Temperature gauge and sender unit - removal and refitting

1 For details of how to remove and replace the temperature

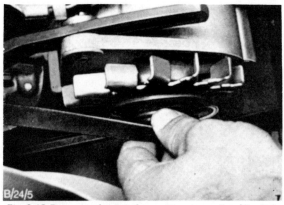

Fig. 2.13 Removing fan belt from alternator pulley (Sec 10)

gauge see Chapter 10.

2 To remove the sender unit, drain half the coolant from the system, disconnect the wire leading into the unit at its connector and undo the unit with a spanner. The unit is located in the cylinder head just below the water outlet elbow on the left side. Replacement is a reversal of the above procedure.

13 Antifreeze solution

1 Apart from the protection against freezing conditions which the use of antifreeze provides, it is essential to minimise corrosion in the cooling system.

2 The cooling system is initially filled with a solution of 45% antifreeze and it is recommended that this percentage is maintained.

3 With long-life types of antifreeze mixtures, renew the coolant every two years or every 36,000 miles (60,000 km) whichever occurs first. With other types, drain and refill the system every twelve months.

4 The following table gives a guide to protection against frost but a mixture of less than 30% concentration will not give protection against corrosion:

Amount of antifreeze	Protection to
45%	$-32^{\circ}C$ ($-26^{\circ}F$)
40%	$-25^{\circ}C$ ($-13^{\circ}F$)
30%	$-16^{\circ}C$ (+ $3^{\circ}F$)
25%	$-13^{\circ}C$ ((+ $9^{\circ}F$)
20%	$- 9^{\circ}C$ (+$15^{\circ}F$)
15%	$- 7^{\circ}C$ (+$20^{\circ}F$)

14 Fault diagnosis - cooling system

Symptom	Reason/s	Remedy
Overheating		
Heat generated in cylinder not being successfully disposed of by radiator	Insufficient water in cooling system	Top up radiator
	Fan belt slipping (accompanied by a shrieking noise on rapid engine acceleration)	Tighten fan belt to recommended tension or replace if worn.
	Radiator core blocked or radiator grill restricted	Reverse flush radiator, remove obstructions.
	Bottom water hose collapsed, impeding flow	Remove and fit new hose.
	Thermostat not opening properly	Remove and fit new thermostat.
	Ignition advance and retard incorrectly set (accompanied by loss of power, and perhaps, misfiring)	Check and reset ignition timing.
	Carburettor(s) incorrectly adjusted (mixture too weak)	Tune carburettor(s).
	Exhaust system partially blocked	Check exhaust pipe for constrictive dents and blockages.
	Oil level in sump too low	Top up sump to full mark on dipstick.
	Blown cylinder head gasket (Water/steam being forced down the radiator overflow pipe under pressure)	Remove cylinder head, fit new gasket.
	Engine not yet run-in	Run-in slowly and carefully.
	Brakes binding	Check and adjust brakes if necessary.
Engine runs cool		
Too much heat being dispersed by radiator	Thermostat jammed open	Remove and renew thermostat.
	Incorrect grade of thermostat fitted allowing premature opening of valve	Remove and replace with new thermostat which opens at a higher temperature.
	Thermostat missing	Check and fit correct thermostat.
Loss of cooling water		
Leaks in system	Loose clips on water hoses	Check and tighten clips if necessary.
	Top, bottom, or by-pass water hoses perished and leaking	Check and replace any faulty hoses.
	Radiator core leaking	Remove radiator and repair.
	Thermostat gasket leaking	Inspect and renew gasket.
	Radiator pressure cap spring worn or seal ineffective	Renew radiator pressure cap.
	Blown cylinder head gasket (Pressure in system forcing water/steam down overflow pipe)	Remove cylinder head and fit new gasket.
	Cylinder wall or head cracked	Dismantle engine, dispatch to engineering works for repair.

Chapter 3 Fuel system and carburation

For modifications, and information applicable to later models, see Supplement at end of manual

Contents

Specifications

Air filter

Element material	Paper
Type	Dry: Summer/Winter setting

Fuel line

Material	Cotton braided PVC nitrile
Inner dia. (mm)	7.47 ± 0.38

Fuel tank

Material finish	Coated steel
Mounting	Bolted
Capacity:	
Initial fill	41 litres/9 gallons
Refill	40 litres/8.8 gallons (Saloon)
	39 litres/8.6 gallons (Van/Estate)

Fuel pump

Type	Diaphragm
Drive	Mechanical from camshaft
Location	Cylinder block, RHS rear
Delivery pressure	3.0 to 5.0 lbf/in^2 (0.21 to 0.35 Kgf/cm^2)

Carburettor

(All dimensions in millimetres with inches in brackets)

Type	751F-9510-LCA	751F-9510-LDA	751F-9510-LEA	751F-9510-CB	751F-9510-BB	711F-9510-HA	761F-9510-AA	751F-9510-GA
Choke plate pull-down setting	3.30±0.25 (0.13±0.01)	3.30±0.25 (0.13±0.01)	3.20±0.25 (0.13±0.01)	3.50±0.25 (0.14±0.01)	3.50±0.25 (0.14±0.01)	4.50±0.25 (0.18±0.01)	3.0 (0.12)	3.0 (0.12)
De-choke	–	–	5.33-0.50 (0.21-0.02)	–	–	–	–	–
Accelerator pump	2.67±0.13 (0.11±0.005)	2.67±0.13 (0.11±0.005)	2.67±0.13 (0.11±0.005)	–	–	–	–	–
Vacuum piston link hole	–	–	Outer	–	–	–	–	–
Thermostat spring slot	–	–	Centre	–	–	–	–	–
'V' mark setting	–	–	2.80 (0.11)	–	–	–	–	–
Throttle barrel diameter	32	34	34	32	32	32	32	32
Venturi diameter	23	25	25	23/24	23/24	23/24	23/24	23/24
Main jet	117	130	127	115/120	120/115	125/130	120/105	105/115
Idling speed (rpm)	800 ±25	800 ±25	800 ±25	800 ±25	800 ±25	800 ±25	800 ±25	800 ±25
Fast idle (rpm)	1100 ±100	1500 ±100	2150 ±100	–	–	–	–	–
Float level	29.50±0.25 (1.16±0.01)	29.50±0.25 (1.16±0.01)	29.50±0.25 (1.16±0.01)	41.00±0.3 (1.61±0.01)	41.00±0.3 (1.61±0.01)	41.00±0.3 (1.61±0.01)	41.00±0.3 (1.61±0.01)	41.00±0.3 (1.61±0.01)
Float travel	5.50 (0.22)	5.50 (0.22)	5.50 (0.22)	11.5 (0.45)	11.5 (0.45)	11.5 (0.45)	11.5 (0.45)	11.5 (0.45)
Choke phasing	–	–	–	2.0 (0.08)	2.0 (0.08)	–	–	–
Exhaust emission % CO	–	–	–	1.5% ±0.25	1.5% ±0.25	3.0% ±0.25	2.0% ±0.25	2.0% ±0.25
High cam idle (rpm)	–	–	–	2100 ±100	2100 ±100	–	2200 ±100	2000 ±100

Torque wrench settings

	lbf ft	kgf m
Fuel pump	12 to 15	1.6 to 2.0
Exhaust manifold to down pipe	15 to 20	2.1 to 2.8
Exhaust manifold to cylinder head	15 to 18	2.1 to 2.5
Exhaust U-bolts and clamps	28 to 33	3.9 to 4.6
Exhaust rear hanger bracket (saloon)	12 to 15	1.6 to 2.0

1 General description

The fuel system comprises a nine gallon (41 litre) fuel tank, a mechanically operated fuel pump and either a Ford or Weber carburettor.

On saloon variants the fuel tank is located within the luggage compartment on the right-hand side of the vehicle, with the filler neck protruding through the right-hand quarter panel. The fuel outlet pipe is located in the bottom of the tank and can be easily removed if the tank needs to be drained. The sender unit is located in the front face of the tank and can be removed with the tank in place. Fuel tank ventilation is achieved via a breather pipe clipped to the tank and protruding through the quarter panel.

On estate car variants the tank is located beneath the load space floor with the combined fuel outlet and sender unit located in the top face of the tank. Ventilation is achieved by a breather pipe behind the right-hand load space trim panel.

The mechanical fuel pump is connected to the carburettor by a nitride pipe and is located on the right-hand side of the engine.

Located inside the pump is a nylon mesh filter and access is gained via the fuel pump cover.

The air cleaner fitted to all models is the renewable paper element type.

2 Air cleaner - removal, servicing and refitting

1 The renewable paper element air cleaner is fitted on to the top of the carburettor installation. Servicing is confined to cleaning, or renewal, of the element at the specified service intervals.

2 Every 6000 miles (96000 km) tap the element on a hard surface or use compressed air from a tyre pump to remove surface dust. Never attempt to clean it in solvent or petrol.

3 Every 18,000 miles (29,000 km) renew the element. Always check the condition of the rubber sealing rings and renew them if they are perished or deformed.

4 To remove the element undo and remove either the three screws (1.1 and 1.3 litre engines) or two nuts (1.1, 1.3 and 1.6 2V. engines) unclip and detach the lid and lift out the element.

5 Should the air cleaner assembly require removal eg; for carburettor servicing this can be easily achieved on 1100cc and 1300cc standard engines by pressing the three air cleaner stays off the lugs on the air cleaner body.

6 On 1300cc 2V engines, the lid and element must first be removed to expose the four nuts and lock plates securing the air cleaner base to the carburettor body. Bend back the lockplates, undo and remove the nuts and lift the cleaner off the carburettor.

7 For 1100 cc and 1600 cc 2V engines, remove the screws and lift the lid and seal off the carburettor body.

8 In all instances replacement is a reversal of the removal procedure.

9 Instead of the straight type of air cleaner intake spout, all models have a variable position at the spout. This position should be positioned 'S' (summer) or 'W' (winter) according to the season. In the winter position, the air is drawn from around the exhaust pipe to prevent ice formation in the carburettor and to reduce condensation in the rocker box which is produced more readily with crankcase emission systems.

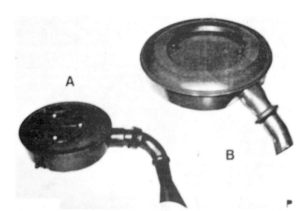

Fig. 3.1 Air cleaner assemblies : A) 1100cc and 1300cc standard engine, B) 1300cc 2V engine (Sec 2)

3 Fuel pump - removal and refitting

1 Disconnect the fuel inlet and outlet pipes. Where crimped hose clips are fitted these should be discarded and replaced by a screw type hose clamp.

2 Unscrew and remove the two securing bolts from the pump flange and remove the pump with gasket from the crankcase.

3 Refitting is a reversal of removal but use a new gasket and make sure that the pump rocker arm is correctly positioned on top of the camshaft eccentric. Tighten the bolts to a torque of between 12 and 15 lb f ft (1.6 to 2.0 kg f m).

4 Fuel pump - testing

1 To test the pump fitted in position on the crankcase, detach the fuel inlet pipe at the carburettor and disconnect the HT lead from the ignition coil.

2 Operate the starter switch when well defined spurts of petrol should be ejected from the disconnected end of the pipe.

3 If the pump is removed from the engine, place a finger over the inlet port and work the rocker arm several times. Remove the finger - a distinct suction noise should be heard.

4 Now place a finger over the outlet port, depress the rocker arm to its fullest extent and immerse the pump in·paraffin. Watch for air bubbles which would indicate leakage at the pump flanges.

Fig. 3.2 Weber carburettor: air cleaner retaining screws (Sec 2)

5 Fuel pump - servicing

1 Remove the single screw securing the fuel pump cover to the pump body and lift off the cover, then detach the cover seal and withdraw the 'top hat' filter from the pump body. (Fig. 3.4)

2 Thoroughly clean the cover, filter and pump body, using a paintbrush and clean petrol to remove any sediment.

3 Reassemble the pump and carryout the test detailed in Section 4. Should the pump prove to be in need of attention it will have to be renewed as a complete unit, as it is not possible to dismantle it, or obtain spare parts.

6 Fuel tank - removal and refitting

1 The fuel tank is positioned in the right-hand rear wing. Remove the filler cap and from under the car, disconnect the flexible fuel pipe from the metal pipe and allow the contents of the tank to drain into a suitable container.

2 Disconnect the battery and then open the boot lid. Pull off the wire from the fuel gauge sender unit; unclip and remove the vent pipe.

Fig. 3.3 Remove existing fuel pump clip and replace with screw type hose clip (Sec 3)

3 Remove the fuel filler cap then unscrew and remove the three screws securing the filler pipe neck to the quarter panel. (Fig. 3.5)

4 From underneath the vehicle undo and remove the two bolts securing the lower edge of the tank to the body.

5 From inside the boot, disengage the sender unit loom then undo and remove the two upper securing bolts and lift the tank from the vehicle. (Fig. 3.6)

6 Replacement is quite straightforward and is a reversal of the removal sequence. Ensure that the grommet at the filler neck aperture in the body is in good condition and renew it if split or

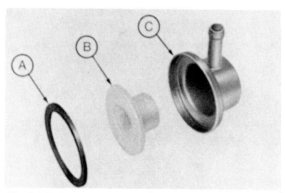

Fig. 3.4 Fuel pump servicing: A) Seal B) Filter C) Cover (Sec 5)

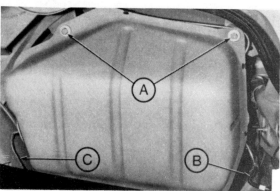

Fig. 3.6 Saloon fuel tank: A) Upper bolts, B) Vent tube,
C = Sender unit loom (Sec 6)

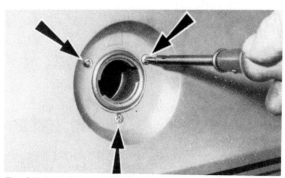

Fig. 3.5 Tank filler neck securing screws on rear quarter panel
(Sec 6)

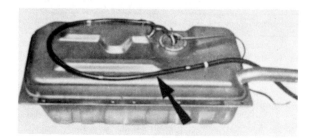

Fig. 3.7 Vent pipe location: estate car fuel tank (Sec 6)

otherwise suspect. Make certain that the fuel pipe grommet is in place and ensure the spacers and washers are correctly positioned. Finally check for leaks.

7 Fuel tank (Estate car and van) - removal and refitting

1   The fuel tank is located under the rear floor pan, and has to be removed from beneath the vehicle. Remove the filler cap and with a 4 ft (1.2 m) length of rubber tubing, syphon the petrol tank contents into a suitable container (no drain plug is fitted). Disconnect the battery.
2   Jack-up the rear of the car and support securely on stands. Remove the spare wheel.
3   Loosen the clips from the filler connecting hose and slide the hose off the tank inlet pipe. Disconnect the fuel gauge sender unit wire, the fuel line, and the vent pipe from the fuel tank.
4   From under the car, undo and remove the bolts and washers which hold the tank in place. Lower the tank to the ground and remove it from under the car.
5   Replacement is a straightforward reversal of the removal sequence.

8 Fuel tank - cleaning and repair

1   With time it is likely that sediment will collect in the bottom of the fuel tank. Condensation, resulting in rust and other impurities, will usually be found in the fuel tank of any car more than three or four years old.
2   When the tank is removed, it should be swilled out using several changes of paraffin and finally rinsed out with clean petrol. Remember that the float mechanism is delicate and the tank should not be shaken violently or turned upside down quickly in case damage to the sender unit is incurred.

3   If the tank is leaking it should be renewed or taken to a specialist firm for repair. Do not attempt to solder, braze or weld it yourself, it can be lethal. A temporary repair may be made with fibreglass or similar material but a new tank should be fitted as quickly as possible.

9 Fuel gauge sender unit - removal and refitting

1   On saloon models, the sender unit can be removed with the tank in position in the vehicle but with estate and van versions, the tank must first be removed as described in the preceding Section.
2   On saloon variants first disconnect the battery, then the lead from the fuel tank sender unit terminal.
3   From both types of fuel tank, unscrew the sender unit retaining ring using a suitably modified 'C' spanner or tapping the projections carefully with a hammer and cold chisel. Remove the sealing ring.
4   Refitting is a reversal of removal but always use a new sealing ring.

10 Carburettors - general description

1   A single venturi (IV) downdraught carburettor is fitted to all vehicles except the two venturi (2V) versions which incorporate a Weber twin barrel carburettor.
2   The single venturi carburettor is basically the same unit whether fitted to an 1100 cc or 1300 cc engine and varies only in the size of internal jets and other components (refer to Specifications Section).
3   Vehicles fitted with automatic transmission, and all 1600 cc models, use a carburettor which incorporates an automatic choke, heated by water from the cooling system.

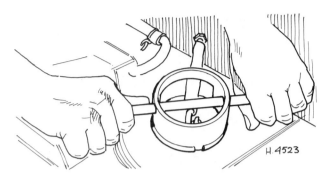

Fig. 3.8 Using Ford special tool to remove estate car tank sender unit (Sec 9)

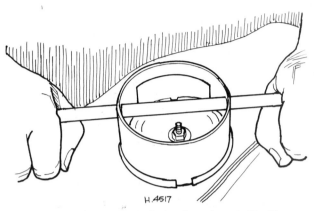

Fig 3.9 Removing saloon fuel tank sender unit (Sec 9)

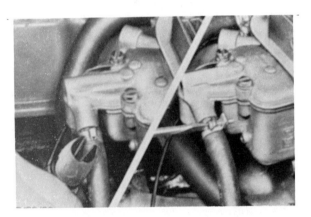

Fig. 3.10 Removing fuel pipe from carburettor (Sec 12)

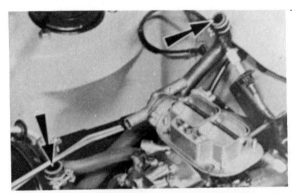

Fig. 3.11 Auto choke hoses positioned aside after their removal. (Sec 12)

11 Motorcraft single venturi carburettor - description

This carburettor is of the single venturi downdraught design incorporating an accelerator pump and power valve, as well as the usual engine idle and main systems. Where specified, a fully automatic strangler type choke system is fitted to ensure easy starting when the engine is cold.

The carburettor body comprises two parts: ie; the upper and lower bodies, with an additional two piece cast housing for the auto choke system.

The upper body houses the float pivot brackets float, fuel inlet connection tube, main jet, float retaining pin, choke plate and forms the cover to the float chamber.

Where specified, the fully automatic choke system comprises an inner and outer housing which is attached to the carburettor upper body. Inside the housing is a thermostatic (bimetal) spring which reacts to the temperature of the engine cooling water passing through the housing. This reaction is transmitted to the choke plate by a lever and shaft assembly located in the inner housing. Also incorporated in the housing is a vacuum pull down piston and lever.

The lower body houses the following major components: throttle barrel with integral choke tube, throttle and lever, adjustment screws, accelerator pump and the distributor auto-advance connection.

12 Motorcraft single venturi carburettor - removal and refitting

1   Remove the air cleaner and disconnect the vacuum and fuel inlet pipes from the carburettor.
2   Free the throttle shaft from the throttle lever by sliding back the securing clip and undo the screw which holds the end of the choke cable in place.

Fig. 3.12 Items to be disconnected before carburettor can be removed (Sec 12)

3   If an automatic choke is fitted drain about 5 pints from the cooling system and loosen the clips which hold the automatic choke water hoses to the carburettor. Pull off the hoses.
4   Undo the two nuts and spring washers which hold the carburettor in place and lift the carburettor off the inlet manifold.
5   Replacement is a straightforward reversal of the removal sequence but note the following points:

   a) *Remove the old inlet manifold to carburettor gasket, clean the mating flanges and fit a new gasket in place.*
   b) *Ensure that the choke knob is in the off position before connecting the inner choke cable at the carburettor. After connection ensure that the choke opens and closes fully with a very slight amount of slack in the cable when the choke control is pushed right in.*

13 Motorcraft single venturi carburettor - cleaning

1 Thoroughly clean the exterior surfaces of the carburettor body.

2 Undo the six screws and washers which hold the carburettor top to the main body.

3 Lift off the top from the main body at the same time un-latching the choke control rod. Ensure that the gasket comes off with the top cover.

4 Turn the carburettor lower body upside-down and allow the accelerator pump discharge ball valve and weight to fall out.

5 From the top cover pull out the float retaining pin and detach the float. With the float removed the needle valve housing assembly can be unscrewed and the upper body gasket lifted off the upper body. Finally, remove the needle valve housing seal and filter, and the main jet from their location in the underside of the upper body.

6 Remove the four screws securing the accelerator pump assembly to the side of the lower body and withdraw the pump from the body, taking care not to lose the two return springs.

7 Remove the volume control (mixture) screw from its location in the lower body.

8 Clean the carburettor and float chamber jets, paying particular attention to those locations shown in Fig. 3.17. Then inspect the float for petrol penetration (ie; holes in the float wall) the pump diaphragm and gasket for splits, and the mixture screw and needle valve for distortion and wear.

9 Refit the volume control screw.

10 Reassemble the accelerator pump assembly in the lower housing, with the steel side of the sealing washer facing away from the body and the tapered end of the spring toward the body.

11 Refit the needle valve, float and main jet in the reverse sequence to their removal, making sure that the needle valve seal and filter are fitted to the needle valve housing **before** the housing is screwed into the upper body.

12 Check and adjust the float level as described in Section 14.

13 Insert the accelerator pump discharge ball valve and weight into their location in the lower body. Align the upper body gasket, reconnect the choke operating linkage and then align and secure the upper body to the lower body with six screws. During this operation ensure that (a) the cranked end of the choke link is fitted at the bottom, and (b) when fitting the upper body ensure that the choke mechanism is held in the fully closed position; this will avoid the choke cam overcentering during the installation.

14 Check and adjust the choke plate pull down as described in Section 15.

15 Check and adjust the accelerator pump stroke as described in Section 16.

14 Motorcraft single venturi carburettor - float setting

1 Since the height of the float is important in the maintenance of a correct flow of fuel, the correct height is determined by measurement and by bending the tab which rests on the end of the needle valve. If the height of the float is incorrect there will either be fuel starvation symptoms or fuel will leak from the joint of the float chamber.

2 To check the fuel level setting turn the carburettor upper body to a vertical position so that the float closes the needle valve by its own weight. This corresponds to its true position in the float chamber when the needle valve is closed and no more fuel can enter the chamber.

3 Measure the distance from the normal base of the float and the metal face of the underside of the upper body. This should be 1.16 in $\pm$ 0.01 in (29.5 $\pm$ 0.25 mm). If this measurement is not correct then bend the tab which rests on the needle valve until the correct measurement is obtained.

4 Turn the body the right way up and take the same measurement with the float in the fully open position. The measurement should now be 1.38 in (35 mm $\pm$ 0.25 mm). If this measurement

Fig. 3.13 Replacing Motorcraft carburettor (Sec 12)

Fig. 3.14 Removing upper body from Motorcraft cover (Sec 13)

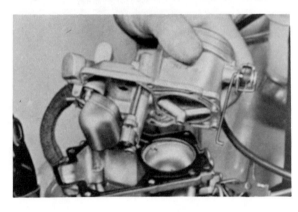

Fig. 3.15 Upper body components: A) Float, B) Main jet, C) Float pivot pin, D) Filter, E) Needle valve housing (Sec 13)

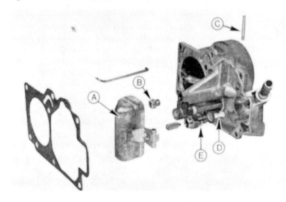

Fig. 3.16 Remove accelerator pump: A) Check valve spring, B) Diaphragm spring (Sec 13)

Fig. 3.17 Jets and orifices to clean (Sec 13)

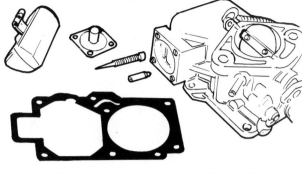

Fig. 3.18 Components to check for wear/damage (Sec 13)

Fig. 3.19 Accelerator pump assembly: A) Diaphragm, B) Sealing washer (Sec 13)

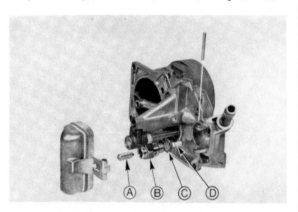

Fig. 3.20 Float assembly: A) Needle, B) Needle valve housing C) Seal, D) Filter (Sec 13)

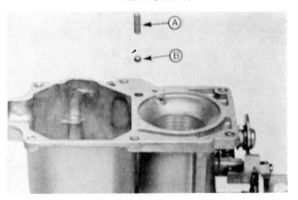

Fig. 3.21 Accelerator pump discharge ball valve (B) and weight (A) (Sec 13)

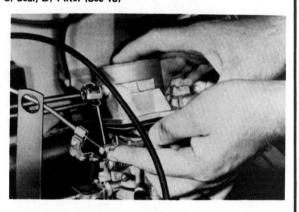

Fig. 3.22 Holding the choke mechanism closed while refitting the upper body (Sec 13)

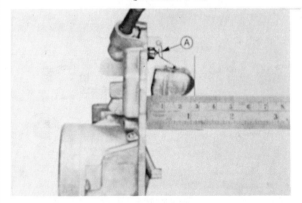

Fig. 3.23 Measuring float level: bend tab 'A' to adjust (Sec 14)

Fig. 3.24 Measuring float travel: bend hinge 'A' to adjust (Sec 14)

Fig. 3.25 Choke plate pull down adjustment: Choke linkage held closed while gap is checked with twist drill (Sec 15)

Fig. 3.26 Accelerator pump adjustment: A) Checking adjustment stroke with 2.67 mm dia drill, B) Open or close gooseneck to effect adjustment (Sec 16)

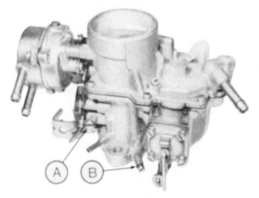

Fig. 3.27 Motorcraft carburettors: A) Idle speed screw, B) Mixture screw (Sec 17)

Fig. 3.28 Removing auto choke cover complete with bi-metal spring off auto choke body (Sec 18)

Fig. 3.29 Removing screw securing choke linkage to auto choke spindle (Sec 18)

Fig. 3.30 Screws (arrowed) holding auto choke body to carburettor body (Sec 18)

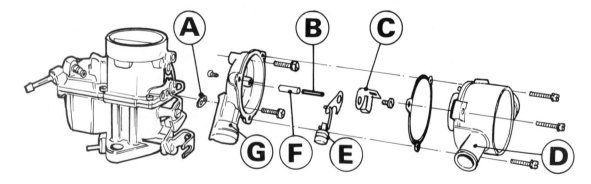

Fig. 3.31 Auto choke assembly. Motorcraft carburettor: A) Gasket, B) Choke spindle, C) Operating link, D) Cover, E) Vacuum piston, F) Sleeve, G) Auto choke body (Sec 18)

is not correct bend the other (hinge) tab until the correct measurement is obtained.

15 Motorcraft single venturi carburettor - choke plate pull down - adjustment

1   Remove the air cleaner and rotate the choke lever until it is against its stop.
2   Depress the choke plate and check the gap between the edge of the plate and the side of the carburettor air intake as shown in Fig. 3.25. The gap is correct when it measures 3.30 mm using the shank of a drill of the correct size as a measuring instrument.
3   If the gap is incorrect bend the tab on the choke spindle until the drill will just fit.

16 Motorcraft single venturi carburettor - accelerator pump adjustment

1   Under normal conditions the accelerator pump requires no adjustment. If it is wished to check the accelerator pump action, first slacken the throttle stop screw so that the throttle plate is completely closed.
2   Press in the diaphragm plunger fully and check that there is then 2.67 mm (0.11 in) clearance between the operating lever and the plunger. The clearance is most easily checked by using a suitably sized drill.
3   To shorten the stroke open the gooseneck of the pump push-rod, and to lengthen the stroke close the gooseneck.
4   If poor acceleration can be tolerated for maximum economy disconnect the operating lever to the accelerator pump entirely.

17 Motorcraft single venturi carburettor - slow-running adjustment

1   Adjustment of the carburettor should only be carried out with the engine at normal operating temperature. Tuning by ear should be regarded as a temporary expedient only and one of two recommended methods (vacuum gauge or 'Colortune') used whenever possible.
2   To adjust the slow-running by ear turn the throttle stop screw so that the engine is running at a fast idle. Turn the volume (mixture) control screw in or out until the engine runs evenly without 'hunting' or 'lumpiness'. Reduce the idling speed and re-adjust the volume control screw.
3   To adjust the slow-running using a vacuum gauge, remove the blanking plug located just below the carburettor mounting flange on the inlet manifold. On vehicles fitted with a semi-closed crankcase ventilation system, remove the fume extraction hose from the manifold nozzle and substitute a tee-connector so that both the fume extraction hose and the vacuum pipe can be connected to the inlet manifold. On vehicles fitted with a semi-closed crankcase ventilation system and a brake vacuum servo unit, pull off the servo flexible hose from the inlet manifold tee-connector and substitute the vacuum gauge pipe. Set the throttle stop screw so that the engine is running at the recommended idling speed (see Specifications) and then turn the volume control screw so that the reading on the vacuum gauge is at maximum obtainable. Re-adjust both screws if necessary to reduce idling speed but maintain maximum vacuum reading.
4   To adjust the slow-running using 'Colortune', follow the manufacturer's instructions.
5   With any of these methods, satisfactory adjustment will not be obtained if there are any air leaks in the system. Check the security of the inlet manifold and carburettor flange gaskets, also the distributor vacuum pipe particularly the rubber or plastic connectors at each end for splits or looseness.

18 Motorcraft single venturi carburettor - automatic choke - removal, overhaul and refitting

1   Remove the carburettor as described in Section 12.
2   Undo and remove the three screws securing the auto choke cover to the auto choke body and lift the cover (complete with bimetal spring) off the auto choke body, together with the cover gasket.
3   Undo and remove the two screws securing the auto choke body to the carburettor and unscrew the single screw securing the choke linkage to the operating spindle. Lift the auto choke body assembly off the carburettor.
4   Unscrew and remove the single screw retaining the operating spindle to the choke body, withdraw the operating spindle and then pull the vacuum piston and linkage from the main choke housing.
5   Clean and inspect all components for damage or wear.
6   Reassembly is a reversal of the removal sequence, but do not forget (a) to fit the operating spindle sleeve, and (b) to assembly all components **dry** (ie; no lubricant of any kind must be used).

19 Motorcraft single venturi carburettors - automatic choke - adjustment

1   The automatic choke adjustment procedure involves correct setting of the 'V' mark, dechoke, and choke plate pull down.

Adjusting the 'V' mark

2   Fasten an elastic band around the choke plate lever and set the band so that it holds the choke plate closed. Operate the throttle lever to open the throttle and allow the choke plate to fully close, then release the throttle.
3   Insert a 2.8 mm diameter drill between the choke plate and the air horn on the accelerator pump side of the carburettor. Allow the fast idle cam to drop into its operating position by partially opening the throttle, then check that the 'V' mark on the cam aligns with throttle lever. (Fig. 3.32)
4   If necessary bend the choke control rod to achieve the correct alignment. (Fig. 3.33)

De-choke adjustment

5   With the choke plate still held in the fully closed position turn the throttle lever so that the throttle is wide open. The choke plate should de-choke (ie; open just before full throttle).
6   If the choke plate action is not correct, check the adjustment by inserting a twist drill of 5.50 mm diameter between the choke plate and the air horn on the accelerator pump side of the carburettor. If necessary bend the de-choke lever on the fast idle cam. (Fig. 3.34)

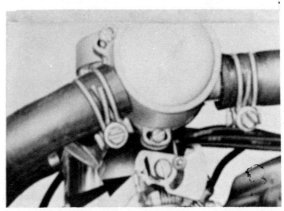

Fig. 3.32 Auto choke 'V' mark aligned with throttle lever (Sec 19)

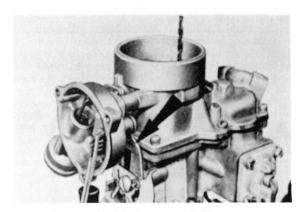

Fig. 3.33 Bend rod (arrowed) to align 'V' mark (Sec 19)

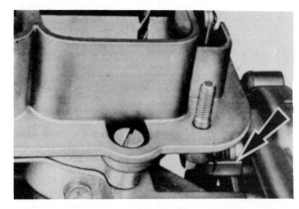

Fig. 3.34 De-choke adjustment: bend tab (arrowed) (Sec 19)

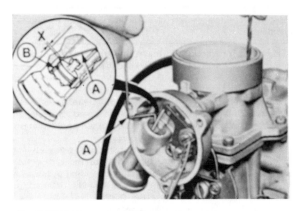

Fig. 3.35 Choke plate pull down: A) 1 mm dia rod, B) Piston, dimension 'X' = 1.0 mm (Sec 19)

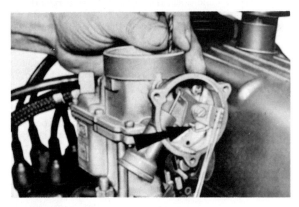

Fig. 3.36 Adjusting choke plate pull down: bend lever (arrowed) to achieve correct adjustment (Sec 19)

Fig. 3.37 Choke cover mark aligned with auto choke bodymark (Sec 19)

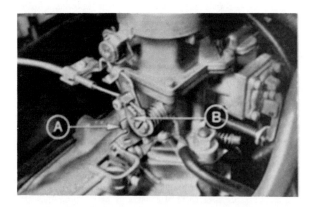

Fig. 3.38 Fast idle tab 'B' on throttle stop 'A' (Sec 20)

Vacuum choke plate pull down adjustment

7   Recheck to ensure that the band is still holding the choke mechanism in the fully closed position. With a 1 mm dia rod (eg; a straightened paper clip) in the slot located inside the front edge of the piston bore, measure the distance between the choke plate and air horn on the accelerator pump side of the carburettor. This distance should be 3.2 mm, and is best measured using the

shank of a suitable twist drill, bend the pull down lever as necessary to achieve a sliding fit condition.
8   When refitting the choke cover and spring assembly to the auto choke housing make sure that the choke spring fits into the correct slot on the operating link (see Specification). Loosely secure the cover with the three screws, then rotate the cover until the mark on the cover lines up with the centre mark on the auto choke housing. Fully tighten the securing screws.

20 Motorcraft single venturi carburettor - fast idling adjustment

1   Remove the air cleaner and rotate the choke lever until it is against its stop.
The fast idle check and any necessary adjustment should only be made after the choke has been checked and adjusted.
2   If the engine is cold, run it until it reaches its normal operating temperature and then allow it to idle naturally.
3   Hold the choke plate in the fully open vertical position and turn the choke lever until it is stopped by the choke linkage. With the choke lever in this position, the engine speed should rise to about 1100 rev/min as the fast idle cam will have opened the throttle very slightly.
4   Check how much radial movement is needed on the throttle lever to obtain this result and then stop the engine.
5   With a pair of mole grips clamp the throttle lever fully open on the stop portion of the casting boss and bend down the tab to decrease, or up to increase, the fast idle speed.
6   Remove the grips and check again if necessary repeating the operation until the fast idling is correct. It may also be necessary to adjust the slow idling speed and recheck the choke setting.
7   For auto choke adjustment, position the throttle lever fast idle tab on the first step of the cam and check the engine speed which should be 2150 rpm. If necessary bend the fast idle tab to bring the engine speed within the range specified.

21 Weber dual venturi carburettor - general description

The Weber carburettor is of the vertical downdraught dual barrel type and incorporates a fully automatic strangler type choke as an easy start device from cold.
The main and idler systems of this carburettor are duplicated for each barrel, although both barrels are fed from a common float chamber their respective systems are separate from each other.
Smooth acceleration from engine idle to the main system is achieved by a single diaphragm type accelerator pump which supplies both barrels of the carburettor.
The carburettor is similar to the Motorcraft with regard to its external connections, those comprise the normal vacuum supply for the distributor advance/retard mechanism and the fuel line from the fuel pump. Internal ventilation of the float chamber is an additional feature of this carburettor.
The carburettor disassembles into the major components, ie; the upper body, the lower body and the auto choke assembly. The upper body houses the fuel feed inlet connection and filter, fuel return connection, the dual barrel air intakes, float mechanism, and air cleaner mounting studs. The float assembly pivots on mounting brackets and reacts to the level of fuel in the chamber by acting on the needle valve and causing it to open or close as necessary.

The lower body of the carburettor comprises the float chamber, throttle barrels, main venturi's accelerator pump body and anti-stall device (1600 cc only). The main venturi's and accelerator pump body are cast as one, and accommodate the air correction jets (main and idle), the emulsion tubes and the accelerator pump discharge valve, all three components being accessible in the top face of the lower body. The main jets are located in the bottom of the float chamber, while the idle jets are housed, on each side of the lower body casting. Located in the top of each barrel, above the main venturi, are the small, anxiliary venturis which incorporate the main system beaks. Also incorporated in the lower body is the 'bypass' idling system (1600 cc only) which allows greater control over the CO content of the exhaust fumes produced while the vehicle is idling. The accelerator pedal linkage acts, via gear sectors, to open and close the throttle spindle. A single idle speed control screw operates on the right-hand spindle to control the engine idle speed, this spindle has a cam attached to it and operates the accelerator pump through a roller and lever system.
The fully automatic choke system is housed in a separate casting attached to the right-hand side of the carburettor body. The choke comprises a bimetal (thermostatic) spring which is senitive to the engine coolant passing through the choke housing and which is linked to the choke plates by a lever and connecting links. An engine fast idle cam which pivots on a bush positioned around the automatic choke shaft is connected to the operating lever via a spring. This cam bears on a further adjustable lever, mounted on the auto choke housing, and connected to the right-hand throttle spindle. This lever is provided with lugs which loosely engage the gear sector, so that when the accelerator pedal is depressed, (with a cold engine) the fast idle setting is obtained. The fast idle linkage incorporates an override system for the choke when the throttle is fully opened. A vacuum diaphragm, housed in the choke body and connected to the barrel below the throttle plate by a system of internal drillings, automatically opens the choke plates by a predetermined amount when the engine is first started.

22 Weber dual venturi carburettor - removal and refitting

1   These operations are carried out in a similar manner to that described for single venturi carburettors (Section 12) but the following points must be observed.
2   The carburettor is secured to the inlet manifold by four nuts.
3   When refitting the air cleaner, first fit a rubber gasket to the top of the carburettor. Then fit the air cleaner body placing a rubber insulator round each mounting stud and a sleeve through each insulator. Place a flat washer and then double type tab washers over the studs and tighten down the securing nuts. Turn up the tab washers to lock the nuts in position.

Fig. 3.39 Removing fuel pipe from carburettor (Sec 22)

Fig. 3.40 Removing Weber carburettor (Sec 22)

23 Weber dual venturi carburettor - cleaning

1 Clean the carburettor exterior surfaces.

2 Using a thin bladed screwdriver carefully prise the choke plate operating link circlip from its location and disconnect the link.

3 Undo and remove the screws which hold the upper body in place and lift off the body and gasket.

4 Unscrew the brass nut adjacent to the fuel intake in the upper body and remove the fuel filter gauze.

5 Pull out the pivot spindle which retains the float in position, then detach the float and float needle. Unscrew the needle housing from the cover and remove the housing sealing washer.

6 Unscrew and remove the three screws which retain the power valve diaphragm assembly in place, then lift off the assembly.

7 Turning to the lower body of the carburettor, the various jets can now be removed for cleaning; in total there are nine components which can be removed at this stage. These are shown in Fig. 3.46 and are:

    1) *Two main correction jets (located in top face of lower body adjacent to float chamber)*

    2) *Two idling jet holders and their idling jets (either side of lower body)*

    3) *Accelerator pump discharge valve (located in top face of lower body between dual barrels)*

    4) *Primary and secondary main jets (from their location in lower side wall of float chamber)*

    5) *Main jet (in bottom of float chamber)*

    6) *Accelerator pump blanking needle (located in top face of lower body between accelerator pump and float chamber)*

8 From the side of the lower body remove the four screws retaining the accelerator pump diaphragm cover and detach the cover, diaphragm and return spring.

Note: On 1600 cc twin venturi carburettors, a similar device is fitted on the opposite side of the carburettor, this is the anti-stall diaphragm and must be removed in the same way as the accelerator pump diaphragm.

9 Turn the carburettor body over and allow the two emulsion tubes, housed in the orifices below the correction jets, to drop out. Keep the tubes seperate as they must be replaced in the same orifices on reassembly.

10 Remove the volume control (mixture) screw from its location in the lower body.

11 Clean all jets, tubes and orifices, paying particular attention to those locations shown in Fig. 3.48. Then inspect the float for leakage, the diaphragm(s) and gasket for splits, or distortion, and the mixture screw, needle valve and throttle spindle for wear.

12 Ensure that the emulsion tubes are returned to their original locations, then refit the two main correction jets.

13 Slide the accelerator pump diaphragm return spring into its recess in the carburettor lower body.

14 Place the diaphragm against the accelerator pump diaphragm cover so that the diaphragm plunger lies in the operating lever recess. Fit the cover to the lower body so that the operating lever engages the cam, then insert and tighten the four retaining screws, at the same time pulling the lever away from the cam to the limit of the diaphragm travel.

Note: Similarly refit the anti-stall diaphragm, using a new gasket.

15 Refit the various jets and tubes removed in sub-operation 7.

16 Commence rebuilding the upper body assembly by refitting the power valve diaphragm. Loosely fit the diaphragm in position with the three retaining screws, then compress the return spring, so that the diaphragm is not distorted, and finally tighten the screws. A check on the efficiency of the diaphragm can be made by blocking the bleed hole ('B' in Fig. 3.45) at the

Fig. 3.41 Choke plate operating link circlip (Sec 23)

Fig. 3.42 Removing upper body (Sec 23)

Fig. 3.43 Weber carburettor: Fuel intake filter (Sec 23)

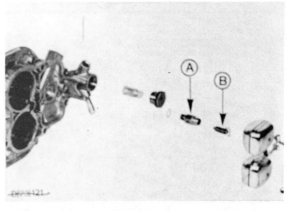

Fig. 3.44 Float and needle assembly: A) Needle housing, B) Needle (Sec 23)

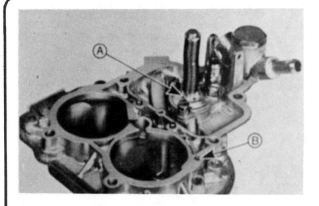

Fig. 3.45 Power valve diaphragm assembly (Sec 23)

A Power valve   *B Diaphragm bleed hole*

Fig. 3.46 Jets for cleaning (Sec 23)

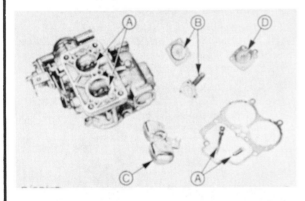

Fig. 3.47 Removing accelerator pump cover (Sec 23)

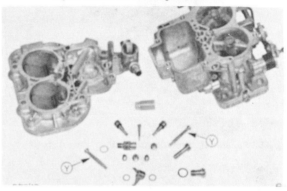

Fig. 3.48 Jets and orifices to clean: item (Y) emulsion tubes must be refitted before air correction jets (Sec 23)

Fig. 3.49 Items checked for damaged or wear: A) Wear, B) Splitting, C) Leaking, D) Splitting (Sec 23)

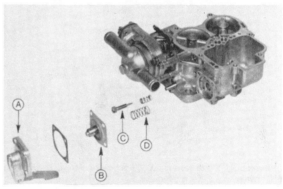

Fig. 3.50 Accelerator pump assembly: A) Cover, B) Diaphragm, D) Return spring, also shown 'C' mixture screw (Sec 23)

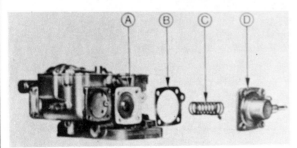

Fig. 3.51 Anti-stall device: A) Diaphragm, B) Seal, C) Spring, D) Cover (Sec 23)

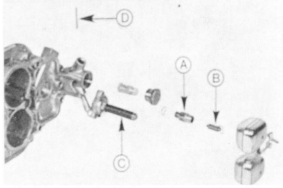

Fig. 3.52 Upper body components: A) Needle valve housing, B) Needle valve, C) Power valve diaphragm, D) Float pivot pin (Sec 23)

same time pushing the diaphragm down. If the diaphragm stays down until the bleed hole is unblocked it is operating correctly.

17 Fit a new seal to the threaded end of the needle valve housing and screw the housing into its location in the upper body. Place a new gasket on the underside of the upper body then replace the float and float spindle.

18 Adjust the float level as described in the next Section.

19 Assemble the top and bottom housings of the carburettor, at the same time replacing the 'U' clip on the choke operating lever, and evenly tighten down the securing screws.

24 Weber dual venturi carburettor - float level setting

1 The setting of the float is vitally important to the maintenance of a correct flow of fuel. Symptoms of mal-adjustment are fuel starvation or fuel leakage particularly from the area of the carburettor float chamber gasket.

2 Hold the upper body vertically so that the float hangs down, and it will be seen that a tab, hooked to the needle control valve is in light contact with the ball, and this should be perpendicular.

Fig. 3.53 Float level: bend tab (arrowed) to adjust (Sec 24)

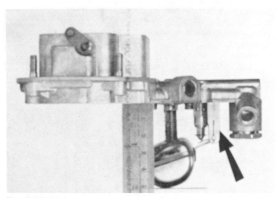

Fig. 3.54 Float travel: bend hinge pivot (arrowed) to adjust (Sec 24)

Fig. 3.55 Manual choke setting: A) Outer cable clamp, B) 10 mm mark, C) Inner cable clamp (Sec 25)

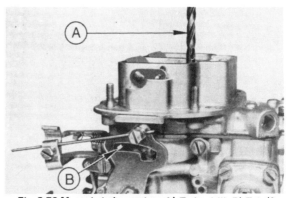

Fig. 3.56 Manual choke setting: A) Twist drill, B) Tab (for adjustment) (Sec 25)

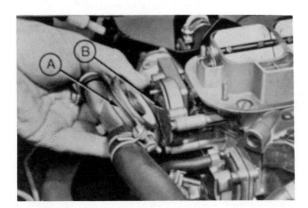

Fig. 3.57 Removing auto choke cover: A) Cover and spring B) Internal heat shield (Sec 26)

Fig. 3.58 Screws (arrowed) holding auto choke to carburettor body (Sec 26)

3 The distance between the float and the upper body at this stage should be 41 mm.

4 If this dimension is incorrect, bend the tabs carefully at the float end.

5 The operating stroke of the float is 11.5 mm so that when the needle valve is fully open, then the float to upper body measurement should be 52.5 mm.

6 Always check the float setting whenever the fuel inlet needle valve has been removed or refitted or when a new inlet valve sealing gasket has been fitted.

25 Weber dual venturi carubrettor - manual choke setting

1 If the choke is not working correctly, the choke plate opening must be checked.

2 To carry out the adjustment procedure a short length of 1.6 mm. dia. rod will be required.

3 Slide the rod through the choke cable outer clamp and the inner cable clamp screw on the choke lever (Fig. 3.55). Fully open the choke mechanism and tighten both the clamp screws.

4 Measure a distance of 10 mm. from the outer cable clamp and make a mark on the rod. Then loosen the outer cable clamp screw and partially close the choke mechanism, so that the 10 mm mark aligns with the outer cable clamp. Retighten the clamp screw at this point.

5 Insert a twist drill of the required diameter (see Specification) between the choke plate and the air horn on the front face of the upper body. Adjust the gap as necessary by bending the tabs (Fig. 3.56) up or down, so that the drill is a tight sliding fit.

26 Weber dual venturi carburettor - automatic choke - removal, overhaul and refitting

1 Remove the carburettor as described in Section 22.

2 Remove the three screws securing the auto choke cover to the choke body and detach the cover complete with bi-metal spring. Lift off the internal heat shield.

3 Remove the 'U' clip and disconnect the choke plate operating link.

4 Disengage the choke linkage at the operating lever, then undo and remove the three screws securing the auto choke body to the main body of the carburettor and detach the choke body.

5 Undo and remove the three screws securing the vacuum diaphragm to the auto choke body and lift the diaphragm off the body.

6 If wear is suspected in the various linkage components they can now be removed, using the illustration provided (Fig. 3.59) as a guide to their removal and assembly. It is important that the various components are assembled **dry** and that no lubricant of any kind is used.

7 Before refitting the diaphragm unit check to ensure that the diaphragm is not split or distorted then refit the assembly using the reverse of its removal procedure.

8 Reconnect the choke linkage and the choke operating link, ensuring that the link to the upper choke linkage is correctly located through the carburettor upper body and that the sealing ('D' in Fig. 3.59) is in place on the auto choke housing.

9 Check and adjust the vacuum pull down as described in Section 27.

10 Check and adjust the auto choke phasing as described in

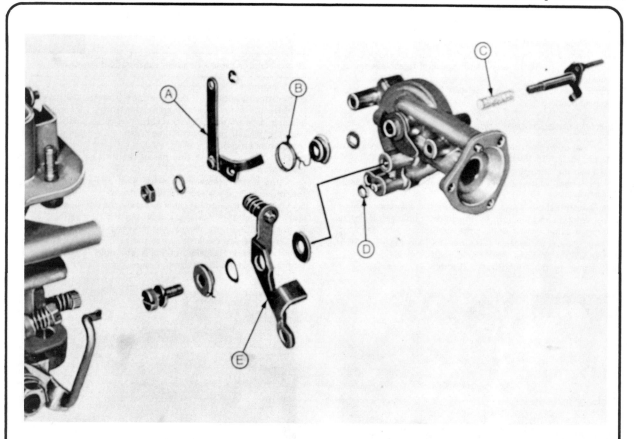

Fig. 3.59 Auto choke assembly, Weber carburettor A) Choke operating link, B) Fast idle cam return spring, C) Sleeve, D) Sealing ring, E) Choke link adjusting screw (Sec 18)

Section 27.
11 Replace the internal heat shield ensuring that the hole in the shield cover is correctly located over the peg on the auto choke body.
12 Reconnect the auto choke cover spring to the choke lever, position the cover on the housing and refit the three retaining screws. Turn the cover to align the cover mark with the mark on the auto choke body, fully tighten the securing screws.
13 Replace the carburettor as described in Section 22.
14 Check and adjust the carburettor fast idle as detailed in Section 27.

27 Weber dual venturi carburettor - automatic choke adjustment

1   The automatic choke adjustment procedure involves the correct setting of the choke plate pull down, choke phasing and the fast idle.
2   Remove the air cleaner as described in Section 2.
3   Undo and remove the three screws securing the auto choke cover to the auto choke body and lift the cover off the body and push the assembly clear of the carburettor body.
4   Lift the internal heat shield off the auto choke body.

Adjusting the vacuum choke plate pull down

5   Wind an elastic band around the choke plate lever and position the band so that it holds the choke plates closed. Open the throttle to allow the choke plates to fully close then release the throttle.
6   Unscrew and remove the plug from the end of the auto choke diaphragm unit. Push the outer body of the diaphragm up to its stop, so that the diaphragm is fully open.
7   Refer to the Specification and select a twist drill of the appropriate size to insert between the choke plate and carburettor body. Use a small electrical screwdriver to turn the adjusting screw (located inside the diaphragm housing) to achieve the correct clearance.
8   When the clearance is correct refit the end plug and detach the elastic band.

Adjusting the auto choke phasing

9   Partially open the throttle and position the fast idle screw on the upper section of the cam.
10 Release the throttle to hold the cam in this position then push the choke plates down until the cam jams against the adjusting screw.
11 Release the choke plates and measure the clearance between the choke plate and air horn on the throttle linkage side of the carburettor using a twist drill of the appropriate size (see Specification). Adjust if necessary by bending the tag (Fig. 3.65).
12 Replace the internal heat shield, and reassemble the auto choke cover to the choke body, (Section 26).

Adjusting the fast idle

13 Run the engine until it reaches its normal operating temperature, then stop the engine.
14 Partially open the throttle, then partially close the choke plates and release the throttle so that the fast idle adjusting screw rests on the intermediate section of the fast idle cam. Close the choke plates so that the cam jams against the screw. At this point the throttle will hold the choke mechanism stationary.
15 Release the choke plates **and without touching the throttle pedal** start the engine and note the engine speed (rpm) this should be 2100 rpm, if necessary adjust by screwing the idle screw in, or out, as required. Note that when the choke plates are released they should return to the fully open positions, if they do not, then either the engine is not fully warmed up, or the auto choke is faulty.

28 Weber dual venturi carburettor - slow running adjustment

1   The alternative methods of carrying out this adjustment are similar to those described in Section 17. However, if there is any possibility that the secondary throttle stop screw has been moved from its original setting, this must be re-adjusted (with the carburettor removed from the engine) to provide a gap of 0.002 in (0.05 mm) between the outer edge of the secondary throttle plate and the throttle barrel.
2   Refer to the Specifications Section for idling speeds and to Fig. 3.66 for location of the throttle speed and volume control (mixture) screws.
3   Bypass idle carburettors require to be adjusted using a CO meter; as they are not generally available cheaply, the work should be entrusted to a Ford dealer.

29 Accelerator cable - removal, refitting and adjustment

1   Disconnect the inner cable from the throttle shaft at the carburettor by sliding off the spring clip from the balljoint.
2   Prise the metal cable retaining clip from its location on the adjuster side of the cable bracket, then press the sides of the plastic cable clip at the same time twisting the cable to disengage it from the bracket.
3   Remove the driver's side parcel shelf to gain access to the accelerator pedal.
4   Using a small screwdriver prise the spring clip which retains the inner cable to the accelerator pedal rod.
5   Unclip the accelerator cable assembly from the point where it passes through the engine rear bulkhead and remove it.
6   Installation of the new cable is a reversal of removal.
7   Screw the cable adjuster in to the bracket as far as possible. Fully depress the accelerator pedal and hold it in this position with a piece of wood, or alternative.

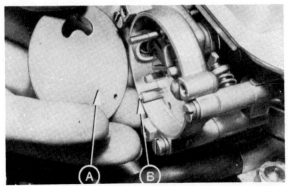

Fig. 3.60 Replacing internal heat shield: A) Shield B) Locating peg on auto body (Sec 26)

Fig. 3.61 Marks (arrowed) on cover and spring shown aligned (Sec 26)

Fig. 3.62 Using small electrical screwdriver to carefully push choke diaphragm open (Sec 27)

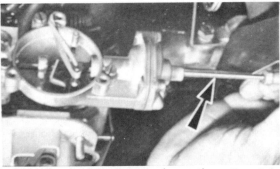

Fig. 3.63 Using electrical screwdriver (arrowed), to adjust choke plate diaphragm (Sec 27)

Fig. 3.64 Idle adjusting screw position on fast idle cam prior to adjusting fast idle (Sec 27)

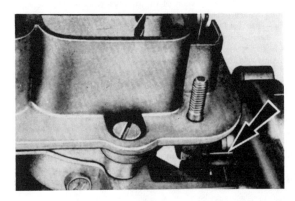

Fig. 3.65 Adjust choke phasing by bending tag (arrowed) (Sec 27)

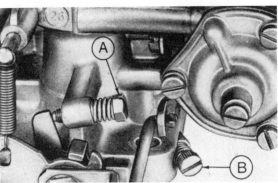

Fig. 3.66 Weber carburettor: A) Idle speed screw, B) Mixture screw (Sec 28)

Fig. 3.67 Weber carburettor (by pass idle type) A) By-pass idle screw B) Mixture screw (Sec 28)

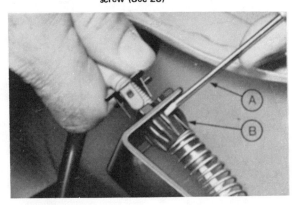

Fig. 3.68 Removing accelerator cable: A) Screwdriver, B) Plastic cable clip (Sec 29)

Fig. 3.69 Removing driver's side parcel tray (Sec 29)

8 Unscrew the adjuster to a point where the carburettor linkage is just in the fully open position.
9 Remove the wood from the accelerator pedal and check that, when the pedal is fully depressed, the fully open throttle position is just achieved.

30 Choke cable - removal, refitting and adjustment

1 Disconnect the battery; remove the air cleaner and disconnect the cable from the carburettor linkage and air cleaner stay. stay.
2 From inside the passenger compartment, reach up behind the heater cover panel and slacken the cable locknut. Then pull the cable through the engine compartment and heater cover panel and remove the cable from the vehicle.
3 Replacement is a reversal of the removal procedure; use Figs. 3.72 and 3.73 to ensure correct cable routing.
4 When the cable is correctly routed pull the choke cable out from the heater cover panel by approximately 6 mm (0.25 inch). Slacken the choke cable clamp screws and manually hold the choke plates fully open, take out all slack from the inner cable and lock up the clamp screws. Push the choke cable fully home, then check that the cable operates the choke flap freely.

31 Exhaust system - general description

The exhaust system is of a two piece design consisting of a front downpipe and a length incorporating a front and rear muffler assembly. Running down the left-hand side of the car the system is supported by rubber 'O' rings at the front and rear mufflers.

When a part, or complete exhaust system, other than the front pipe, is replaced for the first time a special sleeve and two 'U' clamps are necessary to connect the replacement sections of the front and rear muffler assembly. This is because the system is fitted whole in production and must be cut (to clear the rear suspension) to enable its removal.

The sleeve is obtainable from Ford dealers and its location, together with the saloon and estate car systems is shown in Fig. 3.74.

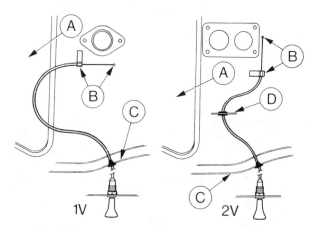

Fig. 3.72 Choke cable routing: RHD models (Sec 30)

A - Rocker cover   C - Dash panel
B - Carburettor bracket   D - Throttle bracket
and linkage

Fig. 3.70 Choke cable connections at carburettor: A) Outer cable clamp screw, B) Inner cable clamp screw (Sec 30)

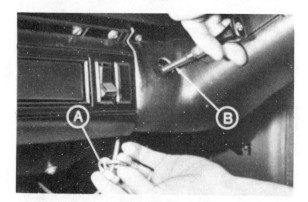

Fig. 3.71 Removing choke cable: A) Locknut and washer B) Cable (Sec 30)

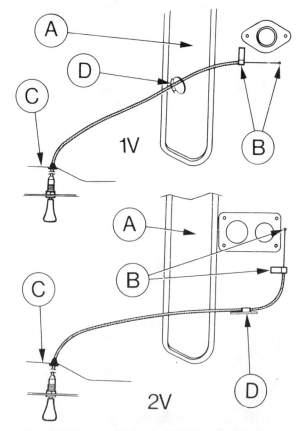

Fig. 3.73 Choke cable routing: LHD models (Sec 30)

A - Rocker cover   C - Engine compartment
B - Carburettor bracket   rear bulkhead
and linkage   D - Air cleaner stay

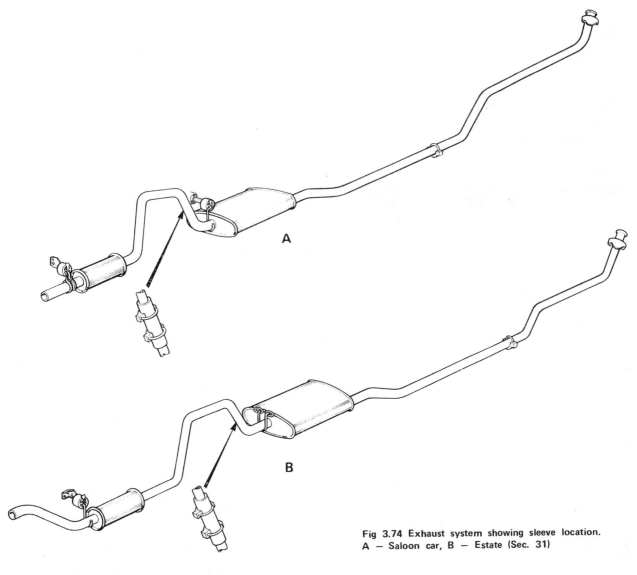

Fig 3.74 Exhaust system showing sleeve location.
A — Saloon car, B — Estate (Sec. 31)

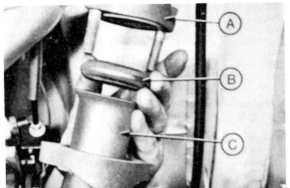

Fig. 3.75 Front pipe to manifold location: A) Manifold,
B) Sealing ring, C) Front pipe (Sec 32)

32 Exhaust pipe (front) - removal and refitting

1   Raise the front end of the vehicle.
2   Use quantities of any suitable penetrating fluid on the manifold studs and the front pipe to rear muffler 'U' clamp threads.
3   Undo and remove the two manifold nuts, slide the clamp
down the pipe and remove the sealing ring from its location
between the pipe and manifold.
4   Slacken the 'U' clamp and drive the front pipe out of the rear
pipe.
5   Replacing the front pipe is a reversal of the removal procedure.

33 Exhaust pipe (front and rear muffler) - removal and refitting

1   Remove the front pipe as described in the previous Section,
and lower the front rear muffler section.
2   Measure the distance shown in Fig. 3.76 and cut the pipe at
this point, then remove the defective section from the vehicle.
3   Loosely align the two sections of the front/rear muffler pipe.
Measure a distance of 45 mm (1.8 in) from the end of each pipe
and scribe a line on the pipe surface.
4   Slide the connecting sleeve and clamps on one pipe end up to
the scribed line on the pipe, then insert the remaining pipe into
the sleeve up to the scribed line on the pipe. Tighten the clamps
at this point and rehang the exhaust system (Fig. 3.77).

Fig. 3.76 Cutting point: Dia A) 210 mm (saloon) 206 mm (estate) (Sec 33

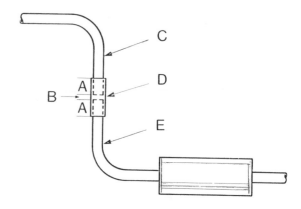

Fig. 3.77 Dimension A 45mm (1.77 in), Dimension B 10 mm (0.39 in), C Pipe from front muffler, D Service sleeve, E Pipe to rear muffler (Sec. 33)

34 Fuel system - fault diagnosis

There are three main types of fault to which the fuel system is prone, and they may be summarised as follows:
  a) *Lack of fuel at engine*
  b) *Weak mixture*
  c) *Rich mixture*

Lack of fuel at engine

1   If it is not possible to start the engine, first positively check that there is fuel in the fuel tank, and then check the ignition system as detailed in Chapter 4. If the fault is not in the ignition system then disconnect the fuel inlet pipe from the carburettor and turn the engine over by the starter relay switch.

2   If petrol squirts from the end of the inlet pipe, reconnect the pipe and check that the fuel is getting to the float chamber. This is done by unscrewing the bolts from the top of the float chamber and lifting the cover just enough to see inside.

3   If fuel is there, then it is likely that there is a blockage in the starting jet, which should be removed and cleaned.

4   No fuel in the float chamber is caused either by a blockage in the pipe between the pump and float chamber or a sticking float chamber valve. Alternatively, on the twin choke carburettor the gauze filter at the top of the float chamber may be blocked. Remove the securing nut and check that the filter is clean. Washing in petrol will clean it.

5   If it is decided that it is the float chamber valve that is sticking, remove the fuel inlet pipe, and lift away the cover, complete with valve and floats.

6   Remove the valve spindle and valve and thoroughly wash them in petrol. Petrol gum may be present on the valve or valve spindle and this is usually the cause of a sticking valve. Replace the valve in the needle valve assembly, ensure that it is moving freely, and then reassemble the float chamber. It is important that the same washer is placed under the needle valve assembly as this determines the height of the floats and therefore the level of petrol in the chamber.

7   Reconnect the fuel pipe and refit the air cleaner.

8   If no petrol squirts from the end of the pipe leading to the carburettor, then disconnect the pipe leading to the inlet side of the fuel pump. If fuel runs out of the pipe, then there is a fault in the fuel pump and the pump should be checked as has already been detailed.

9   No fuel flowing from the tank when it is known that there is fuel in it indicates a blocked pipe line. The line to the tank should be blown out. It is unlikely that the fuel tank vent would become blocked, but this could be a reason for the reluctance of the fuel to flow. To test for this, blow into the tank down the

filler orifice. There should be no build up of pressure in the fuel tank, as the excess pressure should be carried away down the vent pipe.

Weak mixture

1   If the fuel/air mixture is weak there are six main clues to this condition:
  a) *The engine will be difficult to start and will need much use of the choke, stalling easily if the choke is pushed in.*
  b) *The engine will overheat easily.*
  c) *If the spark plugs are examined (as detailed in the Section on engine tuning), they will have a light grey/white deposit on the insulator nose.*
  d) *The fuel consumption may be light*
  e) *There will be a noticeable lack of power.*
  f) *During acceleration and on the over-run there will be a certain amount of spitting back through the carburettor.*

2   As the carburettors are of the fixed jet type, these faults are invariably due to circumstances outside the carburettor. The only usual fault likely in the carburettor is that one or more of the jets may be partially blocked. If the car will not start easily but runs well at speed, then it is likely that the starting jet is blocked, whereas if the engine starts easily but will not rev then it is likely that the main jets are blocked.

3   If the level of petrol in the float chamber is low, this is usually due to a sticking valve or incorrectly set floats.

4   Air leaks either in the fuel lines, or in the induction system should also be checked for. Also check the distributor vacuum pipe connection as a leak in this is directly felt in the inlet manifold.

5   The fuel pump may be at fault as has already been detailed.

Rich mixture

1   If the fuel/air mixture is rich there are also six main clues to this condition:
  a) *If the spark plugs are examined they will be found to have a black sooty deposit on the insulator nose.*
  b) *The fuel consumption will be heavy.*
  c) *The exhaust will give off a heavy black smoke, especially when accelerating.*
  d) *The interior deposits on the exhaust pipe will be dry, black and sooty (if they are wet, black and sooty, this indicates worn bores, and much oil being burnt).*
  e) *There will be a noticeable lack of power.*
  f) *There will be a certain amount of back-firing through the exhaust system.*

2   The faults in this case are usually in the carburettor and the most usual is that the the level of the petrol in the float chamber is too high. This is due either to dirt behind the needle valve, or a

leaking float which will not close the valve properly, or a sticking needle.

3 With a very high mileage (or because someone has tried to clean the jets out with wire), it may be that the jets have become enlarged.

4 If the air correction jets are restricted in any way, the mixture will tend to become very rich.

5 Occasionally it is found that the choke control is sticking or has been maladjusted.

6 Again, on rare occasions, the fuel pump pressure may be excessive so forcing the needle valve open slightly until a higher level of petrol is reached in the float chamber.

35 Fuel gauge and sender unit - fault diagnosis

1 If the fuel gauge fails to give a reading with the ignition on or reads 'Full' all the time, then a check must be made to see if the fault is in the gauge, sender unit, or wire in between.

2 Turn the ignition on and disconnect the wire from the fuel tank sender unit. Check that the fuel gauge needle is on the empty mark. To check if the fuel gauge is in order now earth the fuel tank sender unit wire. This should send the needle to the full mark.

3 If the fuel gauge is in order check the wiring for leaks or loose connections. If none can be found, then the sender unit will be at fault and must be replaced.

4 Should both the fuel gauge and where fitted, the temperature gauge fail to work, of if they both give unusually high readings, then a check must be made of the instrument voltage regulator which is positioned behind the speedometer.

36 Fault diagnosis - fuel system and carburation

Symptom	Reason/s	Remedy
Fuel consumption excessive		
Carburation and ignition faults	Air cleaner choked and dirty giving rich mixture	Remove, clean and replace air cleaner.
	Fuel leaking from carburettor, fuel pump or fuel lines	Check for and eliminate all fuel leaks. Tighten fuel line union nuts.
	Float chamber flooding	Check and adjust float level.
	Generally worn carburettor	Remove, overhaul and replace.
	Distributor condenser faulty	Remove, and fit new unit.
	Balance weights or vacuum advance mechanism in distributor faulty	Remove, and overhaul distributor.
Incorrect adjustment	Carburettor incorrectly adjusted, mixture too rich	Tune and adjust carburettor.
	Idling speed too high	Adjust idling speed.
	Contact breaker gap incorrect	Check and reset gap.
	Valve clearances incorrect	Check rocker arm to valve stem clearances and adjust as necessary.
	Incorrectly set spark plugs	Remove, clean and regap.
	Tyres under-inflated	Check tyre pressures and inflate if necessary.
	Wrong spark plugs fitted	Remove and replace with correct units.
	Brakes dragging	Check and adjust brakes.
Insufficient fuel delivery or weak mixture due to air leaks		
Dirt in system	Petrol tank air vent restricted	Remove petrol tank and clean out air vent pipe.
	Partially clogged filters in pump and carburettor	Remove and clean filters.
	Dirt lodged in float chamber needle housing	Remove and clean out float chamber and needle valve assembly.
	Incorrectly seating valves in fuel pump	Remove, dismantle, and clean out fuel pump.
Fuel pump faults	Fuel pump diaphragm leaking or damaged	Remove, and overhaul fuel pump.
	Gasket in fuel pump damaged	Remove, and overhaul fuel pump.
	Fuel pump valves sticking due to petrol gumming.	Remove, and thoroughly clean fuel pump.
Air leaks	Too little fuel in fuel tank (prevalent when climbing steep hills)	Refill fuel tank.
	Union joints on pipe connections loose	Tighten joints and check for air leaks.
	Split in fuel pipe on suction side of fuel pump	Examine, locate and repair.
	Inlet manifold to block or inlet manifold to carburettor gasket leaking	Test by pouring oil along joints - bubbles indicate leak. Renew gasket as appropriate.

Chapter 4 Ignition system

For modifications, and information applicable to later models, see Supplement at end of manual

Contents

Specifications

Coil

Type	Oil filled low voltage
Resistance @ 20°C:	
Primary	1.3 to 1.6 ohms. (Bosch) 0.95 to 1.35 ohms. (All other types)
Secondary	7000 to 9300 ohms. (Bosch), 5900 to 7200 ohms. (All other types)
Output at 1200 rpm	36 to 39.5 KV. (Bosch) 31 to 37.5 (All other types)
Compensating resistance	1.45 to 1.55 ohms

Condenser

Type	Motorcraft
Capacitance	0.21 to 0.25 mf.

Plug leads

Type	Graphitised resistance conductor
Insulation	Hypalon
Plug connector	Hypalon sleeve

Spark plugs

Type:	
1300 2V and 1600 2V	AGR12*
Other models	AGR22
Gap	0.6 mm (0.025in)
Thread size x length	M14 x 1.25 x 0.75 in.

Ignition timing mark location

On distributor:	Rotor and distributor housing
On engine:	Front cover and pulley

No. 1 cylinder location: ... ... Front

Firing order: ... ... 1—2—4—3

Distributor

Rotation of rotor:	Anticlockwise
Automatic advance:	Mechanical and vacuum
Dwell angle:	48° to 52°
Contact breaker gap:	0.56 to 0.71 mm (0.022 to 0.028 in)
Contact breaker spring pressure:	487 to 595 g
Initial (static) advance:	
1.1 engines	6° BTDC
1.3 LC economy engines (from November 1977)	12° BTDC
1.3 HC economy engines (from November 1977)	10° BTDC
1.3 engines (all other versions)	6° BTDC
1.6 engines	10° BTDC

Torque wrench settings

	lb f ft	kg f m
Spark plugs	22 - 28	2.9 - 3.9

Also see Chapter 13, Section 6

1 General description

In order that the engine can run correctly it is necessary for an electrical spark to ignite the fuel/air mixture in the combustion chamber at exactly the right moment in relation to engine speed and load. The ignition system is based on feeding low tension voltage from the battery to the coil where it is converted to high tension voltage. The high tension voltage is powerful enough to jump the spark plug gap in the cylinders many times a second under high compression, providing that the system is in good condition and that all adjustments are correct.

The ignition system is divided into two circuits, the low tension circuit and the high tension circuit.

The low tension (sometimes known as the primary) circuit consists of the battery, lead to the control box, lead to the ignition switch, lead from the ignition switch to the low tension or primary coil windings (terminal SW), and the lead from the low tension coil windings (coil terminal CB) to the contact breaker points and condenser in the distributor.

The high tension circuit consists of the high tension or secondary coil windings, the heavy ignition lead from the centre of the coil to the centre of the distributor cap, the rotor arm, and the spark plug leads and spark plugs.

The system functions in the following manner. Low tension voltage is changed in the coil into high tension voltage by the opening and closing of the contact breaker points in the low tension circuit. High tension voltage is then fed via the carbon brush in the centre of the distributor cap to the rotor arm of the distributor cap, and each time it comes in line with one of the four metal segments in the cap, which are connected to the spark plug leads, the opening and closing of the contact breaker points causes the high tension voltage to build up, jump the gap from the rotor arm to the appropriate metal segment and so via the spark plug lead to the spark plug, where it finally jumps the spark plug gap before going to earth.

The ignition is advanced and retarded automatically, to ensure that the spark occurs at just the right instant for the particular load at the prevailing engine speed.

The ignition advance is controlled both mechanically and by a vacuum operated system. The mechanical governor mechanism comprises two weights, which move out from the distributor shaft as the engine speed rises due to centrifugal force. As they move outwards they rotate the cam relative to the distributor shaft, and so advance the spark. The weights are held in position by two light springs and it is the tension of the springs which is largely responsible for correct spark advancement.

The vacuum control consists of a diaphragm, one side of which is connected via a small bore tube to the carburettor, and the other side to the contact breaker plate. Depression in the inlet manifold and carburettor, which varies with engine speed and throttle opening, causes the diaphragm to move, so moving the contact breaker plate, and advancing or retarding the spark. A fine degree of control is achieved by a spring in the vacuum assembly.

2 Contact breaker - adjustment

1 To adjust the contact breaker points to the correct gap, first pull off the two clips securing the distributor cap to the distributor body, and lift away the cap. Clean the cap inside and out with a dry cloth. It is unlikely that the four segments will be badly burned or scored, but if they are the cap will have to be renewed.

2 Inspect the carbon brush contact located in the top of the cap - see that it is unbroken and stands proud of the plastic surface.

3 Check the contact spring on the top of the rotor arm. It must be clean and have adequate tension to ensure good contact.

4 Gently prise the contact breaker points open to examine the condition of their faces. If they are rough, pitted or dirty, it will be necessary to remove them for resurfacing, or for new points to be fitted.

5 Assuming the points are satisfactory, or that they have been cleaned and replaced, measure the gap between the points by turning the engine over until the heel of the breaker arm is on the highest point of the cam.

6 An 0.025 inch (0.64 mm) feeler gauge should now just fit between the points.

7 If the gap varies from this amount slacken the contact plate securing screw.

8 Adjust the contact gap by inserting a screwdriver in the notched hole in the breaker plate. Turn clockwise to increase and anticlockwise to decrease the gap. When the gap is correct, tighten the securing screw and check the gap again.

9 Making sure the rotor is in position replace the distributor cap and clip the spring blade retainers into position.

Fig. 4.1 Contact breaker point gap measuring point (A) (Sec 2)

Note that the fibre heel of point assembly rests on high point of cam

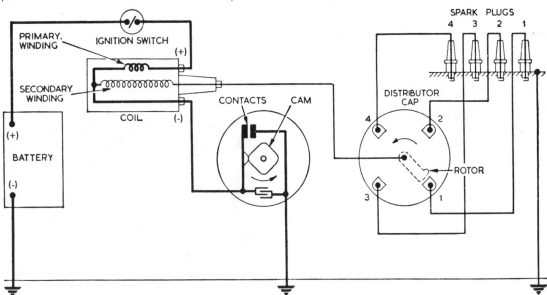

Fig.4.2 Theoretical ignition circuit diagram. Heavier line indicates LT (primary) circuit

3 Contact breaker points - removal and refitting

1 If, on inspection, the faces of the contacts are burned, pitted or worn, the contact breaker points must be removed for refacing or renewal.

2 Lift off the rotor arm by pulling it straight up from the spindle.

3 Slacken the self-tapping screw holding the condenser and low tension leads to the contact breaker and slide out the forked ends of the leads.

4 Remove the points by taking out the two retaining screws and lifting off the points assembly.

5 Dress the face of each contact squarely on an oilstone or a piece of fine emery cloth until all traces of 'pips' or 'craters' have been removed. After two or three times, regrinding of the points in this manner will reduce the thickness of the metal so much that a new contact set will have to be fitted. Before fitting the points, clean them with methylated spirit.

6 Refitting the points assembly is a reversal of removal but take care not to trap the wires between the points and the contact breaker plate.

7 Set the points gap as described in the preceding Section.

8 Refit the rotor arm and the distributor cap.

9 Whenever the contact breaker points are serviced or adjusted, the distributor should be lubricated. Smear the high points of the cam with petroleum jelly and apply two or three drops of engine oil to the felt pad which is located at the top of the cam assembly. Squirt a few drops of engine oil through the distributor baseplate to lubricate the mechanical advance and retard assembly. Do not lubricate the distributor too liberally otherwise the points will become contaminated and misfiring will occur.

4 Condenser - removal, testing and refitting

1 The purpose of the condenser (capacitor) is to ensure that when the contact breaker points open, there is no sparking across them which would waste voltage and cause wear.

2 The condenser is fitted in parallel with the contact breaker points. If it develops a short circuit, it will cause ignition failure as the points will be prevented from interrupting the low tension circuit.

3 If the engine becomes very difficult to start or begins to miss after several miles running and the breaker points show signs of excessive burning, then the condition of the condenser must be suspect. A further test can be made by separating the points by hand with the ignition switched on. If this is accompanied by a flash it is indicative that the condenser has failed.

4 Without special test equipment the only sure way to diagnose condenser trouble is to replace a suspected unit with a new one and note if there is any improvement.

5 To remove the condenser from the distributor, take off the distributor cap and rotor arm. Slacken the self-tapping screw holding the condenser lead and low tension lead to the points, and slide out the fork on the condenser lead. Undo the condenser retaining screw and remove the condenser from the breaker plate.

6 To refit the condenser simply reverse the order of removal. Take care that the condenser lead is clear of the moving part of the points assembly.

5 Distributor - removal, dismantling and inspection

1 To remove the distributor from the engine, pull off the four leads from the spark plugs.

2 Disconnect the high tension and low tension leads from the distributor.

3 Pull off the rubber union holding the vacuum pipe to the distributor vacuum advance housing.

4 Using a suitably sized spanner on the crankshaft pulley bolt turn the engine to T.D.C. on No. 1 cylinder. This can be readily

achieved by noting the position of the rotor arm; when the rotor arm reaches the point where it would normally be opposite the No. 1 contact in the distributor cap No. 1 cylinder is approaching T.D.C. Continue turning the engine until the notch in the crankshaft pulley aligns with the appropriate timing mark on the front cover.

5 Remove the distributor body clamp bolt which holds the distributor clamp plate to the cylinder block. Pull the distributor from the block, marking the position of the rotor arm relative to the body.

6 With the distributor on the bench, pull off the two spring clips retaining the cover and lift the cover off (if not already removed).

7 Pull the rotor arm off the distributor camshaft. Remove the

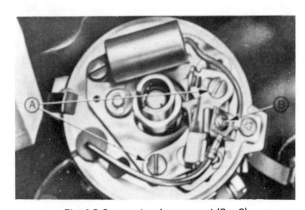

Fig. 4.3 Contact breaker removal (Sec 3)

Screws at (A) retain assembly to base plate, screw at (B) holds condenser and LT lead to assembly

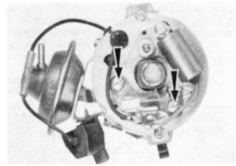

Fig. 4.4 Contact breaker assembly retaining screws (Sec 3)

Fig. 4.5 Greasing cam lobes (Sec 3)

A - Grease   B - Cam

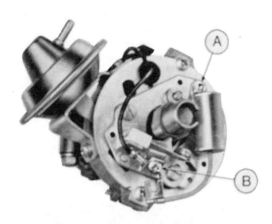

Fig. 4.6 Condenser removal: screw at (A) retains condenser to base plate, screw at (B) retains condenser lead to contact breaker assembly (Sec 4)

Fig. 4.7 Engine and rotor positions for TDC on No 1 cylinder (Sec 5)

A   Rotor arm adjacent to No 1 contact
B   Timing notch on pulley next to TDC mark on front cover

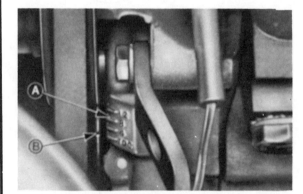

Fig. 4.8 Crankshaft pulley timing notch (B) and 8° BTDC mark (A) shown arrowed. Note that as shown engine is in TDC position on Nos 1 or 4 cylinders (Sec 5)

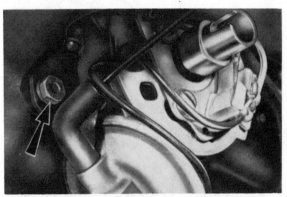

Fig. 4.9 Distributor clamp plate screw retaining plate to cylinder block (Sec 5)

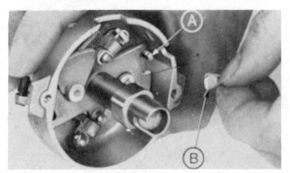

Fig. 4.11 Removing bump stop plastic cover (B) from bump stop (A) (Sec 5)

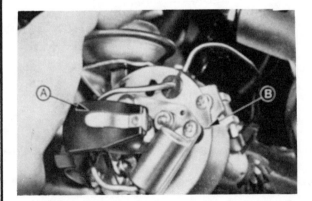

Fig. 4.10 Rotor (A) alignment relative to scribed line (B) on distributor body (Sec 5)

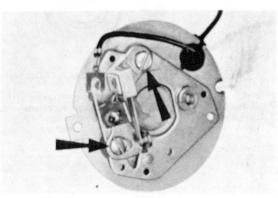

Fig. 4.12 Contact breaker assembly retaining screws (Sec 5)

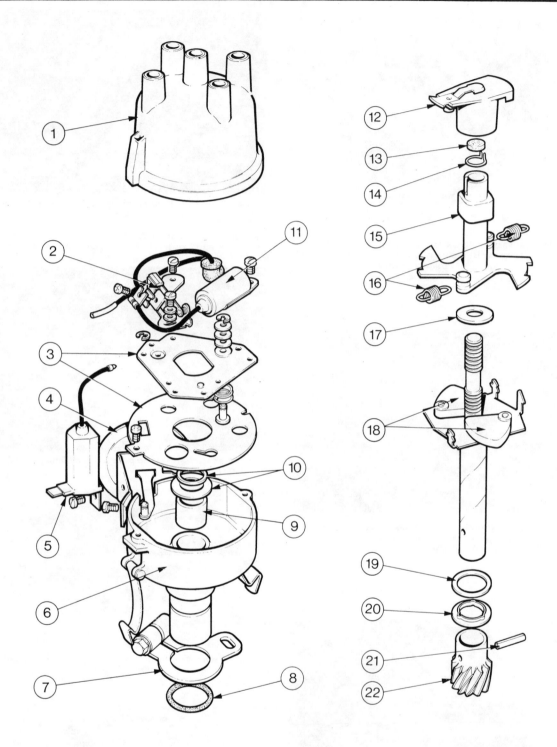

Fig. 4.13 Distributor assembly - exploded view

1 Cap	7 Body clamp plate	13 Felt wick	18 Mechanical advance
2 Contact breaker assembly	8 Cylinder block seal	14 Circlip	weights
3 Base plate	9 Bush (not serviced)	15 Cam spindle	19, 20 Washers
4 Vacuum unit	10 Thryst washers	16 Mechanical advance	21 Pin
5 Suppressor	11 Condenser	springs	22 Gear
6 Distributor body	12 Rotor arm	17 Washer	

Measuring plug gap. A feeler gauge of the correct size (see ignition system specifications) should have a slight 'drag' when slid between the electrodes. Adjust gap if necessary

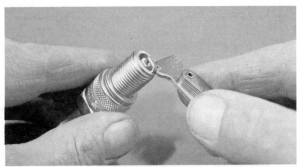

Adjusting plug gap. The plug gap is adjusted by bending the earth electrode inwards, or outwards, as necessary until the correct clearance is obtained. Note the use of the correct tool

Normal. Grey-brown deposits, lightly coated core nose. Gap increasing by around 0.001 in (0.025 mm) per 1000 miles (1600 km). Plugs ideally suited to engine, and engine in good condition

Carbon fouling. Dry, black, sooty deposits. Will cause weak spark and eventually misfire. Fault: over-rich fuel mixture. Check: carburettor mixture settings, float level and jet sizes; choke operation and cleanliness of air filter. Plugs can be re-used after cleaning

Oil fouling. Wet, oily deposits. Will cause weak spark and eventually misfire. Fault: worn bores/piston rings or valve guides; sometimes occurs (temporarily) during running-in period. Plugs can be re-used after thorough cleaning

Overheating. Electrodes have glazed appearance, core nose very white – few deposits. Fault: plug overheating. Check: plug value, ignition timing, fuel octane rating (too low) and fuel mixture (too weak). Discard plugs and cure fault immediately

Electrode damage. Electrodes burned away; core nose has burned, glazed appearance. Fault: pre-ignition. Check: as for 'Overheating' but may be more severe. Discard plugs and remedy fault before piston or valve damage occurs

Split core nose (may appear initially as a crack). Damage is self-evident, but cracks will only show after cleaning. Fault: pre-ignition or wrong gap-setting technique. Check: ignition timing, cooling system, fuel octane rating (too low) and fuel mixture (too weak). Discard plugs, rectify fault immediately

points from the breaker plate as detailed in Section 3.

8 Undo the condenser retaining screw and take off the condenser.

9 Next prise off the small circlip from the vacuum unit pivot post.

10 Take out the two screws holding the breaker plate to the distributor body and lift away. Where a vehicle is fitted with a VHF (F.M.) radio there may be a suppressor fitted to the vacuum unit bracket. Remove this suppressor by unscrewing the single screw holding it to the bracket.

11 Take off the circlip flat washer and wave washers from the pivot post. Separate the two plates by bringing the holding down screw through the keyhole slot in the lower plate. Be careful not to lose the spring now left on the pivot post.

12 Pull the low tension wire and grommet from the lower plate.

13 Undo the two screws holding the vacuum unit to the body. Take off the unit.

14 Prise the plastic bump stop tubing off the advance stop in the distributor body.

15 The mechanical advance is next removed but first make a careful note of the assembly, particularly which spring fits which post and the position of the advance springs. Then remove the advance springs.

16 Prise off the circlips from the governor weight pivot pins and take out the weights.

17 Dismantle the shaft by taking out the felt pad in the top of the spindle. Expand the exposed circlip and take it out.

18 Now mark which slot in the mechanical advance plate is occupied by the advance stop which stands up from the action plate, and lift off the cam spindle (Fig. 4.19).

19 It is only necessary to remove the lower shaft and action plate if it is excessively worn. If this is the case, with a small punch, drive out the gear retaining pin and remove the gear with the two washers located above it. Withdraw the shaft from the distributor body and take off the two washers from below the action plate. The distributor is now completely dismantled.

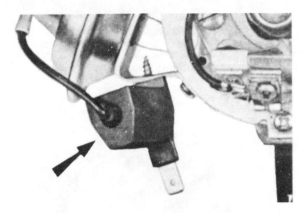

Fig. 4.14 Radio suppressor location on vacuum bracket (Sec 5)

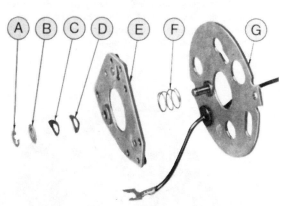

Fig. 4.15 Distributor base plate - exploded view (Sec 5)

A Circlip   E Upper plate
B Washer   F Spring
C & D Wave washers   G Lower plate

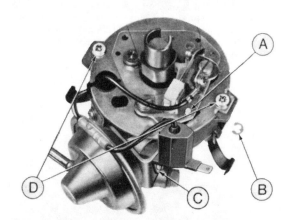

Fig. 4.16 Base plate removal: the vacuum unit pivot post (A) circlip (B) must be removed together with base plate retaining screws (D). Also arrowed is screw (C) holding the radio suppressor to the vacuum unit bracket (Sec 5)

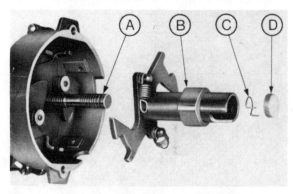

Fig. 4.18 Cam spindle assembly (Sec 5)

A Shaft   C Circlip
B Cam spindle   D Felt wick

Fig. 4.17 Screws (arrowed) retaining vacuum unit to distributor body (Sec 5)

20 Check the points, as described in Section 3. Check the distributor cap for signs of tracking, indicated by a thin black line between the segments. Renew the cap if any signs of tracking are found.

21 If the metal portion of the rotor arm is badly burned or loose, renew the arm. If only slightly burned, clean the end with a fine file. Check that the contact spring has adequate pressure and the bearing surface is clean and in good condition.

22 Check that the carbon brush in the distributor cap is unbroken and stands proud of its holder.

23 Examine the fly weights and pivots for wear and the advance

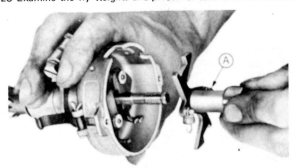

Fig. 4.19 Withdrawing cam spindle (A) from distributor body (Sec 5)

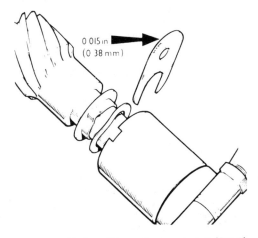

Fig. 4.20 Shaft endfloat adjustment plate (Sec 6)

springs for slackness. They can best be checked by comparing with new parts. If they are slack they must be renewed.

24 Check the points assembly for fit on the breaker plate, and the cam follower for wear.

25 Examine the fit of the lower shaft in the distributor body. If this is excessively worn, it will be necessary to fit a new assembly.

6 Distributor - reassembly and installation

1 Reassembly is a reversal of dismantling but observe the following points:

2 Apply a film of engine oil to the shaft and mechanical advance assembly before fitting.

3 When fitting the lower shaft, first replace the thrust washers below the action plate before inserting into the distributor body. Next fit the wave washer and thrust washer at the lower end and replace the drive gear. Secure it with a new pin.

4 Assemble the upper and lower shaft with the advance stop in the correct slot (the one which was marked) in the mechanical advance plate.

5 After assembling the advance weights and springs check that they move freely without binding, then replace the advance stop tubing.

6 Before assembling the breaker plates, make sure that the three nylon bearing studs are properly located in their holes in the upper breaker plate, and that the small earth spring is fitted on the pivot post.

7 As you refit the upper breaker plate, pass the holding down spindle through the keyhole slot in the lower plate.

8 Hold the upper plate in position by refitting the wave washer, flat washer and large circlip.

9 When all is assembled, remember to set the contact breaker gap to 0.025 inch (0.64 mm).

10 If a new gear or shaft is being fitted, it is necessary to drill a new pin hole. Proceed this way.

11 Make a 0.015 inch (0.38 mm) thick forked shim to slide over the driveshaft (Fig. 4.20).

12 Assemble the shaft, wave washer, thrust washer, shim and gear wheel in position in the distributor body.

13 Hold the assembly in a large clamp such as a vice or carpenter's clamp using only sufficient pressure to take up all end play.

14 There is a pilot hole in a new gear wheel for drilling the new hole. Set this pilot hole at 90° to the existing hole in an old shaft if the old shaft is being re-used. Drill an 1/8 inch (3.18 mm) hole through both gear and shaft.

15 Fit a new pin in the hole. Release the clamp and remove the shim. The shaft will now have the correct amount of clearance.

16 Hold the distributor above its crankcase opening so that the vacuum advance unit is pointing to the rear of the car and set the

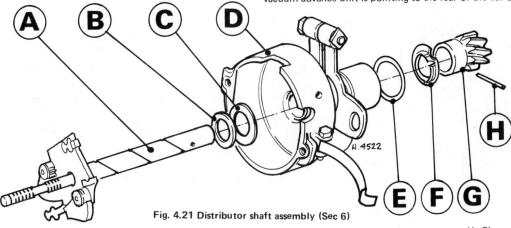

Fig. 4.21 Distributor shaft assembly (Sec 6)

A Shaft
B & C Thrust washers
D Distributor body
E Wave washer
F Washer
G Gear
H Pin

contact end of the rotor arm to align with No 2 inlet port. Insert the distributor; as its driveshaft meshes with the camshaft gear the rotor will rotate slightly and take up a position of approximately 90° to the centre-line of the engine.

17 Fit the clamp plate retaining bolt to hold the assembly to the engine block and tighten it.

18 Loosen the clamp-plate pinch-bolt and turn the distributor body clockwise slightly until the contact breaker points are just about to open.

19 Refit the electrical leads, vacuum pipe and distributor cap.

20 Check and adjust the ignition timing as described in Section 7.

7 Ignition timing

1 One of two methods may be used to check the ignition timing. With the first method, connect a test bulb between the distributor LT terminal and earth.

2 Rotate the crankshaft until No 1 piston is rising on its compression stroke (see paragraph 4 of Section 5). Continue turning until the notch on the crankshaft pulley is opposite the timing mark on the engine timing cover scale (see Specifications).

3 Switch on the ignition and release the distributor clamp pinch-bolt. Turn the distributor clockwise until the test bulb just lights up which indicates that the contact breaker points have just opened.

4 Tighten the pinch-bolt without moving the position of the distributor.

5 Remove the test bulb and switch off the ignition.

6 With the second method, a more precise setting is obtained.

7 Mark the notch on the crankshaft pulley and the timing mark on the timing cover scale with white paint or chalk.

8 Disconnect the vacuum pipe from the distributor and plug the pipe.

9 Connect a timing light (stroboscope) in accordance with the manufacturer's instructions. This is usually between the end of No.1 spark plug lead and the spark plug terminal.

10 Start the engine and let it idle, making sure that the idling speed is as given in the Specifications.

11 Point the stroboscope at the white marks when they will appear stationary and, if the timing is correct, in alignment. If the marks do not appear to be in alignment, release the distributor clamp-plate pinch-bolt and turn the distributor body fractionally in either direction until the timing marks coincide.

12 Retighten the pinch-bolts, switch off the engine and remake the original connections.

8 Spark plugs and HT leads

1 The correct functioning of the spark plugs is vital for the correct running and efficiency of the engine.

2 At intervals of 6000 miles (9600 km) the plugs should be removed, examined, cleaned, and if worn excessively, renewed. The condition of the spark plugs will also tell much about the overall condition of the engine.

3 If the insulator nose of the spark plug is clean and white, with no deposits, this is indicative of a weak mixture, or too hot a plug. (A hot plug transfers heat away from the electrode slowly - a cold plug transfers it away quickly).

4 The plugs fitted as standard are Autolite as listed in the Specifications at the head of this Chapter. If the tip and insulator nose is covered with hard black looking deposits, then this is indicative that the mixture is too rich. Should the plug be black and oily, then it is likely that the engine is fairly worn, as well as the mixture being too rich.

5 If the insulator nose is covered with light tan to greyish brown deposits, then the mixture is correct and it is likely that the engine is in good condition.

6 If there are any traces of long brown tapering stains on the outside of the white portion of the plug, then the plug will have to be renewed, as this shows that there is a faulty joint between the plug body and the insulator, and compression is being lost.

7 Plugs should be cleaned by a sand blasting machine, which will free them from carbon more thoroughly than cleaning by hand. The machine will also test the condition of the plugs under compression. Any plug that fails to spark at the recommended pressure should be renewed.

8 The spark plug gap is of considerable importance, as, if it is too large or too small, the size of the spark and its efficiency will be seriously impaired. The spark plug gap should be set to the figure given in the Specifications at the beginning of this Chapter.

9 To set it, measure the gap with a feeler gauge, and then bend open, or close, the **outer** plug electrode until the correct gap is achieved. The centre electrode should **never** be bent as this may crack the insulation and cause plug failure if nothing worse.

10 When replacing the plugs, remember to replace the leads from the distributor in the correct firing order, which is 1, 2, 4, 3 No 1 cylinder being the one nearest the radiator.

11 The plug leads require no routine attention other than being kept clean and wiped over regularly. At intervals of 6000 miles (9600 km), however, pull the leads off the plugs and distributor

Fig. 4.22 Distributor body clamp screw (Sec 6)

Fig. 4.23 Removing HT lead from distributor cap. Note that lead is gripped around moulded cover. (Sec 8)

one at a time and make sure no water has found its way onto the connections. Remove any corrosion from the brass ends, wipe the collars on top of the distributor and refit the leads.

12 Every 10,000 to 12,000 miles (16,000 to 19,000 km) it is recommended that the spark plugs are renewed to maintain optimum engine performance.

13 Later vehicles are fitted with carbon cored HT leads. These should be removed from the spark plugs by gripping their crimped terminals. Provided the leads are not bent in a tight loop and compressed there is no reason why this type of lead should fail. A legend has arisen which blames this type of lead for all ignition faults and many owners replace them with the older copper cored type and install separate suppressors. In the majority of cases, it would be more profitable to establish the real cause of the trouble before going to the expense of new leads.

9 Ignition system - fault diagnosis

By far the majority of breakdown and running troubles are caused by faults in the ignition system either in the low tension or high tension circuit. There are two main symptoms indicating ignition faults. Either the engine will not start or fire, or the engine is difficult to start and misfires. If it is a regular misfire, ie the engine is only running on two or three cylinders, the fault is almost sure to be in the secondary, or high tension, circuit. If the misfiring is intermittent, the fault could be in either the high or low tension circuits. If the car stops suddenly, or will not start at all, it is likely that the fault is in the low tension circuit. Loss of power and overheating, apart from faulty carburation settings, are normally due to faults in the distributor or incorrect ignition timing.

Engine fails to start

1 If the engine fails to start and the car was running normally when it was last used, first check there is fuel in the petrol tank. If the engine turns over normally on the starter motor and the battery is evidently well charged, then the fault may be in either the high or low tension circuits. First check the HT circuit. **Note**: if the battery is known to be fully charged; the ignition light comes on, and the starter motor fails to turn the engine, **check the tightness of the leads on the battery terminals** and the security of the earth lead to its **connection to the body**. It is quite common for the leads to have worked loose, even if they look and feel secure. If one of the battery terminal posts gets very hot when trying to work the starter motor, this is a sure indication of a faulty connection to that terminal.

2 One of the commonest reasons for bad starting is wet or damp spark plug leads and distributor. Remove the distributor cap. If condensation is visible internally dry the cap with a rag and wipe over the leads. Replace the cap.

3 If the engine still fails to start, check that current is reaching the plugs, by disconnecting each plug lead in turn at the spark plug end, and holding the end of the cable about 3/16 inch (5 mm) away from the cylinder block. Spin the engine on the starter motor.

4 Sparking between the end of the cable and the block should be fairly strong with a regular blue spark. (Hold the lead with rubber to avoid electric shocks). If current is reaching the plugs, then remove them and clean and regap them to 0.025 inch (0.64 mm). The engine should now start.

5 If there is no spark at the plug leads, take off the HT lead from the centre of the distributor cap and hold it to the block as before. Spin the engine on the starter once more. A rapid succession of blue sparks between the end of the lead and the block indicate that the coil is in order and that the distributor cap is cracked, the rotor arm faulty or the carbon brush in the top of the distributor cap is not making good contact with the spring

on the rotor arm. Possibly the points are in bad condition. Clean and reset them.

6 If there are no sparks from the end of the lead from the coil, check the connections at the coil end of the lead. If it is in order start checking the low tension circuit.

7 Use a 12 volt voltmeter or a 12 volt bulb and two lengths of wire. With the ignition switch on and the points open test between the low tension wire to the coil (it is marked SW or +) and earth. No reading indicates a break in the supply from the ignition switch. Check the connections at the switch to see if any are loose. Refit them and the engine should run. A reading shows a faulty coil or condenser or broken lead between the coil and the distributor.

8 Take the condenser wire off the points assembly and with the points open, test between the moving point and earth. If there now is a reading, then the fault is in the condenser. Fit a new one and the fault is cleared.

9 With no reading from the moving point to earth, take a reading between earth and the CB or (−) terminal of the coil. A reading here indicates a broken wire which must be renewed between the coil and distributor. No reading confirms that the coil has failed and must be renewed. Remember to connect the condenser wire to the points assembly. For these tests it is sufficient to separate the contact breaker points with a piece of paper.

Engine misfires

1 If the engine misfires regularly, run it at a fast idling speed. Pull off each of the plug caps in turn and listen to the note of the engine. Hold the plug cap in a dry cloth or with a rubber glove as additional protection against a shock from the HT supply.

2 No difference in engine running will be noticed when the lead from the defective circuit is removed. Removing the lead from one of the good cylinders will accentuate the misfire.

3 Remove the plug lead from the end of the defective plug and hold it about 3/16 inch (5 mm) away from the block. Restart the engine. If the sparking is fairly strong and regular, the fault must lie in the spark plug.

4 The plug may be loose, the insulation may be cracked, or the points may have burnt away, giving too wide a gap for the spark to jump. Worse still, one of the points may have broken off. Either renew the plug, or clean it, reset the gap, and then test it.

5 If there is no spark at the end of the plug lead, or if it is weak and intermittent, check the ignition lead from the distributor to the plug. If the insulation is cracked or perished, renew the lead. Check the connections at the distributor cap.

6 If there is still no spark, examine the distributor cap carefully for tracking. This can be recognised by a very thin black line running between two or more electrodes, or between an electrode and some other part of the distributor. These lines are paths which now conduct electricity across the cap, thus letting it run to earth. The only answer is a new distributor cap.

7 Apart from the ignition timing being incorrect, other causes of misfiring have already been dealt with under the section dealing with the failure of the engine to start. To recap, these are that:

a) The coil may be faulty giving an intermittent misfire.
b) There may be a damaged wire or loose connection in the low tension circuit.
c) The condenser may be short circuiting.
d) There may be a mechanical fault in the distributor (broken driving spindle or contact breaker spring).

8 If the ignition timing is too far retarded, it should be noted that the engine will tend to overheat, and there will be a quite noticeable drop in power. If the engine is overheating and the power is down, and the ignition timing is correct, then the carburettor should be checked, as it is likely that this is where the fault lies.

Chapter 5 Clutch

For modifications, and information applicable to later models, see Supplement at end of manual

Contents

Specifications

Type	Single dry plate, diaphragm spring
Actuation	Cable
Diameter - driven plate (friction disc)	7.5 in. (190.5 mm)
Thickness - driven plate (friction disc)	0.124 in (3.15 mm)
Minimum lining thickness	0.118 in (3.00 mm)
Effective clutch lining area	40.7 in (26221 mm)
Clutch plate spring pressure	847 lb (385 kg)
Clutch pedal free-travel	0.87 ± 0.16 in (22.0 mm ± 4.0 mm)
Number of torsion springs	4
Release bearing type	Sealed ball

Torque wrench setting	lb f ft	kg f m
Clutch pressure plate to flywheel bolts	13 to 15	1.7 to 2.1

1 General description

All models in the Escort range employ a 7.5 in (191 mm) clutch of either Borg and Beck or Laycock manufacture.

The clutch assembly comprises a steel cover which is dowelled and bolted to the rear face of the flywheel and contains the pressure plate diaphragm spring and fulcrum rings.

The clutch disc is free to slide along the splined gearbox first motion shaft and is held in position between the flywheel and the pressure plate by the pressure of the pressure plate spring. Friction lining material is riveted to the clutch disc and it has a spring cushioned hub to absorb transmission shocks and to help ensure a smooth take-off.

The circular diaphragm spring is mounted on shouldered pins and held in place in the cover by two fulcrum rings. The spring is also held to the pressure plate by three spring steel clips which are riveted in position.

The clutch is actuated by a cable controlled by the clutch pedal. The clutch release mechanism consists of a release fork and bearing which are in permanent contact with the release fingers on the pressure plate. There should therefore never be any free play at the release fork. Wear of the friction material in the clutch is taken up by means of a cable adjuster on the clutch bellhousing.

Depressing the clutch pedal actuates the clutch release arm by means of the cable.

The release arm pushes the release bearing forward to bear against the release fingers, so moving the centre of the diaphragm spring inward. The spring is sandwiched between two annular rings which act as fulcrum points. As the centre of the spring is pushed in, the outside of the spring is pushed out, so moving the pressure plate backward and disengaging the pressure plate from the clutch disc.

When the clutch pedal is released, the diaphragm spring forces the pressure plate into contact with the high friction linings on the clutch disc and at the same time pushes the clutch disc a fraction of an inch forward on its splines so engaging the clutch disc with the flywheel. The clutch disc is now firmly sandwiched between the pressure plate and the flywheel so the drive is taken up.

2 Clutch - adjustment

1 Every 6,000 miles (9,600 km) the clutch pedal backlift must be checked and adjusted if necessary to compensate for wear in the friction linings.

2 Slacken the locknut on the threaded portion of the outer cable at the clutch bellhousing.

3 Check that the cable is not kinked, or frayed, then grasp the outer case of the cable and pull the cable forward to take up any free-play in the cable.

4 Turn the adjusting nut down the adjuster thread until it contacts the cable bush in the bellhousing, then press the pedal to the floor several times to ensure all components are properly seated.

5 Reset the adjusting nut until there is a free backlift movement of 22.0 mm ± 4.0 mm at the clutch pedal pad. Before checking the backlift push the pedal slowly down to the floor and, equally slowly, allow it to return to the 'rest' position. Allowing the pedal to spring back to the 'rest' position may not necessarily cause it to reach its normal 'rest' position.

6 If the pedal backlift movement is too small *slacken* the adjusting nut, if too great *tighten* the adjusting nut.

7 When the adjustment is correct tighten the locknut without disturbing the adjusting nut, then recheck the backlift.

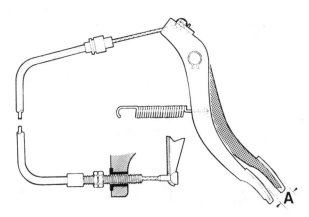

Fig. 5.1 Clutch pedal free movement. BACKLIFT at 'A' on the pedal pad must be 22.0 mm ± 4.0 mm (0.87 ±0.16 in) (Sec 2)

Fig. 5.2 Clutch disc and cover plate assembly (Sec 3)

Fig. 5.3 Assembling clutch cover plate. Note that clutch disc is held centrally on the flywheel by use of a suitably sized mandrel (A) (Sec 4)

3 Clutch - removal

1 Remove the gearbox, as described in the next Chapter.
2 Scribe a mating line from the clutch cover to the flywheel to ensure identical positioning on replacement and then remove the clutch assembly by unscrewing the six bolts holding the cover to the rear face of the flywheel. Unscrew the bolts diagonally half a

turn at a time to prevent distortion of the cover flange.
3 With all the bolts and spring washers removed, lift the clutch assembly off the locating dowels. The driven plate may fall out at this stage as it is not attached to either the clutch cover assembly or the flywheel.

4 Clutch - installation

1 It is important that no oil or grease gets onto the clutch disc friction linings, or the pressure plate and flywheel faces. It is advisable to replace the clutch with clean hands and to wipe down the pressure plate and flywheel faces with a clean, dry rag before assembly begins.
2 Place the clutch disc against the flywheel with the longer end of the splined hub facing toward the flywheel.
3 Locate the clutch cover/pressure plate assembly on the dowels with the mating marks in alignment.
4 Insert the six bolts and their spring washers finger tight so that the driven plate is just gripped but can be slid sideways.
5 The clutch driven plate must now be centralised so that when the gearbox is mated to the engine, the gearbox first motion shaft will pass smoothly through the splined hub of the driven plate.
6 Centralising is best carried out using an old first motion shaft but a rod of equivalent diameter with a stepped end to engage in the spigot bush located in the centre of the flywheel will serve as a good substitute.
7 Insert the centralising tool and move it in all directions to centralise the driven plate. The tool should be easy to withdraw without any side pressure.
8 Tighten the clutch cover to flywheel bolts evenly in diagonal sequence and finally tighten to a torque of between 13 and 15 lbf ft (1.7 and 2.1 kgf m).
9 Refit the gearbox as described in the next Chapter.

5 Clutch assembly - servicing

1 It is recommended that the driven plate is exchanged for a factory reconditioned unit. Do not attempt to fit new friction linings yourself. This is seldom satisfactory and the small saving in cost is not worthwhile.
2 The pressure plate assembly should also be renewed on an exchange basis as if dismantled, it requires the use of jigs and considerable skill to set up.
3 If the driven plate is being renewed, always renew the release bearing at the same time to avoid later dismantling (see Section 7).
4 The driven plate should be renewed if the friction linings have worn down to, or almost down to, the rivets. If the linings are oil stained, renew the friction plate and establish and rectify the cause which will almost certainly be the gearbox front oil seal or the crankshaft rear oil seal having failed.

6 Clutch cable - renewal

1 Slacken the locknut on the threaded portion of the outer cable. This is located at the clutch bellhousing.
2 Unscrew the adjusting nut so that the clutch inner cable becomes quite slack.
3 From inside the vehicle pull the cable into the vehicle as far as possible and remove the cable retaining pin from its location in the cable and clutch pedal. Withdraw the cable into the engine compartment. (Fig. 5.4).
4 Peel back the dust excluding gaiter from the bellhousing aperture through which the release arm emerges and then detach the clutch cable from the release arm by passing the inner cable through the slot in the arm (Fig. 5.5).
5 Fitting the new cable is a reversal of removal but grease the pivot pin before fitting and adjust the free-movement, as described in Section 2.

Fig. 5.4 Clutch cable retaining pin (arrowed) in clutch pedal (Sec 6)

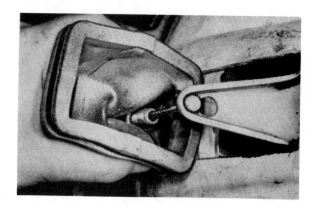

Fig. 5.5 Removing clutch lever gaiter on side of clutch housing to expose clutch cable location in release lever (Sec 6)

7 Release bearing - removal and refitting

1 Whenever the gearbox is withdrawn for servicing of the clutch to be carried out, the clutch release bearing, which is located within the bellhousing on the clutch release arm, should be renewed.
2 Detach the release arm dust excluding gaiter and withdraw the release arm and bearing assembly. Unhook the release bearing from the release arm.
3 Using a suitable piece of tube as a distance piece, press the bearing from its retaining hub.
4 To install the bearing, first locate the release arm within the clutch bellhousing and then fit the bearing to it. Make sure that the projecting tags of the release arm engage securely with the hooked ends of the release bearing and apply a smear of high melting point grease to the clutch release arm pivot post.

8 Clutch - fault diagnosis

There are four main faults to which the clutch and release mechanism are prone. They may occur by themselves or in conjunction with any of the other faults. They are clutch squeal, slip, spin and judder.

Clutch squeal
1 If, on taking up the drive or when changing gear, the clutch squeals, this is a sure indication of a badly worn clutch release bearing.
2 As well as regular wear due to normal use, wear of the clutch release bearing is much accentuated if the clutch is ridden, or held down for long periods in gear, with the engine running. To minimise wear of this component, the car should always be taken out of gear at traffic lights and for similar hold-ups.
3 The clutch release bearing is not an expensive item, but difficult to get at.

Clutch slip
1 Clutch slip is a self-evident condition which occurs when the clutch friction plate is badly worn, oil or grease have got onto the flywheel or pressure plate faces, or the pressure plate itself is faulty.
2 The reason for clutch slip is that, due to one of the faults listed above, there is either insufficient pressure from the pressure plate, or insufficient friction from the friction plate to ensure solid drive.

3 If small amounts of oil get onto the clutch, they will be burnt off under the heat of the clutch engagement and in the process, gradually darkening the linings. Excessive oil on the clutch will burn off leaving a carbon deposit which can cause quite bad slip, or fierceness, spin and judder.
4 If clutch slip is suspected, and confirmation of this condition is required, there are several tests which can be made.
5 With the engine in second or third gear and pulling lightly up a moderate incline, sudden depression of the accelerator pedal may cause the engine to increase its speed without any increase in road speed. Easing off on the accelerator will then give a definite drop in engine speed without the car slowing.
6 In extreme cases of clutch slip the engine will race under normal acceleration conditions.

Clutch spin
1 Clutch spin is a condition which occurs when the release arm travel is excessive, there is an obstruction in the clutch, either on the primary gear splines, or in the operating lever itself, or the oil may have partially burnt off the clutch linings and have left a resinous deposit which is causing the clutch disc to stick to the pressure plate or flywheel.
2 The reason for clutch spin is that due to any, or a combination, of the faults just listed, the clutch pressure plate is not completely freeing from the centre plate even with the clutch pedal fully depressed.
3 If clutch spin is suspected, the condition can be confirmed by extreme difficulty in engaging first gear from rest, difficulty in changing gear, and very sudden take-up of the clutch drive at the fully depressed end of the clutch pedal travel as the clutch is released.
4 Check that the clutch cable is correctly adjusted and if in order, then the fault lies internally in the clutch. It will then be necessary to remove the clutch for examination and to check the gearbox input shaft.

Clutch judder
1 Clutch judder is a self-evident condition which occurs when the gearbox or engine mountings are loose or too flexible, when there is oil on the faces of the clutch friction plate, or when the clutch pressure plate has been incorrectly adjusted during assembly.
2 The reason for clutch judder is that due to one of the faults just listed, the clutch pressure plate is not freeing smoothly from the friction disc, and is snatching.
3 Clutch judder normally occurs when the clutch pedal is released in first or reverse gears, and the whole car shudders as it moves backward or forward.

Chapter 6
Manual gearbox and automatic transmission

For modifications, and information applicable to later models, see Supplement at end of manual

Contents

Specifications

Manual Gearbox

Number of gears	4 forward, 1 reverse	
Type of gears	Helical constant mesh	
Synchromesh	All forward gears	

Gearbox ratios	Standard	Heavy duty
First	3.656 to 1	3.337:1
Second	2.185 to 1	1.995:1
Third	1.425 to 1	1.418:1
Top	1.000 to 1	1.000:1
Reverse	4.235 to 1	3.867:1

Oil capacity	1.6 Imp. pints, 0.90 litres
Countershaft gear train endfloat	0.006 to 0.018 in. (0.15 to 0.45 mm)
Countershaft diameter	0.624 to 0.625 in. (15.852 to 15.865 mm)

Selective circlips (available for gearbox re-building)

Mainshaft bearing to extension housing:

	Colour Code
0.0679 to 0.0689 in. (1.725 to 1.750 mm)	Magenta
0.0691 to 0.0701 in. (1.755 to 1.781 mm)	Violet
0.0703 to 0.0713 in. (1.786 to 1.811 mm)	Blue
0.0715 to 0.0724 in. (1.826 to 1.839 mm)	Plain
0.0725 to 0.0736 in. (1.842 to 1.869 mm)	Orange
0.0738 to 0.0748 in. (1.875 to 1.900 mm)	Red
0.0750 to 0.0760 in. (1.905 to 1.930 mm)	Green

1st/2nd gear synchroniser to mainshaft:

	Colour Code
0.0602 to 0.0612 in. (1.529 to 1.554 mm)	Brown
0.0614 to 0.0624 in. (1.560 to 1.585 mm)	Black
0.0626 to 0.0636 in. (1.590 to 1.615 mm)	Blue
0.0638 to 0.0648 in. (1.621 to 1.646 mm)	Plain
0.0650 to 0.0659 in. (1.651 to 1.674 mm)	Copper

Front bearing to input shaft (small circlip):

	Colour Code
0.0505 to 0.0524 in. (1.280 to 1.331 mm)	Plain
0.0528 to 0.0548 in. (1.341 to 1.392 mm)	Blue
0.0552 to 0.0571 in. (1.402 to 1.450 mm)	Orange
0.0575 to 0.0591 in. (1.461 to 1.501 mm)	Magenta

Mainshaft bearing to mainshaft:

	Colour Code
0.059 to 0.061 in. (1.499 to 1.549 mm)	Plain
0.061 to 0.062 in. (1.549 to 1.575 mm)	Blue
0.062 to 0.064 in. (1.575 to 1.626 mm)	Violet
0.064 to 0.065 in. (1.626 to 1.651 mm)	Magenta
0.065 to 0.067 in. (1.651 to 1.702 mm)	Orange

The foregoing circlip selection tables should be read in conjunction with Fig. 6.1.

Automatic transmission

Type	Ford C3 (Bordeaux)

Gear ratios:

1st	2.47 : 1
2nd	1.47 : 1
3rd	1 : 1
Reverse	2.11 : 1

Stall speed	1700 rpm (min), 2600 (max)
Operating temperature of fluid	65° C
Fluid capacity	11.4 Imp. pints (6.5 litres) with converter and oil cooler

Torque wrench settings (manual gearbox)

	lbf ft	kgf m
Top cover to gearbox	7 to 8	0.9 to 1.1
Drive gear bearing retainer	7 to 8	0.9 to 1.1
Extension housing to gearbox	33 to 37	4.5 to 5.0
Clutch housing to engine		
3/8 inch	22 to 27	3.0 to 3.7
10 mm	29 to 35	3.9 to 4.8
Gearbox to rear engine mounting	37 to 42	5.0 to 5.7
Rear engine mounting to floor pan	12 to 15	1.6 to 2.0

Torque wrench settings (automatic transmission)

	lbf ft	kgf m
Drive disc to converter	26 to 30	3.6 to 4.1
Oil pan to transmission housing	12 to 17	1.6 to 2.4
Downshaft cable bracket	12 to 17	1.6 to 2.4
Downshift lever nut		
inner	30 to 39	4.1 to 5.4
outer	7 to 11	1.0 to 1.5
Starter inhibitor switch	12 to 14	1.6 to 2.0
Oil line to connector	7 to 10	0.9 to 1.4
Oil cooler line to connector	12 to 14	1.6 to 2.0
Oil line connecter to transmission housing ...	10 to 14	1.4 to 2.0
Converter housing to engine	22 to 27	3.0 to 3.7
Converter drain plug	20 to 29	2.7 to 4.0

Manual gearbox

1 General description

The gearbox fitted to all models contains four constant mesh helically cut forward gears and one straight cut reverse gear. Synchromesh is fitted between 1st and 2nd, 2nd and 3rd, and 3rd and 4th. The iron bellhousing and gearbox casing are a combined casting. Attached to the rear of the gearbox casing is an aluminium alloy extension which supports the rear of the mainshaft and the gearchange shaft cum selector rod arm.

The gearbox is of a simple but clever design, using the minimum of components to facilitate speed of assembly; and the minimum of matched items to simplify fitting. Where close tolerances and limits are required, manufacturing tolerances are compensated for excessive endfloat or backlash eliminated by fitting selective circlips. These are fitted in positions 1, 4, 5 and 6 as shown in Fig. 6.1. When overhauling the gearbox, always use new circlips, never replace circlips that have already been used.

The availability of circlips is shown in the Specifications at the beginning of this Chapter.

The gear selector mechanism is unusual in that the selector forks are free to slide on the one selector rod which also serves as the gearchange shaft. At the gearbox end of this rod lies the selector arm, which, depending on the position of the gearlever, places the appropriate selector fork in the position necessary for the synchroniser sleeve to engage with the dog teeth on the gear selected. Another unusual feature is that some of the bolts are metric sizes. In particular this applies to the top cover bolts and some of the bellhousing bolts. The reverse idler shaft thread is also metric (a bolt is only inserted here when it is wished to remove the shaft).

It is impossible to select two gears at once because of an interlock guard plate which pivots on the right-hand side of the gearbox casing. The selector forks, when not in use, are positively held by the guard plate in their disengaged positions.

2 Gearbox — removal and installation

1 The gearbox can be removed in unit with the engine through the engine compartment as described in Chapter 1. Alternatively, the gearbox can be separated from the rear of the engine at the bellhousing and the gearbox lowered from under the car.

2 If a hoist or an inspection pit are not available, then run the back of the car up a pair of ramps or jack it up and fit stands. Jack up the front of the car and fit stands.

3 From inside the car, lift up the gearlever gaiter, and then remove the circlip from its groove in the gearlever to release the tension in the spring. The circlip is fitted adjacent to the smaller diameter of the spring (arrowed in photo).

4 Bend back the lock tab and with a pair of mole grips or similar across the flats undo the plastic dome nut and lift out the gearlever from the car.

5 With the bonnet opened, undo the clamp securing the exhaust manifold to the exhaust downpipe, and disconnect the battery by removing the earth (negative) lead.

6 When underneath the car, it will be necessary to disconnect the clutch cable from the clutch release arm. So that this can be done later, while still working in the engine compartment, loosen the clutch cable at the adjuster on the rear bulkhead or clutch bellhousing to make the cable as slack as possible.

7 At the engine undo the four bellhousing bolts accessible from inside the engine compartment and then move under the car.

8 Support the rear of the engine on a jack. Undo the nut which holds the starter motor lead to the starter motor and then undo the three bolts (two bolts on models fitted with a pre-engaged starter) which hold the starter motor in place. Take off the starter motor.

9 Free the speedometer cable from the gearbox extension

housing by extracting the circlip which holds the cable in place. Disconnect the lead from the reversing light switch where fitted.

10 Push away the rubber gaiter on the clutch release arm, push the clutch cable forward, and then slide it out of the slot in the end of the release arm.

11 Scratch a mating line across the propeller shaft and rear axle flanges, and then undo the four nuts and bolts which hold the flanges together. Drop the rear of the propeller shaft and pull the front off the gearbox mainshaft splines. Place a bowl under the rear of the extension housing to catch the oil which will now leak out.

12 Undo the bolts which hold the flywheel dust cover in place. Undo the four bolts, two at each end, which hold the gearbox crossmember to the bodyshell.

13 Undo the two remaining bellhousing to engine bolts, lower

the jack slightly and pull the gearbox off the rear of the engine. Take great care that the gearbox does not hang on the input shaft. It is preferable to have an assistant available to help with the removal of the gearbox as it is a heavy unit. Alternatively, if a trolley jack is available, this can be placed under the gearbox to take much of the weight, the jack and gearbox being rolled back together.

14 To separate the gearbox from the crossmember simply remove the central bolt.

15 Replacement commences by fitting the crossmember to the rubber mounting and securing them to the gearbox by the large central bolt and washer which should be tightened to 37 to 42 lbf ft (5.0 to 5.7 Kgf m).

16 Check that the adaptor plate is in place on the rear of the engine and then fit the gearbox. A certain amount of movement and positioning may be necessary to get the input shaft splines

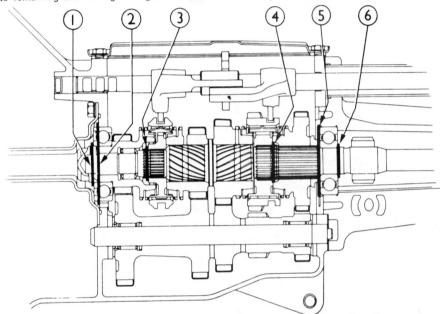

Fig. 6.1 Circlip locations in manual gearbox (Sec 1)

1	Bearing to input shaft (small circlip	4	1st/2nd synchroniser to mainshaft
2	Bearing to input shaft (outer circlip)	5	Mainshaft bearing to extension housing
3	3rd/4th synchroniser circlip	6	Mainshaft bearing to mainshaft

Numbers 1, 4 5 and 6 are selective (see Specifications)

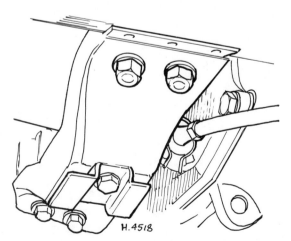

Fig. 6.2 Location of speedometer drive circlip and crossmember (manual gearbox) (Sec 2)

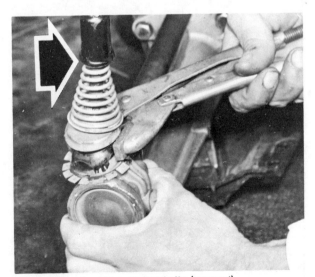

2.3 Location of gearlever spring circlip (arrowed)

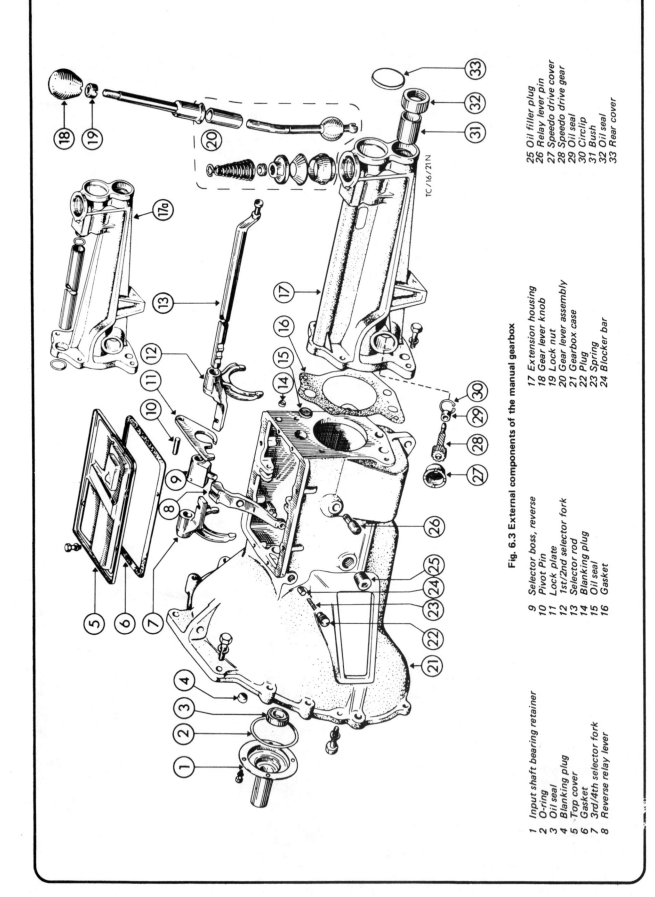

Fig. 6.3 External components of the manual gearbox

1 Input shaft bearing retainer
2 O-ring
3 Oil seal
4 Blanking plug
5 Top cover
6 Gasket
7 3rd/4th selector fork
8 Reverse relay lever

9 Selector boss, reverse
10 Pivot Pin
11 Lock plate
12 1st/2nd selector fork
13 Selector rod
14 Blanking plug
15 Oil seal
16 Gasket

17 Extension housing
18 Gear lever knob
19 Lock nut
20 Gear lever assembly
21 Gearbox case
22 Plug
23 Spring
24 Blocker bar

25 Oil filler plug
26 Relay lever pin
27 Speedo drive cover
28 Speedo drive gear
29 Oil seal
30 Circlip
31 Bush
32 Oil seal
33 Rear cover

TC/16/21N

fully into the splined hub in the middle of the clutch. When the gearbox is fully home, replace the two lower bellhousing bolts.

17 Then refit the four crossmember bolts and spring washers, refit the flywheel dust cover, and replace and reconnect the starter motor.

18 Reconnect the propeller shaft, gearbox end first, and ensure that the mating marks across the rear axle and rear propeller shaft flanges align.

19 Refit the speedometer cable to the extension housing and the clutch cable to the release arm. Where applicable, reconnect the lead to the reversing light switch. Remove the jack from the rear of the engine.

20 From inside the engine compartment refit the remaining bellhousing to engine backplate bolts, noting that the top two are 9/16 inch AF, while the others are 17 mm.

21 Adjust the clutch pedal free movement as described in the preceding Chapter.

22 Connect the exhaust downpipe to the exhaust manifold.

23 Reconnect the battery.

24 Refit the gearlever. On early models without a tab locking plate, smear Loctite over the threads on the plastic dome and over the threads in the extension housing, and allow to partly dry before screwing the dome nut down.

25 Fill the gearbox with a recommended lubricant.

3 Gearbox - dismantling

1 Undo and remove the eight bolts and spring washers which hold the gearbox cover in place. (photo)

2 Lift the cover off and place on one side.

3 Undo the plug from the left-hand side of the gearbox (photo) and remove the spring and plunger from the drilling. It may be necessary to shake the plunger out.

4 Carefully tap out the spring pin (photo) which holds the gear selector arm in place on the gearchange shaft.

5 Then undo the four bolts and spring washer holding the rear extension to the back of the gearbox casing. (photo)

6 With the aid of a sharp screwdriver, carefully prise out the speedometer drive pinion cap (photo), taking great care not to distort the rim of the cap or damage the housing orifice.

7 Remove the speedometer drive pinion and its shaft from the extension. (photo)

8 Knock out the large plug using a soft drift and a hammer at the rear of the remote control extension tube casing. (photo)

9 The gearchange shaft/selector rod can now be removed rearwards. It may be necessary to tap it gently with a soft drift and hammer (photo) to get it started.

10 The selector forks and the selector lever can then be lifted out from the gearbox. (photo)

11 Tap the extension housing slightly rearward and then rotate it until the end of the layshaft fits into the cutaway in the extension housing flange. Drive the layshaft rearward from inside the bellhousing with a metal drift. (photo)

12 The layshaft can then be pulled out from the rear of the gearbox casing. (photo)

13 The extension complete with mainshaft can now be pulled away and out from the back of the gearbox. (photo)

14 Inside the bellhousing unscrew the four bolts and spring washers (photo) which hold the input shaft bearing retainer in place and remove the retainer.

15 The input shaft complete with bearing can then be withdrawn from the front of the gearbox casing through the bellhousing. (photo)

16 With the aid of a thin metal drift, tap out the pivot pin from the lug on the right-hand side of the gearbox (photo) and remove the interlock plate.

17 Remove the laygear through the mainshaft bearing hole in the rear of the gearbox. (photo)

18 Screw a suitably sized bolt into the metric thread cut in the centre of the reverse gear idler shaft and then with one of the

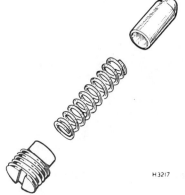

Fig. 6.4 Gear selector plunger, spring and retaining plug (Sec 3)

3.1 Removing gearbox cover bolt

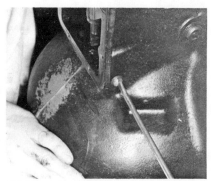

3.3 Removing selector plunger plug

3.4 Drifting out selector arm pin

3.5 Removing extension housing bolt

3.6 Prising out speedometer drive pinion cap

3.7 Withdrawing speedometer drive gear

3.8 Removing extension housing blanking plate

3.9 Removing gearchange/shaft selector rod

3.10 Removing selector forks and lever

3.11 Tapping layshaft from gearbox

3.12 Extracting layshaft from rear of gearbox

3.13 Extracting mainshaft with extension housing

3.14 Removing input shaft bearing retainer

3.15 Withdrawing input shaft and bearing

3.16 Drifting out interlock plate pivot pin

3.17 Withdrawing laygear

3.18 Levering idler shaft from gearbox

jaws of a large spanner resting under the head of the bolt (photo) lever the idler shaft out of the gearbox. Lift out the reverse idler gear.

4 Gearbox - examination and renovation

1 Clean all dismantled components in paraffin and examine them for wear, distortion, cracks or chipped teeth.
2 Examine the gearwheels for excessive wear and chipping of the teeth. Renew them as necessary. If the laygear endfloat is above the permitted tolerance of between 0.006 and 0.018 in (0.15 and 0.45 mm) the thrust washers must be renewed. New thrust washers will almost certainly be required on any car that has completed more than 30,000 miles (48,000 km).
3 Examine the layshaft for signs of wear, where the laygear needle roller bearings bear. If a small ridge can be felt at either end of the shaft, it will be necessary to renew it.
4 The four synchroniser rings (4, 25, 28, 38) (Fig. 6.5) are bound to be badly worn and it is a false economy not to renew them. New rings will improve the smoothness and speed of the gearchange considerably.
5 The needle roller bearing and cage (24) located between the nose of the mainshaft and the annulus in the rear of the input shaft is also liable to wear and should be renewed as a matter of course. Check that the nose of the mainshaft has not worn too.
6 Examine the condition of the two ball bearing assemblies, one on the input shaft (22) and one on the mainshaft (41). Check them for noisy operation, looseness between the inner and outer races, and for general wear. Normally they should be renewed on a gearbox that is being rebuilt.
7 If either of the synchroniser units (6 and 7, 31 and 32) are worn, it will be necessary to buy a complete assembly as the parts are not sold individually.
8 Examine the ends of the selector forks where they rub against the channels in the periphery of the synchroniser units. If possible compare the selector forks with new units to help determine the wear that has occurred. Renew them if worn.
9 If the bush bearing in the extension is badly worn it is best to take the extension to your local Ford garage to have the bearing pulled out and a new one fitted.
10 The rear oil seal should be renewed as a matter of course. Drive out the old seal with the aid of a drift or broad screwdriver.
11 The seal is surrounded by a metal ring and comes out fairly easily.
12 With a piece of wood to spread the load evenly, carefully tap a new seal into place, ensuring that it enters its bore in the extension squarely.
13 It is unlikely that any of the mainshaft bearing surfaces will be worn, but if there is any sign of scoring, picking up, or flats on the shaft, then it must be renewed.

5 Input shaft - dismantling and reassembly

1 The only reasons for dismantling the input shaft are to fit a new ball bearing assembly or, if the input shaft is being renewed and the old bearing is in excellent condition, then the fitting of a new shaft to an old bearing.
2 With a pair of expanding circlip pliers, remove the circlip from the input shaft. (photo)
3 With a soft headed hammer, gently tap the bearing forward and then remove it from the shaft. (photo)
4 When fitting the new bearing, ensure that the groove cut in the outer periphery faces away from the gear. If the bearing is fitted the wrong way round, it will not be possible to fit the large circlip which retains the bearing against the gearbox casing.
5 Using the jaws of a vice as a support behind the bearing, tap the bearing squarely into place by hitting the rear of the input shaft with a plastic or hide faced hammer. (photo)
6 Fit the widest circlip that will fit in the groove in the input shaft. (see circlip selection table - Section 1).

6 Mainshaft - dismantling and reassembly

1 Before the mainshaft can be fully dismantled, it has to be removed from the extension housing. Mount the extension housing between two flat pieces of wood in the jaws of a vice.
2 With a pair of circlip pliers, remove the circlip (3) (Fig. 6.5) (photo) which holds the 3rd and 4th gear synchroniser hub assembly in place.
3 Slide the synchroniser assembly (6, 7) complete with its sleeve forwards off the nose of the mainshaft and follow it with the 4th gear (26) (photo). To get the gear started may call for a little prising between the gear and the raised shoulder on the mainshaft because of the raised shoulder round the periphery of the mainshaft.
4 With a pair of thin nosed pliers, squeeze together the ends of the circlip (40) in the extension housing (photo) and remove the circlip from its groove in the housing.
5 With a soft faced hammer, tap the rear end of the mainshaft (photo) until the large bearing (41) is clear of the housing.
6 The mainshaft can now be completely removed from the extension housing.
7 To remove the speedometer drive gear (43) and the bearing (41) can be very difficult as they are both a very tight interference fit on the mainshaft. Ideally they should be removed in a hydraulic press. They can be removed with the aid of long tyre levers (photo) or similar, but only if the bearing is going to be renewed as the levers have to rest against the side face of the bearing and this is almost sure to damage it.
8 The speedometer drive may be obstinate to remove right up to the last 1/16 inch (1.58 mm) of its shoulder. To enable the

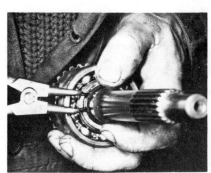
5.2 Extracting input shaft bearing circlip

5.3 Tapping bearing from input shaft

5.5 Refitting input shaft bearing

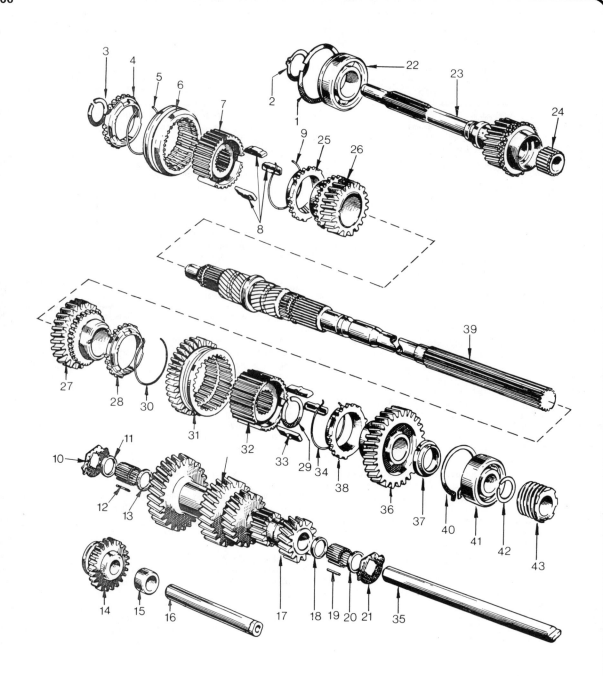

Fig. 6.5 Internal components of the manual gearbox

1 Input shaft bearing circlip (external)	12 Needle roller bearings	22 Input shaft bearing	32 Synchro hub
2 Bearing to shaft circlip	13 Needle bearing thrust washer	23 Input shaft	33 Blocker bars
3 3rd/4th synchroniser circlip	14 Reverse idle gear	24 Needle roller bearings	34 Synchro hub spring
4 3rd/4th synchroniser baulk ring	15 Spacer	25 3rd/4th synchroniser baulk ring	35 Layshaft
5 Synchro hub springs	16 Reverse gear shaft	26 Third gear	36 1st gear
6 Synchro sleeve	17 Laygear	27 Second gear	37 Spacer/oil slinger
7 Synchro hub	18 Needle bearing thrust washer	28 1st/2nd synchroniser baulk ring	38 1st/2nd synchro baulk ring
8 Blocker bars	19 Needle rollers	29 Circlip	39 Mainshaft
9 Synchro hub spring	20 Needle bearing thrust washer	30 Synchro hub spring	40 Circlip
10 Laygear thrust washer	21 Laygear thrust washer	31 1st/2nd synchro sleeve and reverse gear	41 Mainshaft bearing
11 Needle bearing thrust washer			42 Circlip
			43 Speedometer drive gear

6.2 Extracting 3rd/4th synchro hub circlip

6.3 Removing 3rd/4th synchro assembly and 3rd gear

6.4 Extracting mainshaft bearing to extension housing circlip

6.5 Tapping mainshaft from extension housing

6.7 Levering speedometer drive gear and bearing from mainshaft

6.9 Extracting mainshaft bearing circlip

6.10 Levering bearing from mainshaft

6.11 Sliding spacer/oil slinger, 1st gear and synchro ring from mainshaft

6.12 Extracting 1st/2nd synchro circlip

levers to continue leverage when the gap between the drive and the bearing becomes very large, fit a spanner adjacent to the bearing over the mainshaft to take up some of the gap.

9 With a pair of circlip pliers, remove the circlip (42) which holds the main bearing in place on the mainshaft. (photo)

10 The bearing must then be removed from the shaft in exactly the same way as the speedometer drive (photo). Take the greatest care if using tyre levers or similar tools not to chip any of the teeth on 1st gear.

11 The spacer washer or oil slinger (37), 1st gear (36), and the synchroniser ring (38) can now be slid from the mainshaft. (photo).

12 Remove the circlip (29) which holds the 1st and 2nd gear synchroniser assembly (31, 32) in place. (photo)

13 Once again with the aid of screwdrivers or tyre levers, carefully lever the synchroniser assembly and second gear (27) off the mainshaft (photo). The mainshaft is now completely dismantled.

14 If a new synchroniser assembly is being fitted it is necessary to take it to pieces first to clean off all the preservative. These instructions are also applicable in instances where the outer sleeve has come off the hub accidentally during dismantling.

15 To dismantle an assembly for cleaning slide the synchroniser sleeve off the splined hub and clean all the preservative from the blocker bars, spring rings, the hub itself and the sleeve.

16 Oil the components lightly and then fit the sleeve to the hub. Note the three slots in the hub and fit a blocker bar in each.

17 Fit the two spring rings one on the front and one on the rear face of the inside of the synchroniser sleeve under the blocker bars with the tagged end of each spring locating the 'U' section of the same bar. One spring must be put on anticlockwise and one clockwise (Fig. 6.6). When either side of the assembly is then viewed, the directional pattern of the two springs will appear to coincide.

Fig. 6.6 Synchroniser hub, spring rings and blocker bars (Sec 6)

6.13 Levering 1st/2nd synchro unit and 2nd gear from mainshaft

6.18 Fitting 2nd gear and synchro ring to mainshaft

6.19 Fitting 1st/2nd synchro baulk ring

6.20 Synchro ring alignment (arrowed)

6.21 Fitting synchro hub circlip

6.22 Fitting 1st gear and spacer/oil slinger

6.23 Driving mainshaft bearing into position

6.24 Installing mainshaft bearing circlip

6.26 Driving speedo drive gear into mainshaft

6.28 Tapping mainshaft into extension housing

6.29 Fitting mainshaft bearing outer circlip to extension housing

18 Reassembly of the mainshaft commences by replacing 2nd gear (27) and a new synchroniser ring (28) on the longer portion of the mainshaft (photo). Ensure that the gearwheel teeth lie adjacent to the shoulder on the mainshaft.

19 Then slide the 1st and 2nd gear synchroniser sleeve and hub (31, 32) into place, with the straight cut gear teeth adjacent to 2nd gear. Follow on with the synchroniser ring (38). (photo)

20 Make certain that the cut-outs in the synchroniser rings (28, 38) (arrowed in photo) fit over the blocker bars in the synchroniser hub and that any marks on the mainshaft and hub are in line.

21 Then replace the circlip which holds the synchroniser hub in place on the mainshaft (photo). Circlips are available in a variety of thicknesses (see Specifications). It is essential that the thickest circlip that will fit the groove is used so that all endfloat is eliminated.

22 Refit 1st gear (36), cone side facing towards the 1st and 2nd gear synchroniser hub and follow with the spacer washer (oil slinger) (37) so that the larger diameter on the spacer lies adjacent to the gearwheel. (photo)

23 To drive on the mainshaft bearing (41) use a length of suitable diameter tubing so that the end of the tube just fits over the mainshaft and bears against the *inner* race of the bearing (photo). Several heavy blows to the top end of the tube will drive the bearing fully home.

24 Select the thickest circlip (42) which will fit in the groove adjacent to the bearing and with the aid of a pair of circlip pliers, fit the circlip in place. (photo)

25 Then place the large circlip (40) loosely behind the bearing. This large circlip holds the bearing in place in the extension housing. This is a selective circlip and once again it is essential that the largest circlip that will fit the groove in the housing is used. Circlips are available in a variety of thicknesses (see Specifications) and can be fitted to, or removed from, the mainshaft while it is in position in the extension housing.

26 Next fit the speedometer drive to the mainshaft using the same method described in paragraph 23. (photo)

27 Ensure that a new oil seal has been fitted to the rear of the extension (See Section 4).

28 Heat the front end of the extension in boiling water and then fit the mainshaft, tapping the front end of the shaft with a soft headed hammer (photo) until the bearing is fully home in its housing in the extension.

29 With a pair of thin nosed pliers, fit the large circlip into the groove in the extension (photo) so securing the mainshaft ball bearing.

30 Fit a new rubber seal in the groove round the gearchange shaft tube in the front of the extension. (photo)

31 Then fit a new gasket in place on the extension front face. (photo)

32 Slide 3rd gear (26) into place on the mainshaft so the helically cut teeth face 2nd gear and then fit a new synchroniser ring. (photo)

33 Then fit the 3rd and 4th gear synchroniser assembly (6, 7) in place, ensuring that the cut-outs on the outside periphery of the synchroniser ring line up with the blocker bars in the synchroniser hub and sleeve. (photo)

34 Fit the thickest circlip (3) that will fit the groove in front of the synchroniser assembly. (photo)

35 Then slide the caged roller bearing (24) into place on the nose of the mainshaft (photo). The mainshaft is now fully assembled.

7 Gearbox - reassembly

1 Fit the reverse gear relay lever, the reverse idler gear and the shaft to the gearbox casing so that the bottom end of the lever seats in the groove on the forward end of the gearwheel.

2 Slide a thrust washer into either end of the laygear so that

6.30 Fitting gearchange shaft tube oil seal

6.31 Locating extension housing gasket

6.32 Fitting 3rd gear and synchromesh ring

6.33 Fitting 3rd/4th synchro assembly

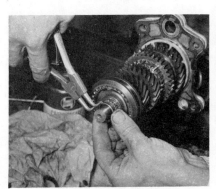
6.34 Fitting synchro assembly circlip

6.35 Fitting needle roller bearing to mainshaft

they abut the internal machined shoulders. Smear thick grease in the laygear orifice and fit the needle rollers one at a time until all are in place at each end. Then fit a thrust washer (photo) to each end of the laygear orifice.

3 Smear the front end of the laygear with grease and fit the thrust washer.

4 Then fit a thrust washer to the other end of the laygear in similar fashion.

5 Insert the laygear (large gearwheel first) into the gearbox through the large hole in the rear of the gearbox casing. (photo)

6 Carefully position the laygear so it lies in the bottom of the gearbox with the tabs on the thrust washers engaged in the cut-aways.

7 Then fit the input shaft with the circlip already in place round the outside periphery of the bearing. Tap the bearing in until it is fully home and the circlip is up tight against the front face of the casing.

8 Then fit the input shaft bearing retainer and ensure that the oil hole in the nose of the retainer faces downward to the bottom of the bellhousing. (photo)

9 Securely tighten up the four nuts and bolts which hold the input shaft bearing retainer in place. (photo)

10 Ensure that the remaining synchroniser ring is in place over the nose of the input shaft gearwheel and the cut-outs align with the blocker bars and then carefully slide the mainshaft into the rear of the gearbox. (photo)

11 Turn the extension so that the cut-out in the extension flange lines up with the hole for the layshaft. Bring the laygear into mesh with the mainshaft by carefully turning the gearbox upside down so that the laygear is at the top. Line up the laygear and thrust washer at the rear of the gearbox using a rod or screwdriver (photo). Take the greatest care not to displace any of the rollers. Repeat at the front of the gearbox.

12 Then fit the layshaft (flat end first) into the gearbox casing from the rear. (photo)

13 Ensure that the lug on the rear of the layshaft is horizontal

and then with the aid of a soft drift or hammer tap the layshaft fully home (photo). Ensure that the lug protrudes so that it can locate in the recess in the extension housing.

14 Pull back the extension housing half an inch, rotate it until the bolt holes are in the correct position and then push the extension housing fully home. Replace and tighten down to a torque of between 33 to 37 lbf ft (4.5 to 5.0 kgf m) the bolts and spring washers which hold the extension housing to the end of the gearbox. (photo)

15 Turn the gearbox the right way up and fit the interlock plate in position between the two lugs on the inside of the gearbox. (photo)

16 Tap the pivot pin which holds the interlock plate into place. (photo)

17 Fit the 1st and 2nd gear selector fork to the gearbox so that the prongs of the fork locate in the groove in the 1st and 2nd gear synchroniser sleeve. (photo)

18 Then fit the 3rd and 4th gear selector fork so that the prongs of the fork locate in the groove of the 3rd and 4th gear synchroniser sleeve. (photo)

19 The arm of the 3rd and 4th gear selector fork (arrowed) should lie on top of the 1st and 2nd gear arm. (photo)

20 Fit the gear selector arm in the hole in the interlock plate so that the selector arm pin (arrowed) rests in the 'V' shaped cutaway of the interlock plate. (photo)

21 Slide the gearchange shaft arm selector rod into the gearbox from the rear of the extension. (photo)

22 First slide the shaft through the hole in the 1st and 2nd gear selector fork. (photo)

23 Drop the interlock plate and selector arm into place and then slide the shaft through the holes in the gear selector arm and the 3rd and 4th gear selector fork. Ensure that the cut-outs on the forward end of the shaft face toward the left-hand side of the gearbox.

24 When the hole in the gearchange shaft lines up with the small

7.2 Inserting thrust washer to laygear

7.5 Inserting laygear into gearbox

7.8 Correct location of input shaft bearing retainer oil hole

7.9 Tightening input shaft bearing retainer bolts

7.10 Inserting mainshaft assembly into gearbox

7.11 Aligning laygear and thrust washer

7.12 Installing layshaft

7.13 Tapping layshaft fully home

7.14 Tightening extension housing to gearbox bolts

7.15 Fitting interlock plate

7.16 Driving interlock pivot pin

7.17 Fitting 1st/2nd selector fork

7.18 Fitting 3rd/4th selector fork

7.19 Correct location of 3rd/4th selector fork arm

7.20 Correct location of gear selector arm pin

7.21 Inserting gearchange shaft arm selector rod

7.22 Selector rod passing through 1st/2nd selector fork

7.24 Driving in gearchange arm to shaft pin

hole in the gear selector arm, drive in the spring pin which holds the arm to the shaft. (photo)

25 Replace the detent plunger and spring in the drilling in the side of the gearbox. (photo)

26 Then replace the plug (photo) and screw it in tightly.

27 Refit the gearlever to the extension housing. The slot in the base of the lever goes over the gearchange shaft. (photo)

28 Screw down the domed nut (photo) and lock in place by turning down some of the tabs on the tab washer on the base of the dome.

29 Compress the conical spring and slide the circlip down the gearlever (photo) until it rests in its groove and locates the spring

securely. Check that all the gears are working correctly by turning the input shaft with the gearlever, engaging each gear in turn.

30 Fit a new gasket to the gearbox cover, replace the cover and tighten down the eight bolts and spring washers which hold it in place. (photo)

31 Replace the speedometer drive pinion and the retainer cup (photo). Smear the edges of the cup with jointing compound to ensure that no oil leaks develop.

32 Smear the edges of the extension plug with jointing compound and fit the blanking plate to the rear of the extension. (photo) Reassembly of the gearbox is now complete.

7.25 Fitting detent plunger and spring

7.26 Screwing in detent plunger plug

7.27 Installing gearchange lever in extension housing

7.28 Tightening the gearlever domed nut

7.29 Fitting the gearlever spring circlip

7.30 Tightening top cover bolts

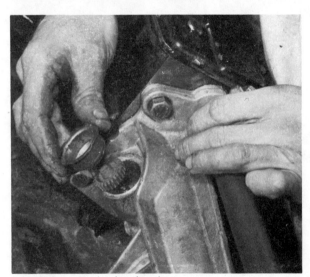

7.31 Fitting extension housing plug

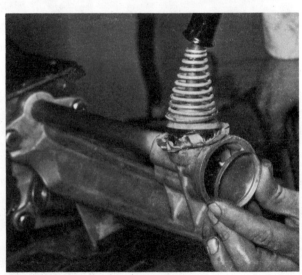

7.32 Fitting extension housing rear blanking plate

8 Fault diagnosis - manual gearbox

Symptom	Reason/s	Remedy
Weak or ineffective synchromesh General wear	Baulk ring synchromesh dogs worn, or damaged	Dismantle and overhaul gearbox. Fit new baulk ring synchromesh.
Jumps out of gear General wear or damage	Broken gearchange fork rod spring Gearbox coupling dogs badly worn Selector fork rod groove badly worn Selector fork rod securing screw and locknut loose	Dismantle and renew spring. Dismantle gearbox. Fit new coupling dogs. Fit new selector fork rod. Remove side cover, tighten securing screw and locknut.
Excessive noise Lack of maintenance	Incorrect grade of oil in gearbox or oil level too low Bush or needle roller bearings worn or damaged Gearteeth excessively worn or damaged Laygear thrust washers worn allowing excessive end play	Drain, refill, or top up gearbox with correct grade of oil. Dismantle and overhaul gearbox. Renew bearings. Dismantle, overhaul gearbox. Renew gearwheels. Dismantle and overhaul gearbox. Renew thrust washers.
Excessive difficulty in engaging gear Clutch not fully disengaging	Clutch pedal adjustment incorrect	Adjust clutch pedal correctly.

Automatic Transmission

9 General description

The three speed, Ford C3, automatic transmission, is available as a production option on 1300cc high compression engines and all 1600cc engines.

Forward movement is obtainable when the selector lever is placed in 'D', '2' or '1'; when 'D' is selected automatic up or down gearchanges occur as a function of the speed of the vehicle. 'Kick-down' is also available in this position and occurs when the accelerator pedal is held at maximum downward travel. With the selector lever in '1', the transmission is held locked in first gear, similarly when '2' is selected the transmission is locked in second gear. In either position no automatic changes will occur.

In addition to the forward movement positions, three further positions are available for selection (ie; 'P', 'R' or 'N'). In the 'P' position the rear wheels of the vehicle are locked by a pawl which engages the parking gear wheel, the 'P' position must only be selected when the vehicle is stationary. Similarly, the 'R' or reverse gear, position should only be selected when the forward movement has ceased. The 'N' position puts the transmission into neutral at which point no further gear changing operation take place.

Should it become necessary to tow a vehicle with automatic transmission the selector lever should be set at 'N' and the handbrake released. The towing speed should not exceed 25 mph and the maximum distance the vehicle should be towed is 12 miles. For distances in excess of 12 miles the driveshaft should be removed before towing commences.

Normally, carburettors with automatic chokes are fitted with automatic transmission.

The unit comprises a three element hydrokinetic torque converter coupling, capable of torque multiplication at an infinitely variable ratio between 2 : 1 and 1 : 1; a torque/speed responsive and hydraulically operated epicyclic gearbox comprising a planetary gearset providing three forward ratios and one reverse ratio. Fluid cooling it achieved via a separate circuit through the bottom of the radiator.

Due to the complexity of the automatic transmission unit, if performance is not up to standard, or overhaul is necessary, it is imperative that this be left to a main agent who will have the special equipment and knowledge for fault diagnosis and rectification.

The contents of the following Sections are therefore confined to supplying general information and any service information and instruction that can be used by the owner.

10 Maintenance

1 It is important that transmission fluid manufactured only to the correct specification, (ie; Ford SQM-2C-9007-AA), is used. The capacity of the complete unit is 11.4 pints (6.5 litres). Drain and refill capacity will be less as the torque converter cannot be completely drained but this operation should not be necessary except for repairs to the internal mechanism.

2 Ensure that the exterior of the converter housing and gearbox is always kept free from dust or mud, otherwise overheating will occur.

3 At the recommended intervals check the fluid lever as described in the Routine Maintenance Section of this manual.

4 If the unit has been drained, it is recommended that only new fluid is used. Fill up to the correct 'MAX' level gradually refilling the unit, the exact amount will depend on how much was left in the converter after draining.

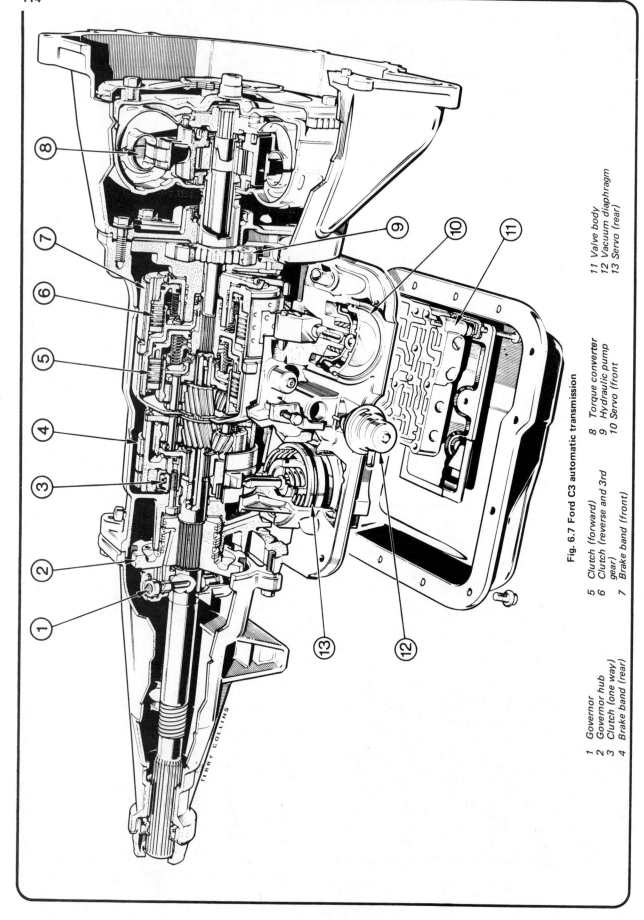

Fig. 6.7 Ford C3 automatic transmission

1 Governor
2 Governor hub
3 Clutch (one way)
4 Brake band (rear)
5 Clutch (forward)
6 Clutch (reverse and 3rd gear)
7 Brake band (front)
8 Torque converter
9 Hydraulic pump
10 Servo (front)
11 Valve body
12 Vacuum diaphragm
13 Servo (rear)

TERRY COLLINS

11 Removal and installation

1 Disconnect the lead from the battery negative terminal.
2 Either jack-up the car and support securely on stands, or position it over a pit or on ramps.
3 Where a metal engine splash shield is fitted this must be removed by unscrewing the six retaining screws and lifting the shield off the underbody.
4 Mark the edges of the propeller shaft rear flange and the rear axle pinion flange and remove the four connecting bolts. Push the propeller shaft slightly forward to separate the two flanges and then withdraw the shaft. If the propeller shaft is a centre bearing type, the removal procedure is the same except that the two centre bearing bolts must first be removed.
5 Have a container ready to catch any fluid, then unscrew the two unions securing the oil cooler pipes to the transmission casing, and pull the pipes out of their location.
6 Disconnect the starter motor cable and remove the starter motor.
7 Disengage the two clips ('A' Fig. 6.22) securing each end of the selector rod and detach the rod.
8 Disconnect the speed selector cable from the operating lever on the side of the transmission casing, also from the support bracket.
9 Disconnect the leads from the inhibitor switch which is secured into the side of the transmission unit.
10 Disconnect the speedometer cable from the transmission extension housing by removing the bolt and clip.
11 Slacken the hose clip securing the vacuum pipe to the vacuum diaphragm, then carefully pull the pipe off the diaphragm inlet stub.

Fig. 6.8 Engine splash shield securing screws (Sec 11)

Fig. 6.9 Driveshaft centre bearing and rear axle flange fixings (Sec 11)

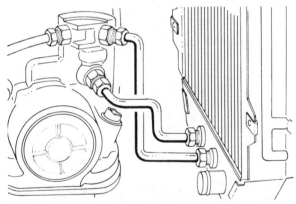

Fig. 6.10 Oil cooler pipe location on transmission and radiator (Sec 11)

Fig. 6.11 Starter motor assembly (Sec 11)

Fig. 6.12 Speedometer cable location in transmission: A) Cable, Cable clip (arrowed) (Sec 11)

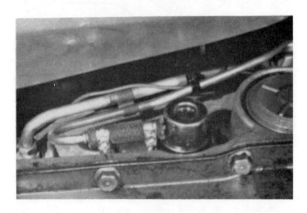

Fig. 6.13 Hose connection to vacuum diaphragm body (Sec 11)

12 Unscrew each of the drive-plate to converter bolts. These are accessible one at a time through the starter motor aperture - the engine will have to be rotated to bring each bolt into view.

13 Disconnect the exhaust downpipe from the manifold.

14 Support the weight of the transmission unit with a trolley jack and remove the rear supporting crossmember. To prevent the engine dropping too low once the rear crossmember has been removed, insert a piece of wood between the engine sump and front crossmember.

15 Unscrew and remove the upper engine to converter housing bolts, noting that one bolt secures the combined dipstick/filler tube.

16 Pull the oil filler pipe out of its transmission case stub, and close the stub opening to avoid oil loss, or dirt ingress.

17 Lower the trolley jack slightly and then support the rear of the engine sump with a second jack.

18 Remove the remaining engine to converter housing bolts.

19 Lower both jacks together until the transmission unit can be **removed toward the rear and drawn out from underneath the vehicle.**

20 Installation is a reversal of removal but the following points must be observed.

21 The converter oil drain plug must be in line with the opening in the drive plate.

22 When the torque converter hub is fully engaged in the pump **gear,** the distance 'A' (as shown in Fig. 6.17) between the converter flange and the stub face must be 25 mm (1.0 in) minimum.

23 When the torque converter is mated with the engine ensure that the converter can rotate freely before finally tightening the converter housing bolts.

24 Adjust the selector cable and inhibitor switch as described later in this Chapter.

25 Check the oil level before starting the engine.

---

12 Downshift cable - adjustment

1 Before attempting any adjustment of the downshift cable ensure that:
   a) *The engine and transmission are at normal operating temperature.*
   b) *The throttle linkage is correctly adjusted and no wear is evident.*
   c) *The engine idling speed is correctly set (see Specifications).*
   d) *The throttle is open fully when the pedal is fully depressed.*
2 Remove the air cleaner.
3 Adjust the cable by:
   a) *Depressing the accelerator pedal until the throttle plates are fully open, hold the pedal in this position.*

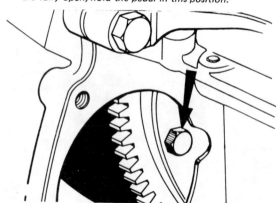

Fig. 6.14 Torque converter plate bolts (arrowed) accessible through starter motor aperture (Sec 11)

   b) *Using a screwdriver press the downshift cable lever away from the operating shaft lever then turn the downshift cable adjuster, as nececessary to obtain a clearance of 0.5 to 1.3 mm (0.02 to 0.05 in), between the downshift cable connecting lever and the operating shaft lever. Tighten the adjuster locknut.*
4 Remove the pedal hold and replace the air cleaner.

---

13 Downshift cable - removal and refitting

1 Remove the split pin securing the end of the downshift cable to the carburettor operating shaft lever and detach the end of the cable from the lever.
2 Slacken the adjuster locknut and screw the cable adjuster out of the cable bracket, pull the outer cable clear of the bracket and disengage the inner cable via the slot in the bracket.
3 From underneath the vehicle, slacken the cable locknut on the transmission casing bracket and slide the cable out of the bracket via the slot. Unhook the cable from the down shift lever and remove it from the vehicle.
4 Install the new cable by reversing the removal procedure, and adjust as described in the previous Section.

---

14 Speed selector linkage - adjustment

1 Remove the clips from the ends of the selector rod ('A' Fig. 6.22) and detach the rod.
2 From inside the vehicle engage the selector lever in the 'D' position.
3 From underneath the vehicle engage the selector lever on the side of the transmission in the 'D' position (ie; two notches back from the front position).
4 Refit the selector rod, without moving the transmission selector lever from the 'D' position. If necessary slacken the selector rod locknut and lengthen or shorten the rod at its adjustable end so that the holes in the selector rod and transmission lever perfectly align. Tighten the locknut, making sure that the adjustable end of the rod remains vertical, then refit the pin and clip.
5 Have an assistant move the selector lever to each position. A distinct click should be heard from the selector lever as each position is selected and the lever should not be subjected to any tension from the linkage in any one position.

---

15 Starter inhibitor switch - removal and refitting

1 From underneath the vehicle, pull the loom multiplug off the inhibitor switch.
2 Unscrew the switch and lift it off the transmission case

Fig. 6.15 Rear crossmember assembly: remove 2 bolts from each side a single bolt from centre (Sec 11)

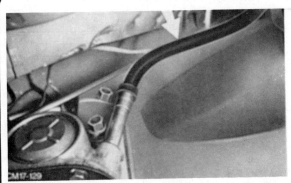

Fig. 6.16 Oil filler tube (arrowed) assembly into gearbox (Sec 11)

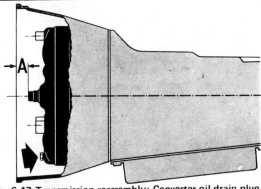

Fig. 6.17 Transmission reassembly: Converter oil drain plug (arrowed) must be in line with hole in drive plate. Dimension 'A' between centering stub face and torque converter flange must be 25mm (1 in) minimum (Sec 11)

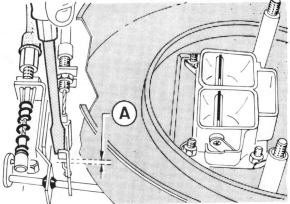

Fig. 6.18 Adjusting downshift cable: A) 0.5 to 1.3 mm (0.02 to 0.05 in) (Sec 12)

Fig. 6.19 Downshift cable attachment at carburettor:
A) Adjuster, B) Split pin, C) Carburettor operating lever (Sec 13)

Fig. 6.20 Down shift cable attachment on transmission: cable passes through bracket (arrowed) before hooking on to transmission lever 'A' (Sec 13)

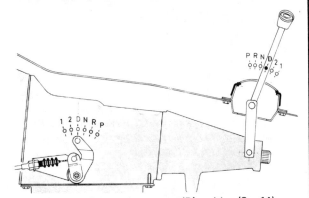

Fig. 6.21 Selector levers set at 'D' position (Sec 14)

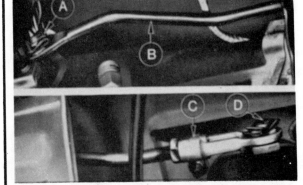

Fig. 6.22 Selector rod assembly: A) Clip, B) Rod, C) Adjuster, D) Clip (Sec 14)

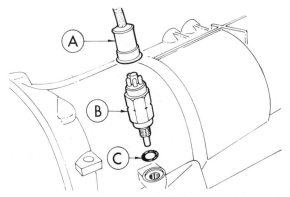

Fig. 6.23 Inhibitor switch assembly: A) Loom connection, B) Switch, C) Seal (Sec 15)

together with its 'O' ring seal.

3   Reassembly is a reversal of the removal procedure.

16 Selector inhibitor cable - adjustment

1   The selector inhibitor cable runs from the 'T' of the selector lever, through the lever shaft and is connected to the selector lever pawl at the base of the shaft.

2   Commence the adjustment procedure by lifting the selector lever quadrant off its housing then remove the rubber plug from the side of the housing.

3   Turn the locknut ('X' Fig. 6.24) to give a clearance of 0.004 to 0.008 in (0.10 to 0.20 mm) between the inhibitor stub and the notch in the selector housing ('Y' Fig. 6.24).

4   Replace the plug and quandrant.

17 Selector lever assembly - removal and refitting

1   Carefully lift the quandrant off the selector lever housing and remove the quadrant light from the holder on the selector lever.

2   Chock the front wheels, jack-up the rear of the vehicle and support on firmly based stands.

3   From underneath the vehicle, disengage the spring clip, withdraw the pin and separate the selector rod from the selector lever.

4   Undo and remove the four bolts and spring washers securing the selector housing and lift away the complete selector assembly, together with its sealing gasket.

5   Refitting the selector lever assembly is the reverse of its removal sequence. If necessary adjust, as described in Section 14.

18 Selector lever assembly - overhaul

1   Refer to Section 17, and remove the lever assembly.

2   Carefully remove the plug from the selector lever housing. Unscrew the nut and press the lower lever arm out of the housing. Recover the bushes.

3   Unscrew and remove the operating cable lower nut and withdraw the selector pawl, spring and guide bush from the selector lever.

4   Using an Allen key, remove the grub screw from the top of the selector lever handle and detach the handle from the shaft.

5   The release button may now be withdrawn from the handle.

6   Using a suitably sized parallel pin punch, drive the roll pin out of the inhibitor release unit and remove the release unit, complete with cable from the lever arm.

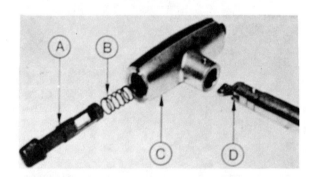

Fig. 6.25 Selector lever assembly: A) Bush, B) Spring, C) Pawl, D) Lock adjuster nut, E) Lever (Sec 18)

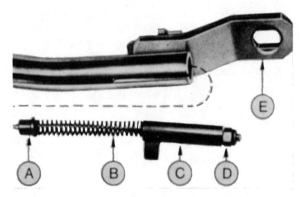

Fig. 6.26 Selector lever handle: A) Inhibitor push button, B) Spring, C) 'T' handle, D) Lever (Sec 18)

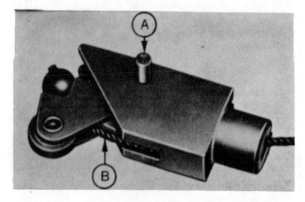

Fig. 6.27 Inhibitor mechanism at handle: A) Pin, B) Cable (Sec 18)

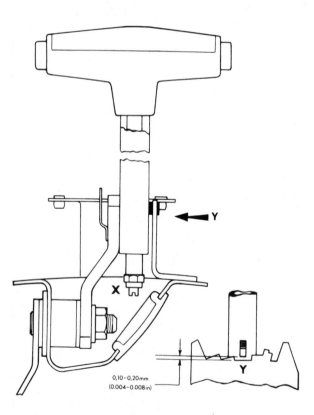

0,10 - 0,20 mm
(0.004 - 0.008 in)

Fig. 6.24 Selector cable adjustment: turn nut (X) to obtain clearance at 'Y' (Sec 16)

7   Reassemble the unit in the reverse order to its removal and adjust the cable, as described in Section 16.

19 Transmission fluid level - checking

1   The fluid level is checked, and if necessary corrected, via the combined dipstick oil filler tube. The level is checked with the engine idling and the selector mechanism in 'P'. It is important that the check is carried out with the fluid at normal operating temperature (ie; after a fairly long test run).
2   Drive the vehicle on to level ground and apply the handbrake, with the engine idling move the selector through all positions at least three times.
3   Move the selector to 'P' and allow the engine to idle for a further three minutes.
4   With the engine still idling, remove the dipstick, wipe with a non-fluffy rag then re-insert and withdraw. The level should be between 'MIN' and 'MAX' on the dipstick.

20 Fault diagnosis (automatic transmission) - stall test procedure

The function of a stall test is to determine whether the torque converter and gearbox are operating satisfactorily.
1   Check the condition of the engine. An engine which is not developing full power will affect the stall test readings.

2   Allow the engine and transmission to reach correct working temperatures.
3   Connect a tachometer to the vehicle.
4   Chock the wheels and apply the handbrake and footbrake.
5   Start the engine and move the selector lever several times through all the positions with the exception of 'P' and 'N'. Fully depress the throttle pedal to the 'kick-down' position and read the engine speed on the tachometer when the needle has stabilised; the reading should be a maximum of 2,600 rpm. If the reading is below 1000 rpm, suspect the torque convertor for stator slip; if it is above 2,600 rpm, the brake bands may be binding or the clutch assemblies slipping. **Note:** do not carry out a stall test for a longer period than 5 seconds and when moving the selector lever, pause for an interval of 20 seconds between positions. If this action is not taken, the transmission could overheat.
6   Inability to start on steep gradients, combined with poor acceleration from rest and low stall speed (1000 rpm) indicate that the converter stator uni-directional clutch is slipping. This condition permits the stator to rotate in an opposite direction to the impeller and turbine, and torque multiplication cannot occur.
7   Poor acceleration in 3rd gear above 30 mph and reduced maximum speed indicates that the stator uni-direction clutch has seized. The stator will not rotate with the turbine and impeller and the 'fluid flywheel' phase cannot occur. This condition will also be indicated by excessive overheating of the transmission although the stall speed will be correct.

Chapter 7 Propeller shaft

For modifications, and information applicable to later models, see Supplement at end of manual

Contents

Specifications

Type

1100cc	Single section open shaft with two universal joints
1300cc	Two section open shaft with three universal joints and centre support bearing
1600cc	Two section open shaft with two universal and one constant velocity joints with centre support bearing

Single section shaft length ... ... 1204.2 mm (47.41 in)

Two section shaft length

Manual transmission	1193.8 mm (47.0 in)
Auto transmission	1130.8 mm (44.52 in)

Number of splines

Manual transmission	16
Auto transmission	25

Torque wrench settings

	lb f ft	kg f m
Universal joint flange to rear axle pinion flange bolts ...	44 - 48	6.0 to 6.5
Centre bearing to underbody bolts	13 to 17	1.8 to 2.3

1 General description

On 1100 cc models drive is transmitted from the gearbox to the rear axle by a single finely balanced tubular propeller shaft. Fitted at each end of the shaft is a universal joint which allows vertical movement of the rear axle. Each universal joint comprises a four-legged centre spider, four needle roller bearings and two yokes.

On 1300 cc models, the drive is transmitted by a two section tubular shaft supported at its centre by a rubber insulated bearing which is bolted to the underbody. The universal joints on both types of propeller shaft are not repairable and in the event of wear occurring, the complete shaft assembly must be renewed.

On 1600 cc variants an additional, constant velocity, joint is incorported in the two piece shaft immediately behind the centre bearing housing.

All universal joints are of lubricant-sealed type and require no maintenance.

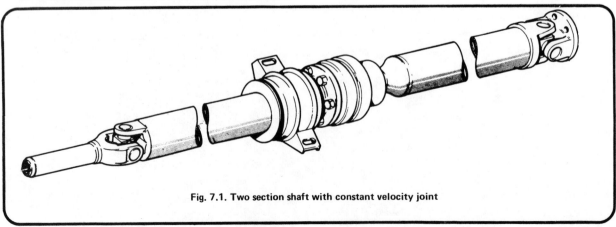

Fig. 7.1. Two section shaft with constant velocity joint

On all models the movement of the rear axle is absorbed by a sliding spline in the front of the propeller shaft which slides over a mating spline on the rear of the gearbox mainshaft. A supply of oil through very small oil holes from the gearbox lubricates the splines.

2 Single section propeller shaft - removal and installation

1 Jack-up the rear of the car, or position the rear of the car over a pit or on a ramp.
2 If the rear of the car is jacked up, supplement the jack with support blocks so that danger is minimised, should the jack collapse.
3 If the rear wheels are off the ground, place the car in gear or put the handbrake on to ensure that the propeller shaft does not turn when an attempt is made to loosen the four nuts securing the propeller shaft to the rear axle.
4 Unscrew and remove the four self-locking nuts, bolts and securing washers which hold the flange on the rear axle.
5 The propeller shaft is carefully balanced to fine limits and it is important that it is replaced in exactly the same position it was in prior to its removal. Scratch a mark on the propeller shaft and rear axle flange edges to ensure accurate mating when the time comes for reassembly.
6 Slightly push the shaft forward to separate the two flanges and then lower the end of the shaft and pull it rearward to disengage the gearbox mainshaft splines.
7 Place a large can or tray under the rear of the gearbox extension to catch any oil which is likely to leak through the spline lubricating holes, when the propeller shaft is removed.
8 Replacement of the propeller shaft is a reversal of the above procedure. Ensure that the mating marks scratched on the propeller shaft and rear axle flanges line up.
9 Finally, tighten the flange bolts to a torque of between 44 and 48 lbf ft (6.0 and 6.5 kgf m), and top up the gearbox with oil as necessary.

3 Single section propeller shaft joints - examination

1 Wear in the needle roller bearings is characterised by vibration in the transmission, 'clonks' on taking up the drive, and in extreme cases of lack of lubrication, metallic squeaking, and ultimately grating and shrieking sounds as the bearings break up.
2 It is easy to check if the needle roller bearings are worn with the propeller shaft in position, by trying to turn the shaft with one hand, the other hand holding the rear axle flange when the rear universal is being checked, and the front half coupling when the front universal is being checked. Any movement between the propeller shaft and the front and the rear half couplings is indicative of considerable wear.
3 Examine the propeller shaft splines for wear. If worn it will be necessary to purchase an exchange propeller shaft.

4 Two section propeller shaft - removal and installation

1 The method of removal of this type of shaft is identical to that described in Section 2 except that the two bolts which secure the centre bearing to the bodyframe must also be unscrewed and removed.
2 Installation is a reversal of removal.
However the following points should be borne in mind. The 'U' shaped packing washers underneath the centre bearing bolt location points control the angular relationship of the front and rear section of the shaft. It is important that these washers are replaced exactly as they were removed.
3 On vehicles fitted with constant velocity shafts the rear of the vehicle must be raised so that the rear axle hangs down freely.
4 Pull the wings of the centre bearing housing towards the front of the vehicle (so that the front section of the shaft and centre bearing move as one unit) until the constant velocity joint

is felt to bear against the rear of the centre bearing.
5 With the centre bearing held in this position fully tighten the bearing bolts to the specified torque.

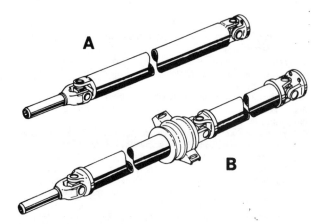

Fig. 7.2 Single and two section propeller shafts

A *Single section shaft (1100cc models)*
B *Two section shaft (1300cc models)*

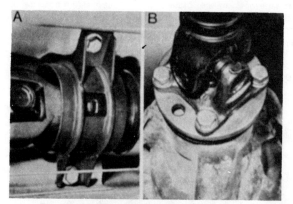

Fig. 7.3 Drive shaft retaining bolts (Sec 2)

A *Centre bearing to underbody*
B *Driveshaft to drive pinion flange*

Fig. 7.4 Tightening centre bearing bolts (Sec 4)

5 Two section propeller shaft - centre bearing removal and refitting

1   Mark the relative positions of the front and rear sections of the propeller shaft so that they will be in their original alignment when refitted.

2   Refer to Figs. 7.5 and 7.6 and knock back the tab washer and slacken the bolt (4) and then remove the 'U' ring (Fig. 7.5) from underneath it.

3   With the 'U' ring removed the rear yoke can now be drawn off the splines of the front section. The centre bolt and its washer remain attached to the splined front section.

4   Slide the bearing housing with its rubber insulator from the shaft. Bend back the six metal tabs on the housing and remove the rubber insulator.

5   The bearing and its protective caps should now be withdrawn from the splined section of the propeller shaft by careful levering with two large screwdrivers or tyre levers. If a suitable puller tool is available this should always be used in preference to any other method as it is less likely to cause damage to the bearing.

6   Fill the area between the bearing and its protective caps with grease to Ford specification S—M1C—4515A.

7   To replace the bearing, select a piece of piping or tubing for use as a tubular drift. Place the splined part of the drive shaft upright in a vice, position the bearing on the shaft and using a soft hammer on the end of the piece of tubing, drive the bearing firmly and squarely onto the shaft.

8   Replace the rubber insulator in the bearing housing, ensuring that the boss on the insulator is at the top of the housing and will be adjacent to the underframe when the propeller shafts are replaced.

9   When the insulator is correctly positioned bend back the six metal tabs and slide the housing and insulator assembly over the bearing.

10 Slide the splined end of the shaft into the rear yoke, ensuring

that the previously scribed mating marks are correctly aligned.

11 Replace the 'U' ring under the centre bolt with its smooth surface facing the front section of the propeller shaft. Tighten down the centre bolt to a torque of 28 lb f ft (3.9 kg f m) and bend up its tab washer to secure it.

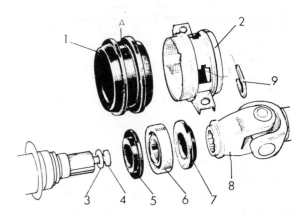

Fig. 7.5 Centre bearing - exploded view (Sec 5)

A	Insulator boss	5 & 7	Caps
1	Insulator	6	Bearing
2	Housing	8	Yoke
3	Lockplate	9	'U' ring
4	Bolt		

Fig. 7.7 Bending back metal tabs on insulator housing (Sec 5)

Fig. 7.6 'U' ring located under short section retaining bolt (Sec 5)

Fig. 7.9 When replacing insulator housing cut-out (arrowed) must face front of vehicle (Sec 5)

Fig. 7.8 Pulling centre bearing off shaft (Sec 5)

Chapter 8 Rear axle

For modifications, and information applicable to later models, see Supplement at end of manual

Contents

Specifications

Timken Rear Axle

	1100 cc	1300 cc LC	1300 cc HC	1300 cc 2v	1600 cc 2v
Rear axle ratio	4.125	3.89	3.89/4.44	4.125	3.54
No. of teeth on:					
Crownwheel	33	35	35/40	33	39
Drive pinion	8	9	9/9	8	11
Speedometer worm gear	6	7	7/6	6	7
Speedometer pinion	23	25	25	23	23

Van rear axle (Timken type)

			Standard		Heavy Duty	
	1100 cc	1300 cc HC	1100 cc	1300 cc	1300 cc Auto
Rear axle ratio	4.125	4.125	4.44	4.125	4.125
No. of teeth on:					
Crownwheel	33	33	40	33	33
Drive pinion	8	8	9	8	8
Speedometer worm gear	6	6	6	6	6
Speedometer pinion	23	23	25	23	23

Salisbury Rear Axle

	1100 cc	1100 cc 2v	1300 cc HC & LC	1300 cc 2v	1100 2v
Rear axle ratio	4.11	4.44	3.89	4.11	—
No. of teeth on:					
Crownwheel	37	40	35	37	—
Drive pinion	9	9	9	9	—
Speedometer worm gear	6	6	7	6	—
Speedometer pinion	23	25	25	23	—

	Timken	Salisbury
Backlash (crownwheel/drive pinion)	0.13 to 0.18 mm (0.005 to 0.007 in)	0.10 to 0.2 mm (0.004 to 0.008 in)
Differential preload	function of backlash	0.03 to 0.07 mm (0.001 to 0.003 in)
Collapsible spacer length	48.7 to 48.9 mm	11.5 to 11.7 mm
Oil specification	SAE 90	SAE 90
Oil capacity	1.1 litres (2 Imp pints)	0.9 litres (1.6 Imp pts)

Torque wrench settings

Timken Axle	lb f ft	kg f m
Differential to axle housing carrier bolts	26 to 30	3.58 - 4.14
Half shaft to axle flange plate bolts	15 to 18	2.07 - 2.48
Bearing cap bolts	46 to 51	6.35 - 7.04
Crownwheel to differential case bolts	50 to 55	6.91 - 7.59
Plug	26 to 31	3.59 - 4.28

Salisbury Axle	lb f ft	kg f m
Differential cover bolts	26 to 33	3.58 - 4.55
Half shaft to axle flange plate bolts	20 to 24	2.76 - 3.31
Bearing cap bolts	44 to 50	6.07 - 6.91
Crownwheel to differential case bolts	58 to 63	8.00 - 8.69
Plug	29 to 37	4.00 - 5.11

1 General description

Escort models may be fitted with either a Timken or Salisbury type rear axle. As the axles are physically different it is fairly easy to identify which is which. The Timken axle can be identified by the forward facing bolt-on differential assembly. On this type of axle the differential assembly can be removed with the axle in-situ. The Salisbury axle has the differential assembly mounted directly in the axle casing. To carry out repairs to the Salisbury type axle the axle must first be removed from the vehicle.

Timken axle

The axle casing of banjo design carries the differential assembly. This comprises a crownwheel and pinion mounted in the differential carrier which is bolted to the front of the axle casing.

The pinion is mounted on two taper roller bearings which are preloaded to partially collapse the tubular spacer which is located between them. The crownwheel is bolted to the differential case which is also supported on two taper roller bearings.

The axle-shafts (halfshafts) are splined to the differential side gears and run in ball races in the axle casing at their outer ends. The ball races have integral oil seals.

Salisbury axle

As in the Timken axle the drive pinion in this assembly runs in two taper roller bearings which are preloaded by collapsing a tubular spacer between them. This preload is achieved by tightening the nut on the drive pinion flange.

The crownwheel runs in adjustable taper roller bearings. adjustment is obtained by spreading the differential casing by means of a special tool, and inserting shims of varying thicknesses between the differential casing and the bearings.

The correct depth of mesh between the drive pinion and crownwheel is achieved by the insertion of shims between the drive pinion head and the rear bearing. The halfshafts are splined at their differential ends, to engage similar splines in the differential side gears, and run in sealed ball bearings at their outer ends.

Both types

Overhaul of the differential assembly is beyond the scope of the home mechanic due to the need for special tools and gauges but the design of the Timken rear axle makes the renewal of the differential assembly on an exchange basis a relatively simple matter.

The owner is not recommended to proceed beyond the operations described in this Chapter.

No provision is made for draining the rear axle but the oil level should be checked regularly, as described in the Routine Maintenance Section.

2 Rear axle - removal and installation

1 Remove the rear wheel hub caps and loosen the wheel nuts.
2 Raise and support the rear of the body and the differential casing with clocks or jacks so that the rear wheels are clear of the ground. This is most easily done by placing a jack under the centre of the differential, jacking up the axle and then fitting chocks under the mounting points at the front of the rear springs to support the body.
3 Remove both rear wheels and place the wheel nuts in the hub caps for safe keeping.
4 Mark the propeller shaft and differential drive flanges to ensure replacement in the same relative positions. Undo and remove the nuts and bolts holding the two flanges together.
5 Release the handbrake inside the car, then disconnect the handbrake lever clevis from the lever of the right-hand side backplate. Withdraw the spring clip from the cable sheath at the handbrake rod bracket on the axle tube, compress the spring and pull the cable back so that the inner cable can be slid out of the slit in the bracket.

Fig. 8.1 Rear of vehicle supported on axle stands: locate stands between front spring mounting bracket and axle tube (Sec 2)

Fig. 8.2 Handbrake cable attachments (Sec 2)

A *Spring clip retaining cable to axle case bracket*
B *Clevis pin securing cable to drum actuating lever*

Fig. 8.3 Withdrawing handbrake cable from axle tube bracket (Sec 2)

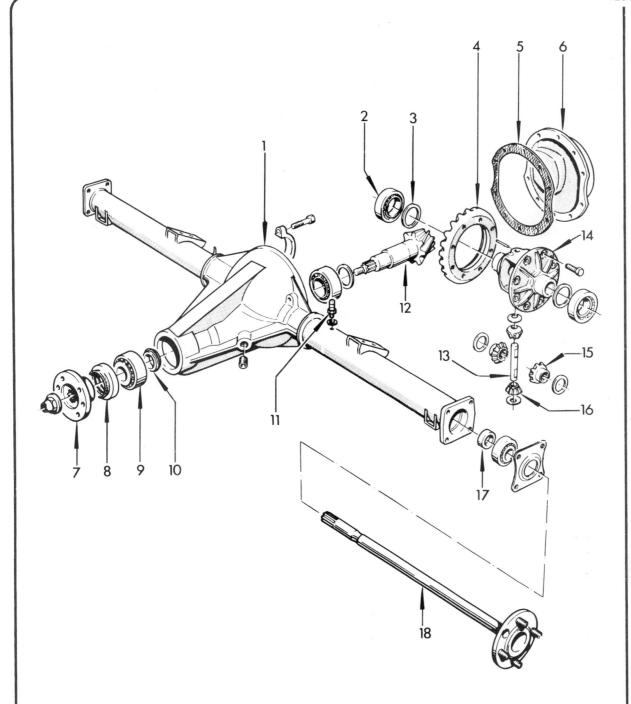

Fig. 8.4 Salisbury type axle

1	Rear axle housing	
2	Differential case taper roller bearing	
3	Shim	
4	Crown wheel	
5	Gasket	
6	Cover	
7	Drive pinion flange	
8	Oil seal	
9	Drive pinion taper roller bearing	
10	Collapsible spacer	
11	Vent valve	
12	Drive pinion	
13	Differential pinion gear shaft	
14	Differential case	
15	Differential side gear	
16	Differential pinion gear	
17	Retaining ring	
18	Half shaft	

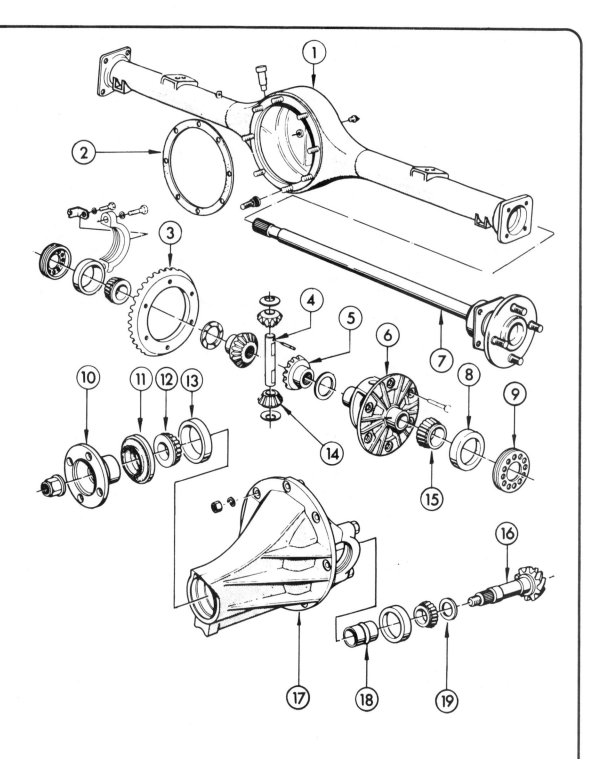

Fig. 8.5 Timken type axle

1	Rear axle housing	8	Taper roller bearing outer race	14	Differential pinion gear
2	Gasket	9	Adjusting nut	15	Inner race with taper rollers
3	Crown wheel	10	Drive pinion flange	16	Drive pinion
4	Differential pinion gear shaft	11	Oil seal	17	Differential carrier
5	Differential side gear	12	Inner race with taper rollers	18	Collapsible spacer, drive pinion
6	Differential case	13	Taper roller bearing outer race	19	Drive pinion shim
7	Half shaft				

6 Unscrew the union on the brake pipe at the junction on the rear axle and have handy either a jar to catch the hydraulic fluid or a plug to block the end of the pipe.

7 Using a suitable lever between the stabiliser bar and the axle casing, lever the bar rearwards to relieve tension on the axle clamp plates. Remove the two bolts retaining each plate to its axle bracket and detach the plates.

8 Undo the self-locking nuts holding the shock absorbers to the spring plates thus freeing their lower ends. It may be necessary to slightly raise the jack under the axle casing to successfully free the shock absorbers.

9 Unscrew the nuts from under the spring retaining plates. These nuts screw onto the ends of the inverted 'U' bolts which retain the axle to the spring. Remove the 'U' bolts, bump stops and spring retaining plates.

10 The axle assembly will now be resting free on the centre jack and can now be removed by lifting it through the space between the road spring and the bodyframe sidemember.

11 Installation is a direct reversal of the removal procedure, but the spring U-bolts should not be finally tightened until the full weight of the car is on the suspension (refer to Chapter 11, Section 21, Paragraph 7). Finally, bleed the brakes as described in Chapter 9.

3 Axle-shafts (halfshafts) - removal and refitting

1 Jack-up the car, remove the roadwheel and then unscrew the brake drum retaining screw and withdraw the brake drum. If the

drum is tight, slacken the shoe adjuster right off and then tap the drum from its location using a block of wood and a wooden or plastic mallet.

2 Unscrew and remove the four self-locking nuts which secure the flange plate to the axle casing end flanges.

3 A slide hammer should now be attached to the hub studs and the axle-shaft withdrawn. A slide hammer can be made up quite easily, but an alternative method of removing the shaft is to bolt

Fig. 8.6 Removing stabiliser bar clamp plates from axle tube brackets (Sec 2)

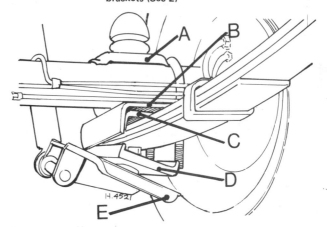

Fig. 8.8 Rear spring mounting assembly (Sec 2)

A Bump rubber
B Insulator retainer

Cand D Upper and lower insulators
E Mounting plate

Fig. 8.7 Underside of rear spring 'U' bolt mounting plate and lower shock absorber mounting (Sec 2)

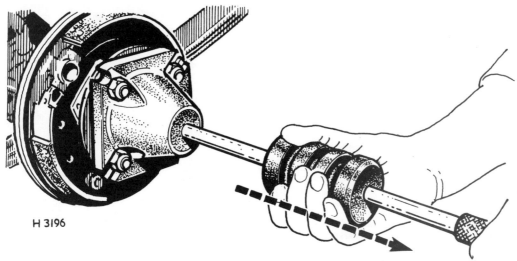

Fig. 8.9 Withdrawing an axle-shaft using a slide hammer (Sec 3)

on the roadwheel and strike it simultaneously on both inside edges of the rim at opposite points. It must be emphasised that it is quite useless to attempt to try and pull the axle-shaft from the axle casing as you will only succeed in pulling the vehicle off the jacks or stands.

4   Refitting is a reversal of removal. Pass the axle-shaft into the axle casing holding the shaft horizontally until the splines at its inner end engage with the splines in the differential gears. Tap the hub/bearing assembly fully home with a hammer and wooden block.

4   Hub bearing/oil seal - renewal

1   The combined bearing and oil seal, also the bearing retaining collar, are an interference fit on the axle-shaft. The removal and refitting of these components must be carried out using a press and correct bearing support tools.

2   It is therefore recommended that the axle-shaft is removed as described in the preceding Section and taken to a Ford dealer for the work to be carried out.

5   Pinion bearing oil seal - renewal

1   The rear axle pinion bearing oil seal may be renewed with the axle in position in the vehicle provided the following operations are adhered to.

2   Disconnect and remove the propeller shaft from the rear axle as described (according to type) in the preceding Chapter.

3   The rear axle pinion must now be held quite still during removal of the pinion flange nut. To do this, either fit two old bolts into the flange holes and position a rod between them to act as a lever or alternatively, drill two holes in a length of flat steel bar and bolt it to the flange.

4   Carefully mark the relative position of the pinion flange nut to the flange so that the nut can be tightened to exactly the same position on refitment. An alternative method of establishing the pinion pre-load is to jack up the rear axle, remove the roadwheels and brake drums and then using a spring balance with a length of cord attached to it and wound round the pinion flange, rotate the flange by pulling on the spring balance. Read off the force required to rotate the pinion, this is the bearing preload.

5   Holding the pinion flange quite still with the tool previously described, unscrew the pinion flange nut.

6   Remove the flange, dust deflector and prise out the defective

oil seal. This can usually be done by carefully drifting in one side of the seal which will have the effect of ejecting the opposite side, it can then be gripped and pulled out of the differential housing.

7   Tap the new seal into position using a suitable tubular drift to bear upon its outside edge. Make sure that the face of the seal is flush with the differential housing.

8   Fit the dust deflector and the pinion flange but grease the lips of the seal before inserting the flange.

9   Examine the pinion flange nut. This is of self-locking type and may be removed and refitted on up to six occasions. If it did not provide much resistance when unscrewing however, always renew it.

10 Hold the pinion flange quite still and screw on the securing nut until either (i) the positioning mark made before removal is in alignment or (ii) by using the spring balance and cord method, the preload matches that existing before dismantling. The running torque at the flange nut should be approximately 22 to 23 lbf in (25 to 27 Kgf cm). **Tighten the flange nut only a fraction of a turn at a time before re-checking, whichever method is used.** If the nut is tightened beyond its original setting, it cannot be backed off to correct the situation as the collapsible spacer will have over-compressed and the pinion bearing will have to be removed to fit a new spacer.

6   Differential carrier - Timken axle - removal and installation

1   Jack-up the rear of the vehicle, remove both roadwheels and withdraw the axle-shafts, as described in Section 3.

2   Disconnect and remove the propeller shaft from the rear axle as described (according to type) in Chapter 7.

3   Unscrew the eight self-locking nuts holding the differential carrier assembly to the axle casing. Pull the assembly slightly forward and allow the oil to drain into a suitable tray or bowl. The carrier, complete with crownwheel, can now be lifted clear with the gasket.

4   Before refitting, carefully clean the mating surfaces of the carrier and axle casing and always fit a new gasket. Installation is then a direct reversal of the removal procedure; the eight nuts retaining the differential carrier assembly to the axle casing should be tightened to a torque of 26 to 30 lbf ft (3.5 to 4.1 Kgf m).

5   Finally, fill the rear axle with the correct quantity and grade of oil, adjust the handbrake (Chapter 9) and lower the car to the ground.

Chapter 9 Braking system

For modifications, and information applicable to later models, see Supplement at end of manual

Contents

Specifications

| Type ... ... | Disc or drum at front, drum rear |

| System ... ... | Hydraulic, dual line, on all four wheels, dual line split front/rear |

| Handbrake ... ... | Mechanical on rear wheels only |

Footbrake

All 1100 cc (except 2V)	Drum (203 mm) front, drum (203 mm) rear
All 6 cwt 1300 cc vans	Drum (203 mm) front, drum (203 mm) rear
Option on all 1100 cc (except 2V) and 6 cwt vans	Disc front, drum (203 mm) rear
All 1300 and 1600 cc and 1100 cc 2V	Disc front, drum (203 mm) rear
All 1300 and 1600 2V	Disc front, drum (228 mm) rear

	1100 cc	1100 cc	1300 cc	1300 cc/ 1600 cc 2V	6 cwt van	9 cwt van
	Drum/Drum	Disc/Drum				

Master cylinder

Type			Tandem			
Bore ... ... 17.78 mm	19.05 mm	19.05 mm	19.05 mm	19.05 mm	19.05 mm
Stroke ... ... 32.0 mm	34.9 mm	34.9 mm	33.4 mm	33.4 mm	34.9 mm

Pedal to master cylinder ratio

| On bulkhead ... ... | 4.61 : 1 |
| On servo ... ... | 3.96 : 1 |

Servo

Manufacturer	Teves or Girling
Dia. of vacuum cylinder	152.4 mm
Amplification factor	2.2 : 1

Front brakes (Drum)

Drum material	Cast iron
Drum diameter	203.2 mm
Brake lining:	
length	194.2 mm
width	38.1 mm
thickness (new)	4.8 mm
thickness (minimum permissible)	To rivet head or 1 mm (0.04 in) bonded linings
material	M79/1GG
fixing	rivetted

Swept brake area	489.0 cm^2 (75.5 in^2) 2 wheels
Wheel cylinder bore	20.64 mm
Adjustment	Manual
Brake hose material	SAE J140 1

Front brakes (Disc)

Caliper type	M16
Disc material	Cast iron, grade D
Disc diameter inner/outer	139.8/247.5 mm
Effective disc diameter	196.6 mm
Disc thickness	12.77 mm
Permissible disc run-out (incl hub)	0.05 mm
Brake pad:	
length (radial)	50.8 mm
width	76.6 mm
thickness (new)	9.65 mm
thickness (minimum)	3 mm
material	DON 227 FG or V1431FF
fixing	Moulded
swept brake area	1175 cm^2 (182 in^2) 2 wheels
No. of pistons per caliper	2
Caliper bore diameter	54 mm
Brake hose material	SAE J1401

Rear brakes (Drum)

	203.2 mm dia. drum	228.6 mm dia. drum
Material	Cast iron	Cast iron
Brake lining:		
length	159.4 mm	178.9 mm
width	38.1 mm	44.5 mm
minimum permissible lining thickness	1 mm/0.040 in. (bonded), to rivet head (rivetted)	
No. of linings per brake	2	2
Fixing	Bonded (leading shoe), rivetted (trailing shoe)	
Material	M79/1GG	DUN 242FE
Adjustment	Self adjusting via brake pedal	

Wheel cylinder bore diameter:	
1100 cc Saloon, Estate, 6 cwt van	19.05 mm
1100 cc 2V, 1300 cc Saloon, Estate and Van	20.64 mm
1300 cc and 1600 cc 2V	17.78 mm
9 cwt Van	20.68 mm

Torque wrench settings

	lbf ft	kgf m
Caliper to front suspension unit .... 35 to 50	4.8 to 6.9	
Brake disc to hub ... ... 30 to 34	4.2 to 4.7	
Brake backplate		
Timken axle	15 to 18	2.1 to 2.5
Salisbury axle ... ... 20 to 23	2.8 to 3.2	
Hydraulic unions ... ... 5 to 7	0.7 to 1.0	
Bleed valves (maximum) 8	1.1	

1 General description

According to model, either disc or drum brakes are fitted to the front wheels while all models have single leading shoe drum brakes at the rear. The mechanically operated handbrake operates on the rear wheels only.

Where front drum brakes are fitted, these are of the two leading shoe type with a separate cylinder for each shoe. Two adjusters are provided on each front wheel so that wear can be taken up on the brake linings. It is unusual to have to adjust the handbrake system as the efficiency of this system is largely dependent on the condition of the rear brake linings and the adjustment of the brake shoes. The handbrake can however be adjusted separately to the footbrake operated hydraulic system (Section 19).

The hydraulic brake system on drum brakes operates in the following manner: On application of the brake pedal, hydraulic fluid under pressure is pushed from the master cylinder to the brake operating cylinders in each wheel by a union, steel pipelines and flexible hoses.

The hydraulic fluid moves the pistons out of the wheel cylinders so pushing the brake shoes into contact with the brake drums. This provides an equal degree of retardation on all four wheels in direct proportion to the brake pedal pressure. Return springs draw the shoes together again when the brake pedal is released.

The front disc brakes fitted to certain models (Specifications) are rotating disc and static caliper type, with one caliper per disc. The caliper is positioned to act on the trailing edge of the disc. Each caliper contains two piston operated friction pads, which on application of the footbrake, pinch the disc between them.

Application of the footbrake creates hydraulic pressure in the master cylinder and fluid from the cylinder travels via steel and flexible pipes to the cylinders in each half of the calipers, thus pushing the pistons, to which are attached the friction pads, into contact with either side of the disc.

Two seals are fitted to the operating cylinders, the outer seal prevents moisture and dirt entering the cylinder, while the inner seal which is retained in a groove inside the cylinder, prevents fluid leakage.

As the friction pads wear so the pistons move further out of

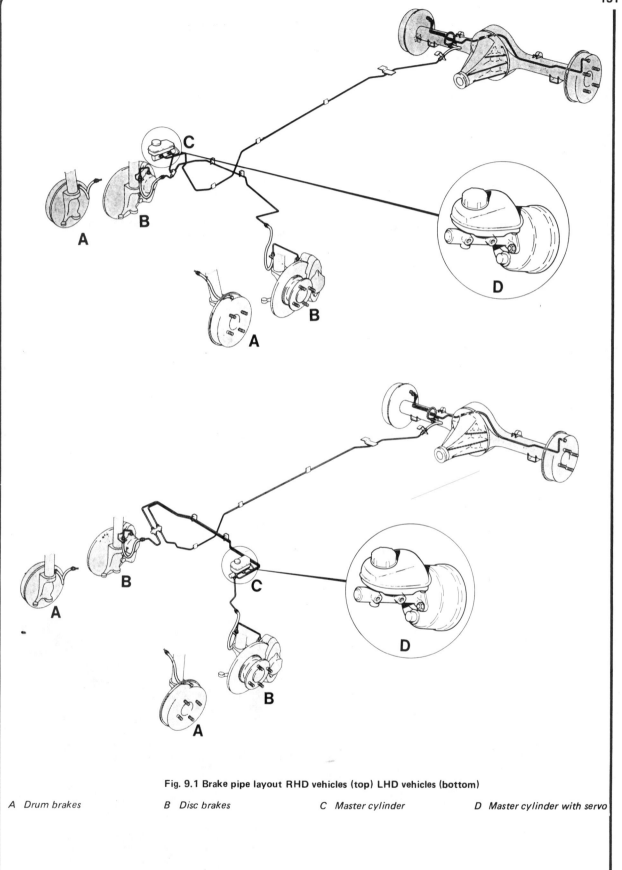

Fig. 9.1 Brake pipe layout RHD vehicles (top) LHD vehicles (bottom)

A Drum brakes   B Disc brakes   C Master cylinder   D Master cylinder with servo

the cylinders and the level of the fluid in the hydraulic reservoir drops. Disc pad wear is therefore taken up automatically, and eliminates the need for periodic adjustment by the owner.

The handbrake lever on all models is located between the front seats. A single cable runs from the lever to an equaliser bracket on the left of the rear axle. The cable runs through the equaliser and operates the right-hand rear brake. At the same time the bracket is deflected and a solid rod attached to it running across the rear of the axle casing, operates the left-hand rear brake.

A mechanical servo, suspended vacuum type, is fitted as standard on all high performance models. A dual circuit braking system is fitted to all models, the circuits being split between front and rear brakes at the master cylinder.

Should one circuit fail, the other circuit is unaffected and the car can still be stopped. On some models a warning light is fitted on the facia which iluminates should either circuit fail. The bulb in the light can also be tested by means of the switch provided.

Either front disc brakes or servo assisted braking can be fitted as an optional extra on any model of the Escort range. The rear brakes are self-adjusting through the operation of the footbrake. The self-adjusting mechanism is located within the rear brake drum and is made up of the handbrake actuating lever, connecting link, serrated wheel and arm. The adjuster arm has serrations along its curved end which engage with similar serrations in the serrated wheel. The other end of the adjuster arm locates in a cut-out in the leading shoe.

The clearance shown at 'B' (Fig. 9.15) determines the brake shoe to drum clearance which is not adjustable. As the brake shoes progressively wear the clearance at 'B' is first reduced and then eliminated, continuing wear causes the brake shoe to exert an increasing pressure on the arm until finally the arm moves one, or two, serrations around its curved end. This has the effect of restoring the clearance at 'B' and the whole process starts again.

2 Braking system - maintenance and inspection

1 Check the fluid level in the reservoir as described in the Routine Maintenance Section at the beginning of this manual. Always use the specified fluid for topping-up or refilling the system. The use of other fluid could result in brake failure caused by perishing or swelling of the seals within the master and operating cylinders.
2 If topping-up becomes frequent, then check the metal piping and flexible hoses for leaks, and check for worn brake or master cylinders which will also cause loss of fluid.
3 At intervals of 3000 miles (4800 km) or more frequently if pedal travel becomes excessive, adjust the brake shoes to compensate for wear of the brake linings.

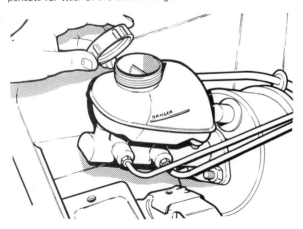

Fig. 9.2 Check brake fluid level (Sec 2)

4 Every 6000 miles (9600 km) in the case of drum brakes, remove the drums, inspect the linings for wear and renew them as necessary. At the same time, thoroughly clean out all dust from the drum using a dry cloth. With disc brakes, remove the pads and examine them for wear. If they are worn down to 1/8 inch or less (the distance being measured between the contact face of the pad and the face of the brake pad support plate) then they should be renewed.
5 Every 36,000 miles (58,000 km) or three years, whichever comes sooner, it is advisable to change the fluid in the braking system and at the same time renew all hydraulic seals and flexible hoses. At the same mileage, it is recommended that the vacuum servo unit (where fitted) is renewed on an exchange basis.

3 Drum brakes (front) - adjustment

1 Jack-up one side of the car to attend to the brakes on that side.
2 The brakes are taken up by turning square headed adjusters on the rear of each backplate. The edges of the adjuster are easily burred if an ordinary spanner is used. Use a square headed brake adjusting spanner if possible.
3 Two adjusters are fitted to each of the front wheels (Fig 9.3).
4 Turn the adjuster a quarter of a turn at a time until the wheel is locked. Then turn back the adjuster one notch so that the wheel will rotate without binding.
5 Spin the wheel and apply the brakes hard to centralise the shoes. Recheck that it is not possible to turn the adjusting screw further without locking the shoe. A rubbing noise when the wheel is spun is usually due to dust in the brake drum. If there is no obvious slowing of the wheel due to brake binding there is no need to slacken off the adjusters. Better to remove the drum and blow out the dust.
Note: Avoid inhaling the brake lining dust, as asbestos dust, when inhaled, can be injurious to health.

4 Front drum brake shoes - inspection and renewal

1 Every 6000 miles (9600 km) the brake drums should be removed and the linings and drums brushed free from dust and inspected.
2 Remove the hub cap, slacken off the wheel nuts, securely jack up the car and remove the roadwheel.
3 Slacken off the brake adjusters two or three turns, then referring to Fig. 9.4, carefully prise off the dust cover (2) and remove the split pin (1) (photo) from the castellated nut retainer (3).
4 Remove the castellated nut retainer (3) and undo the hub

Fig. 9.3 Location of front drum brake shoe adjusters (Sec 3)

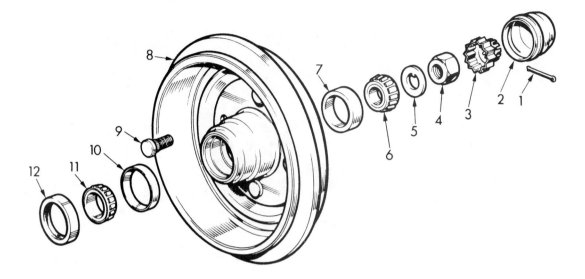

Fig. 9.4 Front hub/drum assembly

1	Split pin	5	Thrust washer	9	Wheel stud
2	Dust cover	6	Outer bearing	10	Bearing cap
3	Nut retainer	7	Bearing cap	11	Inner bearing
4	Nut	8	Drum	12	Grease seal

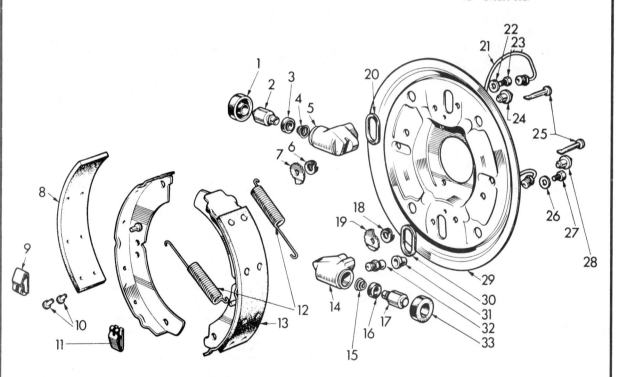

Fig. 9.5 Left-hand front drum brake (note position of leading edge of shoe; this is reversed on right-hand brake)

1	Dust excluding boot	12	Shoe return springs	23	Bolt
2	Piston	13	Shoe	24	Adjuster stud
3	Seal	14	Operating cylinder	25	Shoe steady posts
4	Spring	15	Spring	26	Washer
5	Operating cylinder	16	Seal	27	Bolt
6	Spring	17	Piston	28	Adjuster stud
7	Cam (snail) adjuster	18	Spring	29	Backplate
8	Friction lining	19	Cam (snail) adjuster	30	Rubber gasket
9	Shoe steady post clip	20	Rubber gasket	31	Bleed nipple dust cap
10	Rivets	21	Hydraulic interconnecting pipe	32	Bleed nipple
11	Shoe steady post clip	22	Washer	33	Rubber dust excluding boot

4.3 Withdrawing split pin from axle nut
retainer

4.4 Removing front hub outer bearing
and thrust washer

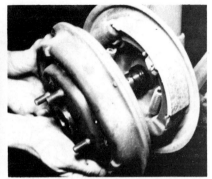

4.5 Withdrawing a front brake drum

4.7 Removing shoe steady post retaining
spring

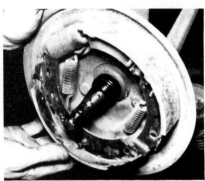

4.8 Detaching lower shoe of front wheel
brake

4.9 Shoe return spring hole marked for
identification

adjusting nut (4). Then pull off the thrust washer (5) and the
conical outer bearing (6) (photo).

5   Remove the brake drum (photo); if it proves obstinate, tap
the rim gently with a soft headed hammer to free it. The shoes
are now exposed for inspection.

6   The brake linings should be renewed if they are so worn that
the rivet heads are flush with the surface of the lining. Where
bonded linings are fitted, they must be removed when the
material has worn down to 1 mm (0.04 in). at its thinnest point.
If the shoes are being removed to give access to the wheel cylinders, then cover the linings with masking tape to prevent any
possibility of their becoming contaminated with grease or oil.

7   Depress the retaining clips which hold the brake steady pins
in place, remove the clips (photo), by turning the steady pin
through 90° and withdraw the pins through the brake backplate.

8   Detach the bottom of the rear brake shoe from its slot in the
lower wheel cylinder (photo), lift it up to allow the spring to
fully compress, then detach the spring from the brake shoe, but
leave the other end in the brake backplate.

9   Scribe a mark on the hole from which the spring was removed in the shoe to ensure correct reassembly (photo). Now
repeat the same procedure on the other brake shoe.

10 Place rubber bands over the wheel cylinders to prevent any
possibility of the pistons dropping out.

11 Thoroughly clean all traces of dust from the shoes, backplates, and brake drums with a dry paintbrush and compressed
air, if available. Brake dust can cause squeal and judder and it is
therefore important to clean out the brakes thoroughly.

12 Check that the pistons are free in their cylinders and that the
rubber dust covers are undamaged and in position and that there
are no hydraulic fluid leaks.

13 Prior to reassembly, smear a trace of brake grease on all
sliding surfaces. The shoes should be quite free to slide on the
closed end of the cylinder and the piston anchorage point. It is
vital that no grease or oil comes in contact with the brake drums

or the brake linings.

14 Replacement is a straightforward reversal of the removal
procedure, but note the following points:

   *a) Fully slacken off the two brake adjusters so as to make it
   easier to replace the drum.*
   *b) The hub adjusting nut should be tightened down to a
   torque of 27 lb f ft (3.73 kg f m) whilst the hub is being
   rotated, to ensure correct bedding in of the bearings. When
   fully tightened down, the nut must be slackened back
   90°, the retainer fitted and a new split pin used to secure
   the retainer.*
   c) Finally adjust the brakes (Section 3).

5   Rear drum brake shoes - inspection and renewal

1   Remove the hub cap, loosen off the wheel nuts, then securely
jack-up the car, and remove the roadwheel. Chock the front
wheels and fully release the handbrake.

2   Carefully lift off the drum, if necessary, lever out the
handbrake lever abutment stop on the rear of the backplate
(photo).

3   Remove the small holding down springs from each shoe by
turning the two small top washers through 90°. (photo)

4   Disengage the spring clip and remove the clevis pin and
washers securing the handbrake cable to thr right-hand brake
assembly at the handbrake actuating arm. (on the left-hand
brake assembly the handbrake rod must be disconnected from
the lever.)

5   The abutment stop must now be removed from the backplate. On 203 mm (8 in) brakes the stop takes the form of a
bridge piece held in positon by a rubber dust cover; on 229 mm
(9 in) brakes the stop is a hinged arrangement secured by a nylon
pin. To remove the stop remove the dust cover or lever out the
pin as appropriate.

6   Carefully lever the brake shoes from their bottom guides and

5.2 Removing the brake drum

5.3 To remove the shoe steady springs, push the cap upwards and rotate it through 90 degrees at the same time. The pin can then be withdrawn from the rear of the backplate

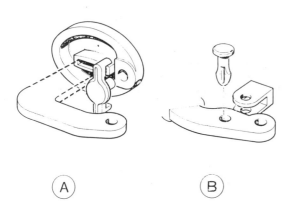

Fig. 9.6 Abutment stop (Sec 5)

A   203 mm (8 in) brakes
B   228 mm (9 in) brakes

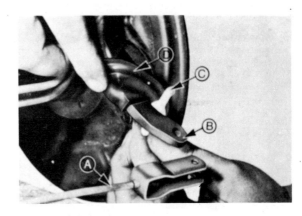

Fig. 9.7 203 mm (8 in) brakes (Sec 5)

A   Handbrake cable
B   Actuating lever
C   Abutment stop bridge piece
D   Actuating lever rubber

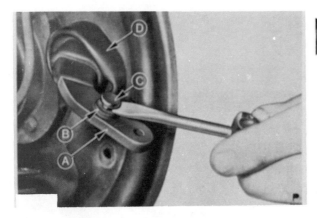

Fig. 9.8 228 mm (9 in) brakes (Sec 5)

A   Actuating lever
B   Abutment stop
C   Pin
D   Actuating lever rubber

Fig. 9.9 Removing brake shoes from lower guides pull off spring 'A' shown arrowed (Sec 5)

detach the lower return spring. Lever the leading shoe from the wheel cylinder slot and self-adjusting arm, disconnect the pull off spring and lift the shoe off the backplate.

7   Unlock the trailing shoe from the actuating lever, disconnect the pull off spring and lift the shoe off the backplate. Note that trailing/leading shoe identification is simplified by the fact that the lining is rivetted to the trailing shoe, and bonded to the leading shoe.

8   The brake linings should be examined and must be renewed if they are so worn that the rivet heads are flush with the surface of the lining. Bonded linings must be renewed when the material has worn down to 1 mm (0.04 in) at its thinnest point.

9   Replacement of the shoe is a direct reversal of the removal procedure but great care must be taken to ensure that the return springs are correctly fitted and that the contact points shown in Fig. 9.12 are lightly greased with brake grease.

10 Reset the self-adjusting mechanism by using a screwdriver to lever the serrated arm away from the wheel at the same time pushing the serrated end of the arm towards the backplate to the limit of the serrations.

11 Adjust the brakes by applying the foot brake two or three times.

---

6   Drum brake wheel operating cylinders - removal and refitting

1   Remove the brake drum and shoes (Sections 4 or 5).

Front brakes

2   Disconnect the flexible hose at its junction with the top wheel cylinder, remembering to plug the pipe to prevent loss of fluid.

3   Remove the small hydraulic pipe connecting the two wheel cylinders.

4   Undo and remove the two bolts and shakeproof washers securing the wheel cylinders to the brake backplate, noting that there is a small rubber sealing ring located between the wheel cylinder and the backplate.

5   This sealing ring must be renewed if it is not in perfect condition.

6   Replacement of the wheel cylinder is a direct reversal of the above procedure. Remember to bleed the brakes when the shoes and drum have been reassembled.

Rear brakes

7   Remove the self-adjusting mechanism components, as described in Section 5, and guide the linkage out of its location between the halfshaft flange and backplate.

8   Free the hydraulic pipe from the wheel cylinders at the union on the brake backplate (there are two unions on the right-hand backplate).

9   Undo and remove the two bolts and spring washers securing the wheel cylinder to the backplate and lift the cylinder off the plate.

10 Replacement is a direct reversal of the removal sequence.

---

7   Wheel operating cylinders - servicing

Front wheel cylinders

1   Clean the exterior of the unit by brushing off all dust and wiping with a piece of rag soaked in methylated spirit.

2   Pull off the rubber dust covers.

3   Eject the piston/seal assembly from its cylinder either by tapping or applying air pressure from a tyre pump at the fluid inlet union.

4   Examine the surfaces of the piston and cylinder bore for scoring or 'bright' wear areas. If these are evident, renew the complete cylinder assembly.

5   Discard the oil seals and purchase a repair kit which will contain all the necessary seals and renewable components.

6   Dip the new seal in clean hydraulic fluid and fit it to the

piston, using only the fingers to manipulate it. Ensure that the flat face of the seal is against the piston rear shoulder. Insert the piston into the cylinder body, taking care not to trap the lips of the seal.

7   Fit a new dust cover.

Rear wheel cylinders

8   Pull the rubber dust covers off the ends of the wheel cylinder.

9   Slide the piston assemblies one from each end out of the cylinder and withdraw the spring from the cylinder bore.

10 Prise the seals from the pistons and then examine the piston and bore for signs of scoring of excessive wear.

11 Fit the new seals as described in paragraphs 5 and 6, then refit the pistons to the wheel cylinder bore.

Fig. 9.10 Removing handbrake actuating lever from brake shoe (Sec 5)

A   Actuating lever   B   Self adjuster assembly

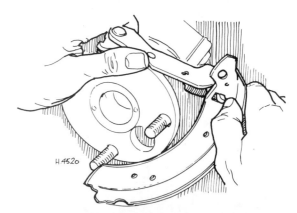

Fig. 9.11 Replacing trailing shoe and spring on adjusting mechanism (Sec 5)

Fig. 9.12 Grease points on rear brake assembly (Sec 5)

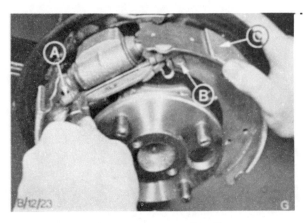

Fig. 9.13 Refitting brake shoes (Sec 5)

A   Upper pull off spring   C   Leading shoe
B   Self adjusting mechanism

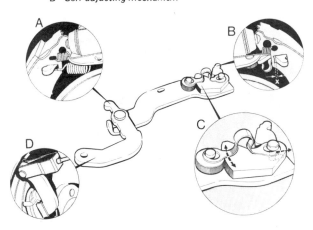

Fig. 9.15 Rear brake self-adjusting mechanism (Sec 5)

A   Shoe end of handbrake actuating lever
B   Shoe to drum clearance 'X' when brakes released
C   Movement of serrated adjuster to reset mechanism
D   Handbrake cable end of actuating lever

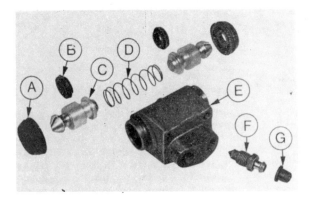

Fig. 9.17 Rear wheel cylinder (Sec 7)

A   Dust cover   E   Wheel cylinder
B   Piston seal   F   Bleed nipple
C   Piston   G   Cap
D   Spring

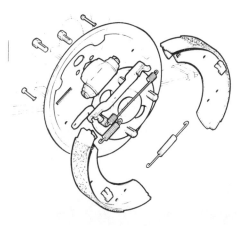

Fig. 9.14 Rear brake drum components (Sec 5)

Fig. 9.16 Removing self adjusting mechanism from backplate
(Sec 6)

8   Disc brake pads - inspection and renewal

1   Remove the front wheels and inspect the amount of friction
material left on the friction pads. The pads must be renewed
when the thickness of the material has worn down to 1/8 inch
(3 mm).
2   With a pair of pliers, pull out the two small wire clips (12)
which hold the main retaining pins in place (Fig. 9.18).
3   Remove the main retaining pins which run through the
caliper, the metal backing of the pads and the shims. (photo)
4   The friction pads and shims can now be removed from the
caliper. If they prove difficult to move by hand, a pair of long
nosed pliers can be used. (photo)
5   Carefully clean the recesses in the caliper in which the
friction pads and shims lie, and the exposed faces of each piston
from all trace of dirt and rust.
6   Release the bleed nipple one half turn on the caliper unit and
press each piston squarely into its cylinder bore. The fluid displaced by this operation will be ejected from the bleed nipple.
7   Fit new friction pads and their shims, the main retaining pins
and their clips.
8   Tighten the bleed nipple and then depress the brake pedal
hard two or three times.
9   Repeat the operation on the opposite caliper and then check
the level in the fluid reservoir and top-up as necessary.

9   Disc calipers - removal, servicing and refitting

1   Jack-up the front of the vehicle, remove the roadwheel,

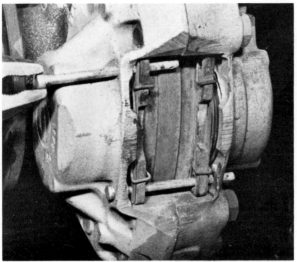

8.3 After removing the spring clips, withdraw the pad retaining pins ...

8.4 ... The pads and shims can then be pulled out. It may be necessary to use pliers

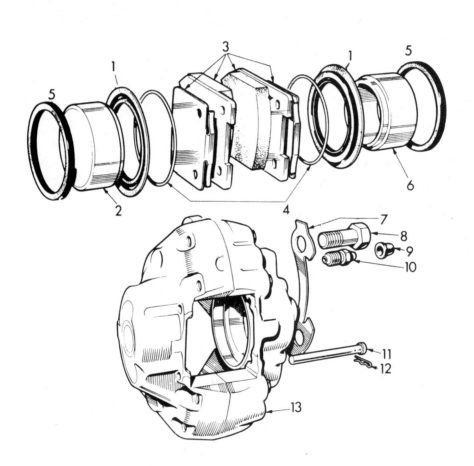

Fig. 9.18 Front caliper unit (Secs 8 and 9)

1 *Dust excluders*	5 *Piston seals*	9 *Dust cap*
2 *Piston*	6 *Piston*	10 *Bleed valve*
3 *Friction pads and shims*	7 *Locking plate*	11 *Pad retaining pin*
4 *Dust excluder retaining rings*	8 *Bolt*	12 *Pin retaining clip*
		13 *Caliper body*

friction pads and shims as previously described.

2   Disconnect the hydraulic fluid line either at the rear of the caliper body or at the suspension leg.

3   Bend back the locking tabs on the caliper mounting bolts and unscrew and remove the bolts. The caliper unit can now be withdrawn from the disc.

4   Remove the retaining rings (4) (Fig. 9.18) and detach the dust excluding covers (1) from each of the cylinders.

5   Apply air pressure from a tyre pump at the fluid inlet port of the caliper and eject the pistons. Do not allow the pistons to fall to the ground during this operation. Mark them with their respective locations using a piece of masking tape.

6   Pick out the rubber seals from the cylinder bores, taking great care not to scratch the surface of the bore.

7   Clean all components in brake fluid or methylated spirit and discard the old seals. Examine the surfaces of the pistons and cylinder bores for scoring or 'bright' wear areas. If these are evident, renew the complete caliper unit.

8   Obtain a repair kit and assemble the seals into the cylinder grooves using only the fingers to manipulate them.

9   Dip the pistons in clean hydraulic fluid and insert them into the cylinder bores. Press each piston as far as it will go into the cylinder, making sure that the piston crown (solid end) enters first.

10 Engage the dust excluders into the piston recessed ends and then attach them to the caliper body; then fit the retaining rings.

11 Refitting is a reversal of removal but tighten the securing bolts to a torque of between 35 and 50 lbf ft (4.8 and 6.9 Kgf m).

10 Brake disc - removal and refitting

1   The brake disc is not normally removed from the hub unless it is to be renewed.

2   Remove the hub and disc assembly complete (Chapter 11, Section 4).

3   Separate the hub from the disc by knocking back the locking tabs and undoing the four bolts. Discard the disc, bolts and locking tabs.

4   Before fitting a new disc to the hub, thoroughly clean the mating surfaces of both components. If this is not done properly, and dirt is allowed to get between the hub and the disc, this will seriously affect disc brake run-out when it is checked after reassembly.

5   Fit the hub and disc together using new locking tabs and nuts. Tighten the nuts down to a torque of 30 to 34 lb f ft (4.15 to 4.70 kg f m) and bend up the locking tabs.

6   Refit the disc and hub assembly.

11 Brake master cylinder - removal and installation

1   Working inside the vehicle, disconnect the pushrod from the brake pedal by removing the spring clip, the clevis pin and bushes.

2   Disconnect the two fluid lines from the master cylinder body.

3   Plug the fluid lines to prevent the ingress of dirt.

4   Unscrew and remove the two nuts and spring washers which secure the master cylinder to the engine rear bulkhead (or brake

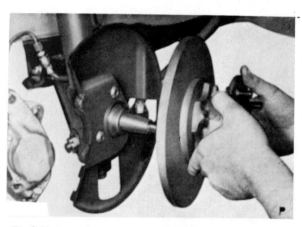

Fig. 9.19 Removing the hub and disc assembly off the stub axle (Sec 10)

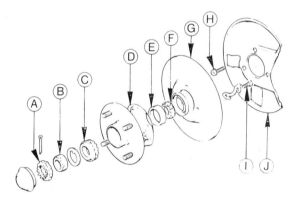

Fig. 9.21 The hub and disc assembly - exploded view (Sec 10)

A   Nut retainer   F   Inner bearing
B   Nut   G   Disc
C   Outer taper bearing   H/I Bolts
D   Hub casting   J   Splash shield
E   Bearing cone

Fig. 9.20 Separating the hub and disc assembly by removing the four retaining bolts after first bending back the lock tabs (Sec 10)

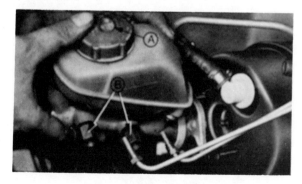

Fig. 9.22 Removing the master cylinder. Note: plasticine plug at A and port plugs at B (Sec 11)

servo unit) and remove it.

5   Installation is a reversal of removal but bleed the brakes as described later in this Chapter when the refitment is completed.

12 Master cylinder - dismantling and reassembly

1   This type of master cylinder is used in conjunction with dual circuit hydraulic systems. Also incorporated is a pressure differential warning actuator, its purpose and servicing being described in Sections 13 and 14.

2   The master cylinder comprises two piston assemblies, one behind the other operating in a common bore. There are two outlets from the master cylinder, one to the front brakes and one to the rear brakes, both going via the pressure differential warning actuator.

3   To dismantle the unit, pull off the rubber dust cover and remove the circlip and washer under the dust cover which holds the pushrod in place. Remove the pushrod.

4   Take the hydraulic fluid reservoir off the cylinder assembly by undoing the screw on each side of the cylinder.

5   From the top of the cylinder, remove the circlip and spring from the primary recuperating valve and with a suitable hexagon headed key, take out the plug which holds this valve in place, then remove the valve assembly.

6   Fit plugs to the two outlet holes and to the primary recuperating valve aperture, then using a suitable air line, blow gently into the other hole on the top of the cylinder. This will remove from the cylinder bore the primary piston and spring,

the secondary piston and the secondary recuperating valve assemblies.

7   Remove the piston seal from the primary piston. Lift the tab on the secondary piston spring retainer and remove the piston. Compress the secondary piston spring, move the retainer to one side and remove the secondary recuperating valve stem from the retainer. Then slide the valve spacer and shim from the valve stem, noting the way in which the shim is fitted.

8   Remove the small rubber valve seal and the secondary piston seal. Examine the state of the cylinder bore for signs of scoring or corrosion. If this is damaged in any way, a new master cylinder must be fitted. It is also advisable to renew all rubber seals as a matter of course, whether they are damaged or not.

9   Clean all parts with approved hydraulic fluid prior to re-assembly in the cylinder bore.

10 Fit a new seal onto the secondary piston and a new seal to the valve stem. Use the fingers only to manipulate them. Replace the shim on the valve stem, making sure that the convex side faces toward the seal spacer which is fitted next, with its legs toward the valve seal.

11 Refit the secondary piston spring over the valve stem, insert the spring retainer, compress the spring and fit the boss in the valve stem into its location in the spring retainer.

12 Place the narrow end of the secondary piston into the spring retainer and secure it by pressing down the tab. Dip the now complete secondary assembly in approved hydraulic fluid and carefully slide it into the cylinder bore with the secondary recuperating valve leading.

13 Place the primary piston spring into the cylinder, fit a new

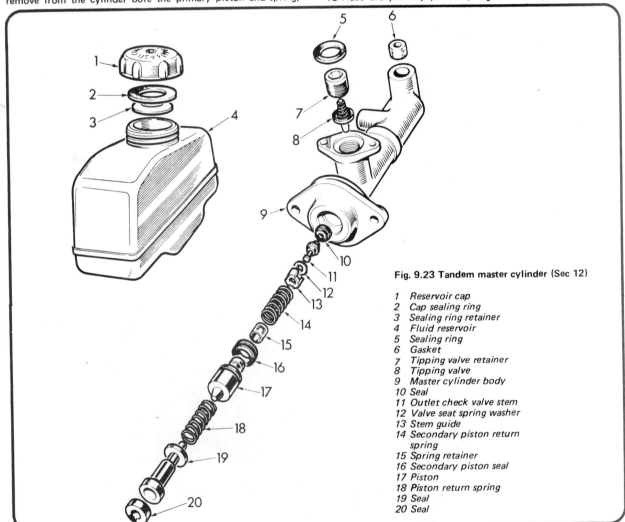

Fig. 9.23 Tandem master cylinder (Sec 12)

1   *Reservoir cap*
2   *Cap sealing ring*
3   *Sealing ring retainer*
4   *Fluid reservoir*
5   *Sealing ring*
6   *Gasket*
7   *Tipping valve retainer*
8   *Tipping valve*
9   *Master cylinder body*
10 *Seal*
11 *Outlet check valve stem*
12 *Valve seat spring washer*
13 *Stem guide*
14 *Secondary piston return spring*
15 *Spring retainer*
16 *Secondary piston seal*
17 *Piston*
18 *Piston return spring*
19 *Seal*
20 *Seal*

rubber seal to the primary piston, dip it in clean brake fluid and carefully slide it into the cylinder, drilled end first.

14 Fit the pushrod into the end of the primary piston and retain it with the washer and circlip.

15 Place the primary recuperating valve into its location in the top of the cylinder and check that it is properly located by moving the pushrod up and down a small amount. Screw the retaining plug into position and refit the spring and circlip to the valve plunger.

16 Move the pushrod in and out of the cylinder and check that the recuperating valve opens when the rod is fully withdrawn and closes again when it is pushed in.

17 Check the condition of the front and rear reservoir gaskets and if there is any doubt as to their condition, new ones must be fitted. Refit the reservoir to the cylinder with its two retaining screws.

13 Pressure differential valve - description

1 On LHD models a brake pressure differential valve is fitted. This valve is essentially a shuttle valve, the opposing sides of which are connected to the front and rear hydraulic brake circuits (dual system). Whilst equal pressure is maintained in both circuits, the valve remains centralised (in balance) but should the pressure drop in either circuit due to a leaking pipe or cylinder seal, then the valve is displaced - blocking the affected circuit and closing an electrical contact to illuminate a warning light on the facia panel.

14 Pressure differential valve - servicing

1 Disconnect the five hydraulic pipes at their unions on the pressure differential valve and to prevent too much loss of hydraulic fluid, either place a piece of polythene under the cap of the master cylinder and screw it down tightly, or plug the ends of the two pipes leading from the master cylinder.

2 Remove the nut and washer securing the differential valve assembly to the fender apron and lift the assembly off the fender, after first disconnecting the switch multiplug.

3 Carefully unscrew and remove the switch unit from the top of the valve body.

4 Unscrew the stop bolt from the end of the valve body and from the opposite end use a thin rod, or electrical screwdriver to push the piston two sleeves and seals out of the valve body bore.

5 Remove the two rubber seals, together with the piston sleeves, off their respective ends of the piston.

6 Clean all components using a Girling cleaning fluid and put them on a clean sheet of paper ready for inspection. Examine the piston for score marks, pitting or signs of corrosion. Similarly, check the condition of the valve body bore, where doubt exists as to the condition of the components they must be renewed.

7 Remember that new seals must never be fitted unless the piston, sleeves and cylinder bore are in perfect condition.

8 Check that the two circlips on the piston body are in good condition then slide the piston sleeves over the end of the piston and secure them in place with two new seals.

9 Insert the piston, sleeve and seal assembly into the valve body after first lubricating the body and assembly with clean brake fluid. Assemble a new washer to the retaining bolt and then screw the bolt into the end of the valve body. Refit the switch unit.

10 Replacement of the valve on the fender apron is a reversal of the removal procedure.

15 Flexible brake hoses - inspection, removal and refitting

1 Inspect the condition of the flexible hydraulic hoses leading from under the front wings to the brackets on the front suspension units, and the single hose on the rear axle casing. If they are swollen, damaged or chafed, they must be renewed.

2 Undo the locknuts at both ends of the flexible hoses and then, holding the hexagon nut on the flexible hose steady, undo the other union nut and remove the flexible hose and washer.

3 Replacement is a reversal of the removal procedure, but carefully check that all the securing brackets are in a sound

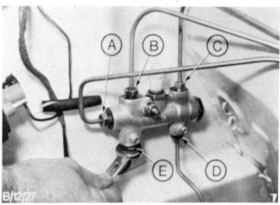

Fig. 9.24 Unscrewing the brake fluid line unions from the differential valve body (Sec 14)

A To LH front brake
B From master cylinder
C From master cylinder
D To rear brake
E To RH front brake

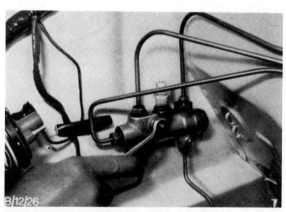

Fig. 9.25 Removing the nut and washer retaining the differential valve to the fender apron (Sec 14)

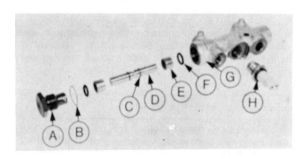

Fig. 9.26 Differential valve - exploded view (Sec 14)

A End bolt
B Washer
C Piston circlip
D Piston
E Sleeve
F Seal
G Valve body
H Switch

condition and that the locknuts are tight. Check the path taken by the hose when installed to ensure that it does not foul the tyres or steering in any position of lock. If this does occur, loosen the union with the rigid pipe and twist the flexible hose not more than one quarter turn in either direction to correct matters. Retighten the union whilst holding the flexible hose perfectly still.

16 Bleeding the hydraulic system

1   Removal of all air from the hydraulic system is essential to the correct working of the braking system, and before undertaking this, examine the fluid reservoir cap to ensure that both vent holes, one on top and the second underneath but not in line, are clear; check the level of fluid and top up if required.
2   Check all brake line unions and connections for possible seepage, and at the same time, check the condition of the rubber hoses which may be perished.
3   If the condition of the wheel cylinders is in doubt, check for possible signs of fluid leakage.
4   If there is any possibility of incorrect fluid having been put into the system, drain all the fluid out and flush through with methylated spirits. Renew all piston seals and cups since these will be affected and could possibly fail under pressure.
5   Gather together a clean jam jar, a 9 inch (230 mm) length of rubber tubing which fits tightly over the bleed nipples, and the correct brake fluid, which has remained unshaken for 24 hours and has been stored in an airtight container.
6   To bleed the system, clean the areas around the bleed valves and start on the front brakes by removing the rubber cup over the bleed valve, if fitted, and fitting a rubber tube in position.
7   Place the end of the tube in a clean glass jar containing sufficient fluid to keep the end of the tube submerged during the operation.
8   Open the bleed valve with a spanner and have an assistant quickly press down the brake pedal. After slowly releasing the pedal, pause for a moment to allow the fluid to recoup in the master cylinder and then depress again. This will force air from the system. Continue until no more air bubbles can be seen coming from the tube.
9   Press the pedal fully to the floor and holding it in this position, tighten the bleed nipple. At intervals, make certain that the reservoir is kept topped up, otherwise air will enter at this point.
10   Repeat this operation on the other front brake and the left-hand rear brake, there being no bleed valve on the right-hand rear brake. When completed, check the level of the fluid in the reservoir and then check the feel of the brake pedal, which should be firm and free from any 'spongy' action, which is normally associated with air in the system.
11   On vehicles fitted with tandem master cylinders, the bleeding operation is similar but the pressure differential actuator valve must be held in a central position (Section 13). Both sections of the fluid reservoir must be kept topped-up throughout the bleeding operation.

17 Vacuum servo unit - removal and refitting

1   Remove the vacuum supply pipe from the servo unit and then undo the brake fluid pipes from the master cylinder. Block the ends of the pipes to prevent the entry of dirt.
2   Take the master cylinder off the front of the servo unit by undoing the two retaining nuts and washers.
3   Detach the servo pushrod from the brake pedal by removing the spring clip, clevis pin and clevis pin bushes.
4   Working underneath the right-hand wing, undo and remove the two nuts and one bolt which hold the servo unit mounting bracket to the side of the car.
5   From under the bonnet, undo and remove the two nuts

Fig. 9.27 Disconnecting the vacuum hose from the brake servo (Sec 17)

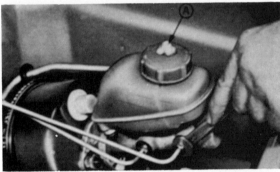

Fig. 9.28 Removing the master cylinder. Note: plasticine plug at A (Sec 17)

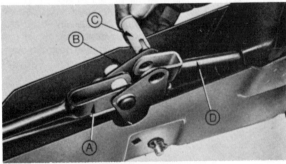

Fig. 9.29 Disconnecting the brake pedal actuating coupling fro the servo (Sec 17)

A Brake pedal connecting rod   C Bush
B Coupling   D Servo rod

Fig. 9.30 Removing brake servo unit (Sec 17)

which hold the rear of the servo mounting bracket to the bulk-head. Remove the servo unit complete with its mounting bracket from the car.

6   From halfway along the mounting bracket, separate the servo pushrod and the pedal pushrod from the pivoted relay lever by removing the spring clip, the clevis pin and clevis bush.

7   Then undo the four nuts and spring washers holding the servo unit to its mounting bracket and detach the servo.

8   Replacement of the servo unit and its mounting bracket are a direct reversal of the above procedure but note the following points.

9   When fitted correctly the pushrod which is attached to the brake pedal must have the yellow paint mark round the hole facing toward the centre of the car.

10   Measure the distance between the centre of the brake push-rod hole and the rear face of the servo mounting bracket. (Fig 9.33). This dimension should be between 3.88 and 3.93 inch (98.6 and 99.8 mm). If found to be incorrect, adjust the length of the pedal pushrod by undoing the locknut at 'A' and adjusting the pushrod to the correct length before tightening down the locknut. The pushrod on some models is not adjustable.

Fig. 9.31 Brake servo unit (Sec 17)

18 Brake pedal - removal and refitting

1   Remove the crosshead screw, nut, bolt and push in clip, securing the driver's side parcel shelf to its various brackets then detach the shelf.

2   Disconnect the brake master cylinder pushrod from the brake pedal, as described in Section 11.

3   Remove the circlip from the end of the pedal shaft, then push the shaft into the pedal box and through the pedal bushes until the pedal can be dropped clear of the box.

4   Disconnect the pedal return spring and remove the pedal from the vehicle.

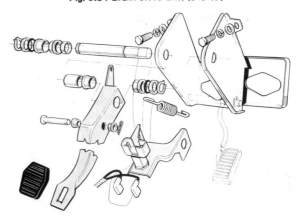

Fig. 9.32 Brake pedal assembly (Sec 18)

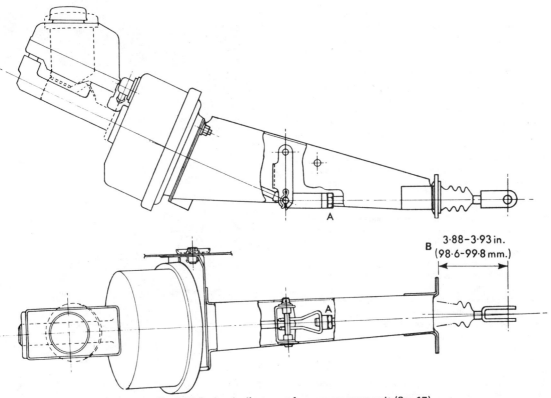

Fig. 9.33 Pushrod adjustment for vacuum servo unit (Sec 17)

A   Adjuster nut   B   Pedal to mounting flange dimension

5   Replacement is a direct reversal of the removal procedure detailed above.

19 Handbrake - adjustment

1   The handbrake is normally adjusted automatically when the adjusters on the brake backplates are rotated to take up wear in the brake shoe linings. However, if the operating cable has stretched or in the event of a new cable having been fitted (Section 20), carry out the following procedure.
2   Chock the front wheels; release the handbrake fully and then jack-up the rear roadwheels.
3   Check that the handbrake cable follows its correct run and is properly located in its guides. then ensure that both levers are fully seated by checking that there is no clearance between the backplate lever and bridge abutment (203 mm/8 in brakes) or the hinge abutment (228 mm/9 in brakes) and the backplate.
4   Locate the cable adjuster on the underside of the floor pan turn the keyed sleeve (C in Fig. 9.35) so that the key engages with the slot on the tunnel bracket.
5   Insert a screwdriver blade between the adjusting nut and keyed sleeve to disengage the nut from the sleeve so that the nut can be freely turned by hand.
6   Turn the nut as necessary to remove all slack from the cable, this is indicated by a clearance 1 to 1.5 mm (0.039 to 0.060 in) at the abutment levers measured at the abutment point.
7   Disengage the sleeve from the abutment bracket.
8   Lower the jack and apply the handbrake. If the adjustment has been correctly carried out, then the rear wheels should be fully locked when the handbrake lever moves through three or four notches of its quadrant.

20 Handbrake cable - renewal

1   Chock the front roadwheels, jack-up the rear of the vehicle and release the handbrake fully.
2   Disconnect the handbrake cable from the brake operating lever by removing the clip (or split pin) and the clevis pin.
3   Turn to the right-hand brake drum and disconnect the cable from the actuating lever in the drum by first removing the spring clip and then pushing out the clevis pin.
4   Prise the clip retaining the cable to the transverse rod off its location and then slide the cable clear of the transverse rod bracket.
5   Finally, slide the cable complete with adjusting nut and keyed sleeve, clear of the cable adjuster bracket on the underside of the foot pan, and then off the vehicle, pulling the cable through the slots in the guide brackets as necessary to disengage the cable from the guides.
6   Fitting the new cable is a reversal of removal but grease the guides and when installed, adjust it as described in Section 19.

21 Handbrake cable transverse rod - removal and installation

1   Chock the front roadwheels, jack-up the rear of the vehicle and fully release the handbrake.
2   Turn to the right-hand brake drum and disconnect the cable from the actuating lever in the drum by first removing the spring clip and then pushing out the clevis pin.
3   Prise the spring clip retaining the cable to the transverse rod off its location, then slide the cable clear of the rod bracket.
4   Disconnect the transverse rod from the actuating lever on the left-hand drum by removing the spring clip and pushing out the clevis pin.
5   Slide the rod through its mounting bush on the axle casing and lift it clear of the vehicle.
6   Replacement of the rod is a direct reversal of the removal procedure, but first check the condition of the axle casing bush and renew if necessary.
7   Grease the rod location at the actuating lever, casing bush,

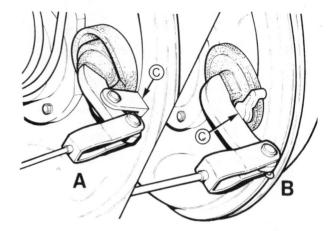

Fig. 9.34 Zero movement at abutment point 'C' (Sec 19)

A   228 mm (9 in) brake
B   203 mm (8 in) brake

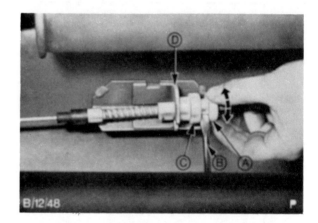

Fig. 9.35 Handbrake cable adjuster (Sec 19)

A   Adjusting nut   C   Keyed sleeve
B   Screwdriver holding nut and   D   Bracket
    keyed sleeve apart

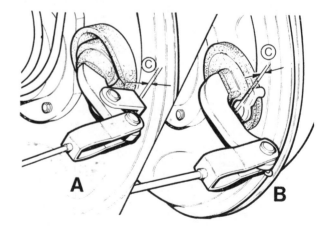

Fig. 9.36 Fully adjusted clearance 1.0 to 1.5 mm at 'C' (Sec 19)

A   228 mm (9 in) brake
B   203 mm (8 in) brake

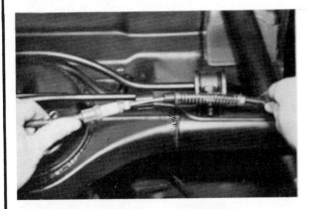

Fig. 9.37 Locating handbrake cable in transverse rod bracket (Sec 20)

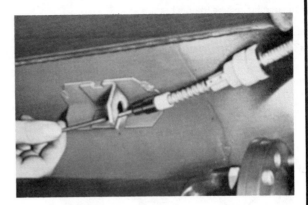

Fig. 9.38 Removing the handbrake cable from its underbody guides, note that guide bush has been slid out of guide and along cable (Sec 20)

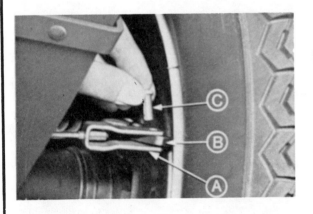

Fig. 9.39 Removing handbrake cable clevis pin from actuating lever (Sec 21)

A Clevis
B Lever
C Clevis pin

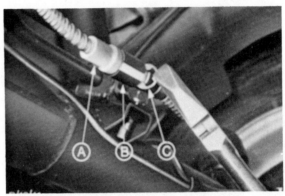

Fig. 9.40 Prising off clip retaining cable to transverse rod bracket (Sec 21)

A Handbrake cable
B Transverse rod bracket
C Clip

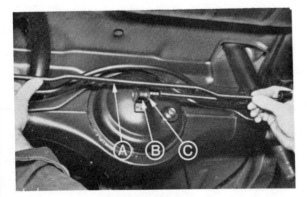

Fig. 9.41 Inserting transverse rod in axle casing bush (Sec 21)

A Rod
B Casing bracket
C Casing bush

Fig. 9.42 Inserting casing bush (B) in axle bracket (A) (Sec 21)

and coupling, with a lithium based grease.

22 Handbrake lever - removal and installation

1   Jack-up the front of the vehicle, chock the rear wheels and fully release the handbrake.
2   From underneath the vehicle, disconnect the cable from the handbrake lever, where the lever protrudes through the floor pan, by removing the spring clip and pushing out the clevis pin.
3   Working inside the passenger compartment carefully pull the carpet (or rubber mat) away from the base of the lever to expose the screws retaining the handbrake lever gaiter.
4   Unscrew and remove the screws then lift away the metal gaiter surround and pull the gaiter off the handbrake lever.
5   Undo and remove the two bolts holding the lever to the floor pan, and remove the lever from the vehicle.
6   Replacement is a reversal of the removal procedure.

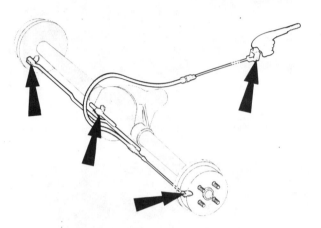

Fig. 9.43 Handbrake cable system grease points (Sec 21)

Fig. 9.44 Disconnecting handbrake cable from handbrake lever pivot by pulling out clevis pin 'A' (Sec 22)

Fig. 9.45 Removing handbrake gaiter retainer (Sec 22)

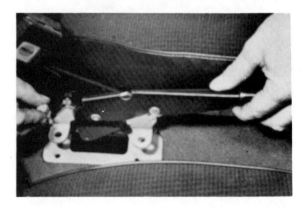

Fig. 9.46 Removing bolts securing handbrake lever to floor pan (Sec 22)

23 Fault diagnosis - braking system

Symptom	Reason/s	Remedy
Pedal travels almost to floor before brakes operate		
Leaks and air bubbles in hydraulic system	Brake fluid level too low	Top up master cylinder reservoir. Check for leaks.
	Wheel cylinder leaking	Dismantle wheel cylinder, clean, fit new rubbers and bleed brakes.
	Master cylinder leaking (Bubbles in master cylinder fluid)	Dismantle master cylinder, clean, and fit new rubbers. Bleed brakes.
	Brake flexible hose leaking	Examine and fit new hose if old hose leaking. Bleed brakes.
	Brake line fractured	Replace with new brake pipe. Bleed brakes.
	Brake system unions loose	Check all unions in brake system and tighten as necessary. Bleed brakes.
Normal wear	Linings over 75% worn	Fit replacement shoes and brake linings.

Symptom	Reason	Remedy
Incorrect adjustment	Brakes badly out of adjustment Master cylinder push rod out of adjustment causing too much pedal free movement (servo system)	Jack up car and adjust brakes. Reset to specification.
Brake pedal feels 'springy' Brake lining renewal	New linings not yet bedded-in	Use brakes gently until springy pedal feeling leaves.
Excessive wear or damage	Brake drums badly worn and weak or cracked	Fit new brake drums.
Lack of maintenance	Master cylinder securing nuts loose	Tighten master cylinder securing nuts. Ensure spring washers are fitted.
Brake pedal feels 'spongy' and 'soggy' Leaks or bubbles in hydraulic system	Wheel cylinder leaking Master cylinder leaking (Bubbles in master cylinder reservoir) Brake pipe line or flexible hose leaking Unions in brake system loose	Dismantle wheel cylinder, clean, fit new rubbers, and bleed brakes. Dismantle master cylinder, clean, and fit new rubbers and bleed brakes. Replace cylinder if internal walls scored. Fit new pipe line or hose. Examine for leaks, tighten as necessary.
Excessive effort required to brake car Lining type or condition	Linings or pads badly worn New linings recently fitted - not yet bedded-in Harder linings or pads fitted than standard causing increase in pedal pressure	Fit replacement brake shoes, linings and pads. Use brakes gently until braking effort normal Remove linings or pads and replace with normal units.
Oil or grease leaks	Linings, brake drums or discs contaminated with oil, grease, or hydraulic fluid	Rectify source of leak, clean brake drums, or discs, fit new linings.
Brakes uneven and pulling to one side Oil or grease leaks	Linings, pads and brake drums or discs contaminated with oil, grease, or hydraulic fluid Tyre pressures unequal Radial ply tyres fitted at one end of car only Brake backplate loose Brake shoes or pads fitted incorrectly Different type of linings fitted at each wheel Anchorages for front suspension or rear axle loose Brake drums or discs badly worn, cracked or distorted	Ascertain and rectify source of leak, clean brake drums, discs or pads and fit new linings. Check and inflate as necessary. Fit radial ply tyres of the same make to all four wheels. Tighten backplate securing nuts and bolts. Remove and fit shoes correct way round. Fit the linings specified by the manufacturers all round. Tighten front and rear suspension pick-up points including spring anchorage. Fit new brake drums or discs.
Brakes tend to bind, drag, or lock-on Incorrect adjustment Wear or dirt in hydraulic system or incorrect fluid	Brake shoes adjusted too tightly Handbrake cable over-tightened Reservoir vent hole in cap blocked with dirt Master cylinder by-pass port restricted - brakes seize in 'on' position Wheel cylinder seizes in 'on' position	Slacken off brake shoe adjusters two clicks. Slacken off handbrake cable adjustment. Clean and blow through hole. Dismantle, clean, and overhaul master cylinder. Bleed brakes. Dismantle, clean, and overhaul wheel cylinder. Bleed brakes.
Mechanical wear	Brake shoe pull off springs broken, stretched or loose	Examine springs and renew if worn or loose.
Incorrect brake assembly	Brake shoe pull off springs fitted wrong way round, omitted, or wrong type used	Examine, and rectify as appropriate.
Neglect	Handbrake system rusted or seized in the 'on' position	Apply 'Plus Gas' to free, clean and lubricate.

Chapter 10 Electrical system

For modifications, and information applicable to later models, see Supplement at end of manual

Contents

Specifications

Battery

Type ...	Lead acid
Location ...	LH side of engine compartment
Fixing ...	Base mounted
Earth terminal ...	Negative (−)
Voltage ...	12
Capacity (AH):	
1.3 and 1.6 manual trans. (UK) ...	38 Femsa battery
1.6 2V and 1.6 auto. trans. ...	44 Femsa battery
1.6 2V auto. trans export or all model options ...	55 Femsa battery
No of plates ...	11 (9-Femsa 38AH)

Starter motor (Bosch)

Type	0.7 PS
Number of brushes	4
Brush material	Carbon Y-31
Min. length of brushes (mm)	10
Brush spring pressure (gm)	900—1,300
Min. diameter of commutator (mm)	32,8
Max. permissible out of round on commutator (mm)	0,3
Armature endfloat (mm)	0,1—0,3
Type of drive	Solenoid
Number of pinion gearteeth	10
Number of flywheel ring gearteeth	135
Max. torque (Nm) at 20°C	10,0
Direction of rotation	Clockwise
Max. draw (watts)	2,400
Voltage	12
Output (watts)	515

Starter motor (Lucas)

Type	**M35J (inertia and pre-engaged)**	**5M90**
Number of brushes	4	4
Brush material	Carbon	Carbon
Min. brush length (mm)	8,0	8,0
Brush spring pressure kg.f (oz f)	28 (0,8)	28 (0,8)
Min. diameter of commutator (mm)	2,05	2,05
Armature endfloat (mm)*	0,25	0,25
Type of drive *	Solenoid	Solenoid
Max. torque (Nm) at 20°C	9,5	10,8
Direction of rotation	Clockwise	Clockwise
Voltage	12	12
Max. current (light running) (amps)	65	65

*Not inertia motor

Alternator (Bosch)

Type	**G1-28A**	**K1-35A**	**K1-55A**
Earth polarity	Negative	Negative	Negative
Nominal rated output at 13.5 volts and 6,000 rpm	28 amp	35 amp	55 amp
Max. continuous alternator speed (rpm)	15,000	15,000	15,000
Stator winding resistance, ohms per phase	0.2 + 0.01	0.13 + 0.007	0.01 + 0.007
Rotor winding resistance, ohms at 20°C	4.0 + 0.4	4.0 + 0.4	4.0 + 0.4
Min. length of slip ring end brushes protruding from brush box in free position	5 mm (0.197 in.)	5 mm (0.197 in.)	5 mm (0.197 in.)
Regulating voltage (Model AD1) at 4,000 rpm and 3 to 7 amp load	13.7 to 14.5 volt	13.7 to 14.5 volt	13.7 to 14.5 volt

Alternator (Lucas)

Type	**15 ACR**	**17 ACR**	**18 ACR**
Earth polarity	Negative	Negative	Negative
Nominal rated output at 13.5 volts and 6,000 rpm	28 amp	35 amp	43 amp
Max. continuous alternator speed (rpm)	15,000	15,000	15,000
Stator winding resistance, ohms per phase	0.198 ± 0.01	0.133 ± 0.007	0.092 ± 0.005
Rotor winding resistance, ohms at 20°C	$3.35 \pm 5\%$	$3.25 \pm 5\%$	$3.25 \pm 5\%$
Min. length of slip ring end brushes protruding from brush box in free position	5 mm (0.197 in.)	5 mm (0.197 in.)	5 mm (0.197 in.)
Regulating voltage (Model 14 TR) at 4,000 rpm and 3 to 7 amp load	14.2 to 14.6 volt	14.2 to 14.6 volt	14.2 to 14.6 volt

Alternator (Femsa)

Type	**ALD 12-32, ALD 12-33**
Earth polarity	Negative
Nominal rated output at 13.5 volts and 6,000 rpm	32 amp
Max. continuous alternator speed (rpm)	15,000
Stator winding resistance, ohms per phase	0.173 ± 0.01
Rotor winding resistance, ohms at 20°C ...	$5.0 + 0.15$
Min. length of slip ring end brushes protruding from brush box in free position	7 mm (0.28 in.)
Regulating voltage (Model GRK 12-16) at 4,000 rpm and 3 to 7 amp load	13.7 to 14.5 volt
Field relay closing voltage	2.0 to 2.8 volt

Fuses (Nos. correspond to fuse block cover numbers)

1   8 amp, 16 amp on later models: ...   .   Cigar lighter, interior light, hazard flashers, (clock and glovebox on later models).

2   8 amp: ...   .   LH side light, LH tail light, licence plate.

3   8 amp: ...   .   RH side light, RH tail light, instrument panel illumination

4   8 amp: ...   .   Main beam headlamps.

5   8 amp: ...   .   Dipped beam headlamps.

6   8 amp, 16 amp on later models: ...   .   Direction indicators, stop lamps, reversing lamps, heater motor.

7   8 amp: ...   .   Windscreen wiper motor, instrument cluster, washer pump.

The fuses listed below are located separately on their respective components

16 amp: ...   .   Heated rear window relay.

2 amp: ...   .   Medium-slow blow fuse in radio circuit.

16 amp: ...   .   Driving lamp relay (Located in engine compartment).

Bulbs

Exterior   Wattage

Headlamp (circular sealed beam) 60/45W

Headlamp (circular semi-sealed) 60/55W

Headlamp (square semi-sealed) 60/55W

Driving lamps (Halogen)   55

Front indicators   21

Rear indicators   21

Side repeater flasher lamps (where fitted)   4

Rear stop tail lamps 21/5

Reversing lamps   21

Licence plate   4

Interior

Interior light   5

Instrument panel warning lights   1,3

Instrument panel illumination   2,6

---

1 General description

The electrical system is a 12 volt negative earth system, the negative terminal of the battery going to earth via the engine block.

The battery supplies a steady amount of current for all the electrical circuits on the vehicle, and provides a reserve of current during the short periods when the current being consumed by the various vehicle circuits exceeds that being produced by the charging circuit.

The alternator fitted to the vehicle will generally be of Lucas manufacture, although Bosch, or Femsa, alternators may be fitted as alternatives. All the alternators are driven from the engine crankshaft pulley via the fan belt, and run in pre-packed no maintenance bearings cooled by their own integral fan. Lucas alternator output is regulated by a regulator housed within the alternator cover; Bosch and Femsa regulators are separately located in the engine compartment.

Either inertia or pre-engaged starter motors are fitted, the type used being dependent on model variant and territory. Where an inertia starter is used it will be the Lucas M35J, this motor being fitted only to vehicles produced in Britain. The alternative pre-engaged motor can be of either Lucas (M35J or 5M90) or Bosch (0.7 ps) manufacture.

Exterior lighting consists of headlamps (with intergral side-lamps), front direction indicators, and rear side/stop/direction indicators combined in one unit. A separate lamp assembly, housed in the rear bumper illuminates the rear number plate. The headlamps can be 7 in. dia. sealed beam (Base and 'L' models built in Britain), 7 in. dia semi-sealed beam (Base and 'L' models built in Germany) or 7 in. dia Halogen semi-sealed beam ('Sport'). The 'XL' and Ghia ranges have 7 in. square, halogen, semi-sealed beams.

The windshield wiper motor is a two-speed, self-parking unit housed inside the vehicle immediately below the passenger side facia. Wiper control is from a steering column mounted switch which also controls the electrically operated screen washing equipment. The windscreen washer reservoir houses the washer pump and is located in the engine compartment.

Instrumentation on 'Base' and 'L' variants consists of speedometer and combined fuel and water temperature gauges; for Sport, GL and Ghia models these instruments are supplemented by the provision of a tachometer. Both types of cluster incorporate a comprehensive range of warning lights including turn indicators, oil pressure and main beam.

---

2 Battery - removal and refitting

1   The battery is positioned on a tray in the front of the engine compartment forward of the nearside suspension.

2   Disconnect the earthed negative lead and then the positive lead by slackening the retaining nuts and bolts or by unscrewing the retaining screws if these are fitted.

3   Remove the battery clamp and carefully lift the battery off its tray. Hold the battery vertically to ensure that no electrolyte is spilled.

4   Replacement is a direct reversal of this procedure. **Note:** Replace the positive lead and the earth (negative) lead, smearing the terminals with petroleum jelly to prevent corrosion. Never use an ordinary grease as applied to other parts of the car.

Fig. 10.1. Battery clamp screw location (Sec. 2)

3 Battery - maintenance and inspection

1 Normal weekly battery maintenance consists of checking the electrolyte level of each cell to ensure that the separators are covered by ¼ inch (6.35 mm) of electrolyte. If the level has fallen top up the battery using distilled water only. Do not overfill. If a battery is overfilled or any electrolyte spilled, immediately wipe away the excess as electrolyte attacks and corrodes any metal it comes into contact with very rapidly.

2 As well as keeping the terminals clean and covered with petroleum jelly, the top of the battery, and especially the top of the cells, should be kept clean and dry. This helps prevent corrosion and ensures that the battery does not become partially discharged by leakage through dampness and dirt.

3 Once every three months remove the battery and inspect the battery securing bolts, the battery clamp plate, tray, and battery leads for corrosion (white fluffy deposits on the metal which are brittle to touch). If any corrosion is found, clean off the deposits with ammonia and paint over the clean metal with an anti-rust// anti-acid paint.

4 At the same time inspect the battery case for cracks. If a crack is found, clean and plug it with one of the proprietary compounds marketed by firms such as Holts for this purpose. If leakage through the crack has been excessive then it will be necessary to refill the appropriate cell with fresh electrolyte as detailed later. Cracks are frequently caused to the top of the battery case by pouring in distilled water in the middle of winter *after* instead of *before* a run. This gives the water no chance to mix with the electrolyte and so the former freezes and splits the battery case.

5 If topping up the battery becomes excessive and the case has been inspected for cracks that could cause leakage, but none are found, the battery is being overcharged and the voltage regulator will have to be checked and reset.

6 Every three months check the specific gravity with a hydrometer to determine the state of charge and the condition of the electrolyte. There should be very little variation between the different cells and if a variation in excess of 0.025 is present, it will be due to either:

   a) *Loss of electrolyte from the battery caused by spillage or a leak resulting in a drop in the specific gravity of the electrolyte. The deficiency was probably made up with distilled water instead of fresh electrolyte.*

   b) *An internal short circuit caused by buckling of the plates or a similar malady pointing to the likelihood of total battery failure in the near future.*

7 The specific gravity of the electrolyte for fully charged conditions at the electrolyte temperature indicated is listed in Table A. The specific gravity of a fully discharged battery at different temperatures of the electrolyte is given in Table B.

Table A

Specific gravity - battery fully charged

1.268 at 100°F or 38°C electrolyte temperature
1.272 at 90°F or 32°C electrolyte temperature
1.276 at 80°F or 27°C electrolyte temperature
1.280 at 70°F or 21°C electrolyte temperature
1.284 at 60°F or 16°C electrolyte temperature
1.288 at 50°F or 10°C electrolyte temperature
1.292 at 40°F or 4°C electrolyte temperature
1.296 at 30°F or -1.5°C electrolyte temperature

Table B

Specific gravity - battery fully discharged

1.098 at 100°F or 38°C electrolyte temperature
1.102 at 90°F or 32°C electrolyte temperature
1.106 at 80°F or 27°C electrolyte temperature
1.110 at 70°F or 21°C electrolyte temperature
1.114 at 60°F or 16°C electrolyte temperature
1.118 at 50°F or 10°C electrolyte temperature
1.122 at 40°F or 4°C electrolyte temperature
1.126 at 30°F or -1.5°C electrolyte temperature

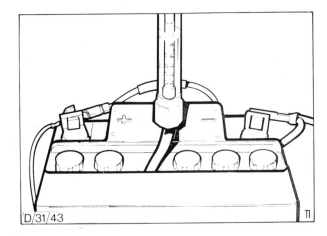

Fig. 10.2. Checking electrolyte specific gravity (Sec. 3)

4 Battery - electrolyte replenishment

1 If the battery is in a fully charged state and one of the cells maintains a specific gravity reading which is 0.025 or more lower than the others, and a check of each cell has been made with a voltmeter to check for short circuits (a four to seven second test should give a steady reading of between 1.2 to 1.8 volts), then it is likely that electrolyte has been lost from the cell which shows the low reading.

2 Top-up the cell with a solution of 1 part sulphuric acid to 2.5 parts of water. If the cell is already fully topped up, draw some electrolyte out of it with a pipette. The total capacity of each cell is ¾ pint.

3 When mixing the sulphuric acid and water **never add water to sulphuric acid** - always pour the acid slowly into the water in a glass container. **If water is added to sulphuric acid it will explode.**

4 Continue to top-up the cell with the freshly made electrolyte and then recharge the battery and check the hydrometer readings.

5 Battery - charging

1 In winter time when heavy demand is placed upon the battery, such as when starting from cold, and much electrical equipment is continually in use, it is a good idea to occasionally have the battery fully charged from an external source at the rate of 3.5 to 4 amps.

2 Continue to charge the battery at this rate until no further rise in specific gravity is noted over a four hour period.

3 Alternatively, a trickle charger charging at the rate of 1.5 amps can be safely used overnight.

4 Specially rapid boost charges which are claimed to restore the power of the battery in 1 to 2 hours are most dangerous as they can cause serious damage to the battery plates through over-heating.

5 While charging the battery, note that the temperature of the electrolyte should never exceed 100°F (37.8°C).

6 Alternator - general description

1 The main advantage of the alternator lies in its ability to provide a high charge at low revolutions. Driving slowly in heavy traffic with a dynamo invariably means no charge is reaching the battery. In similar conditions, even with the wiper, heater, lights and perhaps radio switched on, the alternator will ensure a charge reaches the battery.

2 An important feature of the alternator is a built-in output

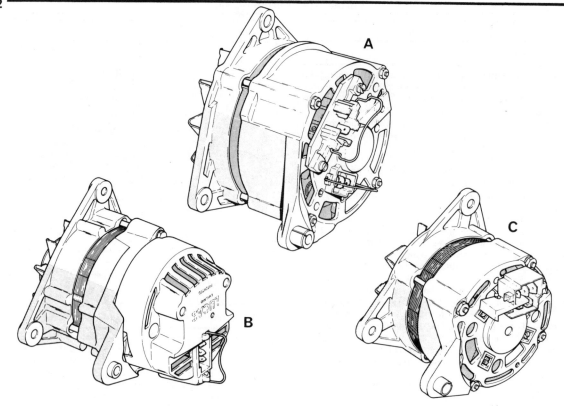

Fig. 10. 3. Alternator types: A) Bosch, B) Lucas, C) Femsa

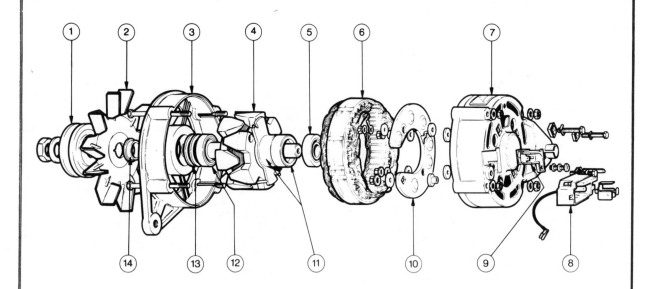

Fig. 10.4. Femsa alternator

1 Pulley	4 Rotor	7 Slip ring end housing	11 Slip ring
2 Fan	5 Slip ring bearing	8 Terminal block	12 Drive end bearing
3 Drive end housing	6 Stator	9 Brush box	13 Washers
		10 Diode pack	14 Spacer

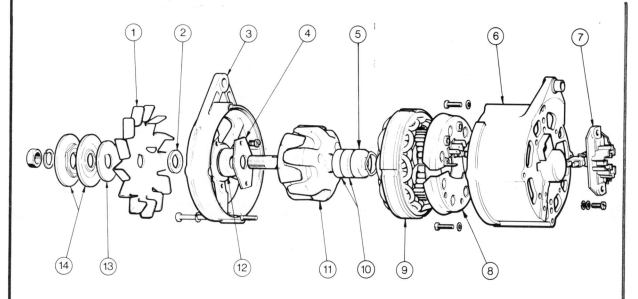

Fig. 10.5. Bosch alternator

1 Fan	4 Thrust plate	7 Brush box	11 Rotor
2 Spacer	5 Slip ring bearing	8 Diode pack	12 Drive end bearing
3 Drive end housing	6 Slip ring end housing	9 Stator	13 Washer
		10 Slip ring	14 Pulley

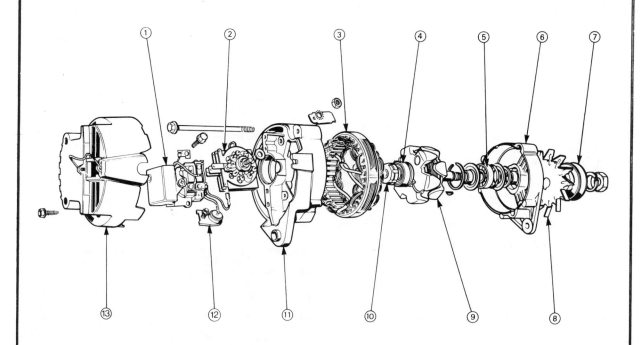

Fig. 10.6. Lucas alternator

1 Regulator	4 Slip ring bearing	7 Pulley	10 Slip ring
2 Diode pack	5 Drive end bearing	8 Fan	11 Slip ring end housing
3 Stator	6 Drive end housing	9 Rotor	12 Diode
			13 Cover

control regulator, based on 'thick film' hybrid integrated micro-circuit technique, which results in the alternator being a self-contained generating and control unit.

3 The system provides for direct connection of a charge indicator light, and eliminates the need for a field switching relay or warning light control unit, necessary with former systems.

4 The alternator is of rotating field, ventilated design. It comprises, principally, a laminated stator on which is wound a star connected three-phase output winding; a twelve pole rotor carrying the field windings - each end of the rotor shaft runs in ball race bearings which are lubricated for life; natural finish aluminium die cast end brackets, incorporating the mounting lugs; a rectifier pack for converting the AC output of the machine to DC for battery charging; and an output control regulator.

5 The rotor is belt driven from the engine through a pulley keyed to the rotor shaft. A pressed steel fan adjacent to the pulley draws cooling air through the alternator. This fan forms an integral part of the alternator specification. It has been designed to provide adequate air flow with minimum noise, and to withstand the high stresses associated with maximum speed. Rotation is clockwise viewed on the drive end. Maximum continuous rotor speed is 15000 rpm.

6 Rectification of the alternator output is achieved by six silicone diodes housed in a rectifier pack and connected as a three-phase full wave bridge. The rectifier pack is attached to the outer face of the slip ring end bracket and contains also three 'field' diodes; at normal operating speeds, rectified current from the stator output windings flows through these diodes to provide the self-excitation of the rotor field, via brushes bearing on face type slip rings.

7 The slip rings are carried on a small diameter moulded drum attached to the rotor shaft outboard of the slip ring end bearing. The inner ring is centered on the rotor shaft axle, while the outer ring has a mean diameter of ¾ inch (19.05 mm) approximately. By keeping the mean diameter of the slip rings to a minimum, relative speeds between brushes and rings, and hence wear, are also minimal. The slip rings are connected to the rotor field winding by leads carried in grooves in the rotor shaft.

8 The brush gear is housed in a moulding screwed to the out-side of the slip ring and bracket. This moulding thus encloses the slip ring and brush gear assembly, and together with the shielded bearing, protects the assembly against the entry of dust and moisture.

9 The regulator is set during manufacture and requires no further attention. Briefly, the 'thick film' regulator comprises resistors and conductors screen printed onto an alumina substrate. Mounted on the substrate are Lucas semi-conductor dice consisting of three transistors, a voltage reference diode and a field recirculation diode, together with two capacitors. The internal connections between these components and the substrate are made by special Lucas patented connectors. The whole assembly is 0.0625 inch (1.588 mm) thick, and is housed in a recess in an aluminium heat sink, which is attached to the slip ring and bracket. Complete hermetic sealing is achieved by a silicone diode rubber encapsulant to provide environmental protection.

10 Electrical connections to external circuits are brought out to Lucar connector blades, these being grouped to accept a moulded connector socket which ensures correct connection.

7 Alternator - maintenance

1 The equipment has been designed for minimum maintenance in service, the only items subject to wear being the brushes and bearings.

2 Brushes should be examined after about 75,000 miles (120,000 km) and renewed if necessary. The bearings are pre-packed with grease for life, and should not require further attention.

3 Check the fan belt every 6,000 miles (9,600 km) for correct adjustment which should be 0.5 inch (13 mm) total movement at the centre of the run between the alternator and water pump

pulleys.

8 Alternator - special procedures

Whenever the electrical system of the car is being attended to, or external means of starting the engine are used, there are certain precautions that must be taken otherwise serious and expensive damage can result.

1 Always make sure that the negative terminal of the battery is earthed. If the terminal connectors are accidentally reversed or if the battery has been reverse charged the alternator diodes will burn out.

2 The output terminal on the alternator marked 'BAT' or B+ must never be earthed but should always be connected directly to the positive terminal of the battery.

3 Whenever the alternator is to be removed or when disconnecting the terminals of the alternator circuit always disconnect the battery earth terminal first.

4 The alternator must never be operated without the battery to alternator cable connected.

5 If the battery is to be charged by external means, always disconnect both battery cables before the external charge is connected.

6 Should it be necessary to use a booster charger or booster battery to start the engine, always double check that the negative cable is connected to negative terminal and the positive cable to positive terminal.

9 Alternator (all types) - removal and refitting

1 Disconnect the battery leads.

2 Note the terminal connections at the rear of the alternator and disconnect the plug or multi-pin connector.

3 Undo and remove the alternator adjustment arm bolt, slacken the alternator mounting bolts and push the alternator inward towards the engine. Lift away the fan belt from the pulley.

4 Remove the remaining two mounting bolts and carefully lift the alternator away from the car.

5 Take care not to knock or drop the alternator otherwise this can cause irreparable damage.

6 Refitting the alternator is the reverse sequence to removal. Adjust the fan belt so that it has 0.5 inch (13 mm) total movement at the centre of the run between the alternator and water pump pulleys.

10 Alternator - fault diagnosis and repair

Due to the specialist knowledge and equipment required to test or service an alternator, it is recommended that if the

Fig. 10.7 Alternator mounting bolts (Sec 9)

performance is suspect, the car be taken to an automobile electrician who will have the facilities for such work. Because of this recommendation, information is limited to the inspection and renewal of the brushes. Should the alternator not charge or the system be suspect, the following points may be checked before seeking further assistance:

1 Check the fan belt tension, as described in Section 7.
2 Check the battery, as described in Section 3.
3 Check all electrical cable connections for cleanliness and security.

---

11 Alternator brushes (Lucas ACR types) - inspection, removal and refitting

1 Undo and remove the two screws which hold on the end cover. Lift away the end cover.
2 To inspect the brushes correctly, the brush holder moulding should be removed by undoing the securing bolts and disconnecting the Lucar connector to the diode plates.
3 With the brush holder moulding removed and the brush assemblies still in position, check that they protrude from the face of the moulding by at least 0.2 inch (5.0 mm). Also check that when depressed, the spring pressure is 7-10 oz (198-283 gms) when the end of the brush is flush with the face of the brush moulding. To be done with any accuracy, this requires a push type spring scale.
4 Should either of the foregoing requirements not be fulfilled, the spring assemblies must be renewed. This can be done by simply removing the holding screws of each assembly and fitting the new components in position.
5 With the brush holder moulding removed, the slip rings on the face end of the rotor are exposed. These can be cleaned with a petrol soaked cloth and any signs of burning may be removed very carefully with fine glass paper. On no account should any other abrasive be used or any attempt at machining be made.
6 When the brushes are refitted they should slide smoothly in their holders. Any sticking tendency may first be rectified by wiping with a fuel soaked cloth, or if this fails, by carefully polishing with a very fine file where any binding marks may appear.
7 Reassemble in the reverse order of dismantling.

---

12 Alternator brushes (Bosch) - inspection, removal and replacement

1 Unscrew and remove the two screws, spring and plain washers securing the brush box to the exterior of the slip ring end housing. Detach the brush box.
2 Check that the carbon brushes are free to slide smoothly in their guides without binding.
3 Ensure that the brush length protuding from the brush box is greater than 0.2 in (5 mm). If the brushes are worn to a greater extent they must be renewed.
4 Using a pair of pliers as a heat shunt, unsolder the brush wire connections and remove the brushes and springs from the brush box moulding.
5 Check that the new brushes are free to slide in the brush box guides; if necessary lightly remove any high spots with a smooth file.
6 Insert the brushes and springs in the guides and solder the brush leads to their respective terminals.
7 Refitting the brush box is a reversal of the removal procedure.

---

13 Alternator brushes (Femsa) - inspection, removal and replacement

1 Disconnect the wire protuding through the slip ring end housing from its terminal on the brush box moulding.
2 Remove the single crosshead screw and withdraw the brush

Fig. 10.8 Brush box retaining screws (Lucas alternator) (Sec 11)

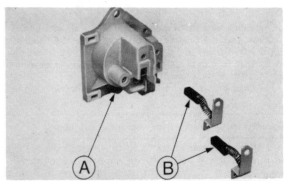

Fig. 10.9 Lucas brush box: A) Box, B) Brushes (Sec 11)

Fig. 10.10. Brush box retaining screws (Bosch alternator) (Sec. 12)

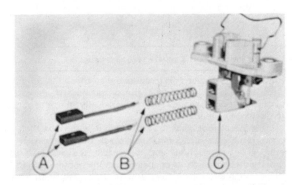

Fig. 10.11 Bosch brush box: A) Brushes, B) Springs, C) Housing, (Sec 12)

Fig. 10.12. Brush box retaining screws (Femsa alternator) (Sec. 13)

box moulding from its location in the slip ring end housing.

3 Check that the brushes are free to slide in their guides and that the free-length of brush protuding from the brush box is greater than 0.28 in (7 mm). If the brushes are worn beyond this point they must be renewed.

4 Replacement is a reversal of the removal process.

14 Starter motor (inertia type) - general description

1 The inertia starter motor fitted to all Escort models is the Lucas M35J. This is a series wound four pole, four brush motor, held in position by three bolts which also serve to clamp the bellhousing flange.

2 The motor has four field coils, four pole pieces and four spring-loaded commutator brushes. Two of these brushes are earthed, and the other two are insulated and attached to the field coil ends.

3 The starter drive is a conventional pinion and spring engaging with a ring gear on either the flywheel or torque converter (automatic transmission).

4 The fully insulated brush gear is housed in a plastic brush box moulding rivetted to the commutator end bracket. The wedge shaped brushes have keyways to ensure their correct fitting in the brush box and are kept in contact with the face type, moulded commutator, by small coil springs.

5 The field winding on this motor is continuously wound with no inter-connecting joints, one end terminating at the brush box moulding with the other end earthed to the yoke, or starter motor casing, via either a rivetted eyelet, or soldered connection.

6 Unlike earlier versions of this starter motor the end brackets are held to the yoke independently of each other, each bracket being secured to its respective location with two screws. At the drive end these screws locate into the pole shoes while at the commutator end the screws locate in tapped holes in the yoke wall.

15 Starter motor (inertia type) - testing on engine

1 If the starter motor fails to operate then check the condition of the battery by turning on the headlamps. If they glow brightly for several seconds and then gradually dim, the battery is in discharged condition.

2 If the headlamps glow brightly and it is obvious that the battery is in good condition, then check the tightness of the battery wiring connections (and in particular the earth lead from the battery terminal to its connection on the bodyframe). If the positive terminal on the battery becomes hot when an attempt is made to work the starter, this is a sure sign of a poor connection on the battery terminal. To rectify, remove the terminal, clean

the inside of the cap and the terminal post thoroughly and reconnect. Check the tightness of the connections at the relay switch and at the starter motor. Check the wiring for breaks or shorts with a suitable meter.

3 If the wiring is in order then check that the starter motor is operating. To do this, press the rubber covered button in the centre of the solenoid under the bonnet. If it is working, the starter motor will be heard to click as it tries to rotate. Alternatively, check it with a voltmeter.

4 If the battery is fully charged, the wiring in order, and the switch working and the starter motor fails to operate, then it will have to be removed from the car for examination. Before this is done, however, ensure that the starter pinion has not jammed in mesh with the flywheel. Check by turning the square end of the armature shaft with a spanner. This will free the pinion if it is stuck in engagement with the flywheel teeth. On some models the square on the end of the shaft will be covered by a metal cap; this can be prised off.

16 Starter motor (inertia type) - removal and refitting

1 Disconnect the battery earth lead from the negative terminal.

2 Disconnect the starter motor cable from the terminal on the starter motor end plate.

3 Remove the upper starter motor securing bolt.

4 Working under the car, loosen and remove the two lower starter motor securing bolts, taking care to support the motor so as to prevent damage to the drive components.

5 Lift the starter motor out of engagement with the flywheel ring gear and lower it out of the car.

6 Replacement is a straightforward reversal of the removal procedure.

17 Starter motor (inertia type) - dismantling and reassembly

1 With the starter motor on the bench, loosen the screw on the cover band and slip the cover band off. With a piece of wire bent into the shape of a hook, lift back each of the brush springs in turn and check the movement of the brushes in their holders by pulling on the flexible connectors. If the brushes are so worn that their faces do not rest against the commutator, or if the ends of the brush leads are exposed on their working face, they must be renewed.

2 If any of the brushes tend to stick in their holders, then wash them with a fuel moistened cloth, and if necessary, lightly polish the sides of the brush with a very fine file, until the brushes move quite freely in their holders.

3 If the surface of the commutator is dirty or blackened, clean it with a fuel dampened rag. Secure the starter motor in a vice and check it by connecting a heavy gauge cable between the starter motor terminal and a 12 volt battery.

4 Connect the cable from the other battery terminal to earth on the starter motor body. If the motor turns at high speed it is in good order.

5 If the starter motor still fails to function, or if it is wished to renew the brushes, it is necessary to further dismantle the motor.

6 Lift the brush springs with the wire hook and lift all four brushes out of their holders one at a time.

7 Remove the terminal nuts and washers from the terminal post on the commutator end bracket.

8 Unscrew the two tie bolts which hold the end plates together and pull off the commutator end bracket. Remove the driving end bracket which will come away complete with the armture.

9 At this stage, if the brushes are to be renewed, their flexible connectors must be unsoldered and the connectors of new brushes soldered in their place. Check that the new brushes move freely in their holders as detailed above. If cleaning the commutator with fuel fails to remove all the burnt areas and spots, then wrap a piece of fine glass paper round the commutator and rotate the armature. If the commutator is very badly worn, remove the drive gear as detailed in the following

Section. Then mount the armature in a lathe and with the lathe turning at high speed, take a very fine cut out of the commutator and finish the surface by polishing with fine glass paper. **Do not undercut the mica insulators between the commutator segments.**

10 With the starter motor dismantled, test the four field coils for an open circuit. Connect a 12 volt battery with a 12 volt bulb in one of the leads between the field terminal post and the tapping ooint of the field coils to which the brushes are connected. An open circuit is proved by the bulb not lighting.

11 If the bulb lights, it does not necessarily mean that the field coils are in order, as there is a possibility that one of the coils will be earthing to the starter yoke or pole shoes. To check this, remove the lead from the brush connector and place it against a clean portion of the starter yoke. If the bulb lights, the field coils are earthing. Replacement of the field coils calls for the use of a wheel operated screwdriver, a soldering iron, caulking and riveting operations and is beyond the scope of the majority of owners. The starter yoke should be taken to a reputable electrical engineering works for new field coils to be fitted. Alternatively, purchase an exchange starter motor.

12 If the armature is damaged, this will be evident after visual inspection. Look for signs of burning, discolouration, and for conductors that have lifted away from the commutator. Reassembly is a straightforward reversal of the dismantling procedure.

18 Starter motor (inertia type) - servicing the drive

1 The starter motor drive is of the outboard type. When the starter motor is operated the pinion moves into engagement with the flywheel gear ring by moving in toward the starter motor.

2 If the engine kicks back, or the pinion fails to engage with the flywheel gear ring when the starter motor is actuated, no undue strain is placed on the armature shaft, as the pinion sleeve disengages from the pinion and turns independently.

3 Whenever the starter motor is removed the drive should be thoroughly washed in paraffin, shaken and a little thin oil applied.

19 Starter motor (inertia type) - drive removal and refitting

1 On early type starter motors, the drive spring is retained and partially compressed by a nut and split pin. Dismantling consists of simply withdrawing the split pin and unscrewing the nut until the spring tension is released.

2 On later type starter motors, the spring is retained by a cup and circlip. The spring must be compressed by using a proprietary compressor (available from most accessory stores) so that the circlip can be extracted from the armature shaft.

3 Once removed, examine the pinion and barrel assembly and

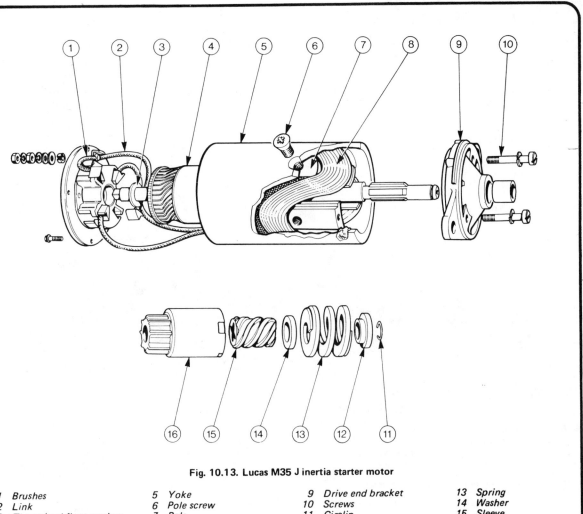

Fig. 10.13. Lucas M35 J inertia starter motor

1	Brushes	5	Yoke	9	Drive end bracket	13	Spring
2	Link	6	Pole screw	10	Screws	14	Washer
3	Thrust/end float washer	7	Pole	11	Circlip	15	Sleeve
4	Armature	8	Field coil	12	Spring cup	16	Barrel and pinion

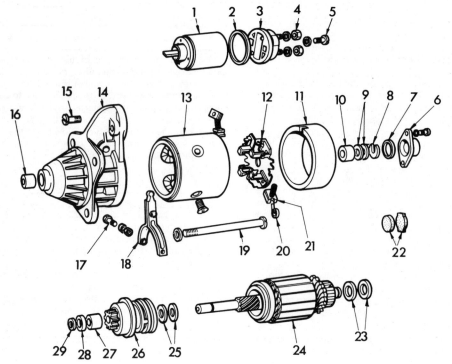

Fig. 10.14 Bosch 0.7 ps. pre-engaged starter motor

1 Solenoid	8 Circlip	15 Screw	22 Pads (lubricating)
2 Ring	9 Thrust washer	16 Bush	23 Thrust washers
3 Terminal block	10 Bearing	17 Pivot pin	24 Armature
4 Nut	11 Commutator end housing	18 Pivot lever	25 Rings
5 Screw	12 Brush mounting plate	19 Bolt	26 Drive assy
6 Cover	13 Yoke	20 Brush spring	27 Bush
7 Spacer	14 Drive end housing	21 Brush	28/29 Stop rings

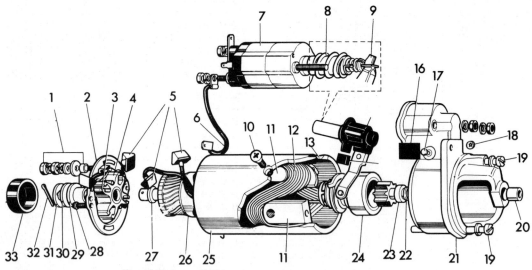

Fig. 10.15 Lucas M35J - pre-engaged starter motor

1 Terminal nut assy	10 Screw	18 Clip	26 Armature
2 Commutator end plate	11 Pole	19 Screws	27 Thrust washer
3 Brush housing	12 Field coil	20 Drive end bush	28 Screws
4 Brush spring location	13 Yoke earth	21 Drive end housing	29 Commutator end bush
5 Brushes	14 Seal	22 Jump ring	30 Thrust plate
6 Solenoid to starter link	15 Dust pad	23 Collar	31 Washer
7 Solenoid assy	16 Dust cover	24 Drive	32 Cotter pin
8 Spring	17 Pivot pin	25 Yoke	33 Cover
9 Engagement lever			

renew them if they are worn or chipped.

4 Refitting is a reversal of removal but ensure that the pinion teeth are toward the armature windings and then lubricate the sliding surfaces with a little thin oil.

20 Starter motor (pre-engaged type) - general description

1 This type of starter motor is normally only fitted as original equipment to cars with 'cold start' specifications, but it can be fitted as an optional extra on all other models.

2 Two types of pre-engaged motor are used depending on model variant and territory. German built vehicles use the Bosch 0.7 PS motor while those models built in Britain have the Lucas M35J (pre engaged) as standard with the Lucas 5M90 as an option.

3 The method of engagement on the pre-engaged starter is that the drive pinion is brought into mesh with the starter ring gear before the main starter current is applied.

4 When the ignition is switched on, current flows from the battery to the solenoid which is mounted on the top of the starter motor body. The plunger in the solenoid moves inward so causing a centrally pivoted lever to move in such a manner that the forked end pushes the drive pinion into mesh with the starter ring gear. When the solenoid plunger reaches the end of its travel, it closes an internal contact and full starting current flows to the starter field coils. The armature is then able to rotate the crankshaft so starting the engine.

5 A special one way clutch is fitted to the starter drive pinion so that when the engine just fires and starts to operate on its own, it does not drive the starter motor.

6 The Bosch 0.7 PS is a four pole, four brush motor utilising a series field and a solenoid controlled roller clutch drive.

7 The brush gear is again fully insulated and is made up of four brushes housed in a metal brush box riveted to the commutator end bracket. Small coil springs keep the brushes in contact with the axially moulded commutator.

8 The field windings are again continuously wound with no inter connecting joints, the end of the windings being connected to the brush gear, while the other is connected to the battery through the solenoid contacts.

9 The operating position of the pivot lever is preset in manufacture and cannot be adjusted. This approach eliminates the need to set the lever to obtain correct operation of the solenoid.

10 Both the Lucas pre-engaged starter motors are similar in construction to the M35J inertia motor previously described. The drive end bracket on these motors is provided with an additional housing which serves both as a mounting point and a cover for the externally located solenoid. The actuating lever position in the drive housing is preset and cannot be adjusted, this eliminates the need to set the lever to obtain correct operation of the solenoid. The lever pivots on a pin set in the drive end bracket.

21 Starter motor (pre-engaged type) - removal and refitting

1 Disconnect the battery by removing the earth lead from the negative terminal.

2 Disconnect the starter motor cable from the terminal on the starter motor end plate.

3 Remove the two solenoid retaining nuts and the connecting strap and lift off the solenoid.

4 Remove the upper starter motor retaining bolt.

5 Working under the car, remove the lower retaining bolt, taking care to support the motor so as to prevent damage to the drive components.

6 Withdraw the starter motor from the bellhousing and lower it from the car.

7 Replacement is a straightforward reversal of the removal procedure.

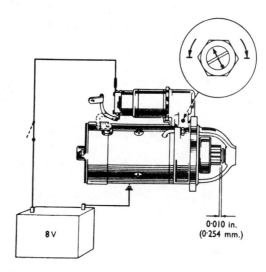

8 V 0·010 in. (0·254 mm.)

Fig. 10.16 Pre-engaged type starter endfloat (solenoid actuated) (Sec 22)

22 Starter motor (pre-engaged type) - dismantling and reassembly

Due to the fact that this type of starter motor uses a face commutator, on which the brushes make contact end on, a certain amount of thrust is created along the armature shaft. A thrust bearing is therefore incorporated in the motor at the commutator end.

1 Remove the split pin from the end of the shaft and slide off the shim(s), washer and thrust plate.

2 Remove the two screws which retain the end plate and pull off the end plate complete with the brush holders and brushes.

3 If the brushes are badly worn, cut off the brush flexible connectors as near to their terminals as possible. Solder the new brush leads to the terminal posts.

4 Cut off the other two brush flexible connectors at a distance of 1/8 inch (3.2 mm) from their connection with the field windings. Solder the new brush leads into position, localise the heat applied.

5 To remove the armature, unscrew the nuts on the holding studs at the drive end bracket.

6 Withdraw the armature complete with the drive and the one-way clutch operating lever.

7 If necessary, clean the end face of the commutator with a petrol soaked cloth. It may be carefully polished with very fine glass paper - **never use emery cloth and never undercut the mica insulation.**

8 Reassembly is a direct reversal of the above procedure, but the armature end float should be measured as indicated in Fig. 10.16. The correct endfloat should be 0.010 inch (0.254 mm) with an 8 volt current activating the solenoid. If the endfloat is found to be incorrect, it can be adjusted by fitting shims between the thrust plate and the split pin. After dismantling, always use a new split pin.

23 Fuses

The fuse box (Fig. 10.17) provides spare positions for accessories at Nos 1, 6 and 7. No 1 is live at all times while 6 and 7 are only live when the ignition is switched on. All fuses are of 8 amp rating.

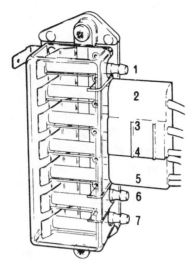

Fig. 10.17. Fuse block (Sec. 23)

1   Interior lamp, cigar lighter
2   L.H. side and tail lamp
    licence plate lamp
3   R.H. side and tail lamp
    instrument illumination
4   Main beam
5   Dipped beam
6   Direction indicators, stop
    lamps, heater motor,
    reversing lamps
7   Wiper motor

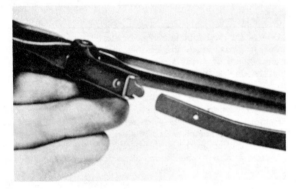

Fig. 10.18 Wiper blade connection to arm (Sec 25)

24 Direction indicator (flasher) circuit - fault tracing and rectification

1   The flasher unit is in a small metal container located in a spring clip under the dashboard on the cowl side panel. The unit is actuated by the direction indicator switch.

2   If the flasher unit fails to operate, or works very slowly or rapidly, check out the flasher indicator circuit, as detailed below, before assuming there is a fault in the unit itself.

 a) Examine the direction indicator bulbs, front and rear for broken filaments.

 b) If the external flashers are working, but the internal flasher warning light has ceased to function, check the filament in the warning light bulb and replace with a new bulb if necessary.

 c) If a flasher bulb is sound but does not work, check all the flasher circuit connections with the aid of the wiring diagram.

 d) In the event of total indicator failure, check fuse No 6 on the fusebox (if fitted). It will be fairly obvious if this fuse has blown as it also protects the stop lamps, heater motor and reversing lights (if fitted).

 e) With the ignition switched on, check that the current is reaching the flasher unit by connecting a voltmeter between the positive terminal and earth. If it is found that current is reaching the unit, connect the two flasher unit terminals together and operate the flasher switch. If the flasher warning light comes on, this proves that the flasher unit itself is at fault and must be renewed as it is not possible to dismantle and repair it.

25 Windscreen wiper blades - removal and refitting

1   The wiper blades should be renewed every year or whenever they fail to wipe the screen cleanly.

2   Lift the wiper arm away from the windscreen and remove the old blade by turning it in toward the arm and then disengage the arm from the slot in the blade.

3   To fit a new blade, slide the end of the wiper arm into the slotted spring fastening in the centre of the blade. Push the blade firmly onto the arm until the raised portion of the arm is fully home in the hole in the blade.

4   Some models use a different method of blade attachment (photo). With this type simply lift the small tang at the end of the arm and then withdraw the blade from the arm.

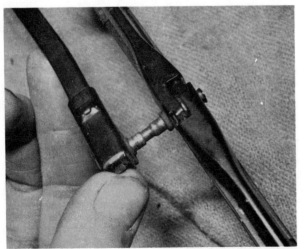

25.4 Alternative wiper blade attachment. Lift tang and withdraw blade assembly from arm

26.2 Lift cover, unscrew nut and withdraw wiper arm from splined driveshaft

26 Windscreen wiper arms - removal and refitting

1 Before removing a wiper arm, turn the windscreen wiper switch on and off to ensure the arms are in their normal parked position parallel with the bottom of the windscreen.
2 To remove an arm lift up the wiper spindle cover to expose the arm retaining nut. Unscrew this nut and detach the washer, then pull the arm off the splined pivot shaft. If the arm proves difficult to remove, a screwdriver with a large blade can be used to lever the wiper arm head off the splines. Care must be taken not to damage the splines. (photo)
3 When replacing an arm, position it so it is in the correct relative parked position and then press the arm head onto the splined drive until it is fully home on the splines.
4 Replace the washer and nut and then the spindle cover.

27 Windscreen wiper mechanism - fault diagnosis and rectification

1 Should the windscreen wipers fail, or work very slowly, then check the terminals on the motor for loose connections, and make sure that the insulation of the wiring is not cracked or broken possibly causing a short circuit. If this is in order, then check the current the motor is taking by connecting an ammeter in the circuit and turning on the wiper switch. Consumption should be between 2.3 and 3.1 amps.
2 If no current is passing through the motor, check that the switch is operating correctly.
3 If the wiper motor takes a very high current, check the wiper blades for freedom of movement. If this is satisfactory, check the gearbox cover and gear assembly for damage ·
4 If the motor takes a very low current ensure that the battery is fully charged. Check the brush gear and ensure the brushes are bearing on the commutator. If not, check the brushes for freedom of movement and, if necessary, renew the tension springs. If the brushes are very worn, they should be replaced with new ones. Check the armature by substitution if this unit is suspect.

28 Windscreen wiper motor - removal and refitting

1 Disconnect the battery by removing the negative earth lead.
2 The wiper motor is accessible from under the facia on the passenger side of the vehicle. Before the wiper motor can be removed on Ghia variants, the glovebox assembly must first be removed.
3 Locate the face level vent hose and pull this off the rear of the face level vent stub.
4 Pull the two moulded multi-plug connectors off their respective terminals on the wiper motor end housing.
5 Remove the three bolts and spring washers securing the wiper motor end housing to the wiper motor bracket. **Do not confuse these screws with the bracket retaining screws.**
6 Slightly lower the motor then unscrew the nut securing the linkage to the motor drive link and detach the motor.
7 Replacement is a reversal of the removal procedure.

29 Windscreen wiper linkage - removal and refitting

1 Refer to Section 26 and remove the windscreen wiper arms.
2 With the arms removed carefully prise the plastic covers off the wiper linkage pivot shafts, then remove the nut, washer, spacer and nylon washer from each shaft.
3 Working inside the vehicle, remove the glovebox (Ghia models only) from the passenger side of the vehicle, then pull the face level vent hose off the face level unit stub.
4 Remove the nut securing the wiper motor linkage assembly to the wiper motor driveshaft.
5 Remove the instrument cluster assembly as described in Section 50.
6 Accessible through the instrument cluster aperture, remove the two bolts securing the demister nozzle to the body. Remove the duct, via the instrument cluster aperture, after first pulling the hose off the duct stub.
7 Remove the single bolt supporting the driven side of the wiper linkage and withdraw the linkage through the instrument cluster aperture.
8 Refitting the windscreen wiper linkage is a reversal of the removal sequence. When connecting the linkage to the motor make sure that the tang on the linkage engages with the keyway on the motor driveshaft.

30 Windscreen wiper linkage pivot shaft - removal and replacement

1 Remove the windscreen wiper motor linkage, as described in Section 29.
2 Lever the pivot shaft out of its plastic balljoint. Note that for the pivot shaft at the motor end of the linkage the motor link balljoint must also be disconnected.
3 Using suitable circlip pliers remove the pivot shaft circlip and

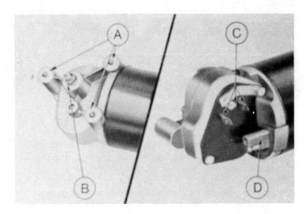

Fig. 10.19. Windscreen wiper motor (Sec. 28)

A Bracket fixing holes
B Linkage location on spindle
C Terminals (two speed control)
D Multiplug (power supply)

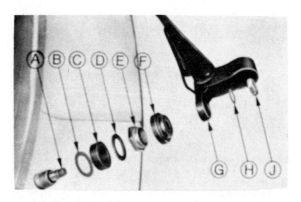

Fig. 10.20. Wiper arm assembly - exploded view (Sec. 29)

A Spindle
B Nylon spacer
C Spacer
D Washer
E Nut
F Cover
G Arm
H Washer
J Nut

Fig. 10.21. Demister duct retaining bolts (arrowed) (Sec. 29)

Fig. 10.22. Wiper linkage support bolt (driver's side, RHD)
(Sec. 29)

Fig. 10.23. Removing windscreen wiper linkage through
instrument cluster aperture

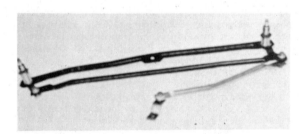

Fig. 10.24 Windscreen wiper linkage (Sec 29)

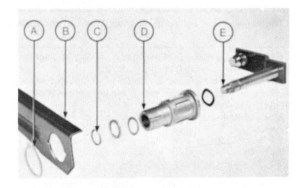

Fig. 10.25 Pivot shaft - exploded view (Sec 30)

A Circlip   D Bush
B Linkage   E Shaft
C Clip

31.1 Location of the windscreen-washer pump

withdraw the pivot shaft assembly from the linkage.
4 Prise the clip from the end of the pivot shaft and withdraw
the shaft from the bush.
5 Assemble the shaft to the bush as shown in Fig. 10.25 then
refit the assembly in the reverse sequence to that described
above.

31 Windscreen washer pump - removal and refitting

1 The windscreen washer pump is a push-fit on a lug located in
a recess in the washer bottle. (photo)

2 To remove the pump first pull the loom connector off the
plug terminals then pull the washer tube off the pump outlet.
3 Before removing the pump, either remove and drain the
washer bottle, or have a drain tray handy to catch the contents
of the bottle when the pump is pulled off its location.
4 Replacement of the pump is a reversal of the removal
process.

32 Windscreen washer jets - removal and refitting

1 Working under the bonnet, undo and remove the self-tapping

screw securing each jet to the cowl.

2   Pull off the washer hose and lift away the jet.

3   Refitting the jet is a reverse sequence to removal. Adjust the position of the jet before finally tightening the retaining screw.

33 Horn - fault diagnosis and rectification

1   If the horn operates weakly or fails to sound at all, check the wiring leading to the horn plug which is located on the body panel next to the horn itself. Also check that the plug is properly pushed home and is in a clean condition, free from corrosion etc.

2   Check that the horn is secure on its mounting and that there is nothing lying on the horn body. (photo)

3   If the fault is not an external one, remove the horn cover and check the leads inside the horn. If these are sound, check the contact breaker contacts. If these are burnt or dirty, clean them with a fine file and wipe all traces of dirt and dust away with a fuel moistened rag.

34 Headlamp - removal and refitting

1   Disconnect the battery by removing the negative earth lead.

2   Remove the radiator grille by removing the twelve retaining screws.

3   Unscrew the four crossheaded screws which retain the lamp

to the body. (photo)

4   From inside the engine compartment disconnect the parking lamp and the multiplug, then carefully detach the lamp assembly from its location.

5   Replacement is a straightforward reversal of the above procedure. After reassembly, check that the headlamps are correctly aligned, before refitting the radiator grille.

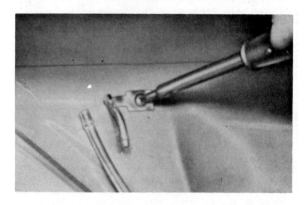

Fig. 10.26. Removing windscreen washer jet screw (Sec. 32)

33.2 Location of horn

34.3 Four crosshead screws secure the headlamp (round type) to the body

Fig. 10.27. Headlamp and mounting plate assembly retaining screws (Sec. 34)

Fig. 10.28 Removing headlamp and mounting plate assembly (Sec 34)

35 Headlamp lens and reflector - removal and refitting

1 Disconnect the battery by removing the negative earth lead.
2 Remove the radiator grille by removing the twelve retaining screws.
3 Remove the single crosshead screw located at the lower inboard edge of the lens rim. Take care not to confuse this screw with either of the headlamp adjusting screws.
4 Carefully turn the lens and reflector body in an anticlockwise direction to disengage the lens retaining slots from the headlamp adjusting screws. Do not attempt to turn these screws as this will alter the adjustment of the headlamp.
5 Lift the unit clear of the body then remove the parking lamp bulb from its location adjacent to the headlamp bulb holder. To remove the bulb holder prise the retaining clip off its location on the holder and carefully detach the holder complete with bulb.
6 Replacement is a straightforward reversal of the above procedure. After reassembly check that the headlamps are correctly aligned before refitting the radiator grille.

36 Headlamp - bulb renewal

1 Remove the headlamp lens and reflector assembly as previously described.
2 Release the bulb holder retaining clip and push the plastic bulb holder cover up the loom wires to give access to the rubber multiplug connection.
3 Disconnect this plug from the bulb terminals then turn the

bulb retaining plate in an anticlockwise direction to disengage the lugs. Lift the retaining plate and spring clear of the bulb then lift the bulb from the reflector. (photos)
4 When handling halogen bulbs it is important that the glass of the bulb is not touched. If the glass is inadvertently handled it **must** be wiped clean with methylated spirits **before** the lamps are switched on. Failure to observe this precaution will result in a 'blown' bulb.
5 Replacement is a straightforward reversal of the above procedure. After reassembly check that the headlamps are correctly aligned before refitting the radiator grille.

37 Headlamps (sealed beam) - alignment

1 It is always advisable to have the headlamps aligned on proper optical beam setting equipment but if this is not available, the following procedure may be used.
2 Position the car on level ground 13 ft (4 m) in front of a dark wall or board. The wall or board must be at right angles to the centre line of the car.
3 Draw a vertical line on the board in line with the centre line of the car.
4 Bounce the car on its suspension to ensure correct settlement and then measure the height between the ground and the centre of the headlamps. (H) (Fig. 10.33).
5 Draw a horizontal line across the board at this measured height, less 20 cm (H-X).
6 On this horizontal line mark a cross on either side of, and equidistant from, the vertical line. The distance between the

Fig. 10.29. Headlamp adjusting screws (A) and retaining screw (B) (Sec. 35)

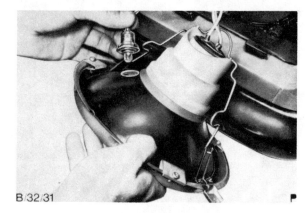

Fig. 10.31. Removing parking lamp bulb holder from reflector body (Sec. 35)

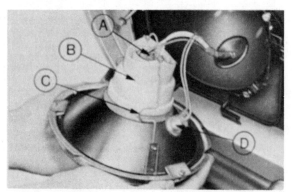

Fig. 10.30. Removing lens and reflector assembly (Sec. 35)

A Multiplug   C Retaining clip
B Cap   D Parking lamp

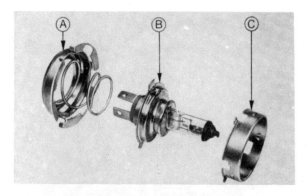

Fig. 10.32. Halogen bulb assembly (Sec. 36)

A Retaining plate   C Locking ring
B Bulb

36.3A Release the spring clip and then remove the plastic cover and the rubber multi-plug

36.3B Turn the bulb retainer anticlockwise to release it

36.3C Withdraw the bulb. If it is of the halogen type do not touch the glass with the fingers (see text)

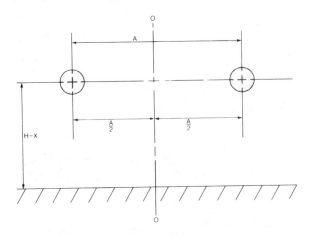

Fig. 10.33. Headlamp alignment - sealed beam (circular only) (Sec. 37)

A = distance between headlamp centres
H = height from around to lamp centres ($X = 8$ in), 0 - 0 = vehicle centre line

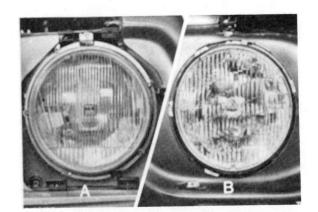

Fig. 10.34 Headlamp identification (Secs 37 and 38)

A   Sealed beam
B   Semi sealed beam

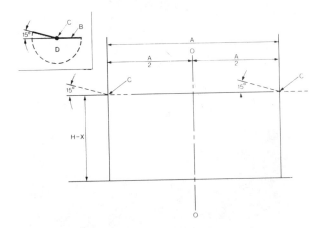

Fig. 10.35. Headlamp alignment - semi sealed beam (circular or square) (Sec. 38)

A =	distance between headlamp centres	0-0 =	vehicle centre line
H =	height from ground to lamp centres ($X = 8.0$ in)	D =	dipped beam pattern,
		C =	dipped beam centre
		B =	light/dark boundary

two crosses must be equal to the distance between the headlamp centres (A).
7   Switch the headlamps on to *dipped* beam.
8   By carefully adjusting the horizontal and vertical adjusting screws on each lamp, align the centres of each beam onto the crosses which you have previously marked on the horizontal line.
9   Bounce the car again and check that the beams return to the correct positions. At the same time check the operation of the headlamp flasher.

38 Headlamps (semi-sealed beam) - alignment

1   Position the car on level ground 33 ft (10 m) in front of a dark wall or board as described in Section 37.
2   Switch the headlamps to *dipped* beam.
3   Cover the right-hand headlamp and, by carefully adjusting the horizontal adjusting screws, align the lamp so that the inter-section of the horizontal and angled light pattern coincides with the vertical line on the aiming board.
4   Similarly adjust the vertical screw so that the light/dark intersection of the beam pattern coincides with the 15° dotted line on the aiming board (see line 'B', inset of Fig. 10.35).
5   Cover the left-hand headlamp and adjust the right-hand lamp horizontal and vertical alignment in the same way as for the left-hand lamp. Switch off the headlamps.

39 Front sidelight bulb - removal and refitting

1   Remove the headlamp lens and reflector assembly as described in Section 35.
2   Pull the sidelight bulb assembly from its location in the headlight body. (photo)
3   Remove the bulb by depressing, twisting and withdrawing from the holder.
4   Refitting the sidelight bulb and holder is the reverse sequence to removal. Make sure the holder fits tightly against the reflector body to prevent water ingress.

40 Front direction indicator lamp assembly - removal and refitting

1   Undo and remove the two bolts retaining the direction indicator lamp to the front bumper.
2   From inside the engine compartment disconnect the lamp wires from the engine compartment loom multiplug and detach the lamp assembly, complete with wire, from the front bumper.
3   Refitting the front direction indicator lamp assembly is the reverse sequence to removal.

41 Front direction indicator lamp bulb - removal and refitting

1   Undo and remove the two crosshead screws securing the lens to the lamp body and lift away the lens.
2   Remove the bulb by depressing, twisting and withdrawing from the holder.
3   Refitting the bulb and lens is the reverse sequence to removal. Make sure that the lens gasket is correctly seated to prevent dirt or water ingress.

42 Auxiliary lamp assembly - removal and refitting

1   Open the bonnet and disconnect the battery, for safety reasons.
2   Remove the nut and washer assembly securing the lamp to its mounting bracket and lift the lamp off the bracket.
3   Detach the lamp lead from the main wiring loom and completely remove the lamp assembly.
4   Refitting the auxiliary lamp is the reverse sequence to its removal. Re-align the beam as described in Section 44.

39.2 The sidelight bulb is simply pulled from its location in the headlamp shell

Fig. 10.36. Headlamp adjusting screws - square headlamps (Sec. 38)

A   Vertical   B   Horizontal

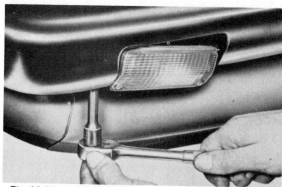

Fig. 10.37. Removing direction indicator lamp body from front bumper

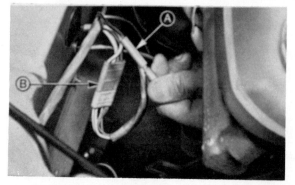

Fig. 10.38. Removing direction indicator lead (A) from headlamp loom (B)

Fig. 10.39. Removing front indicator lamp lens retaining screws

43 Auxiliary lamp bulb - removal and refitting

1 Undo and remove the crosshead screw on the lens rim and draw the lens assembly forward off the lamp body.
2 Disconnect the bulb wire from the loom snap-connector.
3 Release the spring clip and withdraw the bulb from the reflector body.
4 Refitting bulb and lens assembly is the reverse sequence to removal. Make sure that the cut-out at the top of the reflector body engages with the lug on the lamp body.

44 Auxiliary lamp beam alignment

1 It is always advisable to have the auxiliary lamps aligned using special optical beam setting equipment but if this is not available the following procedure may be used.
2 Check the tyre pressures and adjust as necessary. Remove any luggage from the boot or load space then bounce the front of the vehicle to ensure that the suspension has settled.
3 Place the car on level ground and locate a white board marked as shown in Fig.10.42 3 m (10 ft) from the front of the vehicle at 90º to the car axis.
4 Cover the headlamps and the second auxiliary lamp to prevent glare whilst carrying out the adjustment.
5 Adjust the beam so that the centre of brightest illumination lies at the intersection of the horizontal and vertical dividing

lines on the board.
6 Adjust the second auxiliary lamp in a similar manner to the first one.

45 Rear lamp assembly (saloon) - removal and refitting

1 Working inside the boot compartment remove the spare wheel and the plastic caps from the nuts securing the rear lamp body.

Left-hand lamp
2 Undo and remove the two nuts and washers, pull the lamp assembly off the body and remove the lamp leads after first noting the terminal connection. (Fig. 10.44).

Right-hand lamp
3 Undo and remove the crosshead screws securing the lamp lens to the lamp body and detach the lens (Fig. 10.45).
4 Remove the single crosshead screw exposed by the removal of the lamp lens, from its location in the reflector body. Fig. 10.46).
and washer securing the lamp to the vehicle body.
6 Pull the lamp assembly rearwards, off the body and disconnect the lamp leads, after first making a note of their respective positions.
7 Refitting either lamp is a reversal of the removal procedure.

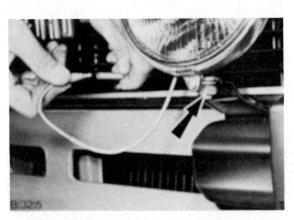

Fig. 10.40 Auxiliary lamp power supply and retaining nut (arrowed) (Sec 43)

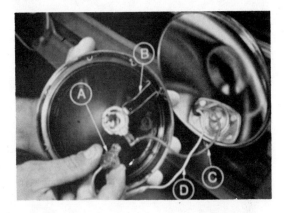

Fig. 10.41 Removing auxiliary lamp bulb (Sec 43)

A *Bulb*   C *Earth lead*
B *Clip*   D *Power supply*

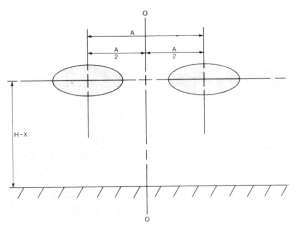

Fig. 10.42 Auxiliary lamp alignment (Sec 44)

A = *Distance between lamp centres*
H = *Height from ground to lamp centres (X = 2.0 in)*
OO = *Vehicle centre line*

Fig. 10.43. Rear lamp body retaining nuts in luggage compartment (Sec. 45)

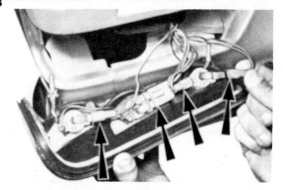

Fig. 10.44 Removing leads from rear lamp terminals (saloon) (Sec 45)

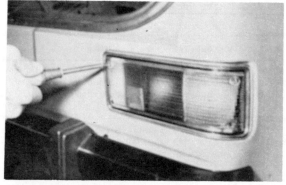

Fig. 10.45 Removing rear lamp lens retaining screws (Sec 45

Fig. 10.46 Rear lamp assembly: rear lamp body retaining screw (arrowed) lens removed (Sec 45)

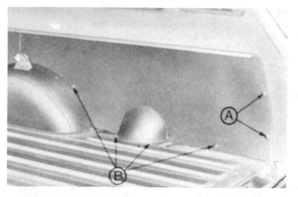

Fig. 10.47 Estate car load space panel retaining screws (Sec 46)

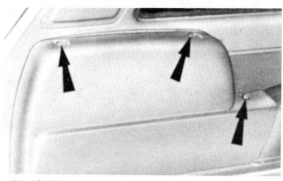

Fig. 10.48 Estate car load space panel retaining screws (spare wheel side) (Sec 46)

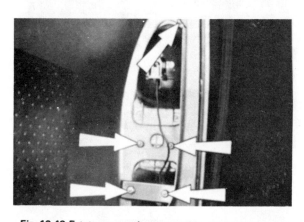

Fig. 10.49 Estate car rear lamp assembly retaining nuts and lower plate (Sec 46)

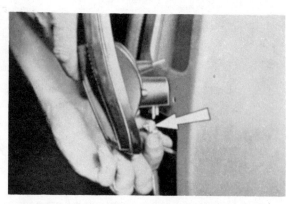

Fig. 10.50 Removing rear lamp assembly (estate car): detaching lower terminal lead (arrowed) (Sec 46)

Fig. 10.51 Removing rear lamp bulb (Sec 4)

46 Rear lamp assembly (estate car) - removal and refitting

1 Open the tailgate and remove the load space trim panel on the appropriate side of the vehicle.
2 Disconnect the upper lead to the rear lamp assembly.
3 The lamp assembly is secured to the body by five nuts. The two lower nuts are used in conjunction with a metal strap. Undo and remove the five nuts and strap, pull the lamp assembly off the body and disconnect the lower lead.
4 Reassembly is a reversal of the removal procedure.

47 Rear lamp bulb - removal and refitting

1 The rear lamp assembly incorporates the following bulbs: reverse, rear/stop and direction indicator.
2 Undo and remove the crosshead screws securing the lens to the lamp body, and lift away the lens.
3 The relevant bulb is removed by depressing, turning anticlockwise and withdrawing from the holder.
4 Refitting a bulb and lens is a reversal of the removal process. Ensure that the small nylon washers are correctly located under the screw heads and that the screws are not overtightened, or cracking of the lens may result.

48 Rear number plate lamp bulb - removal and refitting

1 Depress the spring clips on each end of the lamp and

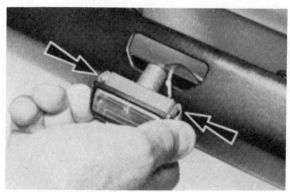

Fig. 10.52. Depressing clips (arrowed) to facilitate removal of licence plate lamp (Sec. 48)

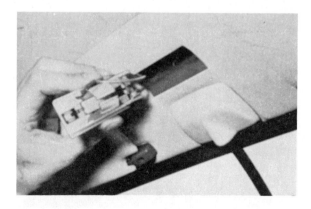

Fig. 10.54 Removing interior lamp assembly from roof (Sec 49)

carefully prise the lamp out of the bumper.
2 From inside the boot disconnect the lamp wires from the main beam.
3 Disengage the bulb cover and lens from the lamp body by disengaging the cover from the lugs on the lamp body.
4 Remove the bulb by depressing, turning anticlockwise and withdrawing from the body.
5 Refitting the bulb is the reverse sequence to removal.

49 Interior bulbs - removal and refitting

Interior light bulb
1 Carefully prise the lamp assembly from its location in the roof panel.
2 Disconnect the leads to the lamp and remove the bulb from its holder.
3 Refitting the bulb and lamp is a reversal of their removal.

Quadrant lamp bulb (automatic transmission)
1 Carefully ease the automatic transmission lever quadrant up and away from the floor.
2 Slide the bulb holder out of its location adjacent to the base of the selector lever and pull the bulb from the holder. (Fig. 10.56).
3 Refitting the bulb and quadrant is the reverse sequence to removal.

Heated rear window warning light bulb
1 Place a wad of padding below the switch and, using a thin

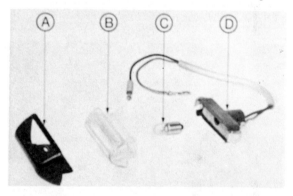

Fig. 10.53. Licence plate lamp - exploded view

A Cover   C Bulb
B Lens   D Body

Fig. 10.55 Removing quadrant (A) to expose bulb holder (B) (Sec 49)

bladed screwdriver, carefully prise the switch from its location in the heater cover panel.

2 The bulb holder is attached to the lower of the two sets of leads entering the rear of the switch. Pull the holder out of its location and remove the bulb.

3 Refitting the bulb and switch is the reverse of the removal procedure.

Hazard warning light bulb

The removal procedure for this bulb is identical to that described above for the HRW bulb.

50 Instrument cluster - removal and refitting

1 For safety reasons, disconnect the battery.

2 Remove one or two screws, holding the edge of the insulator pad to the lower edge of the instrument panel and reach up behind the cluster to disengage the speedometer cable.

3 Remove the upper half of the steering column shroud.

4 Remove the four instrument cluster retaining screws (see Fig. 10.59), pull the cluster away from the dash location and disconnect the wiring loom connectors.

5 Refitting the instrument cluster is a reversal of the removal sequence. Check the gauges, warning lights and instruments at the earliest opportunity.

51 Instrument cluster printed circuit (models with tachometer) - removal and refitting

1 Refer to Section 50 and remove the instrument cluster.

2 With the cluster removed and working on the rear face of the cluster unclip the loom from the lower edge of the cluster and pull the speedometer and tachometer bulb holders from their locations in the rear of these instruments.

3 Undo and remove the terminal nuts from their locations on the rear of the tachometer, then undo the single retaining screw and unclip and detach the printed circuit from the rear of the tachometer.

4 Remove the tachometer, as detailed in Section 60.

5 Remove the speedometer head, as detailed in Section 56.

6 Remove the single screw securing the instrument voltage regulator and lift the regulator off the cluster. Pull the five remaining bulb holders from their locations then unscrew and remove the remaining four terminal nuts and detach the printed circuit.

7 Reassembly of the printed circuit is a reversal of the removal procedure.

52 Instrument cluster printed circuit (models without tachometer) - removal and refitting

1 Refer to Section 50, and remove the instrument cluster.

2 Remove the instrument gauge and speedometer bulb holders and unclip and remove their loom from the rear of the cluster assembly.

3 Undo and remove the four screws holding the speedometer head to the cluster body and, similarly, the screws securing the fuel and temperature gauges, and remove the head and gauges.

4 Dismantle the fuel/temperature gauge assembly, as described in Section 58, and remove the gauge printed circuit.

5 Pull the five warning bulbs from their locations in the centre

Fig. 10.56 Removing quadrant lamp bulb (Sec 49)

A Bulb   B Holder

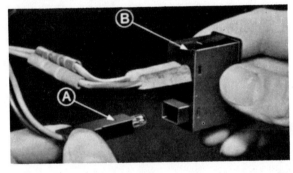

Fig. 10.57 Heated rear window warning lamp bulb (Sec 49)

A Holder   B Switch

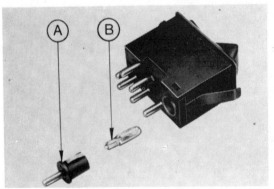

Fig. 10.58. Hazard switch and bulb (Sec. 49)

A Holder   B Bulb

Fig. 10.59. Instrument cluster retaining screws (Sec. 50)

Fig. 10.60. Removing instrument cluster assembly (Sec. 51)

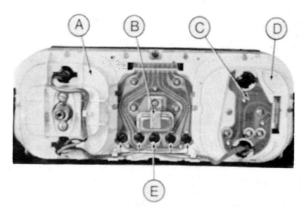

Fig. 10.61. Rear view of instrument cluster (Sec. 50)

A Speedometer   circuit
B Instrument regulator   D Tachometer
C Tachometer printed   E Warning lamps

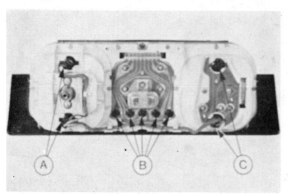

Fig. 10.62. Instrument cluster assembly (Sec. 52)

A Speedometer head bulb   C Tachometer bulb
B Warning lamp bulb

Fig. 10.63 Instrument housing screw locations on cluster bezel (Sec. 53)

removal. Do not forget to wipe off all traces of dust before refitting.

54 Instrument voltage regulator - removal and refitting

1 Refer to Section 50, and remove the instrument cluster.
2 Undo and remove the screw that secures the voltage regulator to the rear of the instrument cluster and detach the regulator and, where fitted, the radio suppressor filter.
3 Refitting the regulator is a reversal of the removal sequence.

55 Instrument cluster bulb - removal and refitting

1 Refer to Section 50 and remove the instrument cluster.
2 Carefully pull the relevant bulb holder from its location on the rear of the cluster and remove the bulb.
3 Refitting the bulb and instrument cluster is the reverse sequence to removal.

Fig. 10.64. Removing speedometer assembly from instrument cluster (Sec. 56)

lower edge of the cluster and detach the printed circuit.
6 Refitting the instrument cluster printed circuit is a reversal of the removal procedure.

53 Instrument cluster glass - removal and refitting

1 Remove the instrument cluster assembly, as described in Section 50.
2 Undo and remove the five screws securing the instrument cluster bezel to the cluster body, detach the bezel and lift away the cluster glass.
3 Refitting the instrument cluster glass is the reverse of its

56 Speedometer head - removal and refitting

1 Remove the instrument cluster assembly, as described in Section 50.
2 Pull the two head illuminating bulb holders, from their location, locally remove the loom and set the loom and holders to one side, clear of the working area.
3 Undo and remove the four screws securing the speedometer head housing to the instrument cluster body and lift away the housing complete with the head.
4 Undo and remove the two screws securing the head to the head housing and detach the head.
5 Refitting the speedometer head is the reverse of its removal.

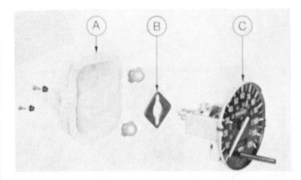

Fig. 10.65. Speedometer assembly exploded view (Sec. 56)

A Housing   B Mounting pad   C Head

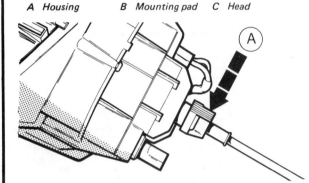

Fig. 10.67. Speedometer cable connection at head - removed cable from head by depressing arrowed section 'A' (Sec. 57)

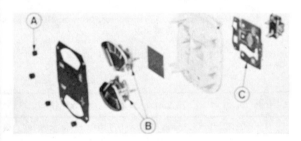

Fig. 10.69. Fuel and temperature gauge assembly - exploded view (Sec. 58)

A Mounting rubbers   C Printed circuit
B Gauges

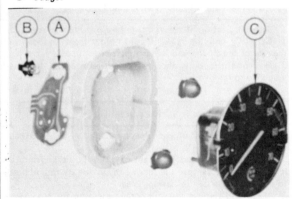

Fig. 10.71. Tachometer assembly - exploded view (Sec. 60)

A Printed circuit   B Bulb   C Head

Fig. 10.66 Speedometer cable location in gearbox casing (Sec 57)

A Cable   B Circlip

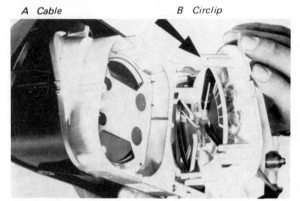

Fig. 10.68. Removing fuel and temperature gauge assembly (Sec. 58)

Fig. 10.70. Removing tachometer assembly from housing

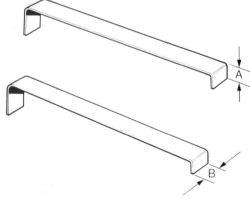

Fig. 10.72 Clock removal strips: dimension A = 4 mm, B = 10 mm (Sec 63)

57 Speedometer inner and outer cables - removal and refitting

1 Chock the rear wheels jack-up the front end of the vehicle and support on firmly based stands.

2 Locate the cable entry in the side of the gearbox, and, using a pair of circlip pliers, remove the retaining circlip and pull the cable from the gearbox.

3 Unclip the cable from its clips along the sidemembers and underbody.

4 From inside the vehicle remove the sound insulating cover sufficiently to gain access to the rear of the instrument cluster. Locate the cable and press down the grooved section of the cable clip to disengage the locking catch; the cable can then be pulled from the speedometer head.

5 The cable can then be pulled through the engine compartment rear bulkhead and into the engine compartment.

6 Refitting the cable is a reversal of the removal procedure.

58 Fuel gauge (instrument clusters without tachometer) - removal and refitting

1 Remove the instrument cluster assembly, as described in Section 50.

2 Remove the gauge illuminating bulb holders and locally detach the bulb loom.

3 Undo and remove the four screws securing the gauge housing to the instrument cluster body and lift away the housing, complete with gauges.

4 Remove the two nuts from the gauge studs and lift the gauge off the gauge housing.

5 Replacement is a reversal of removal, but when inserting the gauge in the cluster body ensure that the four rubber sleeves are correctly located over the housing pegs before fitting the gauge housing.

59 Temperature gauge (instrument clusters without tachometer) - removal and refitting

The procedure for removing and refitting the temperature gauge is identical to that described in Section 58 for the removal and installation of the fuel gauge.

60 Tachometer - removal and refitting

1 Remove the instrument cluster assembly, as described in Section 50.

2 Remove the illuminating bulb holder and locally remove the bulb holder wiring loom.

3 Undo and remove the four screws securing the tachometer housing to the instrument cluster body and lift the housing, complete with tachometer off the body.

4 Undo and remove the two screws and three terminal nuts retaining the tachometer to the housing and detach the tachometer.

5 Replacement of the tachometer is a reversal of the removal procedure.

61 Fuel gauge (instrument clusters fitted with tachometer) - removal and refitting

1 Remove the instrument cluster and then remove the speedometer head and tachometer, as described in Sections 56 and 60 respectively.

2 Remove the single screw securing the voltage regulator and lift the regulator off the cluster body.

3 Undo and remove the four screws securing the gauge housing to the cluster body and lift the housing complete with gauges off the body.

4 Remove the two nuts securing the gauge studs to the housing and withdraw the gauge from the housing.

5 Replacement is a reversal of the removal procedure.

62 Temperature gauge - removal and refitting

The procedure for removing and refitting the temperature gauge is identical to that described in Section 61 for the removal and installation of the fuel gauge.

63 Electric clock - removal and refitting

1 The electric clock is housed in a cut-out in the tunnel mounted centre console. To remove the clock two strips of metal must be formed to the dimensions shown in Fig. 10.72.

2 Insert the metal formers either side of the clock and pull the clock out of its cut-out. Disconnect the wiring leads to the clock and lift the clock and bezel assembly off the centre console.

3 Push the clock assembly out of the bezel.

4 Replacement of the clock and bezel assembly is a reversal of the removal procedure.

64 Cigarette lighter - removal and refitting

1 The cigarette lighter is housed in the heater cover panel and to gain access for its removal the cover panel must first be removed; on certain models this will entail the removal of the radio or centre console. The removal and installation of these components is fully described in Chapter 12.

2 Undo and remove the four screws securing the upper edge of the heater cover panel and the two screws securing the lower edge and pull the cover rearwards off the instrument panel.

3 Pull the element out of the cigarette lighter body and the wiring loom off the rear of the light body.

4 Push the locking collar and integral bulb holder in against spring tension and then turn anticlockwise to disengage the locking tangs. Withdraw the body and plastic collar from the aperture in the heater cover panel.

5 Reassembly of the cigarette lighter and cover panel is a reversal of the removal procedure.

65 Ignition switch - removal and refitting

1 For safety reasons, disconnect the battery.

2 Remove the steering column assembly, as described in Chapter 11.

3 With the column securely held in a vice use a suitable diameter drill to drill out the two shear bolts securing the switch to the column bracket, and lift the switch off the column.

Fig. 10.73. Heater cover panel retaining screws (Sec. 64)

Fig. 10.74. Cigarette lighter assembly, showing combined locking ring and bulb holder (arrowed) (Sec. 64)

Fig. 10.75 Drilling out ignition switch (A) shear bolts (B) (Sec 65)

Fig. 10.76. Light switch (Sec. 66)

A Retaining screws   B Loom multi-plug

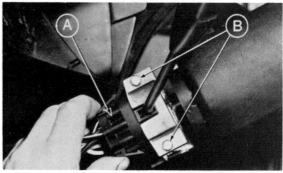

Fig. 10.77. Direction indicator switch (Sec. 67)

A Loom multi-plug   B Retaining screws

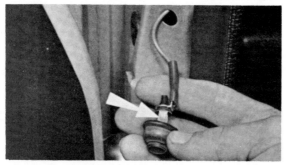

Fig. 10.78 Courtesy light switch (arrowed)

Fig. 10.79. Prising hazard switch from its location in heater cover panel. Note use of protective pad

Fig. 10.80 Heater blower switch (arrowed) on rear of heater control panel

Fig. 10.81 Auxiliary lamp relay location on fender apron; note earth connection under bracket retaining screw (sec. 72).

4   Check that the pawl of the new switch is projecting, engage the pawl with the cut-out in the column and align the body of the switch with the column mounting bracket.

5   Fit the new shear bolts through the bracket into the switch body and tighten the bolts until the heads shear off.

6   Replace the steering column in the vehicle as described in Chapter 11.

66 Light switch - removal and refitting

1   For safety reasons, disconnect the battery.

2   Prise the rubber cap off the head of the screw securing the upper half of the steering column shroud. Undo and remove the screw and lift off the upper half of the shroud.

3   Remove the three screws securing the lower half of the shroud and lower the shroud off the column.

4   Pull the two multiplugs off the switch then undo and remove the two bolts securing the switch and lift the switch off the column.

5   Replacement of the light switch is a reversal of the removal procedure.

67 Direction indicator switch - removal and refitting

The removal and installation of the direction indicator switch is identical to that described in Section 66 for the light switch.

68 Switches - general - removal and refitting

Courtesy light

1   Ease the switch from the door pillar and detach the wiring loom.

2   Refitting the switch is the reverse sequence to removal.

Stoplight

1   Working inside the vehicle remove the insulation panel from under the instrument panel on the driver's side (where fitted).

2   Disconnect the two terminal connectors from the switch, then undo and remove the front locknut securing the switch to the pedal mounting bracket. Lift the switch away from the bracket.

3   Refitting the switch is a reversal of its removal. Before tightening the locknut, position the switch so that the stop-lights operate within 0.2 to 0.8 in (5 to 20 mm) of forward movement of the brake pedal.

Brake warning light (LHD models only)

1   Clean the area around the brake differential valve body, then disconnect the multiplug from the switch body.

2   Wipe the top of the brake master cylinder reservoir, unscrew the cap and place a piece of polythene over the top of the reservoir neck. Refit the cap. This is to prevent the loss of hydraulic fluid during subsequent operations.

3   Unscrew the switch from the differential valve body.

4   Refitting the switch is a reversal of the removal procedure.

69 Heated rear window switch - removal and refitting

1   Place a wad of padding below the switch and using a thin bladed screwdriver, carefully prise the switch from its location in the heater cover panel.

2   Disconnect the leads from the rear of the switch.

3   Refitting the HRW switch is a reversal of the removal procedure.

70 Emergency flasher switch - removal and refitting

The removal and installation of the flasher switch is identical to that described in Section 69 HRW switch removal and refitting.

71 Heater motor switch - removal and refitting

1   Remove the heater control assembly, as described in Chapter 12.

2   From the rear of the control assembly undo and remove the two screws securing the switch and lift the switch off the control panel.

3   Refitting the switch is the reverse sequence to removal.

72 Auxiliary lamp relay - removal and refitting

1   The auxiliary lamp relay is located on the fender apron adjacent to the battery. To remove the relay pull off the multiplug then undo and remove the two crosshead screws securing the relay to the body.

2   Refitting is a reversal of removal.

73 Heated rear window relay - removal and refitting

1   The heated rear window relay is located on the underside of the instrument panel adjacent to the steering column. To remove the relay pull off the multiplug then undo and remove the two crosshead screws securing the relay to the body.

2   Refitting is a reversal of removal.

74 Direction indicator relay - removal and refitting

1   Disconnect the battery, and remove the instrument cluster assembly, as detailed in Section 50.

2   Accessible through the instrument cluster aperture in the instrument panel, unclip the direction indicator relay from its location on the steering column bracket. Disconnect the multiplug from the relay and remove the relay from the vehicle.

3   Replacing the relay is a reversal of the removal procedure.

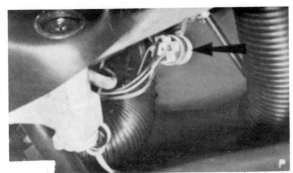

Fig. 10.82. Heated rear window relay (Sec. 73)

Fig. 10.83 Direction indicator relay viewed through instrument cluster aperture (Sec 74)

75 Fault diagnosis - electrical system

Symptom	Reason/s	Remedy
Starter motor fails to turn engine		
No electricity at starter motor	Battery discharged	Charge battery.
	Battery defective internally	Fit new battery.
	Battery terminal leads loose or earth lead not securely attached to body	Check and tighten leads.
	Loose or broken connections in starter motor circuit	Check all connections and tighten any that are loose.
	Starter motor switch or solenoid faulty	Test and replace faulty components with new.
Electricity at starter motor: faulty motor	Starter motor pinion jammed in mesh with flywheel gear ring	Disengage pinion by turning squared end of armature shaft.
	Starter brushes badly worn, sticking, or brush wires loose	Examine brushes, replace as necessary, tighten down brush wires.
	Commutator dirty, worn, or burnt	Clean commutator, recut if badly burnt.
	Starter motor armature faulty	Overhaul starter motor, fit new armature.
	Field coils earthed	Overhaul starter motor.
Starter motor turns engine very slowly		
Electrical defects	Battery in discharged condition	Charge battery.
	Starter brushes badly worn, sticking or, brush wires loose	Examine brushes, replace as necessary, tighten down brush wires.
	Loose wires in starter motor circuit	Check wiring and tighten as necessary.
Starter motor operates without turning engine		
Dirt or oil on drive gear	Starter motor pinion sticking on the screwed sleeve	Remove starter motor, clean starter motor drive.
Mechanical damage	Pinion or flywheel gear teeth broken or worn	Fit new gear ring to flywheel, and a new pinion to starter motor drive.
Starter motor noisy or excessively rough engagement		
Lack of attention or mechanical damage	Pinion or flywheel gear teeth broken or worn	Fit new gear teeth to flywheel, or new pinion to starter motor drive.
	Starter drive main spring broken.	Dismantle and fit new main spring.
	Starter motor retaining bolts loose	Tighten starter motor securing bolts. Fit new spring washer if necessary.
Battery will not hold charge for more than a few days		
Wear or damage	Battery defective internally	Remove and fit new battery.
	Electrolyte level too low or electrolyte too weak due to leakage	Top up electrolyte level to just above plates.
	Plate separators no longer fully effective	Remove and fit new battery.
	Battery plates severely sulphated	Remove and fit new battery.
Insufficient current flow to keep battery charged	Fan/alternator belt slipping	Check belt for wear, replace if necessary, and tighten.
	Battery terminal connections loose or corroded	Check terminals for tightness, and remove all corrosion.
	Alternator not charging properly	Remove and overhaul alternator
	Short in lighting circuit causing continual battery drain.	Trace and rectify.
	Regulator unit not working correctly	Check setting, clean, and renew if defective.
Ignition light fails to go out, battery runs flat in a few days		
Alternator not charging	Fan belt loose and slipping, or broken	Check, renew and tighten as necessary.
	Brushes worn, sticking, broken, or dirty	Examine, clean, or renew brushes as necessary.
	Brush springs weak or broken	Examine and test. Renew as necessary.
Regulator or cut-out fails to work correctly	Regulator incorrectly set	Adjust regulator correctly.
	Cut-out incorrectly set	Adjust cut-out correctly.
	Open circuit in wiring of cut-out and regulator unit	Remove, examine, and renew as necessary.

Failure of individual electrical equipment to function correctly is dealt with alphabetically, item-by-item, under the headings listed below :

Symptom	Reason/s	Remedy
Fuel gauge		
Fuel gauge gives no reading	Fuel tank empty!	Fill fuel tank.
	Electric cable between tank sender unit and gauge earthed or loose	Check cable for earthing and joints for tightness.
	Fuel gauge case not earthed	Ensure case is well earthed.
	Fuel gauge supply cable interrupted	Check and renew cable if necessary.
	Fuel gauge unit broken	Renew fuel gauge.
Fuel gauge registers full all the time	Electric cable between tank unit and gauge broken or disconnected	Check over cable and repair as necessary.
Horn		
Horn operates all the time	Horn push either earthed or stuck down	Disconnect battery earth. Check and rectify source of trouble.
	Horn cable to horn push earthed	Disconnect battery earth. Check and rectify source of trouble.
Horn fails to operate	Blown fuse	Check and renew if broken. Ascertain cause.
	Cable or cable connection loose, broken or disconnected	Check all connections for tightness and cables for breaks.
	Horn has an internal fault	Remove and overhaul horn.
Horn emits intermittent or unsatisfactory noise	Cable connections loose	Check and tighten all connections.
	Horn incorrectly adjusted	Adjust horn until best note obtained.
Lights		
Lights do not come on	If engine not running, battery discharged	Push-start car, charge battery.
	Light bulb filament burnt out or bulbs broken	Test bulbs in live bulb holder.
	Wire connections loose, disconnected or broken	Check all connections for tightness and wire cable for breaks.
	Light switch shorting or otherwise faulty	By-pass light switch to ascertain if fault is in switch and fit new switch as appropriate.
Lights come on but fade out	If engine not running battery discharged	Push-start car, and charge battery.
Lights give very poor illumination	Lamp glasses dirty	Clean glasses.
	Reflector tarnished or dirty	Fit new units.
	Lamps badly out of adjustment	Adjust lamps correctly.
	Incorrect bulb with too low wattage fitted	Remove bulb and replace with correct grade.
	Existing bulbs old and badly discoloured	Renew bulb units.
	Electrical wiring too thin not allowing full current to pass	Rewire lighting system.
Lights work erratically - flashing on and off, especially over bumps	Battery terminals or earth connection loose	Tighten battery terminals and earth connection.
	Lights not earthing properly	Examine and rectify.
	Contacts in light switch faulty	By-pass light switch to ascertain if fault is in switch and fit new switch as appropriate.
Wipers		
Wiper motor fails to work	Blown fuse	Check and renew fuse.
	Wire connections loose, disconnected, or broken	Check wiper wiring. Tighten loose connections.
	Brushes badly worn	Remove and fit new brushes.
	Armature worn or faulty	If electricity at wiper motor remove and overhaul and fit replacement armature.
	Field coils faulty	Purchase reconditioned wiper motor.
Wiper motor works very slowly and takes excessive current	Commutator dirty, greasy, or burnt	Clean commutator thoroughly.
	Drive to wheelboxes too bent or unlubricated	Examine drive and straighten out severe curvature. Lubricate.
	Wheelbox spindle binding or damaged	Remove, overhaul, or fit replacement.
	Armature bearings dry or unaligned	Renew with new bearings correctly aligned.

Symptom	Reason/s	Remedy
	Armature badly worn or faulty	Remove, overhaul, or fit replacement armature.
Wiper motor works slowly and takes little current	Brushes badly worn Commutator dirty, greasy, or burnt Armature badly worn or faulty	Remove and fit new brushes. Clean commutator thoroughly. Remove and overhaul armature or fit replacement.
Wiper motor works but wiper blades remain static	Driving cable rack disengaged or faulty Wheelbox gear and spindle damaged or worn. Wiper motor gearbox parts badly worn	Examine and if faulty, renew. Examine and if faulty, renew. Overhaul or fit new gearbox.

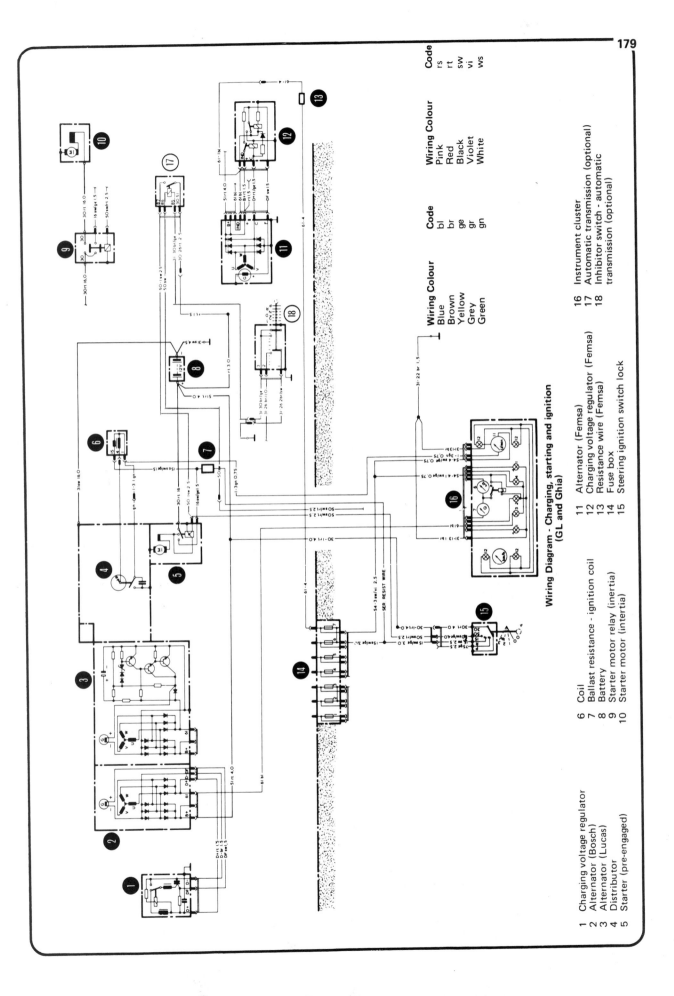

Wiring Diagram - Charging, starting and ignition (GL and Ghia)

1	Charging voltage regulator	6	Coil
2	Alternator (Bosch)	7	Ballast resistance - ignition coil
3	Alternator (Lucas)	8	Battery
4	Distributor	9	Starter motor relay (inertia)
5	Starter (pre-engaged)	10	Starter motor (intertia)

11	Alternator (Femsa)
12	Charging voltage regulator (Femsa)
13	Resistance wire (Femsa)
14	Fuse box
15	Steering ignition switch lock

16	Instrument cluster
17	Automatic transmission (optional)
18	Inhibitor switch - automatic transmission (optional)

Wiring Colour
Blue
Brown
Yellow
Grey
Green

Code
bl
br
ge
gr
gn

Wiring Colour
Pink
Red
Black
Violet
White

Code
rs
rt
sw
vi
ws

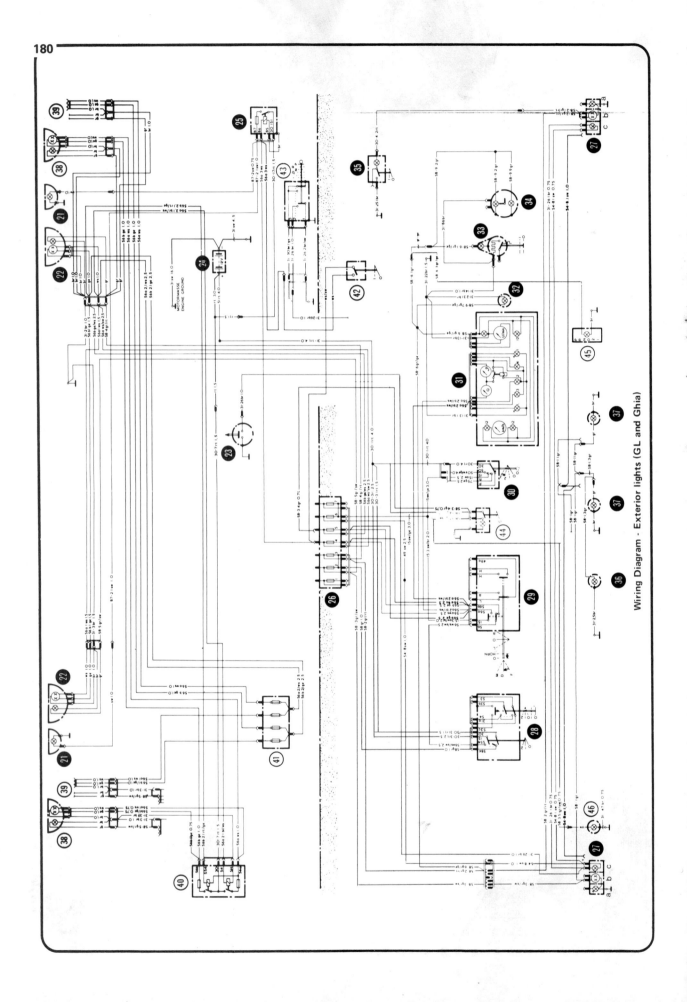

Wiring Diagram - Exterior lights (GL and Ghia)

Key to Wiring Diagram - Exterior lights (GL and Ghia)

21 Auxiliary driving lamp
22 Headlamp - main beam
23 Reversing lamp switch
24 Battery
25 Auxiliary driving lamp relay
26 Fuse box (seven way)
27 Combined tail lamp
    b - tail lamps
    c - reversing lamps
28 Light switch
29 Flasher switch
30 Steering lock ignition switch
31 Instrument cluster
    2 Main beam indicator lamp
    12 Instrument illumination
32 Heater blower switch illumination
33 Cigarette lighter
34 Choke
35 Load compartment lamp (Estate car only)
36 Luggage compartment lamp
37 Numer plate lamps
38 Headlamp - main beam (Sweden)
39 Headlamp - main beam (Italy)
40 Dimmer relay (Sweden)
41 Fuse box (four way)
42 Auxiliary driving lamp switch

Optional extra equipment
43 Inhibitor switch - automatic transmission
44 Rear fog lamp switch
45 Automatic transmission - selector illuminator
46 Rear fog lamp

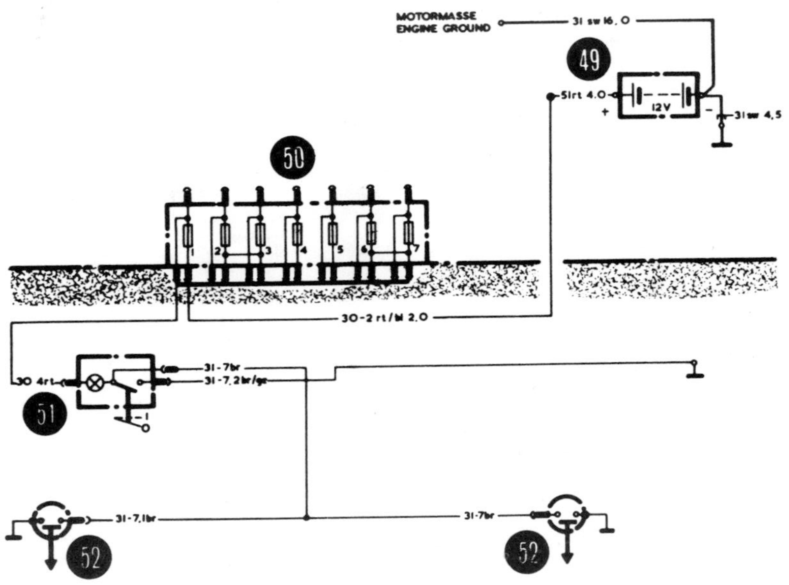

Wiring Diagram - Interior lights (GL and Ghia)

49 Battery
50 Fuse box
51 Interior lamp
52 Courtesy light switch

Wiring Colour		Code
Blue	Blue	bl
Brown	Brown	br
Yellow	Yellow	ge
Grey	Grey	gr
Green	Green	gn

Wiring Colour		Code
Pink	Pink	rs
Red	Red	rt
Black	Black	sw
Violet	Violet	vi
White	White	ws

Wiring Diagram - Horn, indicator and hazard lights (GL and Ghia)

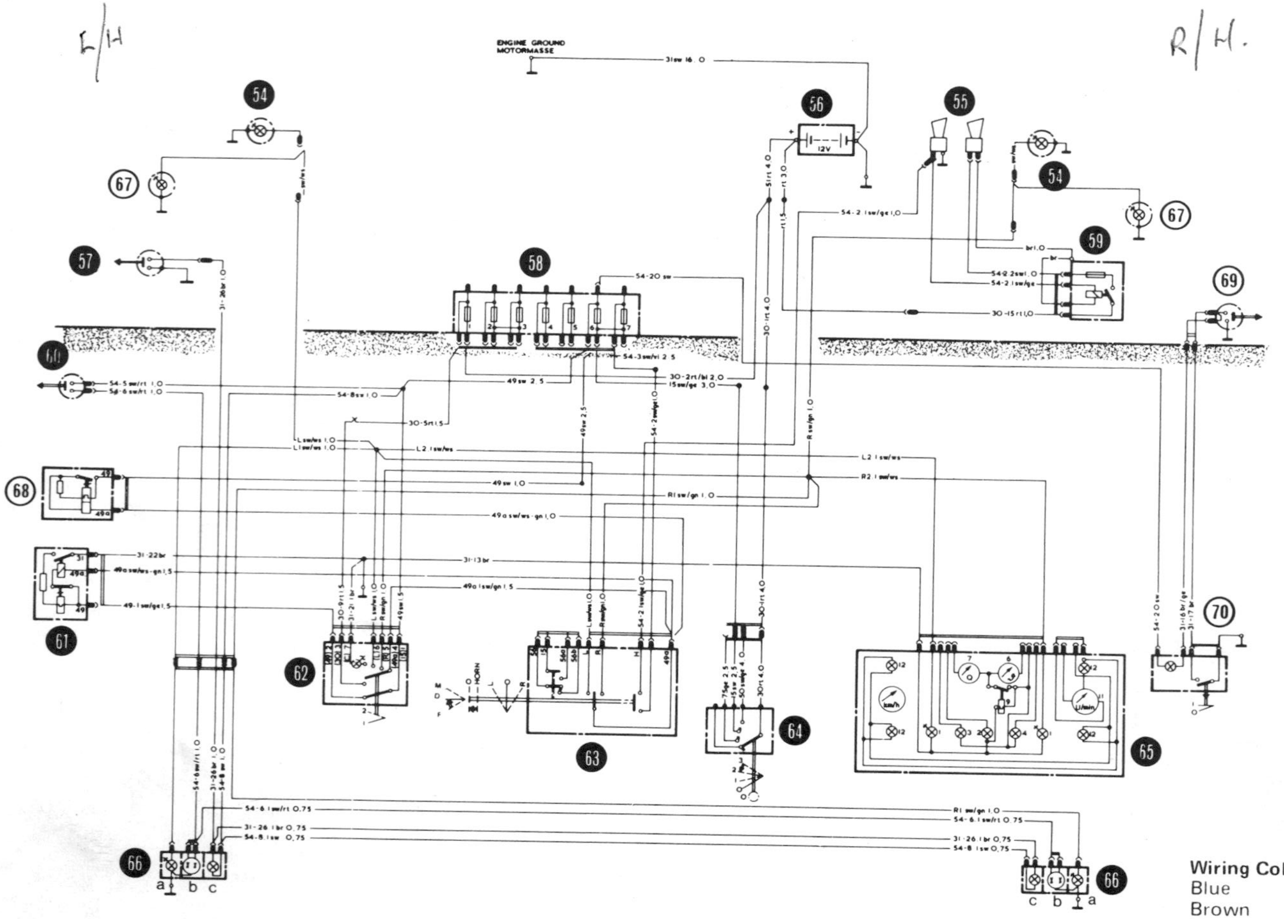

54 Flasher lamps (front)
55 Horn
56 Battery
57 Reversing lamp switch
58 Fuse box
59 Horn relay
60 Stop light switch
61 Flasher unit
62 Hazard flasher switch
63 Multi-function switch
64 Steering lock ignition switch
65 Instrument cluster
66 Combined tail lamp
   1 Flasher warning light (green)
   a) flasher lamps
   b) stop lights
   c) reversing lamps
67 Side repeater flasher lamps
68 Flasher unit (without hazard flasher system)
69 Dual circuit brake warning system switch
70 Dual circuit brake warning system control switch

Wiring Colour	Code		Wiring Colour	Code
Blue	bl		Pink	rs
Brown	br		Red	rt
Yellow	ge		Black	sw
Grey	gr		Violet	vi
Green	gn		White	ws

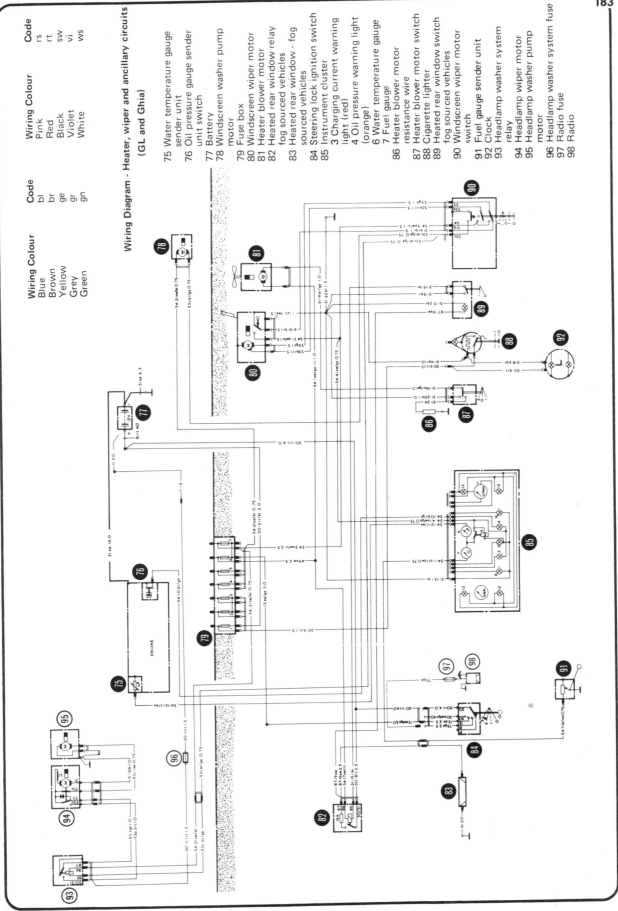

Wiring Diagram - Heater, wiper and ancillary circuits (GL and Ghia)

Wiring Colour	Code
Blue	bl
Brown	br
Yellow	ge
Grey	gr
Green	gn

Wiring Colour	Code
Pink	rs
Red	rt
Black	sw
Violet	vi
White	ws

75 Water temperature gauge sender unit
76 Oil pressure gauge sender unit switch
77 Battery
78 Windscreen washer pump motor
79 Fuse box
80 Windscreen wiper motor
81 Heater blower motor
82 Heated rear window relay fog sourced vehicles
83 Heated rear window - fog sourced vehicles
84 Steering lock ignition switch
85 Instrument cluster
3 Charging current warning light (red)
4 Oil pressure warning light (orange)
6 Water temperature gauge
7 Fuel gauge
86 Heater blower motor resistance wire
87 Heater blower motor switch
88 Cigarette lighter
89 Heated rear window switch fog sourced vehicles
90 Windscreen wiper motor switch
91 Fuel gauge sender unit
92 Clock
93 Headlamp washer system relay
94 Headlamp wiper motor
95 Headlamp washer pump motor
96 Headlamp washer system fuse
97 Radio fuse
98 Radio

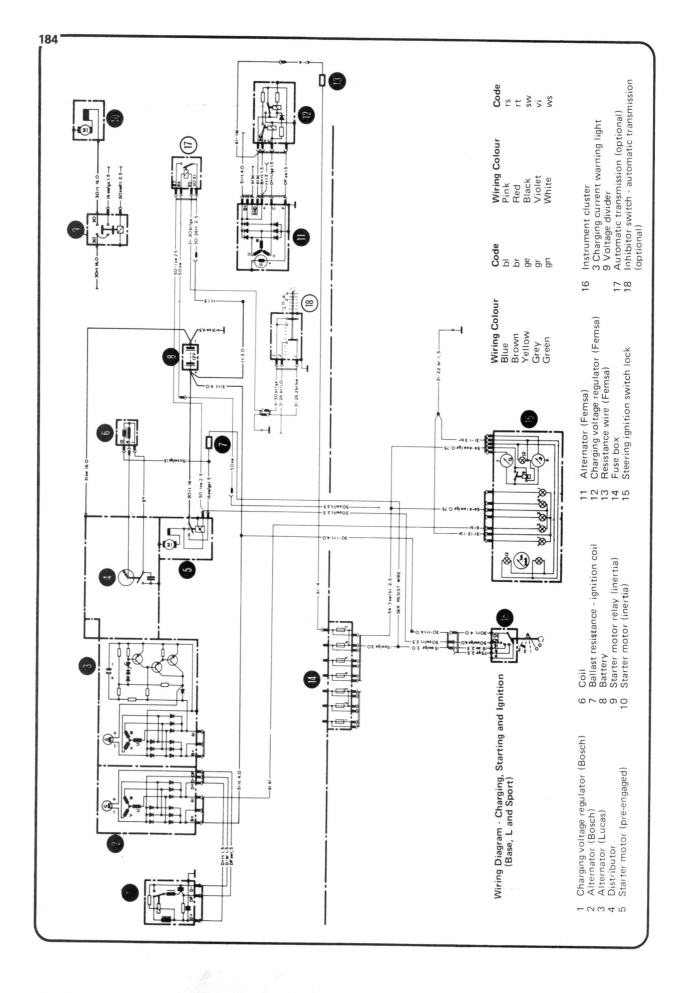

Wiring Diagram - Charging, Starting and Ignition (Base, L and Sport)

1	Charging voltage regulator (Bosch)	6	Coil
2	Alternator (Bosch)	7	Ballast resistance - ignition coil
3	Alternator (Lucas)	8	Battery
4	Distributor	9	Starter motor relay (inertia)
5	Starter motor (pre-engaged)	10	Starter motor (inertia)

11	Alternator (Femsa)	16	Instrument cluster
12	Charging voltage regulator (Femsa)	17	Automatic transmission (optional)
13	Resistance wire (Femsa)	18	Inhibitor switch - automatic transmission (optional)
14	Fuse box		
15	Steering ignition switch lock		

Wiring Colour

Code	
bl	Blue
br	Brown
ge	Yellow
gr	Grey
gn	Green

Wiring Colour

Code	
rs	Pink
rt	Red
sw	Black
vi	Violet
ws	White

3 Charging current warning light
9 Voltage divider

Key to Wiring Diagram on page 186 - Exterior lights (Base, L and Sport)

25 Headlamp - main beam
26 Battery
27 Reversing lamp switch
28 Fuse box (seven way)
29 Light switch
30 Multi-function switch
31 Steering lock ignition switch
32 Instrument cluster
  2 Main beam indicator lamp
12 Instrument illumination
33 Heater blower switch illumination
34 Load compartment lamp (Estate car only)
35 Tail lamps combined
  B Tail lamps
  C Reversing lamps
36 Luggage compartment lamp
37 Number plate lamps
38 Headlamp - main beam (Sweden)
39 Headlamp - main beam (Italy)
40 Dimmer relay (Sweden)
41 Fuse box (four way)

Optional extra equipment
42 Inhibitor switch - automatic transmission
43 Rear fog lamp switch
44 Automatic transmission - selector illumination
45 Cigarette lighter
46 Rear fog lamp

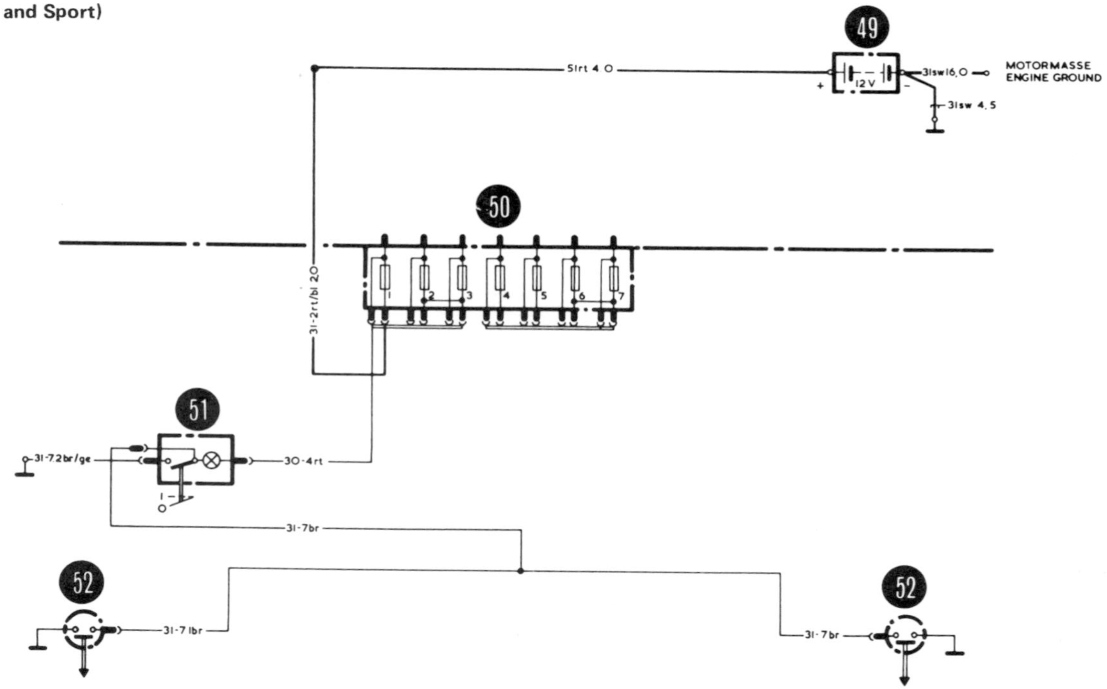

Wiring Colour	Code
Blue	bl
Brown	br
Yellow	ge
Grey	gr
Green	gn

Wiring Diagram - Interior lights (Base, L and Sport)

49 Battery
50 Fuse box
51 Interior lamp
52 Courtesy light switch

Wiring Colour	Code
Pink	rs
Red	rt
Black	sw
Violet	vi
White	ws

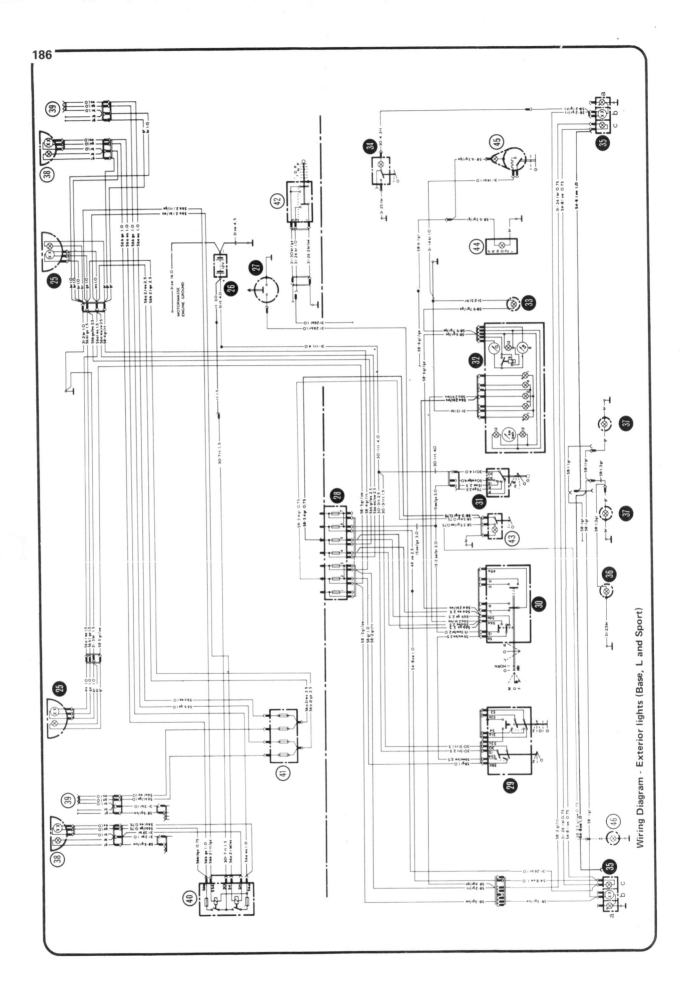

Wiring Diagram - Exterior lights (Base, L and Sport)

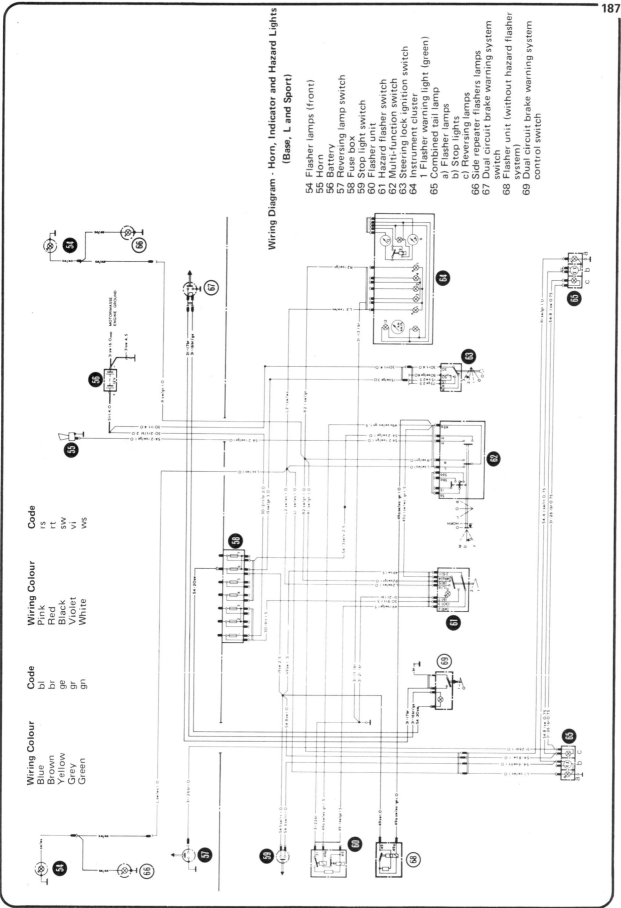

Wiring Diagram - Horn, Indicator and Hazard Lights
(Base, L and Sport)

54 Flasher lamps (front)
55 Horn
56 Battery
57 Reversing lamp switch
58 Fuse box
59 Stop light switch
60 Flasher unit
61 Hazard flasher switch
62 Multi-function switch
63 Steering lock ignition switch
64 Instrument cluster
    1 Flasher warning light (green)
65 Combined tail lamp
    a) Flasher lamps
    b) Stop lights
    c) Reversing lamps
66 Side repeater flashers lamps
67 Dual circuit brake warning system
    switch
68 Flasher unit (without hazard flasher
    system)
69 Dual circuit brake warning system
    control switch

Wiring Colour		Code	
Blue		bl	
Brown		br	
Yellow		ge	
Grey		gr	
Green		gn	

Wiring Colour		Code	
Pink		rs	
Red		rt	
Black		sw	
Violet		vi	
White		ws	

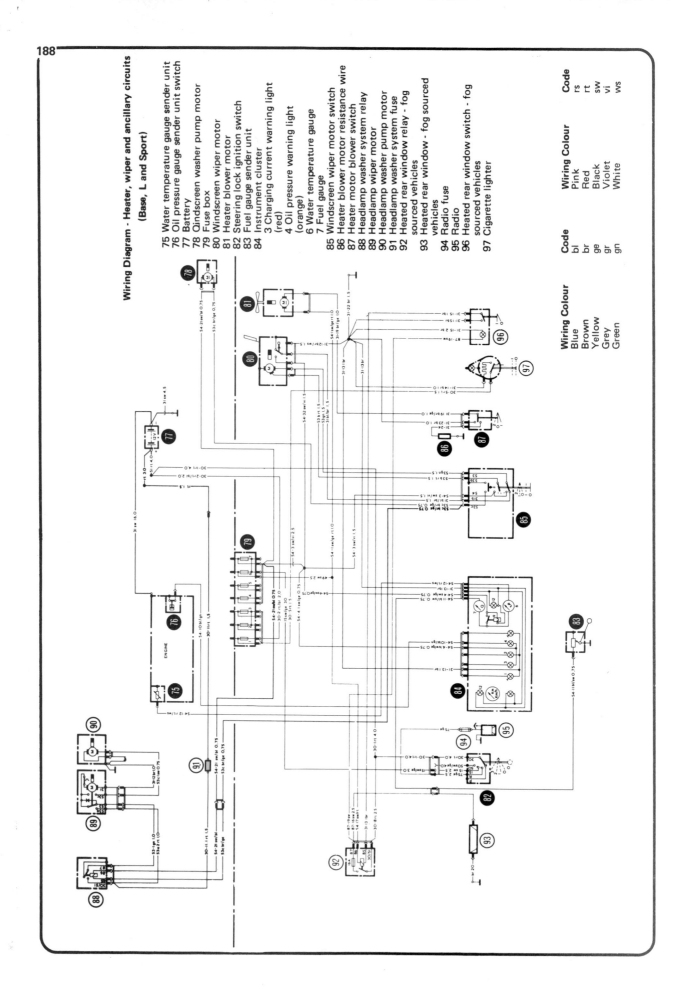

188

Wiring Diagram - Heater, wiper and ancillary circuits (Base, L and Sport)

75 Water temperature gauge sender unit
76 Oil pressure gauge sender unit switch
77 Battery
78 Qindscreen washer pump motor
79 Fuse box
80 Windscreen wiper motor
81 Heater blower motor
82 Steering lock ignition switch
83 Fuel gauge sender unit
84 Instrument cluster
3 Charging current warning light (red)
4 Oil pressure warning light (orange)
6 Water temperature gauge
7 Fuel gauge
85 Windscreen wiper motor switch
86 Heater blower motor resistance wire
87 Heater motor blower switch
88 Headlamp washer system relay
89 Headlamp wiper motor
90 Headlamp washer pump motor
91 Headlamp washer system fuse
92 Heated rear window relay - fog sourced vehicles
93 Heated rear window - fog sourced vehicles
94 Radio fuse
95 Radio
96 Heated rear window switch - fog sourced vehicles
97 Cigarette lighter

Wiring Colour		Code
Blue		bl
Brown		br
Yellow		ge
Grey		gr
Green		gn

Wiring Colour		Code
Pink		rs
Red		rt
Black		sw
Violet		vi
White		ws

Chapter 11 Suspension and steering

For modifications, and information applicable to later models, see Supplement at end of manual

Contents

Specifications

Front suspension

Type	Independent, MacPherson strut.
Control:	
Lateral	Track control arm
Longitudinal	Stabiliser bar
Wheel alignment:	

	Caster angle	Camber angle
Saloon and estate	0^0 44' to 1^0 59'	0^0 14' to 1^0 44'
Saloons and estate (H.D.)	0^0 46' to 2^0 01'	0^0 30' to 2^0 00'
6 and 9 cwt. van	0^0 11' to 1^0 04'	0^0 21' to 1^0 09'
6 and 9 cwt. van (H.D.)	0^0 08' to 1^0 23'	0^0 6' to 1^0 36'
Sport	0^0 20' to 1^0 35'	0^0 26' to 1^0 04'
Sport (H.D.)	0^0 44' to 1^0 59'	0^0 14' to 1^0 44'
Maximum caster angle difference LHS to RHS	0^0 45'	
Maximum camber angle difference LHS to RHS	1^0 00'	
Toe in	0 to 7 mm. (0 to 0.28 in.)	

Shock absorbers:	
Type	Telescopic. hydraulic double acting
Fluid capacity	325 $\pm$ 15 cc. (340 $\pm$ 15 cc. German built)
Fluid type	Ford SM6C - 1003 - A
Front springs:	
Type	Right-hand coil

Model:	Colour Code	Free-length	Wire dia.	Mean load	Total Coils
All saloons	Red/Yellow/Green	329 mm	10.7 mm	520 lb ft.	7.36
10 cwt van and H.D. saloon	Red/White	285 mm	11.2 mm	512 lb ft.	7.09
Sport	Red/Yellow/Orange	294 mm	10.9 mm	539 lb ft.	7.28
Sport (H.D.)	Red/Yellow/Blue	279 mm	11.2 mm	539 lb ft.	7.09
8 and 9 cwt. van	Red/Blue	267 mm	11.5 mm	512 lb ft.	6.96

Tyre Pressures

Model	Tyres	Normal Laden Pressures*		Fully Laden Pressures**	
		Front	Rear	Front	Rear
Saloon:					
1,1	6,00-12 4PR	21 lb sq in. (1,5 kg sq cm)	27 lb sq in (1,9 kg sq cm)	23 lb sq in (1,6 kg sq cm)	30 lb sq in (2,1 kg sq cm)
1,1	155SR 12	21 lb sq in 1,5 kg sq cm	27 lb sq in (1,9 kg sq cm)	24 lb sq in (1,7 kg sq cm)	36 lb sq in (2,5 kg sq cm)
1,1	155SR 13	21 lb sq in (1,5 kg sq cm)	24 lb sq in (1,7 kg sq cm)	24 lb sq in (1,7 kg sq cm)	36 lb sq in (2,5 kg sq cm)
1,3	155SR 13	21 lb sq in (1,5 kg sq cm)	24 lb sq in (1,7 kg sq cm)	24 lb sq in (1,7 kg sq cm)	36 lb sq in (2,5 kg sq cm)
1,6	155SR 13	21 lb sq in (1,5 kg sq cm)	24 lb sq in (1,7 kg sq cm)	24 lb sq in (1,7 kg sq cm)	36 lb sq in (2,5 kg sq cm)
1,3 1,6 Sport	175/70SR 13	21 lb sq in (1,5 kg sq cm)	24 lb sq in (1,7 kg sq cm)	23 lb sq in (1,6 kg sq cm)	28 lb sq in (2,0 kg sq cm)
Estate:					
1,1	6,00-12 6PR	21 lb sq in (1,5 kg sq cm)	27 lb sq in (1,9 kg sq cm)	24 lb sq in (1,7 kg sq cm)	36 lb sq in (2,5 kg sq cm)
1,1	155SR 12	21 lb sq in (1,5 kg sq cm)	27 lb sq in (1,9 kg sq cm)	24 lb sq in (1,7 kg sq cm)	36 lb sq in (2,5 kg sq cm)
1,1	155SR 12 REIN	21 lb sq in (1,5 kg sq cm)	27 lb sq in (1,9 kg sq cm)	24 lb sq in (1,7 kg sq cm)	36 lb sq in (2,5 kg sq cm)
1,1	155SR 13	21 lb sq in (1,5 kg sq cm)	24 lb sq in (1,7 kg sq cm)	24 lb sq in (1,7 kg sq cm)	36 lb sq in (2,5 kg sq cm)
1,3	155SR 13	21 lb sq in (1,5 kg sq cm)	24 lb sq in (1,7 kg sq cm)	24 lb sq in (1,7 kg sq cm)	36 lb sq in (2,5 kg sq cm)
1,1	155SR 13 REIN	21 lb sq in (1,5 kg sq cm)	24 lb sq in (1,7 kg sq cm)	24 lb sq in (1,7 kg sq cm)	36 lb sq in (2,5 kg sq cm)
1,3	155SR 13 REIN	21 lb sq in (1,5 kg sq cm)	24 lb sq in (1,7 kg sq cm)	24 lb sq in (1,7 kg sq cm)	36 lb sq in (2,5 kg sq cm)
Van:					
6 cwt.	6,00-12 6PR LV	24 lb sq in (1,7 kg sq cm)	27 lb sq in (1,9 kg sq cm)	27 lb sq in (1,9 kg sq cm)	46 lb sq in (3,2 kg sq cm)
6 cwt.	155SR 12 REIN	21 lb sq in (1,5 kg sq cm)	27 lb sq in (1,9 kg sq cm)	24 lb sq in (1,7 kg sq cm)	36 lb sq in (2,5 kg sq cm)
6 cwt.	155SR 13 REIN	21 lb sq in (1,5 kg sq cm)	24 lb sq in (1,7 kg sq cm)	24 lb sq in (1,7 kg sq cm)	36 lb sq in (2,5 kg sq cm)
9 cwt.	155SR 13 REIN	21 lb sq in (1,5 kg sq cm)	24 lb sq in (1,7 kg sq cm)	24 lb sq in (1,7 kg sq cm)	46 lb sq in (3,2 kg sq cm)
6 cwt;	5,50-12 LV	24 lb sq in (1,7 kg sq cm)	27 lb sq in (1,9 kg sq cm)	27 lb sq in (1,9 kg sq cm)	46 lb sq in (3,2 kg sq cm)

*Normal laden pressure: vehicle loaded with up to 3 persons
**Fully laden pressure: vehicle loaded in excess of normal load
For sustained high speed increase as follows:

Non'S' tyres	3 lb sq in. (0.21 kg sq cm)
'S' tyres	Nil
'SR' tyres	1.5 lb sq in (0.11 kg sq cm) for every 6 mph above 100 mph

Steering

Type	Rack and pinion
Rack travel	129 mm
Turns (lock-to-lock)	3.5
Helical teeth on pinion	5
Lubricant type	SAE 90 EP
Lubricant capacity	0.15 litre (0.25 Imperial pint)
Adjustment	by shim
Pinion bearing preload shim and gasket:	
71EB-3K544-AA	Steel (0,127 mm; 0.005 in.)
71EB-3K544-BA	Steel (0,178 mm; 0.007 in.)
71EB-3K544-CA	Steel (0,254 mm; 0.010 in.)
71EB-3K544-DA (must always be used)	Steel (2,286 mm; 0.090 in.)
3024E-3581-B	Gasket (0,127 mm; 0.005 in.)
Rack slipper bearing shim:	
3024E-3K544-J	Steel (0,051 mm) (0.002 in.)
3024E-3K544-K	Steel (0,127 mm) (0.005 in.)
3024E-3K544-L	Steel (0,254 mm) (0.010 in.)
3024E-3K544-M	Steel (0,381 mm) (0.015 in.)
3024E-3K544-N	Steel (0,508 mm) (0.020 in.)

Rear Suspension

Type	Semi elliptical longitudinal leaf spring and stabilised
Shock absorber	Double acting, telescopic

Springs:

Type	Semi elliptic
No. of leaves	3 (4 on 9 cwt van)
Width of leaves at centre	60 mm

Spring colour codes:

1100 - 1300 Saloon	Standard: red/yellow/white,	H.D.: green/white
1300 2V Saloon	Standard: red/yellow/white,	H.D.: green/white
1600 2V Saloon	Standard: red/yellow/white,	H.D.:green/white
1100 - 1300 Estate	Standard: green/white,	H.D.: orange/white
Van	Standard: violet/white,	H.D.: pink/white
9 cwt. Van	Standard: red/blue/white,	H.D.: red/green/white

Torque wrench settings

	lb f ft	kg f m
Front suspension cross-member to body side-member	29 to 37	4 - 5.11
Steering rack clamp to cross-member	15 to 18	2.1 - 2.5
Wheel bearing nuts	27	3.73
Brake caliper mounting bolts	35 to 50	4.8 - 6.9
Brake disc to hub assembly	30 to 34	4.2 - 4.7
Lower arm to suspension unit	30 to 35	4.2 - 4.8
Lower arm to cross-member pivot bolts*	18 to 22	2.5 - 3
Stabiliser bar to lower arm*	15 to 45	2.1 - 6.22
Stabiliser bar to body mounting brackets*	21 to 24	2.9 - 3.3
Suspension unit upper mounting bolts	15 to 18	2.1 - 2.5
Track rod to steering arm	18 to 22	2.5 - 3
Suspension unit piston rod nut**	29 to 33	4 - 4.56
Steering gear to crossmember	15 to 18	2.1 - 2.5
Trackrod-end to steering arm	18 to 22	2.5 - 3
Coupling to pinion spline	11 to 13	1.5 - 1.79
Coupling to steering shaft spline	11 to 13	1.5 - 1.79
Steering wheel to steering shaft	20 to 25	2.8 to 3.5
Shock absorber to rear axle:		
Saloon	25 to 31	3.5 - 4.2
Van	27 to 33	3.73 - 4.56
Shock absorber to floor pan.		
Nut:		
Saloon	15 to 21	2.1 - 2.9
Van	9 to 12	1.24 - 1.65
Locknut	12 to 15	1.66 - 2.07
Rear spring front end to floor pan bolts	52 to 66	7.18 - 9.12
Rear spring rear end to floor pan bolts	19 to 23	2.6 - 3.17
'U' bolt	18 to 27	2.5 - 3.73
Stabiliser bar to axle tube bolts	29 to 37	4 - 5.11
Stabiliser bar to sidemember bolts	44 to 52	6.08 - 7.18
Stabiliser bar end bush locknuts	44 to 59	6.08 - 8.15
Wheel nuts (flat faced)	85 to 103	11.7 to 14.2
Wheel nuts (conical)	63 to 85	8.7 to II.7

*These to be tightened with the weight of the car resting on its wheels.
**These to be tightened with the wheels in straight-ahead position and weight of car resting on its wheels and locked by punching slot using a 3 mm (0.10 in.) diameter ball ended punch.

1 General description

Each of the independent front suspension MacPherson strut units consists of a vertical strut enclosing a double acting shock absorber surrounded by a coil spring.

The upper end of each strut is secured to the top of the wing valance under the bonnet by rubber mountings.

The wheel spindle (stub axle) carrying the brake assembly and wheel hub is forged integrally with the suspension unit foot.

The steering arms are connected to each unit which are in turn connected to track rods and thence to the rack and pinion steering gear.

The lower end of each suspension unit is located by a track control arm.

A stabilising torsion bar (anti-roll bar) is fitted between the outer ends of each track control arm and secured at the front to mountings on the body front member.

On all models a rubber rebound stop is fitted inside the suspension unit. This prevents the spring becoming over-extended and jumping out of its mounting plates.

Whenever repairs have been carried out on a suspension unit it is essential to check the wheel alignment as the linkage could be altered which would affect the correct front wheel settings.

Every time the car goes over a bump vertical movement of a front wheel pushes the damper body upward against the combined resistance of the coil spring and the shock absorber piston.

Hydraulic fluid in the shock absorber is displaced and it is then forced through the compression valve into the space between the inner and outer cylinder. On the downward movement of the suspension, the road spring forces the shock absorber body downward against the pressure of the hydraulic fluid which is forced back again through the rebound valve. In this way the natural oscillations of the spring are damped out and a comfortable ride is obtained.

On the front uprights there is a shroud inside the coil spring which protects the machined surface of the piston rod from road

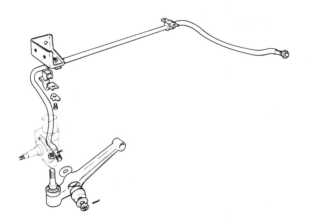

Fig. 11.1 Stabiliser bar bush components

dirt.

The upper mounting assembly consists of a steel sleeve with a rubber bush bonded to it. The steering gear on the Escort is rack and pinion and is located on the front crossmember by two 'U' shaped clamps. The pinion is connected to the steering column by a flexible coupling.

Turning the steering wheel causes the rack to move in a lateral direction and the track rods attached to either end of the rack pass this movement to the steering arms on the suspension/axle units thereby moving the roadwheels.

Two adjustments are possible on the steering gear, namely rack damper adjustment and pinion bearing pre-load adjustment, but the steering gear must be removed from the car to carry out these adjustments. Both adjustments are made by varying the thickness of shim packs.

The rear axle is located by two inverted 'U' bolts at each end of the casing to underslung semi-elliptical leaf springs which provide both lateral and longitudinal location.

Double acting telescopic shock absorbers are fitted between the axle and reinforced mountings in the floor pan. These shock absorbers work on the same principle as the front shock absorbers.

In the interests of lessening noise and vibration, the springs and shock absorbers are mounted on rubber bushes. Similarly the rear anti-roll bar is rubber bushed at its mounting points on the sidemembers and axle casing.

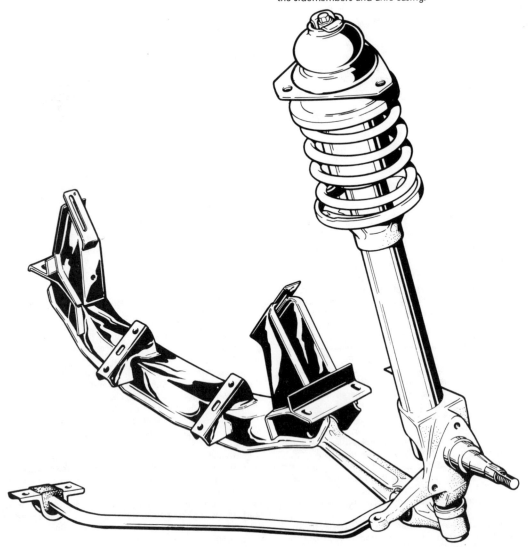

Fig. 11.2 Front suspension components

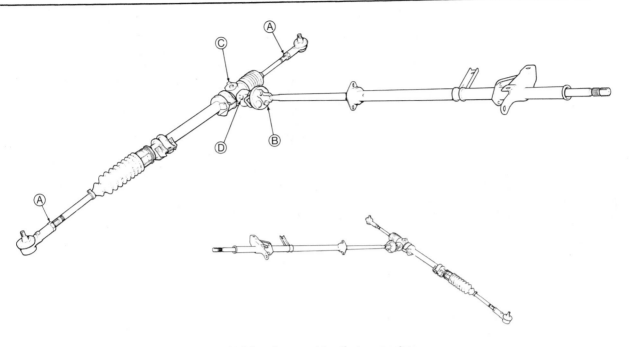

Fig. 11.3 Steering assembly adjustment points

A Toe in adjustment at track rod end
B Coupling shaft adjustment on steering column splines

C Rack adjustment via shim pack and slipper
D Pinion bearing adjustment

2 Suspension and steering - maintenance and inspection

1 Every 6000 miles (9600 km) brush the rear road springs free from dirt and apply either penetrating oil or engine oil to the leaves with a spray or brush. Do not allow oil to come in contact with the rubber bushes at the spring eyes.
2 Check the torque setting of the 'U' bolts and shackle bolts.
3 Inspect the rubber bushes for deterioration or wear and renew if necessary as described later in this Section.
4 At a similar mileage interval, check the condition of the rubber bellows at both ends of the steering rack. Renew them if they are split or perished.
5 Check the condition of the rubber gaiters on all the steering ball joints and renew them if they are split or perished. It is unlikely that the gaiters themselves can be obtained without purchasing a complete ball joint.
6 Check all suspension securing bolts and nuts for correct tightening torque in accordance with the figures specified in the Specifications Section.
7 Examine the front suspension strut for signs of oil leakage ('B' Fig. 11.15), or score marks on the piston rod ('A' Fig. 11.15). Then check the shock absorber movement and determine whether the action feels stiff, or, alternatively, notchy or spongy.
8 If any of the above checks reveal wear or some malfunction the relevant components should be replaced.

3 Front hub/drum assemblies - maintenance, removal and refitting

1 Jack-up the front of the car, remove the roadwheel, the dust cap, split pin, nut retainer, nut, thrust washer, outer bearing and hub/drum assembly.
2 From the back of the drum/hub carefully prise out the grease seal and remove the inner tapered bearing.
3 Carefully clean out the hub and wash the bearings with petrol, making sure no grease or oil is allowed to get onto the brake drum.
4 Working the grease well into the bearings fully pack the bearing cages and roller with Castrol LM Grease or any suitable lithium based grease. Note: Leave the hub and grease seal empty to allow for subsequent expansion of the grease.
5 To reassemble the hub, first fit the inner bearing and then gently tap the grease seal back into the hub. If the seal was at all damaged during removal, a new one must be fitted.
6 Replace the hub and drum assembly on the stub axle and slide on the outer bearing and thrust washer.
7 Tighten down the centre adjusting nut to a torque of 27 lb f ft (3.73 kg fm) whilst rotating the drum to ensure free movement, then slacken the nut off 120° (two flats), then fit the nut retainer and a new split pin.
8 Bend the ends of the split pin, refit the dust cap.
9 Check the adjustment of the front brakes (Chapter 9), refit the roadwheel and then lower the vehicle to the ground.

4 Front hub/disc assemblies - maintenance, removal and refitting

1 Jack-up the front of the vehicle, remove the appropriate roadwheel then slacken the 17 mm nut securing the brake line to the suspension leg bracket at the junction of the flexible and metal pipes.
2 Knock back the locking tabs on the two caliper unit securing bolts. unscrew and remove the bolts.
3 Very carefully, taking care not to twist or damage the brake pipes, guide the caliper unit away from the disc at the same time disengaging the brake line from the suspension strut bracket.
4 Using a suitable length of wire suspend the caliper from the vehicle body away from the work area, making sure that the caliper is securely held and that the brake lines are not twisted. A piece of soft packing between the disc pads will effectively prevent these components closing up.
5 Knock the dust cap from the end of the hub and then withdraw the split pin, nut retainer, nut, thrust washer and outer bearing.

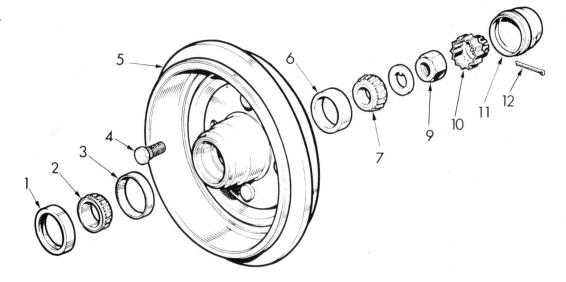

Fig. 11.4 Hub/drum assembly (Sec 3)

1 Grease seal
2 Inner roller bearing
3 Track
4 Road wheel stud
5 Drum/hub assembly
6 Outer bearing track

7 Outer bearing
9 Nut
10 Nut retainer
11 Dust cap
12 Split pin

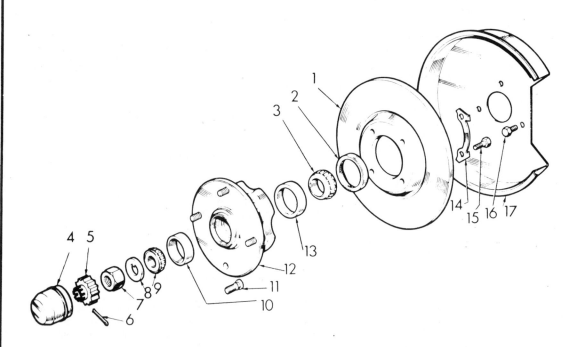

Fig. 11.5 Hub/disc assembly (Sec 4)

1 Disc
2 Grease seal
3 Inner roller bearing
4 Dust cap
5 Nut retainer
6 Split pin
7 Nut
8 Thrust wash

9 Outer bearing
10 Outer bearing track
11 Road wheel stud
12 Hub
13 Inner bearing track
14 Lock plate
15, 16 Bolts
17 Splash shield

Fig. 11.6 Removing the 17 mm lock nut (A) before sliding the pipe/hose assembly out of the suspension leg bracket (Sec 4)

Fig. 11.7 Method of suspending caliper from underbody without breaking fluid lines

Fig. 11.8 Removing the bolts securing the disc assembly to the hub (Sec 4)

Fig. 11.9 Replacing brake disc and hub assembly (Sec 4)

6 Pull the hub/disc assembly from the stub axle.

7 From the back of the hub assembly, carefully prise out the grease seal and remove the inner tapered bearing. Then bend up the lock tabs on the four bolts securing the disc to the hub, remove the bolts and separate the disc and hub assembly.

8 If the hub and disc are being removed for maintenance of, or access to, the hub bearings this can be carried out with the disc in place.

9 Carefully clean out the hub and wash the bearings with petrol, making sure that no grease or oil is allowed to get onto the brake disc.

10 Working the grease well into the bearings, fully pack the bearing cages and rollers with Castrol LM Grease or any suitable lithium based grease. **Note:** Leave the hub and grease seal empty to allow for subsequent expansion of the grease.

11 To reassemble the hub, first fit the inner bearing and then gently tap the grease seal back into the hub. If the oil seal was at all damaged during removal, a new one must be fitted.

12 Reposition the disc on the hub assembly and secure the two components using the four bolts and new tab washers. Torque the bolts to 30 - 34 lb f ft. (4.2 - 4.7 kg fm).

13 Replace the hub and disc assembly on the stub axle and slide on the outer bearing and thrust washer.

14 Tighten down the centre adjusting nut to a torque of 27 lb f ft (3.73 kg fm) whilst rotating the hub and disc to ensure free movement, then slacken the nut off 90° and fit the nut retainer and new split pin but do not bend back the split pin.

15 At this stage it is advisable, if a dial gauge is available, to check the disc for run-out. The measurement should be taken as near

to the edge of the worn, smooth part of the disc as possible and must not exceed 0.002 inch (0.05 mm). If this figure is found to be excessive, check the mating surfaces of the disc and hub for dirt or damage and check the bearings and cups for excessive wear or damage. Renew the disc if the run-out is excessive or it appears deeply scored.

16 Bend the ends of the split pin and refit the dust cap.

17 Carefully push the disc pads apart sufficiently to allow the caliper to align around the disc. Secure the caliper in position, tighten the retaining bolts to 35 - 50 lb f ft (4.8 - 6.9 kg fm), and retain with new tab washers. Carefully guide the brake pipes into the suspension strut bracket and tighten the 17 mm nut.

5 Front hub bearings - checking for wear and renewal

1 To check the condition of the hub bearings, jack-up the front end of the car and grasp the roadwheel at two opposite points to check for any rocking movement in the wheel hub. Watch carefully for any movement in the steering gear, which can easily be mistaken for hub movement. If movement is observed in the ball joints, they must be renewed.

2 If a front wheel hub has excessive movement, this is adjusted by removing the hub cap and then levering off the small dust cap. Remove the split pin through the stub axle and take off the adjusting nut retainer.

3 If a torque wrench is available, tighten the centre adjusting nut down to a torque of 27 lb f ft (3.73 kg fm) and then slacken it off 90° and replace the nut retainer and a new split pin.

4 Where this action does not remove the rocking or if a grinding or grating sound can be heard when the hub is rotated, then the bearings must be renewed.

5 Remove the hub/drum or hub/disc assembly as previously described. Remove the outer bearing.

6 Prise out the grease seal from the back of the hub and remove the inner bearing.

7 Drift out the bearing outer tracks from each end of the hub and then thoroughly clean the grease from the hub interior.

8 It is essential to keep the new bearings in their individual packs until required for fitting. Do not open them and mix the roller races and tracks but keep them as matched pairs.

9 Drift in the new bearing outer tracks using a suitable piece of tubing. Ensure that they are fully home in their recesses. Fit a new grease seal.

10 Fill the intervening space between the two bearings with recommended grease but not by more than 1/3 of the available capacity.

11 Refitting is a reversal of removal. Adjust the bearings as described in Sections 3 or 4.

---

6 Front coil spring - removal and installation

1 Before commencing operations, the spring must be compressed. This can be carried out by having an assistant sit on the front wing and then fitting clips over two or three adjacent coils or by using the screw type compressors. Either item is available from most good accessory stores.

2 With the spring compressed, jack-up the front of the vehicle and support the bodyframe and crossmember adequately on stands.

3 Working under the bonnet, measure the distance that the threads on the top of the piston rod protrude above the nut, then remove the nut and the cranked retainer.

4 Undo and remove the three bolts securing the top of the suspension unit to the side panel.

5 Push the piston rod downward as far as it will go. It should now be possible to remove the top mounting assembly, the dished washer and the upper spring seat from the top of the spring.

6 The spring can now be lifted off its bottom seat and removed over the piston assembly.

7 If a new spring is being fitted, check extremely carefully that it is of the same rating as the spring on the other side of the car. The colour coding of the springs can be found in the Specifications at the beginning of this Chapter.

8 Before fitting a new spring, it must be compressed with the adjustable restrainers and make sure that the clips are placed on the same number of coils, and in the same position as on the spring which has been removed.

9 Place the new spring over the piston and locate it on its bottom seat, then pull the piston upward and fit the upper spring seat so that it locates correctly on the flats cut on the piston rod.

10 Fit the dished washer to the piston rod, ensuring that the convex side faces upward.

11 Now fit the top mount assembly. With the steering in the straight ahead position, fit the cranked retainer facing inward at 90° to the wheel angles and the piston rod nut, having previously applied Loctite or similar compound to the thread. Do not fully tighten down the nut at this stage.

12 If necessary, pull the top end of the unit upward until it is possible to locate correctly the top mount bracket and fit the three retaining bolts from under the bonnet. These nuts must be tightened down to a torque of 15 to 18 lb f ft (2.1 to 2.5 kg fm).

13 Remove the spring clips. fit the roadwheel and lower the car to the ground.

14 Finally, slacken off the piston rod nut, get an assistant to hold the upper spring seat to prevent it turning, and retighten the nut to a torque of 29 to 33 lbf ft (4.1 to 4.6 Kgf m). Check that the same amount of thread is protruding above the nut as was measured in paragraph 3, of this Section. If this is not the

same, it is probable that the upper spring seat is not correctly located or alternatively, that the spring itself is not properly seated.

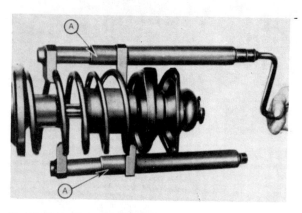

Fig. 11.10 Typical adjustable spring compressors (A) of the type required to compress the front suspension leg spring (Sec 6)

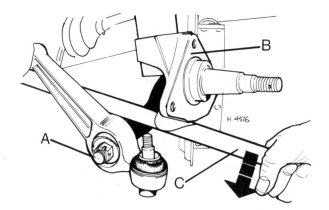

Fig. 11.11 Using lever (C) in direction arrowed to enable stabiliser bar and track control arm (A) to be disengaged from suspension leg (B). Note: Brake disc and splash shield are shown removed for clarity (Sec 7)

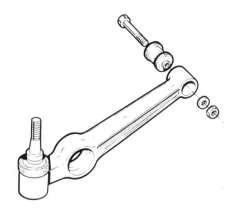

Fig. 11.12 Track control arm mounting bush assembly in front crossmember

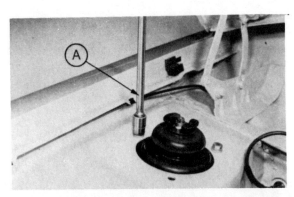

Fig. 11.13 Replacing suspension strut upper mounting bolts (A = torque wrench). Torque: 2.0 - 2.4 kg f m (15 - 18 lb f ft) (Sec 7)

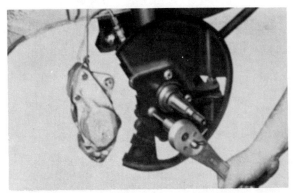

Fig. 11.14 Unscrewing disc splash shield retaining bolts with suspension leg in-situ. Note caliper hanging to one side on suitable wire support (Sec 7)

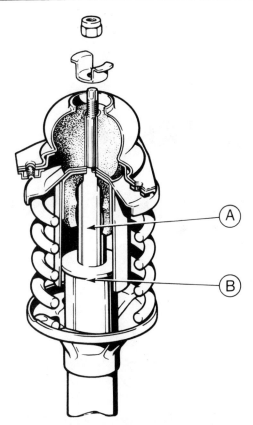

Fig. 11.15 Front suspension unit components. Piston rod (A) must not show signs of scoring and must NEVER be gripped when removing the piston rod nut. The most probable leakage point is shown arrowed at (B) (Secs 2 and 7)

7 Front suspension unit - removal and installation

1 Jack-up the front end of the vehicle and remove the appropriate roadwheel.

2 Remove the hub/drum or hub/disc assembly (Sections 3 or 4).

3 Disconnect the trackrod-end from the base of the suspension unit after removal of the split pin and castellated nut.

4 Remove the split pin and castellated nut securing the track control arm taper to the base of the unit. Disengage the taper and lever the arm clear of the unit.

5 Working under the bonnet, unscrew and remove the three bolts on the side apron holding the top of the suspension unit in place and then lower the unit away from the car.

6 With the unit securely mounted in a bench vice unscrew the three allen screws retaining the brake disc splash shield to the unit and detach the shield.

7 Assemble the spring compressor, previously mentioned, around the spring and tighten each compressor a little, in turn, until the load, or action, of the spring on the top mount is released.

8 Unscrew the piston nut from the piston spindle and remove the cranked retainer, top mount, upper spring retainer, bump roller and spring from the unit. **While unscrewing the piston nut do not grip the piston shaft in order to stop the piston turning with the nut. A flat section is provided at the top of the piston shaft for this purpose.**

9 Replacement is a direct reversal of the removal procedure but remember to use a new split pin on the track control arm to suspension unit castellated nut.

10 The lower control arm to crossmember pivot bolts must be

Fig. 11.16 Removing the bump stop plat form. Note: that the Ford special tool is shown being used; careful use of a round nosed punch will achieve the same results (Sec 8)

tightened to a torque of 18 to 22 lbf ft (2.5 to 3.1 Kgf m), the lower control arm to suspension unit nut to a torque of 30 to 35 lbf ft (4.2 to 4.9 Kgf m) and the top mounting bolts to a torque of 15 to 18 lbf ft (2.0 to 2.4 Kgf m).

8 Front suspension unit - overhaul

1 Remove the suspension unit from the vehicle (Section 7) and remove the bump rubber, topmost end spring (Section 7).

2 The bump stop platform nut normally requires a special tool for removal. However, the nut can be removed using a round

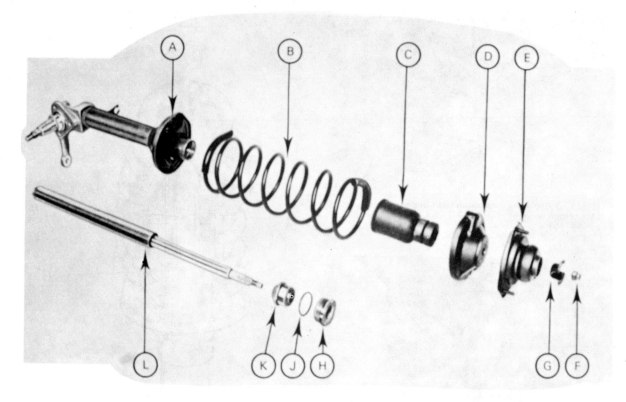

Fig. 11.17 Front suspension unit - exploded view

A Unit	D Upper spring retainer	G Cranked retainer	K Gland
B Front spring	E Top mount assembly	H Bump stop plat form	L Piston and cylinder assembly
C Bump rubber	F Piston rod nut	J Seal	

nosed punch in the two slots cut in the upper surface of the nut.

3   With the platform nut removed withdraw the 'O' ring seal, gland and the piston rod and cylinder assembly from the suspension unit.

4   At the base of the piston rod cylinder there is a castellated valve assembly which is a push fit into the cylinder bore. The valve can be pulled from the cylinder after first imparting a twisting action with a suitable lever.

5   Remove the piston rod and piston from the cylinder and examine for signs of damage or wear, in particular look for signs of scoring on the piston rod around the area of the gland and seal. The piston must not be removed from the rod.

6   Drain the oil from the unit and clean the cylinder piston and unit with a suitable solvent using a non-fluffy cloth. An old chamois leather is useful for finally wiping the components dry.

7   Replacement is a direct reversal of the removal procedure. However, when filling the unit with oil prior to refitting the piston rod and cylinder assembly use **exactly** 326 cc of Ford shock absorber fluid M100502E. To avoid damaging the new unit seals cover the threads of the piston rod with adhesive tape before fitting the seal or gland.

9   Anti-roll bar (front) - removal and refitting

1   Jack-up the front of the vehicle, support the vehicle on suitable stands and remove both front roadwheels.

2   Working under the car at the front, knock back the locking tabs on the four bolts securing the two front clamps which hold the torsion bar to the frame and then undo the four bolts and remove the clamps and rubber insulators.

3   Remove the split pins from the castellated nuts retaining the anti-roll bar to the track control arms then undo the nuts and pull off the large washers, carefully noting the way in which they are fitted.

Fig. 11.18 When the suspension leg assembly has been replaced in the vehicle and the piston rod nut finally tightened, the wall of the nut must be deformed into the piston rod slot (A) using a suitable pin punch (Sec 8)

Fig. 11.19 Stabiliser bar mounting bush clamp. Bend down lock tabs (arrowed) before unscrewing bolts (Sec 9)

4 Pull the anti-roll bar forward out of the two track control arms and remove it from the vehicle.

5 Clean the road dirt and rust from the bar, then slide the rubber mounting bushes around the bar and off the ends. Use rubber lubricant on the bar to assist in the removal of the bushes.

6 Reassembly is a reversal of this procedure, but new locking tabs must be used on the front clamp bolts and new split pins on the castellated nuts. The nuts on the clamps and the castellated nuts on each end of the anti-roll bar must not be fully tightened down until the vehicle is resting on its wheels.

7 Once the vehicle is on its wheels the castellated nuts on the ends of the anti-roll bar should be tightened down to a torque of 15 to 45 lbf ft (2.1 to 6.2 Kgf m) and the new split pins fitted. The four clamp bolts on the front mounting points must be tightened down to a torque of 21 to 24 lbf ft (2.9 to 3.4 Kgf m) and the locking tabs knocked up.

10 Steering gear - removal and installation

1 Before starting this job set the front wheels in the straight ahead position. Then jack-up the front of the vehicle and place blocks under the wheels; lower the vehicle slightly on the jack so that the track rods are in a near horizontal position.

2 Remove the nut and bolt from the clamp at the front of the flexible coupling on the steering column. This clamp holds the coupling to the pinion splines (Fig. 11.20).

3 Working on the front crossmember, knock back the locking tabs on the two nuts on each 'U' clamp, undo the nut and remove the locking tabs and clamps.

4 Remove the split pins and castellated nuts from the ends of each trackrod where they join the steering arms. Separate the trackrods from the steering arms using a ball joint extractor or wedges and lower the steering gear downward out of the car.

5 Before replacing the steering gear, make sure that the wheels have remained in the 'straight-ahead' position. Also check the condition of the mounting rubbers round the housing and if they

appear worn or damaged, renew them.

6 Check that the steering gear is also in the 'straight-ahead' position. This can be done by ensuring that the distances between the ends of both track rods and the steering gear housing on both sides are the same.

7 Place the steering gear in its location on the crossmember and at the same time mate up the splines on the pinion with the splines in the clamp on the steering column flexible coupling.

8 . Replace the two 'U' clamps using new locking tabs under the bolts, tighten down the bolts to a torque of 15 to 18 lbf ft (2.1 to 2.5 Kgf m) and bend up the locking tabs.

9 Refit the trackrod-ends into the steering arms, replace the castellated nuts and tighten them to a torque of 18 to 22 lb f ft (2.5 to 3.0 kg fm). Use new split pins to retain the nuts.

10 Tighten the clamp bolt on the steering column flexible coupling to a torque of 11 to 13 lbf ft (1.4 to 1.7 Kgf m), having first made sure that the pinion is correctly located in the splines.

11 Jack-up the car, remove the blocks from under the wheels and lower the car to the ground. It is advisable at this stage to take your car to your local Ford dealer and have the toe-in checked (Section 16).

11 Steering gear - dismantling and reassembly

1 Remove the steering gear from the car (Section 10).

2 Unscrew the ball joints and locknuts from the end of each trackrod, having previously marked the threads to ensure correct positioning on reassembly. Alternatively, the number of turns required to undo the ball joint can be counted and noted.

3 Slacken off the clips securing the rubber bellows to each track rod and the steering gear housing then pull off the bellows. Have a quantity of rag handy to catch the oil which will escape when the bellows are removed.

4 To dismantle the steering gear, it is only necessary to remove the trackrod which is furthest away from the pinion on either right or left-hand drive cars.

5 To remove the trackrod place the steering gear in a soft jawed vice. Working on the trackrod ball joint, carefully drill out the

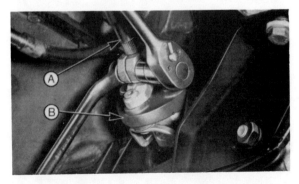

Fig. 11.20 Steering column (A) and coupling (B) assembly shown with socket and ring spanner on clamp bolt (Sec 10)

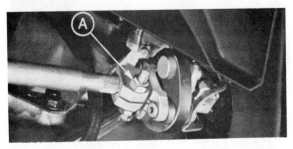

Fig. 11.22 Steering column coupling clamp bolt (A) (Sec 11)

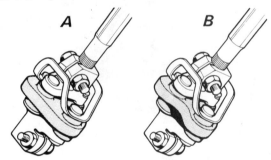

Fig. 11.21 Rubber disc in steering column to pinion shaft coupling. This disc must be assembled without distortion (A) and not as at (B). To relieve the condition shown at (B) slide the coupling up the column splines before tightening the clamp bolts (Sec 10)

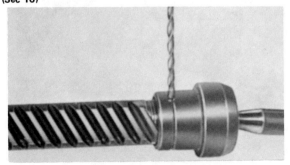

Fig. 11.23 Drilling out track rod housing locking pin (Sec 11)

pin which locks the ball housing to the locknut. Great care must be taken not to drill too deeply or you will drill into the threads on the rack thus causing irreparable damage. The hole should be 3 mm (0.12 in) dia and a maximum of 9.5 mm (0.38 in) deep.

6 Using two pairs of mole wrenches firmly grip the locknut and undo the ball housing from the end of the rack.

7 Take out the spring and ball seat from the recess in the end of the rack and then unscrew the locknut from the threads on the rack. The spring and ball seat must be replaced by new components on reassembly. Repeat for the other trackrod assembly.

8 Now remove the two bolts securing the rack slipper cover plate. This plate is the one on the front face of the rack casting adjacent to the pinion shaft. With the cover removed, detach the shims and withdraw the spring 'O' ring and slipper from the rack.

9 Remove the two bolts from the remaining cover plate immediately below the pinion shaft and detach the shim pack and gasket, together with the pinion shaft lower bearing.

10 Remove the pinion oil seal from the cover plate. The pinion

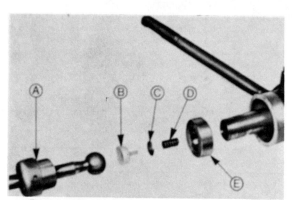

Fig. 11.24 Track rod assembly to rack (Sec 11)

A *Track rod housing*
B *Nylon seating*
C *Washer*
D *Spring*
E *Housing locknut*

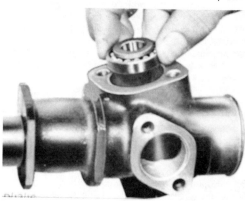

Fig. 11.25 Replacing the pinion lever bearing assembly (Sec 11)

Fig. 11.26 Replacing the pinion and upper bearing assembly (Sec 11)

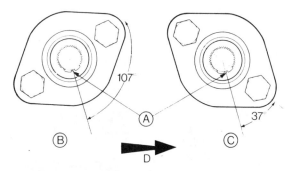

Fig. 11.27 Location of pinion master spline with the steering rack at the mid point of its travel (Sec 11)

A *Master spline*
B *Pinion LHD vehicles*
C *Pinion, right hand drive vehicles*

Note: D = right hand side of vehicle

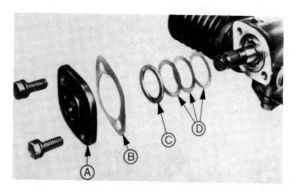

Fig. 11.28 Pinion bearing adjustment (Sec 11)

A *Cover plate*
B *Gasket*
C *Thick shim*
D *Shim pach*

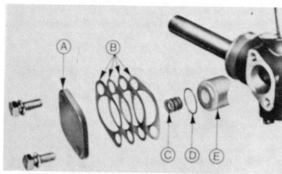

Fig. 11.29 Steering rack adjustment (Sec 11)

A *Cover plate*
B *Shim pack*
C *Spring*
D *Seal*
E *Slipper (or yoke)*

shaft and upper bearing assembly can now be withdrawn from the rack casting. Examine the upper bearing for signs of wear, or damage; if necessary the bearing can be pulled from the shaft after first removing all traces of paint from the splines end.

11 The toothed rack can now be withdrawn from the casting.

12 Carefully examine all parts for signs of wear or damage. Check the condition of the rack support bush at the opposite end of the casing from the pinion. If this is worn, renew it. If the rack or pinion teeth are in any way damaged, a completely new steering gear will have to be fitted.

13 To commence reassembly, fit the lower pinion bearing and thrust washer into their recess in the casing.

14 Replace the rack in the casing from the pinion end and position it in the 'straight-ahead' position by equalising the amount it protrudes at either end of the casing.

15 Replace the remaining pinion bearing and thrust washer onto the pinion and fit the pinion into the casing so that the larger master spline on the pinion shaft is parallel to the rack and on the right-hand side of the pinion. This applies to both right and left-hand drive cars.

16 Replace the pinion bearing cover plate and adjust the shim pack to give the necessary clearance; similarly assemble the rack slipper, spring shims and cover plate again adjusting the shim pack to give the required clearance.

17 To replace each trackrod, in turn first fit a new spring and ball seat to the recess in the end of the rack shaft and replace the locknut onto the threads of the rack.

18 Lubricate the ball, ball seat and ball housing with a small amount of SAE 90 EP oil. Then slide the ball housing over the trackrod and screw the housing onto the rack threads, keeping the trackrod in the horizontal position until the trackrod starts to become stiff to move.

19 Using a normal spring balance hook it round the trackrod a quarter of an inch (6 mm) from the end and check the effort required to move it from the horizontal position (Fig. 11.30).

20 By adjusting the tightness of the ball housing on the rack threads the effort required to move the trackrod must be set at 5 lb (2.8 kg).

21 Tighten the locknut up to the housing and then re-check that the effort required to move the trackrod is still correct at 5 lb (2.8 kg).

22 On the line where the locknut and ball housing meet, drill a 0.12 inch (3 mm) diameter hole which must be 0.38 inch (9.5 mm) deep. Even if the two halves of the old hole previously drilled out align, a new hole must still be drilled.

23 Tap a new retaining pin into the hole and peen the end over to secure it.

24 Replace the rubber bellows and the track rod ends ensuring that they are replaced in exactly the same position from which they were removed.

25 Do not attempt to re-use the wire type clips used in production to retain the ends of the bellows. Special Jubilee type clips are available for use in service and these **must** be used. The inside surface of the bellows should be lightly smeared with grease at the point where it contacts the groove in the trackrod. The trackrod clips should now be fully tightened until the toe-in setting has been adjusted; when the clips are finally tightened the clip bolt heads must face the front of the vehicle and the gaiter must not be twisted.

26 Remove the cover plate and pour in ¼ pint (0.15 litre) of EP 90 grade oil. Alternatively, the oil can be poured into the casing via the pinion end with the bellows removed.

27 Carry out both the adjustments described in Section 12.

28 Refit the steering gear (Section 10) and then have the toe-in checked at your Ford dealer or refer to Section 16.

---

12 Steering gear - adjustments

1 For the steering gear to function correctly, two adjustments must be carried out whenever the unit is dismantled or

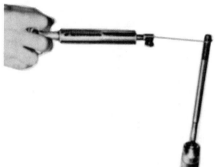

Fig. 11.30 Measuring track rod articulation using a spring balance (Sec 11)

Fig. 11.31 Disconnecting track rod end from suspension unit steering arm (Sec 11)

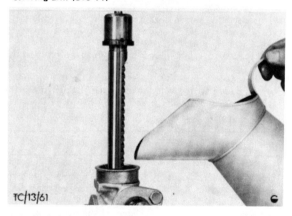

TC/13/61

Fig. 11.32 Method of filling steering rack with oil (Sec 11)

reassembled and the settings must be maintained when wear calls for further adjustment.

2 To carry out these adjustments, remove the steering gear from the car (Section 10), then mount the steering gear in a soft jawed vice so that the pinion is in a horizontal position and the rack damper cover plate to the top.

3 Remove the rack damper cover plate by undoing the two retaining bolts, then take off the gasket and shims from under the plate. Also remove the two small springs and the recessed yoke which bears on the rack.

4 Remove the pinion bearing cover plate, gasket and shim pack.

Pinion bearing adjustment

5 Select three shims one of which must be 2.35 mm (0.093 in) thick and placed immediately against the cover plate. Tighten the cover plate bolts to compress the shim pack then slacken the bolts so that the cover plate just touches the shim pack.

6 Using feeler gauges measure the gap between the underside of

the cover plate and the machined surface of the housing adjacent to each cover plate bolt. This gap should be 0.18 to 0.23 mm (0.007 to 0.009 in), if necessary adjust the shim pack by adding or deleting shims from the following selection.

Steel	0.010 inch (0.254 mm)
	0.005 inch (0.127 mm)
	0.002 inch (0.051 mm)
Paper	0.005 inch (0.127 mm)

The steel 2.286 mm shim must always be used in the shim pack.

7 Remove the cover plate and refit using a new gasket, smear a suitable sealer around the bolt threads and finally tighten the cover bolts to 6 to 8 lb f ft (0.83 to 1.1 kg fm).

Rack slipper adjustment

8 To set the rack damper adjustment, replace the slipper in its location on the rack and make sure it is fully home. Then measure the distance between the uppermost part of the slipper and the top of the steering gear casing.

9 Assemble a shim pack, including gaskets, to give a dimension 0.050 to 0.125 mm (0.002 to 0.005 in) greater than the dimension recorded in paragraph 8 above.

10 An alternative and more accurate method of establishing this dimension is to use a dial gauge zeroed on the rack slipper housing with the stylus of the gauge on the slipper. Traverse the rack until the highest slipper position is obtained and use the reading recorded, (ie; the maximum dial gauge deflection), as the base dimension.

11 Select shims from the following list to give a dimension 0.050 to 0.125 mm (0.002 to 0.005 in) greater than the dimension recorded on the gauge:

Steel 0.051 mm (0.002 in.)
Steel 0.127 mm (0.005 in.)
Steel 0.254 mm (0.010 in.)
Steel 0.381 mm (0.015 in.)
Steel 0.508 mm (0.020 in.)

12 It is important that the slipper adjustment is correctly set if heavy, stiff, steering and 'knocking' from the rack are to be avoided.

13 Refit the spring into its recess in the yoke and position the new shim pack so that the gasket is next to the cover plate. Replace the cover plate having first applied Loctite or similar sealing compound to the bolt threads. Then tighten down the bolts to a torque of 6 to 8 lb f ft (0.9 to 1.1 kg fm).

---

13 Steering wheel and column - removal and refitting

1 Place the vehicle with the wheels in the 'straight-ahead' position, disconnect the battery by removing the negative earth lead, then disconnect the lower end of the steering shaft from the flexible coupling by removing the nut and bolt on the top clamp of the coupling. **Note:** Removal of the flexible coupling clamp bolts can be assisted if the front of the vehicle is raised on stands.

2 Remove the choke cable, as described in Chapter 3.

3 Locate the small rubber screw cap on the surface of the upper half of the steering column shroud. Remove the cap, unscrew the screw exposed by the cap removal, and detach the upper half of the shroud.

4 Remove the screws securing the lower half of the shroud to the steering column bracket and the edge of the facia.

5 Disconnect the multiplug connections jointing the column switch wiring and the ignition switch wiring to the main wiring looms.

6 Remove the bolt securing the underside of the driver's side package tray to the steering column support bracketry.

7 Fold back the carpet from around the area where the steering column passes through the floor, then unbolt the plate from the floor.

8 Undo the two nuts and bolts holding the upper steering column bracket to the underside of the facia panel, then lift the complete steering column assembly into the car, and thence

Fig. 11.33 Using feeler gauges adjacent to the bolt location to measure pinion bearing preload. Note: the gasket is not in place when this measurement is taken (Sec 12)

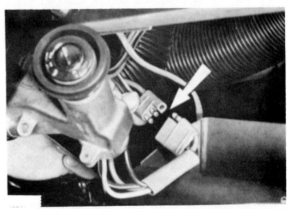

Fig. 11.34 Ignition switch to main loom multiplug (arrowed) shown disconnected (Sec 13)

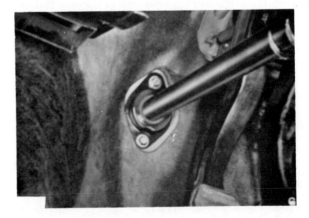

Fig. 11.35 Steering column plate (covered by corset) location in floor pan (Sec 13)

from the vehicle.

9 To replace the steering column in the car, pass it through the hole in the floor and mate up the splines on the shaft with the clamp on the flexible coupling and tighten the nut to a torque of 11 to 13 lbf ft (1.4 to 1.7 Kgf m).

10 Secure the top bracket on the column to the underside of the facia panel with the nuts and bolts, but do not tighten them

Fig. 11.36 Steering column bracket bolt location (arrowed) on underside of facia (Sec 13)

Fig. 11.37 Actuating cam, spring and spacer assembly (steering wheel not shown (Sec 14)

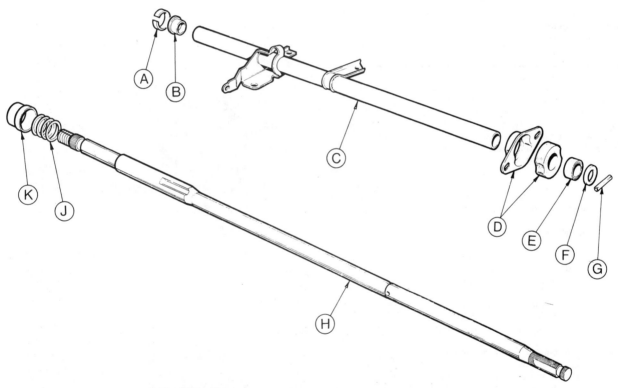

Fig. 11.38 Column and shaft assembly - exploded view (Sec 14)

A Spacer
B Upper bearing assembly
C Steering column tube
D Plate and rubber insulator
E Lower bearing

F Washer
G Pin
H Steering shaft
J Spring
K Actuator cam

Note: *On some versions plate D has a single hole and is welded to the column tube.*

down at this stage.

11 Secure the column lower support bracket to the floor and tighten down the bolts. Now return to the upper bracket and tighten down the nuts and bolts. This order of procedure ensures correct alignment of the steering column.

12 The remainder of the replacement procedure is a direct reversal of the removal sequence.

14 Steering column - servicing

1 Prise out the centre emblem on the steering wheel bar, undo the nut retaining the wheel to the steering shaft and detach the wheel, together with the indicator actuating cam, spring and spacer. Take care not to damage the steering wheel collapsible can.

2 Remove the two bolts clamping the combined indicator and horn switch to the steering column upper bracket and detach the switch.

3 Similarly unscrew the two crosshead screws holding the combined wash/wipe/light switch and bracket assembly to the column and carefully detach the assembly.

4 Remove the lower half of the steering column shroud.

5 Remove the combined ignition switch steering column lock, as described in Chapter 10, Section 65.

6 Tap the roll pin from its location in the lower end of the shaft and withdraw the lower bearing washer.

7 The steering shaft can now be withdrawn from the upper end of the steering column.

8 Remove the upper bearing from its location at the top of the steering column by drifting it out from below using a long rod.

9 Similarly remove the lower bearing from the lower end of the column then pull the plate and insulator rubber off the end of the column.

10 Check that the splines at both ends of the steering shaft are in good order.

11 Reassembly is a reversal of dismantling. Tighten the steering wheel nut to a torque of 20 to 25 lbf ft (2.8 to 3.5 Kgf m).

Fig. 11.39 Removing bolts securing combined indicator/horn switch to steering column bracket (Sec 14)

---

15 Steering column lock - removal and refitting

1 Refer to Chapter 10, Section 65.

---

16 Front wheel alignment

1 Accurate front wheel alignment is essential to provide good steering and slow tyre wear. Before considering the steering angles, check that the tyres are correctly inflated, that the road-wheels are not buckled, that the hub bearings are not worn or incorrectly adjusted and that the steering gear and linkage is in good order without slackness or wear at the joints.

2 Wheel alignment consists of four factors:

Camber — the angle at which the front wheels are set from the vertical when viewed from the front of the car. Positive camber is the angle that the wheels are tilted outward at the top of their vertical centre line.

Castor — the angle between the steering axis and a vertical line when viewed from each side of the vehicle. Positive castor is when the steering axis is inclined rearward at the top.

Steering axis inclination — the angle, when viewed from the front of the vehicle, between the vertical and an imaginary line drawn between the upper and lower suspension/steering pivots.

Toe-in — the amount by which the distance between the front inside edges of the roadwheels (measured at hub height) is less than that measured between the rear inside edges of the wheels.

3 The only steering adjustment which can be made by the home mechanic is for toe-in (tracking) the rest of the geometry having been set in production. It is recommended that the toe-in of the front wheels should be checked and adjusted by a service station having modern wheel alignment gauges but where this is not possible carry out the following procedure.

4 Place the vehicle on level ground with the wheels in the 'straight-ahead' position.

5 Obtain one of the proprietary tracking gauges or make one from a length of tubing, suitably cranked to clear the engine sump and bellhousing and having an adjustment nut and setscrew at one end.

6 With the gauge, measure the distance between the two inner wheel rims at hub height at the front of the roadwheel.

7 Roll the vehicle forward or backward so that a chalk mark made on the tyre wall will move through 180° (½ a turn). Now (without altering the setting previously obtained on the gauge) place the gauge between the inner wheel rims at hub height at the rear of the roadwheel. This measurement should be greater

Fig. 11.40 Removing crosshead screws securing switches and bracket to column (Sec 14)

Fig. 11.41 Replacing steering column lower bearing. Note plate and insulator rubber in place on column (Sec 14)

by up to ¼ inch (6.4 mm). This represents the required toe-in for the front wheels.

8   Where the toe-in is found to be incorrect, slacken both track-rod end locknuts and the outer clips on the rubber steering rack gaiters and ensure that the gaiters are not sticking to the track-rods.

9   Rotate both trackrods equally until the correct toe-in is obtained. Do not rotate the trackrods more than ¼ of a turn at a time before re-checking with the gauge.

10 Tighten the trackrod-end locknuts ensuring that the track-rod-end ball joints are held in the centre of their arc of travel during tightening. Tighten the gaiter clips.

17 Rear shock absorbers - removal and refitting

1   Chock the front wheels and jack-up the rear of the vehicle. The roadwheels need not be removed but it will be more convenient to do so.

2   Open the boot to gain access to the shock absorber top mountings. These can be located beneath the domed covers at the front corners of the boot floor. Remove the covers, unscrew the nut and locknut assemblies and detach the flat washer and bush.

3   From underneath the vehicle remove the nut securing the shock absorber lower mounting to the stud on the spring shackle plate.

4   Pull the shock absorber off the stud and then from its location in the floor pan, compressing the shock absorber as

necessary to enable its removal.

5   Refitting is a reversal of removal.

18 Rear shock absorbers - testing

1   Once removed, the shock absorber should be secured vertically in a vice, the jaws of which grip the lower mounting eye.

2   Fully extend and contract the shock absorber ten or twelve times and observe if there is strong resistance in both directions. It this is so, then the unit is operating satisfactorily and can be refitted. If there is no resistance or the unit jumps erratically during its movement, it must be renewed as it is not repairable.

3   Examine the shock absorber body for fluid leakage, also the rubber mounting bushes for wear or deterioration. If there is evidence of these, renew the unit.

19 Anti-roll bar (rear) - removal and installation

1   Chock the front wheels and jack-up the rear of the vehicle. The roadwheels need not be removed, but it will be more convenient to do so.

2   Remove the nuts securing each anti-roll bar end bush to the rear sidemembers. Extract the bolts from the sidemembers, noting that they are entered from the inside on the right-hand side and the outside on the left-hand side.

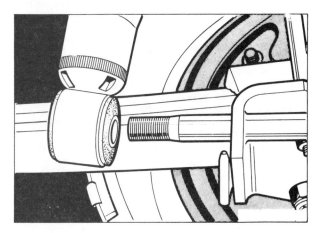

Fig. 11.42 Track rod adjustment: Slacken bellows clip (A) and track rod end lock nut (B) before turning track rod as necessary in direction indicated by arrows (Sec 16)

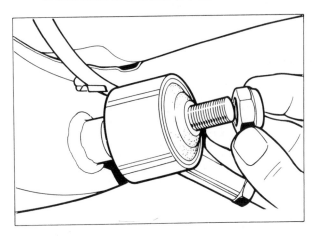

Fig. 11.43 Removing cap from shock absorber upper mounting in front corner of boot floor (Sec 17)

Fig. 11.44 Shock absorber lower mounting on rear spring shackle stud (Sec 17)

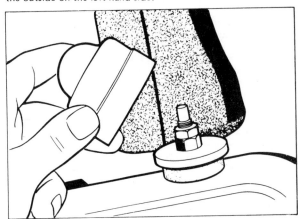

Fig. 11.45 Removing nut from anti-roll bar end bush location on rear side member (Sec 19)

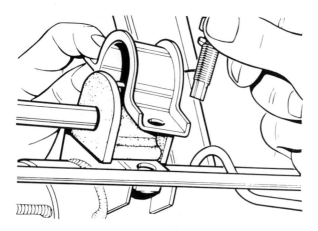

Fig. 11.46 Removing rear stabiliser bar clamp plate bolts from their rear axle tube locations (Sec 19)

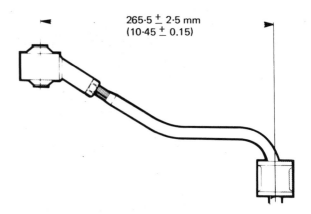

Fig. 11.47 End bush setting dimension relative to centre line of anti-roll bar transverse section (Sec 19)

3   Remove the two bolts securing each roll bar clamp plate to its axle tube bracket. The bar can now be removed from the vehicle.

4   Slacken the locknuts at the end of each end bush housing and unscrew the bushes from the bar followed by each locknut. Slide the rubber mounting bushes off the bar.

5   Refitting is a reversal of removal. However, when replacing the end bush housing ensure that the centreline of the bush is 265.5 ± 2.5 mm (10.4 ± 0.15 in) from the centre line of the transverse section of the bar (Fig. 11.47).

6   Before finally tightening the nuts securing the end bushes to the sidemembers, the weight of the vehicle must be on the wheels and the rear of the vehicle loaded, so that the rear spring eye centres and the centre of the axle tube are in line (Fig. 11.48). Tighten the nuts to the specified torque wrench setting.

20 Anti-roll bar end bushes - removal and installation

1   The rubber bushes can be pressed into and from the anti-roll bar end housings using a suitably sized pipe.

2   When finally assembled the voids in the bush must be vertical to the centreline of the bar.

21 Rear road springs - removal and installation

1   Chock the front wheels to prevent the car moving, then jack--up the rear of the car and support it on suitable stands. To make the springs more accessible, remove the roadwheels.

2   Remove the rear anti-roll bar.

3   Then place a trolley jack underneath the differential housing to support the rear axle assembly when the springs are removed. Do not raise the jack under the differential housing so that the springs are flattened, but raise it just enough to take the full weight of the axle with the springs fully extended.

4   Undo the rear shackle nuts and remove the combined shackle

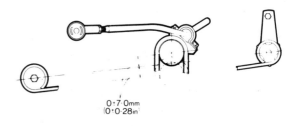

Fig. 11.48 'Loaded' position showing position of spring eyes relative to axle tube before tightening stabiliser bar mounting bolts (Sec 19)

bolt and plate assemblies. Then, if fitted, remove the small rubber bushes from the body aperture.

5   Undo the nut from the front mounting and take out the bolt running through the mounting.

6   Undo the nuts on the ends of the four 'U' bolts and remove the 'U' bolts together with the attachment plate and rubber spring insulators. Also remove the bump stops from the top of the 'U' bolts.

7   The rubber bushes can be pressed or driven out and the new bushes installed as described for the anti-roll bar in the previous Section. A little glycerine or brake fluid will allow the bushes to be pressed in more easily.

8   Replacement is a direct reversal of the above procedure. The nuts on the 'U' bolts, spring front mounting and rear shackles must be torqued down to the figures given in the Specifications at the beginning of this Chapter but only **after** the car has been lowered onto its wheels.

22 Fault diagnosis - suspension and steering

Symptom	Reason/s	Remedy
Steering feels vague, car wanders and floats at speed		
General wear or damage	Tyre pressures uneven	Check pressures and adjust as necessary.
	Shock absorbers worn	Test and renew if worn.
	Spring clips broken	Renew spring clips.
	Steering gear ball joints badly worn	Fit new ball joints.
	Suspension geometry incorrect	Check and rectify.
	Steering mechanism free play excessive	Adjust or overhaul steering mechanism.
	Front suspension and rear axle pick-up points out of alignment	Normally caused by poor repair work after a serious accident. Extensive rebuilding necessary.
Stiff and heavy steering		
Lack of maintenance or accident damage	Tyre pressures too low	Check pressures and inflate tyres.
	Front wheel toe-in incorrect	Check and reset toe-in.
	Suspension geometry incorrect	Check and rectify.
	Steering gear incorrectly adjusted too tightly	Check and readjust steering gear.
	Steering column badly misaligned	Determine cause and rectify (Usually due to bad repair after severe accident damage and difficult to correct).
Wheel wobble and vibration		
General wear or damage	Wheel nuts loose	Check and tighten as necessary.
	Front wheels and tyres out of balance	Balance wheels and tyres and add weights as necessary.
	Steering ball joints badly worn	Replace steering gear ball joints.
	Hub bearings badly worn	Remove and fit new hub bearings.
	Steering gear free play excessive	Adjust and overhaul steering gear.
	Front springs loose, weak or broken	Inspect and overhaul as necessary.

Chapter 12 Bodywork and fittings

For modifications, and information applicable to later models, see Supplement at end of manual

Contents

1 General description

The combined body and underframe is of welded, all steel unit construction. Models are available in two and four door saloon, estate car and van versions.

With these body types there is a choice of 'L', 'GL' or 'Ghia' trim versions. The heating and ventilation system introduces separate fresh air ventilation system through adjustable face level vents for the first time on the Escort range; these vents can be used for side window demisting during damp weather.

Toughened safety glass, tinted on Ghia variants, is fitted all round, although the safer type of laminated screen may be fitted as an option.

All models are fitted with bucket seats at the front, and a bench seat at the rear. The rake of the front seat is infinitely adjustable via a wheel controlled mechanism on the seat side. Ghia variants are also fitted with adjustable head restraints.

2 Maintenance — bodywork and underframe

1 The general condition of a car's bodywork is the thing that significantly affects its value. Maintenance is easy but needs to be regular. Neglect, particularly after minor damage, can lead quickly to further deterioration and costly repair bills. It is important also to keep watch on those parts of the car not immediately visible, for instance the underside, inside all the wheel arches and the lower part of the engine compartment.

2 The basic maintenance routine for the bodywork is washing — preferably with a lot of water, from a hose. This will remove all the loose solids which may have stuck to the car. It is important to flush these off in such a way as to prevent grit from scratching the finish. The wheel arches and underframe need washing in the same way to remove any accumulated mud which will retain moisture and tend to encourage rust. Paradoxically enough, the best time to clean the underframe and wheel arches is in wet weather when the mud is thoroughly wet and soft. In very wet weather the underframe is usually cleaned of large accumulations automatically and this is a good time for inspection.

3 Periodically, it is a good idea to have the whole of the underframe of the car steam cleaned, engine compartment included, so that a thorough inspection can be carried out to see what minor repairs and renovations are necessary. Steam cleaning is available at many garages and is necessary for removal of the accumulation of oily grime which sometimes is allowed to become thick in certain areas. If steam cleaning facilities are not available, there are one or two excellent grease solvents available which can be brush applied. The dirt can then be simply hosed off.

4 After washing paintwork, wipe off with a chamois leather to give an unspotted clean finish. A coat of clear protective wax polish will give added protection against chemical pollutants in the air. If the paintwork sheen has dulled or oxidised, use a cleaner/polisher combination to restore the brilliance of the shine. This requires a little effort, but such dulling is usually caused because regular washing has been neglected. Always check that the door and ventilator opening drain holes and pipes are completely clear so that water can be drained out. Bright work should be treated in the same way as paintwork. Windscreens and windows can be kept clear of the smeary film which often appears, by adding a little ammonia to the

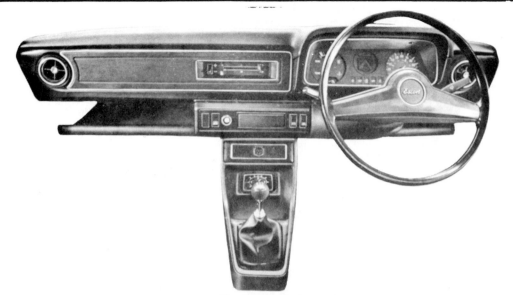

Fig. 12.1 GL Facia

Fig. 12.2 Sport Facia

Fig. 12.3 Ghia Facia

water. If they are scratched, a good rub with a proprietary metal polish will often clear them. Never use any form of wax or other body or chromium polish on glass.

---

3 Maintenance — upholstery and carpets

---

1 Mats and carpets should be brushed or vacuum cleaned regularly to keep them free of grit. If they are badly stained remove them from the car for scrubbing or sponging and make quite sure they are dry before refitting. Seats and interior trim panels can

be kept clean by a wipe over with a damp cloth. If they do become stained (which can be more apparent on light coloured upholstery) use a little liquid detergent and a soft nail brush to scour the grime out of the grain of the material. Do not forget to keep the head lining clean in the same way as the upholstery. When using liquid cleaners inside the car do not over-wet the surfaces being cleaned. Excessive damp could get into the seams and padded interior causing stains, offensive odours or even rot. If the inside of the car gets wet accidentally it is worthwhile taking some trouble to dry it out properly, particularly where carpets are involved. *Do not leave oil or electric heaters inside the car for this purpose.*

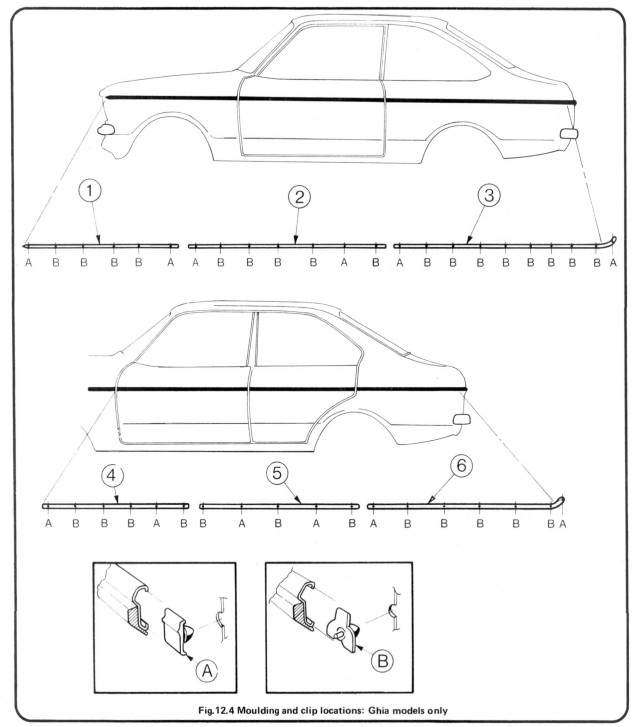

Fig.12.4 Moulding and clip locations: Ghia models only

4 Minor body damage - repair

The photo sequence on pages 222 and 223 illustrates the operations detailed in the following sub-Sections.

Repair of minor scratches in the car's bodywork

If the scratch is very superficial, and does not penetrate to the metal of the bodywork, repair is very simple. Lightly rub the area of the scratch with a paintwork renovator, or a very fine cutting paste, to remove loose paint from the scratch and to clear the surrounding bodywork of wax polish. Rinse the area with clean water.

Apply touch-up paint to the scratch using a fine paint brush; continue to apply thin layers of paint until the surface of the paint in the scratch is level with the surrounding paintwork. Allow the new paint at least two weeks to harden; then blend it into the surrounding paintwork by rubbing the scratch area with a paintwork renovator or a very fine cutting paste. Finally, apply wax polish.

Where the scratch has penetrated right through to the metal of the bodywork, causing the metal to rust, a different repair technique is required. Remove any loose rust from the bottom of the scratch with a penknife, then apply rust inhibiting paint to prevent the formation of rust in the future. Using a rubber or nylon applicator fill the scratch with bodystopper paste. If required, this paste can be mixed with cellulose thinners to provide a very thin paste which is ideal for filling narrow scratches. Before the stopper-paste in the scratch hardens, wrap a piece of smooth cotton rag around the top of a finger. Dip the finger in cellulose thinners and then quickly sweep it across the surface of the stopper-paste in the scratch; this will ensure that the surface of the stopper-paste is slightly hollowed. The scratch can now be painted over as described earlier in this Section.

Repair of dents in the car's bodywork

When deep denting of the car's bodywork has taken place, the first task is to pull the dent out, until the affected bodywork almost attains its original shape. There is little point in trying to restore the original shape completely, as the metal in the damaged area will have stretched on impact and cannot be re-shaped fully to its original contour. It is better to bring the level of the dent up to a point which is about 1/8 inch (3 mm) below the level of the surrounding bodywork. In cases where the dent is very shallow anyway, it is not worth trying to pull it out at all.

If the underside of the dent is accessible, it can be hammered out gently from behind, using a mallet with a wooden or plastic head. Whilst doing this, hold a suitable block of wood firmly against the impact from the hammer blows and thus prevent a large area of bodywork from being 'belled-out'.

Should the dent be in a section of the bodywork which has a double skin or some other factor making it inaccessible from behind, a different technique is called for. Drill several small holes through the metal inside the dent area - particularly in the deeper sections. Then screw long self-tapping screws into the holes just sufficiently for them to gain a good purchase in the metal. Now the dent can be pulled out by pulling on the protruding heads of the screws with a pair of pliers.

The next stage of the repair is the removal of the paint from the damaged area, and from an inch or so of the surrounding 'sound' bodywork. This is accomplished most easily by using a wire brush or abrasive pad on a power drill, although it can be done just as effectively by hand using sheets of abrasive paper. To complete the preparations for filling, score the surface of the bare metal with a screwdriver or the tang of a file, or alternatively, drill small holes in the affected area. This will

provide a really good 'key' for filler paste.

To complete the repair see the section on 'filling and re-spraying'.

Repair of rust holes or gashes in the car's bodywork

Remove all paint from the affected area and from an inch or so of the surrounding 'sound' bodywork, using an abrasive pad or a wire brush on a power drill. If these are not available a few sheets of abrasive paper will do the job just as effectively. With the paint removed you will be able to gauge the severity of the corrosion and therefore decide whether to renew the whole panel (if this is possible) or to repair the affected area. New body panels are not as expensive as most people think and it is often quicker and more satisfactory to fit a new panel than to attempt to repair large areas of corrosion.

Remove all fittings from the affected area except those which will act as a guide to the original shape of the damaged bodywork (eg headlamp shells etc). Then, using tin snips or a hacksaw blade, remove all loose metal and any other metal badly affected by corrosion. Hammer the edges of the hole inwards in order to create a slight depression for the filler paste.

Wire brush the affected area to remove the powdery rust from the surface of the remaining metal. Paint the affected area with rust inhibiting paint; if the back of the rusted area is accessible treat this also.

Before filling can take place it will be necessary to block the hole in some way. This can be achieved by the use of zinc gauze or aluminium tape.

Zinc gauze is probably the best material to use for a large hole. Cut a piece to the approximate size and shape of the hole to be filled, then position it in the hole so that its edges are below the level of the surrounding bodywork. It can be retained in position by several blobs of filler paste around its periphery.

Aluminium tape should be used for small or very narrow holes. Pull a piece off the roll and trim it to the approximate size and shape required, then pull off the backing paper (if used) and stick the tape over the hole; it can be overlapped if the thickness of one piece is insufficient. Burnish down the edges of the tape with the handle of a screwdriver or similar, to ensure that the tape is securely attached to the metal underneath.

Bodywork repairs - filling and re-spraying

Before using this Section, see the Sections on dent, deep scratch, rust hole, and gash repairs.

Many types of bodyfiller are available but generally speaking those proprietary kits which contain a tin of filler paste and a tube of resin hardener are best for this type of repair. A wide, flexible plastic or nylon applicator will be found invaluable for imparting a smooth and well contoured finish to the surface of the filler.

Mix up a little filler on a clean piece of card or board — measure the hardener carefully (follow the maker's instructions on the pack) otherwise the filler will set too rapidly or too slowly.

Using the applicator, apply the filler paste to the prepared area; draw the applicator across the surface of the filler to achieve the correct contour and to level the filler surface. As soon as a contour that approximates to the correct one is achieved, stop working the paste - if you carry on too long the paste will become sticky and begin to 'pick-up' on the applicator. Continue to add thin layers of filler paste at twenty-minute intervals until the level of the filler is just 'proud' of the surrounding bodywork.

Once the filler has hardened, excess can be removed using a Surform plane or Dreadnought file. From then on, progressively finer grades of abrasive paper should be used, starting with a 40 grade production paper and finishing with 400 grade 'wet-and-dry' paper. Always wrap the abrasive paper around a flat rubber, cork, or wooden block - otherwise the surface of the filler will not be completely flat. During the smoothing of the filler surface the 'wet-and-dry' paper should be periodically rinsed in water. This will ensure that a very smooth finish is imparted to the filler at the final stage.

At this stage the 'dent' should be surrounded by a ring of bare metal, which in turn should be encircled by the finely 'feathered' edge of the good paintwork. Rinse the repair area with clean water, until all the dust produced by the rubbing-down operation is gone.

Spray the whole repair area with a light coat of grey primer - this will show up any imperfections in the surface of the filler. Repair these imperfections with fresh filler paste or body-stopper, and once more smooth the surface with abrasive paper. If bodystopper is used, it can be mixed with cellulose thinners to form a really thin paste which is ideal for filling small holes. Repeat this spray and repair procedure until you are satisfied that the surface of the filler, and the feathered edge of the paintwork are perfect. Clean the repair area with clean water and allow to dry fully.

The repair area is now ready for spraying. Paint spraying must be carried out in a warm, dry, windless and dust free atmosphere. This condition can be created artifically if you have access to a large indoor working area, but if you are forced to work in the open, you will have to pick your day very carefully. If you are working indoors, dousing the floor in the work area with water will 'lay' the dust which would otherwise be in the atmosphere. If the repair area is confined to one body panel, mask off the surrounding panels; this will help to minimise the effects of a slight mis-match in paint colours. Bodywork fittings (eg; chrome strips, door handles etc.,) will also need to be masked off. Use genuine masking tape and several thicknesses of newspaper for the masking operation.

Before commencing to spray, agitate the aerosol can, thoroughly, then spray a test area (an old tin, or similar) until the technique is mastered. Cover the repair area with a thick coat of primer; the thickness should be built up using several thin layers of paint rather than one thick one. Using 400 grade 'wet-and-dry' paper, rub down the surface of the primer until it is really smooth. While doing this, the work area should be thoroughly doused with water, and the 'wet-and-dry' paper periodically rinsed in water. Allow to dry before spraying on more paint.

Spray on the top coat, again building up the thickness by using several thin layers of paint. Start spraying in the centre of the repair area and then, using a circular motion, work outwards until the whole repair area and about 2 inches of the surrounding original paintwork is covered. Remove all masking material 10 to 15 minutes after spraying on the final coat of paint.

Allow the new paint at least two weeks to harden, then, using a paintwork renovator or a very fine cutting paste, blend the edges of the paint into the existing paintwork. Finally, apply wax polish.

5 Major body damage - repair

1   Because the body is built on the unitary principle and is integral with the underframe, major damage must be repaired by competent mechanics with the necessary welding and hydraulic straightening equipment.
2   If the damage has been serious, it is vital that the body is checked for correct alignment, as otherwise the handling of the car will suffer and many other faults such as excessive wear in the tyres, transmission and steering may occur.

6 Maintenance - hinges and locks

Once every six months, or 6000 miles (9600 km), the door, bonnet and boot hinges should be oiled with a few drops of engine oil from an oil can.
1   To oil a hinge, first check that the plastic plugs in the ends of the hollow hinge pin, are in place, then prise the top plug out of its location in the pin.
2   Fill the hollow pin with oil and replace the top plug, carefully wiping away any overspill.
3   Open and close the door several times to disperse the oil then repeat the process for the remaining hinges. The door striker plates can be given a thin smear of grease to reduce wear and ensure free-movement.

7 Front bumper - removal and refitting

1   Disconnect the battery, then unscrew the two bolts securing each turn indicator lamp assembly to the front bumper bar. Accessible from within the engine compartment, disconnect the wiring loom from the lamp leads and detach the lamps.
2   Working inside the front wheel arches, first remove the bolt and washer assembly securing the outer ends of the bumper to the fender then the two bolts securing the bumper bar brackets to the body sidemembers.
3   The bumper bar complete with brackets can now be detached from the vehicle.
4   With the bumper bar removed from the body any of the bumper bar components can be removed.
5   The overriders are retained on the bar by a screw and clip arrangement on each end of the overrider, removal can be easily achieved by slackening the screws and sliding the overrider along

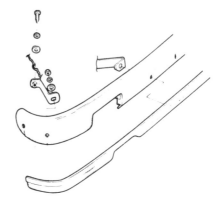

Fig. 12.5 Front bumper and bracket assembly (Sec 7)

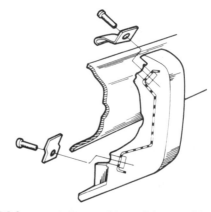

Fig. 12.6 Screw and clip assembly retaining overrider to bumper (Sec 7)

the bumper bar and off the end.

6 The bumper bar trim can be held to the bar either by small metal tangs (inserted through holes in the bar and then bent down), or by nuts and washer assemblies securing studs, integral with the trim. To remove the trim either bend up (ie; straighten), the tangs, or remove the nuts and washer assemblies.

7 Replacement is a reversal of the above procedure, but before finally tightening the bar retaining bolts ensure that the bar is set straight relative to the ground and adjacent body components on each side of the vehicle.

8 Rear bumper - removal and refitting

1 Working inside the boot, take out the spare wheel and undo the bolt at each end of the bumper bar with their washers and spring washers.

2 Similarly remove the bolt and washers assemblies securing the bumper bar brackets to the boot floor.

3 The bar can now be removed but before detaching it from the vehicle remember to disconnect the licence plate lamp wires.

4 Replacement is a reversal of the above procedure.

9 Windscreen glass - removal and installation

1 If you are unfortunate enough to have a windscreen shatter or should you wish to renew your present windscreen, fitting a replacement is one of the few jobs which the average owner is advised to leave to a professional. For the owner who wishes to do the job himself the following instructions are given.

2 Cover the bonnet with a blanket or cloth to prevent accidental damage and remove the windscreen wiper blades and arms.

3 If the screen has shattered, cover the facia demister slots and then knock the crystals out of the rubber frame. Withdraw the rubber surround and clean the glass channel free from mastic or glass crystals. If it is cut or hardened, renew it.

4 If the screen is intact, first check the type of screen fitted to the vehicle, this can be either 'laminated' or 'toughened'. To identify whether the screen is toughened or laminated, locate the manufacturer's trademark which will include either the word 'toughened' or 'laminated' or the letters 'T' or 'L'.

5 Before commencing windscreen removal, remove the windscreen wiper arms and blades, as described in Chapter 10, then cover the windscreen cowl and bonnet to prevent accidental damage to the paintwork.

6 Sitting inside the vehicle, and starting at one corner of the screen, use a blunt ended lever to push the weatherstrip lip under the weatherstrip aperture flange, at the same time pushing the glass forwards to fully disengage the glass and rubber from the flange. Continue the process, working in small lengths at a time, around the periphery of the screen until the glass and weatherstrip assembly is completely out of the screen aperture.

7 An alternative method **not** to be used on laminated screens: put on a pair of soft shoes and sit in one of the front seats. With a piece of soft cloth between the soles of your shoes and the windscreen glass, place both feet in one top corner of the windscreen and push firmly.

8 When the rubber surround has freed itself from the body flange in that area, repeat the process at frequent intervals along the top edge of the windscreen until, from outside the car, the glass and rubber surround can be removed together.

9 Gently prise out the clip which covers the joint of the chromium finisher strip and pull the finisher strip out of the rubber surround. Then remove the rubber surround from the glass.

10 Check the weatherstrip for signs of perishing, cuts, or distortion; if there is any doubt about the condition of a weatherstrip it should be renewed. If the rubber is deemed suitable for further service it must be completely cleaned of all traces of hardened sealer before it is fitted to the new glass.

11 Check the windscreen aperture in the vehicle to ensure that the flange is free from buckles and distortion and that all traces of hardened sealer are removed from both sides of the flange.

12 Apply a suitable sealer such as Expandite SR-51-B to the rubber to body groove. In this groove fit a fine but strong piece of cord right the way round allowing an overlap of about 6 inches (152.4 mm) at the joint.

13 From outside the car, place the windscreen in its correct position, making sure the loose end of the cord is inside the car.

14 With an assistant pressing firmly on the outside of the windscreen get into the car and pull out the cord thus drawing the lip of the rubber surround over the body flange.

15 Apply a further layer of sealer to the underside of the rubber glass groove from outside the car.

16 Replace the chromium finisher strip into its groove in the

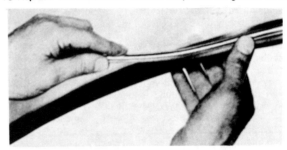

Fig. 12.7 Removing mylar insert from weatherstrip rubber (Sec 9)

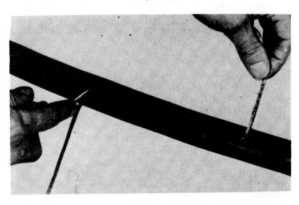

Fig. 12.8 Inserting cord into weatherstrip to body groove. If the cord is first passed through to thin metal tube and the tube then inserted into the weatherstrip groove, positioning the cord is simply a matter of drawing the tube around the periphery of the weatherstrip (Sec 9)

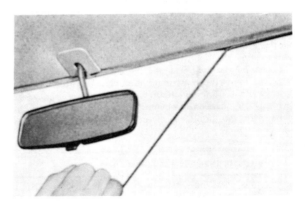

Fig. 12.9 Replacing windscreen glass: Note that cord is being pulled at right angles to the aperture flange (Sec 9)

rubber surround and replace the clip which covers its joint.

17 Carefully clean off any surplus sealer from the windscreen glass before it has a chance to harden and then replace the windscreen wiper arms and blades.

10 Door rattles - tracing and rectification

1 The most common cause of door rattle is a misaligned, loose or worn striker plate, but other causes may be:
   a) *Loose door handles or window winder handles*
   b) *Loose, or misaligned door lock components*
   c) *Loose or worn remote control mechanism*
2 It is quite possible for door rattles to be the result of a combination of the above faults so a careful examination must be made to determine the cause of the fault.
3 If the nose of the striker plate is worn and as a result the door rattles, renew and then adjust the plate, as described in Section 11.
4 Should the inner door handle rattle, this is easily cured by fitting a rubber washer between the escutcheon and the handle.
5 If the door lock is found to be worn and rattles as a consequence, then fit a new lock (Section 11).

11 Door striker plate - removal, refitting and adjustment

1 Mark the position of the striker plate on the door pillar using a soft pencil.
2 Unscrew and remove the four crosshead securing screws and lift the striker plate away.
3 Replace the striker plate by positioning the plate on the door piller within the lines previously described, and loosely securing with the four screws.
4 To adjust the plate, close the door to the first of the two locking positions and visually check the alignment of the outside edge of the striker plate relative to the edge of the lock support plate. This check is best carried out by looking at the lock/striker plate from either the top, or bottom, edges of the door, while shining a light on the lock/striker plate location. The edges of the striker and lockplates should be parallel.
5 Measure the distance the door edge stands proud of the adjacent body panel; for a correctly set door this distance should be 6.00 mm (0.25 in).
6 If necessary the striker plate securing screws must be slackened and the striker plate moved in, or out, until both the parallel condition, and the proud condition, described above are achieved.
7 The lock claw to lock striker clearance must now be measured and, if necessary adjusted. The lock claw is the 'U' shaped portion of the lock (protuding through the door) which responds to the action of the door handle. Before this measurement can be taken the lock must be in the 'open' position (ie; the 'U' of the claw must be facing the striker). The correct setting is best obtained by placing a small ball of plasticine on the top of the striker post and then gently closing and opening the door. The top of the plasticine ball will be flattened by the lock claw and the distance between this flat edge and the striker post is the lock claw to striker clearance. This should be 2.0 mm (0.08 in). If necessary, **and without disturbing the previously obtained settings**, vertically reposition the striker plate until the correct dimension is obtained. When adjustment is correct, fully tighten the securing screws.

12 Door trim pad - removal and refitting

1 Carefully slide the window regulator handle plastic trim upwards (ie; away from the tapered end), to disengage the trim from its retaining slots. With the trim free of the slots it can be lifted clear out of the handle recess to expose the handle retaining screws.
2 Wind the window glass into the closed position, note the

Fig. 12.10 Door lock striker plate fixing screws (Sec 11)

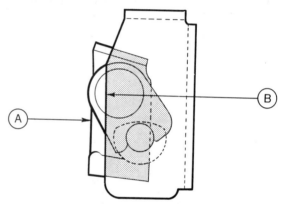

Fig. 12.11 Parallel condition between lock striker (A) and lock support plate (B) (Sec 11)

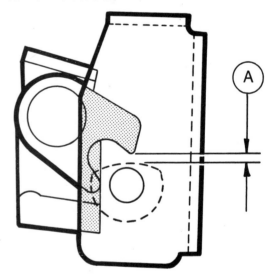

Fig. 12.12 Lock claw to striker clearance 'A' = 2.0 mm (Sec 11)

position of the handle then unscrew the crosshead screw retaining the handle to the shaft and detach the handle and bezel from the shaft. (photo)
3 Undo and remove the two crosshead screws securing the door armrest and lift the armrest off the trim pad. (photo) Unscrew the private lock button. (located in the top corner of the pad) off the private lock rod.
4 Press the trim panel away from the remote control handle bezel at the same time pushing the bezel towards the hinge end

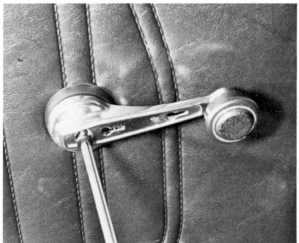

12.2 Unscrew the single crosshead screw and then detach the window winder handle

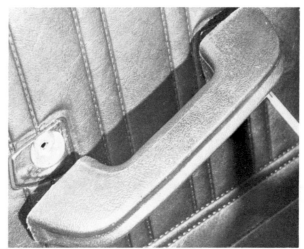

12.3 Unscrew the two crosshead screws securing the armrest to the door panel

12.4 Push the trim panel inwards and then slide the bezel towards the hinge end of the door

12.5 The door trim panel removed. Note the weatherproof sheet attached to the door skin

of the door. This will disengage the bezel retaining lugs from their locations whereupon the bezel can be lifted out of its location. **Do not attempt to lever the bezel out of its location as this will almost certainly result in broken retaining lugs.** (photo)

5 Insert a thin strip of metal with all the sharp edges removed between the recessed trim panel and the door. This will release one or two of the trim panel clips without damaging the trim and the panel can then be gently eased off by hand. A short metal ruler is ideal for this job. (photo)

6 Depending on why the panel is being removed the alkathene waterproof sheeting can now be removed.

7 Replacement is generally a reversal of the removal procedure. However, the following points should be noted. If the alkathene sheet is torn, or badly distorted, it must be replaced to ensure a weatherproof seal. When the defective sheet has been removed, all traces of old adhesive, or tape, must be removed before the new double-sided tape is applied. Apply the new tape so that the edge of the tape is 6 mm. (0.25 in) from the edge of the door inner panel and that the trim clip holes are covered. If a new sheet is being made up, the door trim pad can be used as a template, with the edges of the sheet cut 5.0 mm (0.2 in) inside the periphery of the pad. Start fixing the sheet to the door at the top edge, progressing down the sides and finally pushing the

lower edge of the sheet into the slot at the bottom of the door. Working upwards from the bottom, smooth the sheet down making sure that there are no air bubbles in the sheet, particularly along the bottom and sides. When the sheet has been satisfactorily smoothed down cover the slot with tape.

13 Door lock - removal and refitting

1 Refer to Section 12, and remove the door trim pad.

2 Carefully slide the remote control assembly towards the hinge end of the door to disengage it from the cut-out in the door inner panel. Turn the assembly, as necessary, to unhook the lock control rod and place the assembly to one side.

3 Locate the window frame lower retaining screw on the door inner panel; remove this screw and push the frame to one side to improve access to the lock assembly.

4 Unclip the two rods connecting the lock to the exterior handle linkage; these rods are located in the white bushes on the lock mechanism.

5 From outside the vehicle, unscrew and remove the three screws securing the lock to the door. Turn the lock claw to the 'closed' position (ie; with the 'U' of the claw facing the floor),

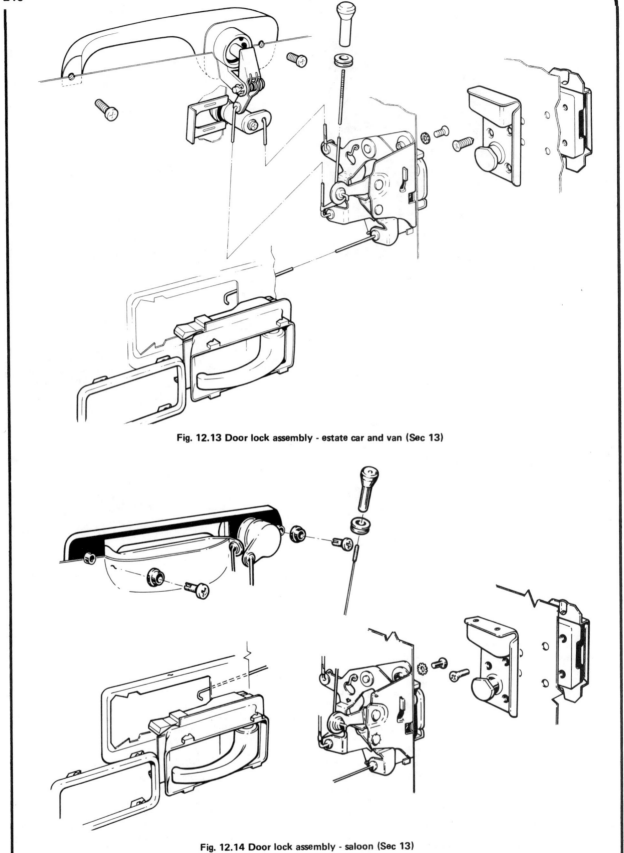

Fig. 12.13 Door lock assembly - estate car and van (Sec 13)

Fig. 12.14 Door lock assembly - saloon (Sec 13)

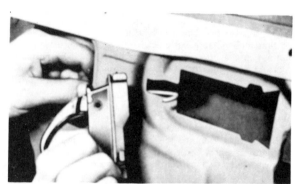

Fig. 12.15 Removing door remote control handle assembly (Sec 13)

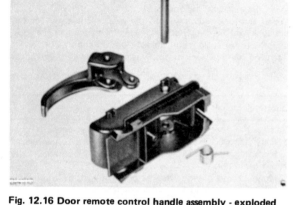

Fig. 12.16 Door remote control handle assembly - exploded view (Sec 13)

Fig. 12.17 Door lock showing black bush (A) and white bushes (B) (Sec 13)

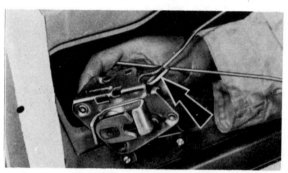

Fig. 12.18 Removing door lock assembly with remote control handle rack (arrowed) disconnected (Sec 13)

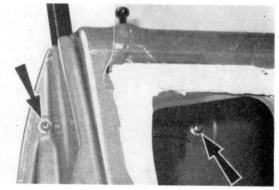

Fig. 12.19 Exterior handle retaining screws on rear of door outer panel. Note: only remove the alkathene sheeting locally, to gain access to the screws and lock rods (Sec 14)

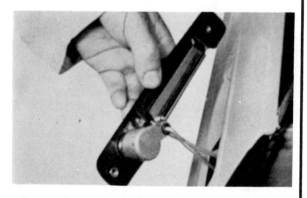

Fig. 12.20 Removing the door exterior handle (Sec 14)

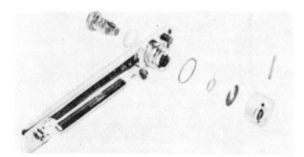

Fig. 12.21 Exterior handle and lock barrel assembly - exploded view (Sec 14)

Fig. 12.22 Removing door window regulator (Sec 15)

and push the lock into the door shell.

6   Lower the lock assembly into the shell sufficiently for the private lock rod to clear its housing, then manoeuvre the lock through the lower cut-out and thence from the shell.

7   Refitting the door lock assembly is the reverse of the removal sequence.

14 Door lock barrel - removal and refitting

1   Remove the door trim pad, as described in Section 12.

2   Locally remove the alkathene sheet in the rear top corner of the door, to expose the exterior handle retaining screws and the door lock assembly.

3   Disconnect the exterior handle connecting rods from their locations in the door lock mechanism (the lock rods are connected to the links with white bushes).

4   Unscrew the two crosshead screws retaining the exterior handle to the door shell and carefully detach the handle, together with the lock rods, from the door.

5   Remove the lock barrel by tapping the roll pin from the end cap and separating the end cap, 'U' washer, return spring and seals. Withdraw the barrel and seal from the exterior handle casting.

6   Refitting the lock barrel and exterior handle is a reversal of the removal process.

15 Door glass regulator - removal and refitting

1   Wind the window down and remove the door remote control handle, the window regulator handle, the arm rest/door pull and trim panel (Section 12).

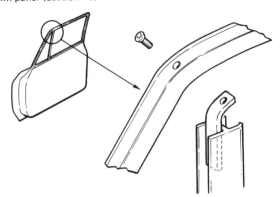

Fig. 12.23 Screw location securing front quarter window dividing channel to window frame (Sec 16)

2   Undo the screws and washers which secure the window regulator assembly. This is best achieved by lowering the window so that the regulator and bracket can be seen through the lower cut-out in the door shell. Remove the screw securing the pivot plate to door inner panel and then push the plate into the door shell so that the regulator handle shaft no longer protudes through the inner panel.

3   Slide the regulator arm along the door glass bracket and into the enlarged area at the end of the bracket. The arm can be disengaged from the bracket at this point. With the arm free, push the glass up into the closed position and withdraw the regulator assembly through the lower door cut-out. If necessary, remove the screw securing the lower end of the frame and push the frame to one side to gain access for removing the regulator.

4   Refitting the regulator is the reverse of the removal sequence.

16 Door glass - removal and refitting

1   Remove the door trim pad, as described in Section 12.

2   Prise the inner and outer door belt weatherstrips from their retaining clips in the upper gap between the door inner and outer panels.

3   Remove the screw securing the upper end of the quarter window dividing channel to the frame, and the single screw securing the lower end to the door inner panel. Tilt the dividing channel as necessary to enable its removal from the door shell.

4   Remove the door window glass by sliding the glass along the regulator arm until the arm can be disengaged from the glass retaining bracket.

5   Push the regulator arm clear of the glass and withdraw the glass from the shell, passing the window frame on the passenger compartment side.

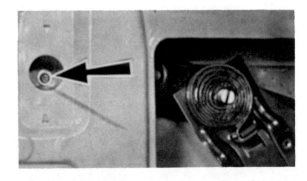

Fig. 12.24 Screw location for lower fixing door quarter window dividing channel (Sec 16)

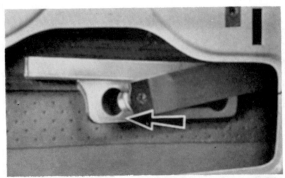

Fig. 12.25 Window regulator to glass bracket engagement. Slide regulator in direction of arrow into enlarged area of bracket to disengage (Sec 16)

Fig. 12.26 Removing door window glass. Note that the glass passes the window frame on the passenger compartment side (Sec 16)

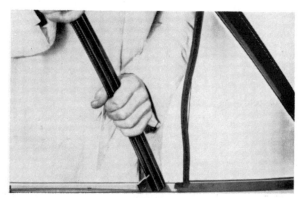

Fig. 12.27 Removing quarter window dividing channel (Sec 17)

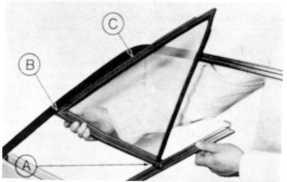

Fig. 12.28 Replacing fixed door quarter window glass. Ensure that 'U' shaped end of weatherstrip (A) is around channel and that weatherstrip 'C' starts to engage 'U' channel of frame at approximately part 'B' (Sec 17)

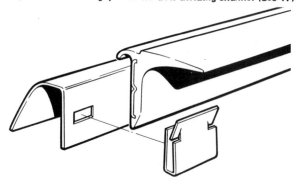

Fig. 12.29 Door belt weatherstrip and moulding assembly (Sec 18)

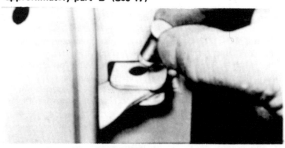

Fig. 12.30 Removing the door check arm pin (Sec 19)

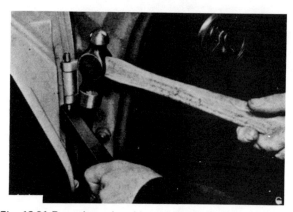

Fig. 12.31 Removing a door hinge pin with Ford tool 41 - 002 and a hammer (Sec 19)

Fig. 12.32 Door hinge retaining nuts (lower) (Sec 19)

6   Refitting the door glass is the reverse sequence to removal.

---

17 Door fixed quarterlights - removal and refitting

1   Commence removal of these components from the front door by first removing the inner and outer weather sealing strips and their clips.

2   Remove the screw which secures the top of the quarter window dividing channel to the door frame.

3   Remove the door interior trim panel as previously described and then remove the screw and washer securing the bottom of the dividing channel.

4   Pull the sliding channel down and then incline it toward the rear of the vehicle. The ventilator or fixed quarterlight may now be lifted from the door frame.

5   Refitting is a reversal of removal.

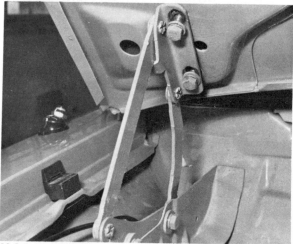

20.3 Release the bolts securing the bonnet to the hinges and carefully lift the bonnet away. Do not forget to scribe around the hinges before slackening the bolts

18 Door belt weatherstrips (outer) - removal and refitting

1 Wind the window down to its fullest extent. Carefully prise the weatherstrips and moulding assembly out of the retaining clips along the top edge of the door shell.
2 With the weatherstrip and moulding assembly clear of the door belt, carefully prise the 'U' clips securing the moulding and weatherstrip together off the assembly, and separate the moulding and weatherstrip.
3 Refit the weatherstrip by first aligning it along the moulding and securing with the 'U' clips, and then replacing the combined moulding and weatherstrip in the door shell clips.

19 Front and rear door - removal and refitting

Ford tool No 41 - 002, or equivalent, will be needed for this operation.
1 Open the door and disconnect the check arm by removing its pivot pin.
2 Fit tool 41 - 002 through one of the hinge pins as shown in Fig. 12.31 and remove the hinge pin downwards by striking the tool with a hammer. Repeat the operation on the other hinge. It is advisable to have an assistant support the door.
3 Lift the door off the hinges. If it is to be re-used, stand it on an old blanket or similar item and protect it from abrasion if it is leaning against a wall.
4 Refit in the reverse order to removal, using tool 41 - 002 to pull the hinge pins into position.
5 If adjustment of the door is necessary, first remove the door striker plate as described in Section 11. Remove the trim panel and slacken the hinge retaining nuts slightly. Adjust the door by lifting or lowering the rear corner until it sits correctly in its aperture, then tighten the hinge nuts.
6 Adjust the striker plate as described in Section 11.

20 Bonnet - removal and replacement

1 Open the bonnet and support it open using the bonnet stay. To act as a datum for refitting, scribe round the position of the hinge brackets on the underside of the bonnet.
2 With the assistance of a second person hold the bonnet in the open position and release the stay.
3 Undo and remove the two bolts, spring and plain washers that secure each hinge to the bonnet, and lift the bonnet of the vehicle, taking care not to damage the tops of the fenders. (photo)
4 Lean the bonnet against a wall with the contact points suitably padded to protect the paintwork against damage.
5 Refitting the bonnet is the reverse sequence to removal. If the hinge brackets are correctly aligned to the previously scribed lines the bonnet should be correctly aligned in its aperture. However, if the adjustment has been disturbed the bonnet can be re-adjusted as follows: Remove the conical-end bonnet lock striker after first slackening the locknut.
6 Slacken the locknuts on the rubber bump stops at either end of the front crossmember and screw the bump stops fully into their locations.
7 Close the bonnet and check the gaps on either side of the bonnet between the fenders and the gap between the rear edge of the bonnet and the cowl panel. These must be equal along this length and, in the case of the bonnet to fender gap, equal on either side of the bonnet. If necessary move the bonnet on the hinges to achieve the necessary alignment, then fully tighten the hinge bolts.
8 Check the height of the front of the bonnet relative to the adjacent fenders. Progressively screw the bump stops out of their locations until the bonnet is flush with the tops of the fenders. Tighten the locknuts on the rubbers when this stage of the bonnet adjustment is correct.

Fig. 12.33 Bonnet adjustment points (Sec 20)

A *Bump stops*   C *Hinges*
B *Bonnet lock spring* D *Striker*

Fig. 12.34 Replacing bonnet striker: when striker is finally set fully tighten locknut 'A' (Sec 20)

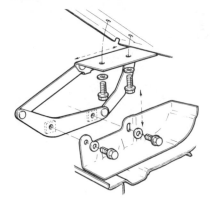

Fig. 12.35 Bonnet hinge assembly (Sec 20)

side of the bonnet and screw the striker in, or out, to achieve the following condition:
  i) *When released from a height of 300 mm (11.8 in) above the 'pop-up' position the bonnet must fully engage.*
  ii) *When released from a height of up to 75 mm (3 in) above the 'pop-up' position only the safety catch must engage.*

When these conditions are fulfilled tighten the striker locknut.

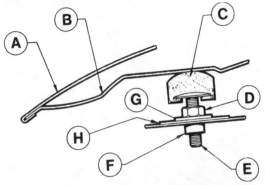

Fig. 12.36 Bonnet bump stop assembly (Sec 20)

A Bonnet panel
B Bonnet inner panel
C Bump rubber
D Locknut

E Bump stop thread
F Weld nut
G and H Front
    crossmember

Fig. 12.37 Bonnet release cable clamp location (Sec 21)

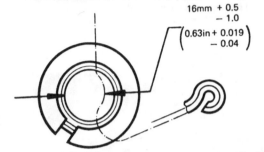

$$16\text{mm} \begin{array}{l} + 0.5 \\ - 1.0 \end{array}$$

$$\left(0.63\text{in} \begin{array}{l} + 0.019 \\ - 0.04 \end{array}\right)$$

Fig. 12.39 Bonnet release spring setting dimension (Sec 21)

Fig. 12.38 Releasing bonnet release cable clamp bolt by inserting suitable size socket through bars of grille (Sec 21)

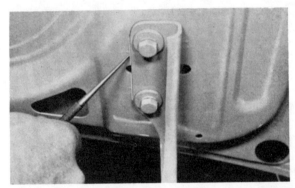

Fig. 12.40 Scribing line around boot lid hinge prior to removing lid (Sec 23)

Fig. 12.41 Boot lid lock assembly (Sec 23)

A Clip
B Lock
C Boot lid

D Lock barrel
E Lock striker plate

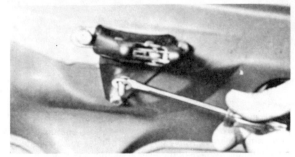

Fig. 12.42 Prising clip off boot lid lock spindle (Sec 23)

This sequence of photographs deals with the repair of the dent and paintwork damage shown in this photo. The procedure will be similar for the repair of a hole. It should be noted that the procedures given here are simplified — more explicit instructions will be found in the text

In the case of a dent the first job — after removing surrounding trim — is to hammer out the dent where access is possible. This will minimise filling. Here, the large dent having been hammered out, the damaged area is being made slightly concave

Now all paint must be removed from the damaged area, by rubbing with coarse abrasive paper. Alternatively, a wire brush or abrasive pad can be used in a power drill. Where the repair area meets good paintwork, the edge of the paintwork should be 'feathered', using a finer grade of abrasive paper

In the case of a hole caused by rusting, all damaged sheet-metal should be cut away before proceeding to this stage. Here, the damaged area is being treated with rust remover and inhibitor before being filled

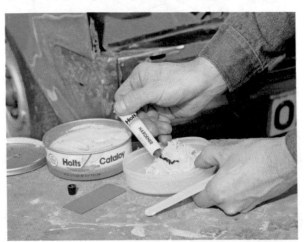

Mix the body filler according to its manufacturer's instructions. In the case of corrosion damage, it will be necessary to block off any large holes before filling — this can be done with zinc gauze or aluminium tape. Make sure the area is absolutely clean before...

...applying the filler. Filler should be applied with a flexible applicator, as shown, for best results; the wooden spatula being used for confined areas. Apply thin layers of filler at 20-minute intervals, until the surface of the filler is slightly proud of the surrounding bodywork

Initial shaping can be done with a Surform plane or Dreadnought file. Then, using progressively finer grades of wet-and-dry paper, wrapped around a sanding block, and copious amounts of clean water, rub down the filler until really smooth and flat. Again, feather the edges of adjoining paintwork

The whole repair area can now be sprayed or brush-painted with primer. If spraying, ensure adjoining areas are protected from over-spray. Note that at least one inch of the surrounding sound paintwork should be coated with primer. Primer has a 'thick' consistency, so will fill small imperfections

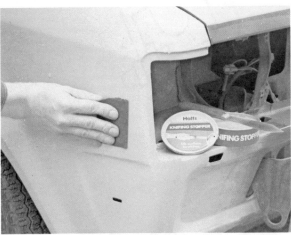

Again, using plenty of water, rub down the primer with a fine grade of wet-and-dry paper (400 grade is probably best) until it is really smooth and well blended into the surrounding paintwork. Any remaining imperfections can now be filled by carefully applied knifing stopper paste

When the stopper has hardened, rub down the repair area again before applying the final coat of primer. Before rubbing down this last coat of primer, ensure the repair area is blemish-free — use more stopper if necessary. To ensure that the surface of the primer is really smooth use some finishing compound

The top coat can now be applied. When working out of doors, pick a dry, warm and wind-free day. Ensure surrounding areas are protected from over-spray. Agitate the aerosol thoroughly, then spray the centre of the repair area, working outwards with a circular motion. Apply the paint as several thin coats

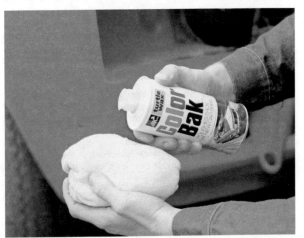

After a period of about two weeks, which the paint needs to harden fully, the surface of the repaired area can be 'cut' with a mild cutting compound prior to wax polishing. When carrying out bodywork repairs, remember that the quality of the finished job is proportional to the time and effort expended

21 Bonnet release cable - adjustment

1 The bonnet release cable is adjusted by applying tension to the cable until the bonnet release spring is pulled into a set position relative to the spring aperture. The cable is then clamped in position.
2 The cable clamp screw is located on the rear of the front body panel adjacent to the radiator. To gain access to the screw head first remove the radiator grille. Alternatively, if a suitably sized socket set is available the screw can be slackened by inserting the socket attachment through the bars of the grille.
3 Unclip the cable from its retaining clips around the side of the engine compartment and pull the cable through the clamp until the bonnet lock spring setting is as shown in Fig. 12.39 (16.0 mm $^+$ 0.5 mm - 1.0 mm).
4 Hold the cable in this position and retighten the clamp bolt. Close the bonnet and operate the release lever. The bonnet should 'pop-up' freely, if it does not, recheck the spring setting, if this is correct, re-adjust the hood lock striker.

22 Bonnet release spring - removal and refitting

1 Slacken the bonnet release cable clamp screw.
2 Unscrew the screw retaining the bonnet release spring clamp plate. Withdraw the spring arm from the aperture in the lock support plate and manoevre the spring until the release cable loop can be disengaged from the release spring arm.
3 When the cable has been disconnected manoevre the spring around in the lock support plate and out of its location via the aperture in the rear of the crossmember.
4 Refitting is a reversal of the removal procedure. Before finally tightening the cable clamp screw adjust the release spring, as described in Section 21.

23 Luggage boot lid and lock - removal and refitting

1 Open the boot lid and mark the position of the hinge plates using a sharp pencil.
2 Release the cranked end of the torsion bar (used to counterbalance the lid) from its retaining bracket. Disconnect the double cranked end from the hinge and withdraw the torsion bar.
3 Remove the hinge securing bolts and their washers and lift the lid away.
4 The boot lock can be removed without removing the luggage boot lid.
5 To remove the lock assembly remove the spring clip from the end of the lock spindle and remove the three bolts which secure the lock to the boot lid.
6 To remove the lock barrel from two door models, insert a pair of long nosed pliers through the aperture left after withdrawal of the lock mechanism, and compress the legs of the lock barrel retaining clip.
7 Refitting of all components is a reversal of removal but if necessary adjust the lock striker by slightly loosening its retaining bolts to provide positive closure of the boot lid without any rattling.

24 Estate car tailgate lock - removal and refitting

1 Remove the tailgate trim panel in a similar manner to that described for doors (Section 12).
2 Disconnect the operating rod from the tailgate handle.
3 Unscrew and remove the three screws which retain the lock assembly to the tailgate and withdraw the lock complete with its operating rod through the small aperture in the tailgate panel.
4 Refitting is a reversal of removal.

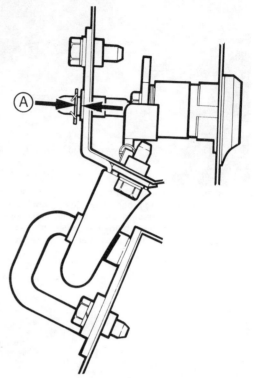

Fig. 12.43 Position of clip on boot lid lock barrel spindle (Sec 23)

A = 2.0 mm $\pm$ 1.0 mm

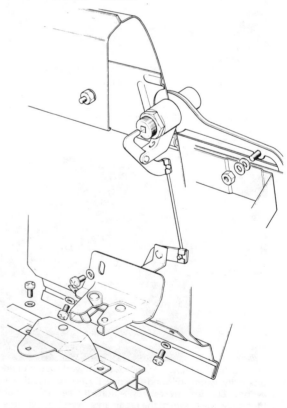

Fig. 12.44 Tailgate exterior handle and lock assembly (Sec 24)

25 Estate car tailgate - removal and refitting

1 Open the tailgate door to its full extent. Remove the trim panel from the hinge assemblies.
2 Mark the position of the hinge plates on the tailgate and then unscrew and remove the two bolts from each hinge plate and lift the tailgate away.
3 Refitting is a reversal of removal.

26 Estate car tailgate hinge and torsion bar assembly - removal and installation

1 Remove the tailgate (Section 25).
2 Unscrew and remove the four bolts which retain each of the hinge/torsion bar assemblies to the body. **On no account remove the nut from the torsion bar locking plate bolt.**
3 If further dismantling is essential, lay the assembly upside down (to its normal location in the vehicle) on a block of wood positioned under the locking plate of one hinge.
4 Obtain the help of an assistant to stand on the hinge baseplate and unscrew the torsion bar locking plate bolt of this particular hinge. Gradually release the tension of the torsion bar by allowing the hinge and baseplate to rise against the combined weights of yourself and your assistant.
5 Remove the other torsion bar locking plate, the two locating spacers and then withdraw the torsion bars from the hinges.
6 To reassemble the hinge/torsion bar assemblies, position the baseplate on the floor with the hinge arms uppermost at approximately the correct distance apart.
7 Locate the torsion bar which has a single right angled bend at one end in the baseplate and secure it with a locking plate and bolt.
8 Fit the other end of the torsion bar in the opposite baseplate and position a spacer between the short section of the torsion bar (which is parallel to the main bar) and the hinge arm pin.
9 Locate the end of the torsion bar which has a double right angled bend in the baseplate to which the torsion bar with the single right angled bend was first connected.
10 Position the second spacer between the hinge arm pin and the end of the torsion bar. The remaining unattached end of the second torsion bar should now be at an angle of about 120° to the baseplate to which it is to be attached. Should it be only about 15° however, the torsion bars will have to be dismantled and reversed.
11 Turn the hinge and torsion bar assembly over and support the unattached end of the torsion bar on a block of wood.
12 Locate the remaining locking plate under the unattached end of the torsion bar.
13 Turn the baseplate over and then with the combined weights of two people standing on it, bolt the locking plate into position. It is imperative that the foregoing instructions are rigidly adhered to otherwise personal injury can be caused by the sudden release of the torsion bar tension.

27 Van rear door lock and lock bar - removal and refitting

1 Remove the trim panel from the right hand door.
2 Unscrew and remove the three lock securing screws and withdraw the lock through the door aperture.
3 The exterior handle is withdrawn after removal of the two escutcheon plate securing screws.
4 To remove the locking bar from the opposing door, unscrew and remove the screws from the pivot plate and pull the lock bar outward to free the ends of the bars from their guides (Fig. 12.46).
5 Refitting is a reversal of removal.

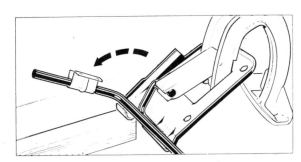

Fig. 12.45 Releasing estate tailgate torsion bar (Sec 26)

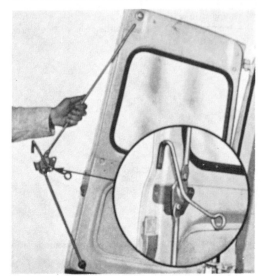

Fig. 12.46 Removing van rear door lock bar (Sec 27)

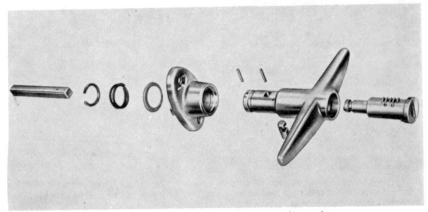

Fig. 12.47 Van rear door lock components (Sec 27)

28 Rear window glass - removal and replacement

The procedure for removing the rear window glass is identical to that described for the windscreen glass.

29 Tailgate window glass - removal and replacement

The procedure for removal and replacement of the tailgate window glass is basically identical to that for the windscreen glass. However, at all times during the removal and installation process great care must be taken not to damage the heated rear screen elements.

30 Fixed rear quarter window glass - removal and replacement

1 Have an assistant ready to catch the glass as it is released from the body aperture. Working from inside the vehicle use a blunt screwdriver to carefully ease the weatherstrip rubber off the aperture flange, at the same time pushing on the glass to release the glass and rubber from the aperture.
2 Remove the weatherstrip from the glass and remove all traces of old sealer from the glass to weatherstrip groove. Inspect the weatherstrip for signs of splitting, or deterioration. If there is any doubt about the condition of the weatherstrip it must be renewed.
3 Check that the window aperture moulding is correctly positioned on the aperture flange and that the double sided sponge sealing strip is in good condition.
4 Fit a length of cord in the weatherstrip to body groove, so

that the ends of the cord have a crossover of approximately 150 mm (6.0 in) at the bottom centre of the glass.
5 Offer the glass and weatherstrip assembly to the aperture with the ends of the cord inside the vehicle. Engage the weatherstrip with the flange along the top of the window aperture and push the lower edge firmly into contact with the bottom flange. With an assistant working inside the vehicle, and pulling one end of the cord, **at right-angles to the glass,** push, or tap the glass very firmly adjacent to the cord, to assist in pulling the weatherstrip over the flange.
6 Seal the weatherstrip to glass location with a suitable glass sealer.

31 Radiator grille - removal and refitting

Open the bonnet and support in the open position. Undo and remove the screws that secure the radiator grille to the front body crossmembers, and lift the grille away from the body. Replacement is a reversal of removal, but first check to ensure that the special grille nuts are in place in their locations on the crossmembers.

32 Heater unit - removal and refitting

1 Disconnect the battery by removing the negative earth lead and drain the radiator.
2 Disconnect the choke cable from the carburettor. This cable must be released in order to remove the heater cover panel.
3 Working under the bonnet, slacken off the two cable clips on the heater water pipes and then pull the pipes off the bulkhead.

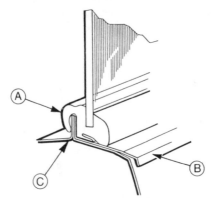

Fig. 12.48 Fixed rear quarter window glass assembly (Sec 30)

A Weatherstrip rubber   B Moulding   C Flange

Fig. 12.49 Offering fixed rear quarter window into body aperture. Note cord crossover at centre of lower edge of glass (Sec 30)

Fig. 12.50 Radiator grille special nut locations on front crossmembers. Note: that only one half of grille is shown as nut locations are symmetrical about the centre line of the grille (Sec 31)

Fig. 12.51 'Ford' letters on radiator grille: the letter can be prised out or pushed into place individually (Sec 31)

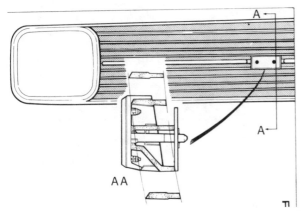

Fig. 12.52 'Ford' motif on grille. Section 'AA' shows method of fixing motif to centre of grille (Sec 31)

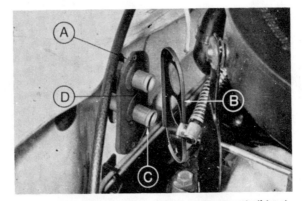

Fig. 12.53 Heater assembly at engine compartment bulkhead

A Foam gasket   C Inlet sutb
B Cover plate   D Outlet stub

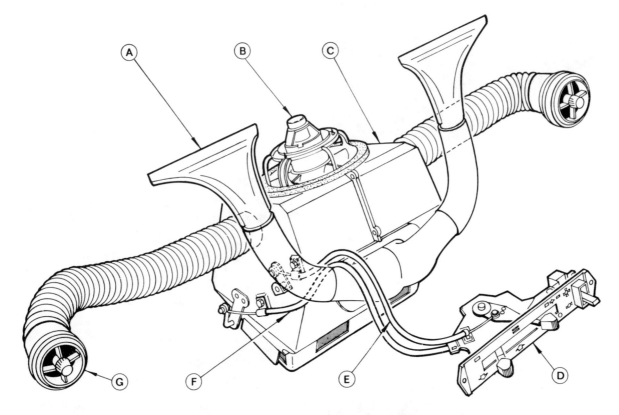

Fig. 12.54 Heating and ventilating components (Sec 32)

A Demister duct   C Heater   E Hot/cold valve cable   G Face level vent
B Heater motor   D Control panel   F Distribution valve cable

Remove the heater pipe sealing plate and gasket from the bulkhead by undoing the two retaining screws.

4 Unscrew the four screws retaining the top edge of the heater cover panel and the two screws securing the lower edge. Lower the panel sufficiently to gain access to the rear of the switch assemblies and disconnect the multiplugs. Continue lowering the panel clear of the working area.

5 Remove the trim clips securing the front passenger side parcel shelf to its support bracket on the cowl side trim panel, then undo the two bolts holding the shelf to the heater and lift the shelf away.

6 Unscrew the single screw securing the heater cover panel bracket and detach the bracket.

7 Carefully pull the demister hoses and the face level vent hoses off their respective heater outlets.

8 Unscrew the two nuts securing the passenger side demister duct to the cowl panel and detach the duct. Note: removing this duct provides access for the subsequent removal of the heater unit.

9 Disconnect the leads to the heater, at their snap connectors.

10 Carefully disconnect the inner heater control cables from their slots on the two arms on the heater, then remove the clips

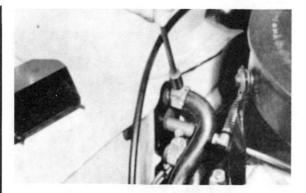

Fig. 12.55 Unscrewing heater hose clamp bolts (Sec 32)

Fig. 12.56 Heater inlet and outlet stubs on engine compartment rear bulkhead (Sec 32)

Fig. 12.57 Removing lower screws retaining heater cover panel (Sec 32)

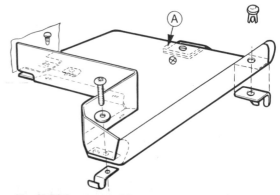

Fig. 12.58 Passenger's side parcel shelf fixings (Sec 32)

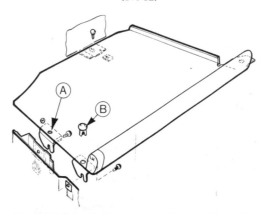

Fig. 12.59 Driver's side parcel shelf fixings (Sec 32)

Fig. 12.60 Removing crosshead screw securing heater cover mounting bracket (Sec 32)

Fig. 12.61 Demister duct retaining nuts (arrowed) (Sec 32)

Fig. 12.62 Cable clamp locations (arrowed) on heater box (Sec 32)

Fig. 12.63 Bolt location (arrowed) two each side retaining heater unit to cowl panel (Sec 32)

Fig. 12.64 Lifting heater assembly off cowl panel block outlet (arrowed) against accidental water spillage (Sec 32)

Fig. 12.65 Heater unit assembly (Sec 32)

Fig. 12.66 Crosshead screws securing motor to mounting plate (Sec 33)

Fig. 12.67 Removing clips securing motor mounting plate to heater (Sec 33)

Fig. 12.68 Removing Allen screw securing fan to motor shaft (Sec 33)

Fig. 12.69 Installed position for heater radiator (Sec 34)

Fig. 12.70 Heater radiator and seal assembly (Sec 34)

Fig. 12.71 Removing heater control panel bezel (Sec 35)

Fig. 12.72 Location of screw securing upper edge of heater control panel (Sec 35)

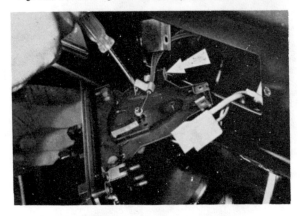

Fig. 12.73 Disconnecting the cable clips from the heater control assembly (Sec 35)

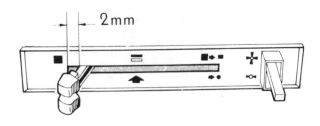

Fig. 12.74 Control level position prior to adjusting cables (Sec 35)

on the heater body holding the cables in place. Tuck the cables out of harms way.

11 Undo the four bolts holding the heater mechanism to the bulkhead and remove the heater from its location via the passenger side of the vehicle.

12 Replacement of the complete mechanism is a direct reversal of the above procedure.

13 Remember to refill the cooling system with the heater control lever set to full on.

33 Heater motor - removal and refitting

1 Remove the heater assembly from the car (Section 32).

2 Disengage the four clips securing the motor mounting plate to the heater and detach the motor plate assembly.

3 Using a suitably sized key slacken the allen screw in the fan hub and pull the fan off the motor shaft.

4 Undo the three screws holding the blower motor to the mounting plate and remove the motor.

5 Refitting is a reversal of removal.

34 Heater matrix - removal, servicing and refitting

1 Withdraw the heater assembly (Section 32).

2 Unscrew and remove the four bolts holding the heater matrix cover plate to the heater assembly. Withdraw the heater radiator and detach the radiator seal from the heater assembly.

3 Flush the unit through with cold water. If it is clogged, try reverse flushing it with a hose. If this does not clear it, exchange

it for a reconditioned unit. Do not be tempted to use chemical cleansers as they will only loosen deposits which will in turn cause further clogging of the fine cooling tubes. If the matrix leaks, do not attempt to solder it as this work seldom proves satisfactory.

4 Reassembly is a reversal of removal, but when replacing the matrix ensure that it does not contact the heater assembly.

35 Heater controls - removal and refitting

1 Disconnect the battery and remove the heater cover panel (for fuller details, refer to Section 32).

2 Carefully prise the heater control bezel out of its location in the control aperture.

3 Unscrew and remove the two screws securing the sides of the control panel to the facia and the single screw securing the upper edge.

4 Pull the controls out of the control aperture and disconnect the blower switch multiplugs. Prise the cable clips off their locations and disengage the cable loops from their respective levers.

5 Reassembly is a reversal of the removal procedure.

36 Face level vent - removal and refitting

1 Using two suitably sized rods in the holes in the vent fixing ring, unscrew and remove the ring (Figs. 12.75 and 12.76).

2 Accessible from the rear of the facia, pull the face level vent stub from its location and disconnect the vent hose.

Fig. 12.75 Using suitably sized rods to remove vent retaining ring (Sec 36)

Fig. 12.76 Removing ring from face level vent: note keyway in periphery of vent thread (Sec 36)

Fig. 12.77 Replacing hose on face level vent stub (Sec 36)

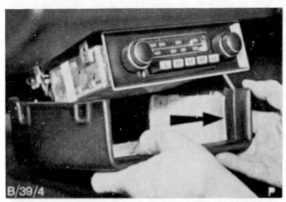

Fig. 12.78 Removing the radio receiver surround from the radio mounting bracket (Sec 37 - without centre console)

Fig. 12.79 Pulling the radio control knobs off the switch stalks (Sec 37 - without centre console)

Fig. 12.80 Switch stalk nut and washer assemblies retaining the radio escutcheon panel (Sec 37)

Fig. 12.81 Pop rivets (arrowed) retaining radio mounting plate to console aperture (Sec 37 - with centre console)

Fig. 12.82 Removing radio from centre console aperture (Sec 37 - with centre console)

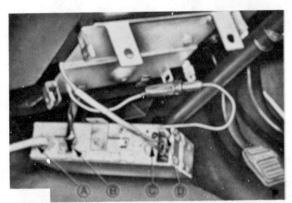

Fig. 12.83 Rear of radio receiver (Sec 37 - Without centre console)

A   Aerial lead   C   Loudspeaker leads
B   Earth lead   D   Power supply

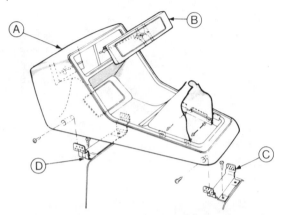

Fig. 12.84 Centre console assembly - GL models (Sec 39)

A   Centre console   C and D   Tunnel mounted
B   Radio aperture cover plate   fixing brackets

Fig. 12.85 Using cranked screwdriver (A) to remove loudspeaker
retaining screws (B) (Sec 38)

Fig. 12.86 Removing the loudspeaker via the instrument cluster
aperture (Sec 38)

3   Assemble the stub into its facia location, ensuring that the groove, in the stub aligns with the key in the facia cut out. Secure the vent with the fixing ring and reconnect the hose.

37 Radio - removal and refitting

Without centre console

1   Open the bonnet and disconnect the battery.
2   Remove the four screws and flat washers, two each side, securing the radio receiver surround to the radio bracket and detach the surround.
3   Pull the radio control knobs off the switch stalks and remove the nut and washer assemblies securing each stalk to the radio bracket.
4   Undo and remove the single screw securing the rear of the receiver to the bracket, then lower the receiver off the bracket before disconnecting the aerial, earth, speaker, and supply leads. Remove the receiver from the vehicle.
5   Installation of the radio receiver is a reversal of removal process, however when finally installed the receiver must be tuned to the aerial. To do this first select a weak medium wave station, turn the volumn to maximum and, using a small electrical screwdriver turn the aerial screw (located in the top RH corner of the front face of the receiver) a half turn in either direction until maximum volume is obtained.

With centre console

6   Follow the procedure given in paragraphs 1 and 3.
7   The radio mounting plate is held in the radio aperture by two pop rivets. These must now be drilled out and the mounting plate removed.

8   Once the mounting plate has been removed, the radio can be withdrawn from the radio aperture and the speaker, aerial, earth and power supply leads disconnected from the receiver.
9   Refitting is the reversal of the removal procedure, not forgetting to tune the aerial, as described in paragraph 5.

38 Radio loudspeaker - removal and refitting

1   Open the bonnet and disconnect the battery.
2   Remove the instrument cluster as described in Chapter 10, Section 50.
3   Working through the instrument cluster aperture, disconnect the loudspeaker leads from the rear of the receiver.
4   Using a suitable cranked screwdriver, remove the two loudspeaker securing screws, then remove the loudspeaker via the instrument cluster aperture.
5   If necessary, detach the loudspeaker mounting plate.
6   Refitting the loudspeaker is a reversal of the removal procedure.

39 Centre console - removal and refitting

1   Remove the radio as described in Section 37.
2   Remove the clock as described in Chapter 10, Section 63.
3   Unscrew the gear lever knob and knob locknut from the gearlever, then unscrew the two screws from each side of the centre console and lift the console off its tunnel mounting brackets.
4   Refitting the centre console is a direct reversal of the removal procedure

Chapter 13 Supplement:
Revisions and information on later models

Contents

1 Introduction

Since its introduction in early 1975, the New Escort has had a number of modifications and improvements in order to keep pace with current technical and servicing innovations. Most significant of these were the introduction in July 1975 of the Escort Popular and Popular Plus versions which were equipped with a special economy carburettor, and the fitting

of a viscous-coupled fan in April 1979. All other modifications which were made, up to the introduction of the New Escort in September 1980, are included in this Supplement.

In order to use the Supplement to the best advantage it is suggested that it is referred to *before* the main Chapters of the manual; this will ensure that any relevant information can be collected and accommodated into the procedures given in Chapters 1 to 12. Time and cost will therefore be saved and the particular job will be completed correctly.

2 Specifications

The specifications listed here are revised or supplementary to the main specifications given at the beginning of each Chapter

Engine
1100 Popular
Specifications as 1100 engine, Chapter 1 with the following exceptions

Compression ratio	9.0 : 1
Engine output (DIN)	41 BHP at 5300 rpm
Engine torque (DIN)	71 Nm at 3000 rpm

Cylinder head (all models)
Valve seat angle (all models from April 1980)	46°

Fuel system and carburation
Sonic Idle carburettors (1V)

	1100 cc	1300 cc	1300 cc
Engine			
Transmission	Manual	Manual	Automatic
Type	761F-9510-KAA	761F-9510-KBA	761F-9510-KCA

Throttle barrel diameter	32 mm	34 mm	34 mm
Venturi diameter...	24 mm	25 mm	25 mm
Main jet	117	122	117
Idle speed rpm	800 ± 25	800 ± 25	800 ± 25
Mixture % CO	2.0 ± 0.2	1.5 ± 0.2	1.5 ± 0.2
Fast idle speed rpm	1000 ± 100	1400 ± 100	2100 ± 100
Float level setting	29.0 ± 0.75 mm (1.14 ± 0.03 in)	29.0 ± 0.75 mm. (1.14 ± 0.03 in)	29.0 ± 0.75 mm (1.14 ± 0.03 in)
Choke plate pull down:			
Setting	4.0 ± 0.25 mm (0.16 ± 0.01 in)	3.0 ± 0.25 mm (0.12 ± 0.01 in)	3.0 ± 0.25 mm (0.12 ± 0.01 in)
De-choke	—	—	5.3 ± 0.5 mm (0.21 ± 0.02 in)
Accelerator pump stroke	2.2 ± 0.13 mm (0.09 ± 0.005 in)	2.6 ± 0.13 mm (0.10 ± 0.005 in)	2.6 ± 0.13 mm (0.10 ± 0.005 in)
Vacuum piston link hole	—	—	Outer
Thermostatic spring slot	—	—	Centre
V-mark setting	—	—	4.2 mm (0.17 in)

Sonic Idle carburettor (1V) - economy

Engine	1100 cc
Transmission	Manual
Type	761F-9510-LHA
Throttle barrel diameter	30 mm
Venturi diameter	21.5 mm
Main jet	110
Idle speed rpm	800 ± 25
Mixture % CO	2.75 ± 0.25
Fast idle speed rpm	1500 ± 100
Float level setting	29.0 ± 0.75 mm (1.14 ± 0.03 in)
Choke plate pull down setting	4.5 ± 0.25 mm (0.18 ± 0.01 in)
Accelerator pump stroke	2.0 ± 0.13 mm (0.08 ± 0.005 in)

Weber carburettors (2V)

Engine	1100 cc	1300 cc	1600 cc	1600 cc
Transmission	Manual	Manual	Manual	Automatic
Type	761F-9510-DA	761F-9510-AA	761F-9510-BA	761F-9510-CA
Throttle barrel diameter	32/32	32/32	32/32	32/32
Venturi diameter...	21/24	23/24	23/24	23/24
Main jet	105/115	120/105	120/115	115/120
Idle speed rpm	930 ± 20	800 ± 20	800 ± 20	800 ± 20
Mixture % CO	2.0 ± 0.25	2.0 ± 0.25	1.5 ± 0.25	1.5 ± 0.25
Fast idle speed rpm (phase point method) ...	2750 ± 100	2200 ± 100	1900 ± 100	1900 ± 100
Fast idle speed rpm cold climates (phase point method)	—	—	2100 ± 100	2100 ± 100
Fast idle speed rpm (high cam method) ...	—	—	2800	3000
Float level setting	41.0 ± 0.5 mm (1.61 ± 0.02 in)	41.0 ± 0.5 mm (1.61 ± 0.02 in)	41.0 ± 0.5 mm (1.61 ± 0.02 in)	41.0 ± 0.5 mm (1.61 ± 0.02 in)
Choke plate pull down setting	2.8 ± 0.5 mm (0.11 ± 0.02 in)	3.0 ± 0.5 mm (0.12 ± 0.02 in)	6.5 ± 0.25 mm (0.26 ± 0.01 in)	6.5 ± 0.25 mm (0.26 ± 0.01 in)
Choke phasing	—	—	2.0 ± 0.25 mm (0.08 ± 0.01 in)	2.0 ± 0.25 mm (0.08 ± 0.01 in)

Tamperproof carburettor (1V)

Engine	1100 cc	1300 cc	1300 cc
Transmission	Manual	Manual	Automatic
Type	771F-9510-KAA 771F-9510-KFA	771F-9510-KBA 771F-9510-KGA	771F-9510-KCA —
Choke	Manual	Manual	Automatic
Vacuum pull down (automatic choke)	—	—	3.0 ± 25 mm (0.12 ± 0.01 in)

Note: *All other specifications identical to Sonic idle carburettors (1V)*

Tamperproof carburettors (Weber 2V)

Engine	1100 cc	1300 cc	1600 cc	1600 cc
Transmission	Manual	Manual	Manual	Automatic
Type	771F-9510-DA	771F-9510-AA	771F-9510-BA	771F-9510-CA
Choke	Manual	Manual	Automatic	Automatic
Fast idle speed rpm	—	—	2000 ± 100	2000 ± 100
Choke phasing	—	—	2.8 ± 0.25 mm (0.11 ± 0.01 in)	2.8 ± 0.25 mm (0.11 ± 0.01 in)
Bi-metal adjustment	—	—	On index	On index

Note: *All other specifications identical to Weber carburettors (2V)*

Tamperproof Motorcraft carburettor (1V)

Engine	1300 cc Ecomomy
Type suffix	9510-KJA
Transmission	Manual
Main jet	117
Idle speed rpm	800 ± 50
Mixture % CO	2.0 ± 0.5
Fast idle speed rpm	1000 ± 100
Accelerator pump stroke	2.2 ± 0.13 mm (0.09 ± 0.005 in)
Choke plate pull down	2.6 ± 0.25 mm (0.10 ± 0.01 in)

Note: *All other specifications identical to Sonic idle carburettors (1V), 1300 cc manual*

Torque wrench settings

	lbf ft	kgf m
Exhaust manifold-to-head nuts	15 to 18	2.0 to 2.5
Exhaust manifold U-bolt nuts (2V engines)	18 to 22	2.5 to 3.0

Rear axle

Timken type (except Van) - Ford type C model

Axle ratio:

1.1 LC/HC (manual)	4.44 : 1*
1.1 LC/HC (manual with 12 in wheels)	3.89 : 1
1.1 HC (1V) economy (manual with 12 in wheels and radial ply tyres)	3.77 : 1
1.1 HC (1V) economy (manual with 12 in wheels and cross-ply tyres or 13 in wheels)	3.89 : 1
1.3 LC (manual)	4.125 : 1*
1.3 HC (manual)	4.125 : 1*
1.3 HC 2V (manual)...	4.44 : 1*

Salisbury type - Ford type E

Axle ratio:

1.1 LC/HC (manual)	4.44 : 1*
1.3 LC/HC (manual)	4.11 : 1*
1.3 HC 2V (manual)	4.44 : 1*

Timken type (Van only) - Ford type C

Axle ratio:

1.1 LC/HC (manual with 12 in wheels) - standard	4.125 : 1
1.1 LC/HC (manual) - standard	4.44 : 1*
1.1 HC 1V economy (manual with 12 in wheels) - standard ...	3.77 : 1
1.1 HC 1V economy (manual with 13 in wheels) - standard ...	3.89 : 1
1.3 LC/HC (manual) - heavy duty	4.44 : 1*

* Optional

Braking system

Pedal free height ... ... | 6.70 ± 0.4 in (170 ± 10 mm)

Escort Popular and Popular Plus

System type (1100 models)	Drum brakes front and rear
System type (1300 models)	Disc brakes front, drum brakes rear

Torque wrench settings

	lbf ft	kgf m
Brake tube/hose connection	9 to 11	1.2 to 1.5
Brake tube/hose locknut	10 to 12	1.3 to 1.6

Electrical system

Starter motor (Nippondenso)

Minimum brush length	0.5 in (13.0 mm)
Minimum commutator diameter	1.21 in (30.7 mm)
Commutator undercut	0.020 to 0.032 in (0.5 to 0.8 mm)

Starter motor (Femsa)

Number of brushes	2
Minimum brush length	0.47 in (12 mm)
Brush spring force	1.54 to 3.08 lbf (0.7 to 1.4 kgf)
Minimum commutator diameter	1.18 in (30 mm)
Maximum current draw	325 amp

Bulbs

	Wattage
Rear fog light	21
Side/parking lights	4

Suspension and steering
Wheel alignment (September 1976 to August 1978)

	Caster angle	Camber angle
Saloon, Estate, Sport (HD), and Ghia	0° 38' to 1° 53'	0° 06' to 1° 36'
Saloon (HD), Estate (HD), and Ghia (HD)	0° 46' to 2° 01'	0° 30' to 2° 00'
Sport	0° 20' to 1° 35'	0° 28' to 1° 02'
6 and 9 cwt Vans	0° 13' to 1° 02'	0° 33' to 1° 07'
6 and 9 cwt Vans (HD)	0° 06' to 1° 21'	0° 03' to 1° 33'

Wheel alignment (off-set coil springs — August 1978 on)

	Caster angle	Camber angle
6 and 9 cwt Vans	-0° 55' to $+0^o$ 20'	-0° 26' to $+1^o$ 04'
6 and 9 cwt Vans (HD)	-0° 13' to $+1^o$ 02'	0° 05' to 1° 35'
Saloon, Sport, and Estate	0° 02' to 1° 17'	-0° 13' to $+1^o$ 17'
Sport (HD)	0° 13' to 1° 28'	0° 05' to 1° 35'
Saloon and Estate (HD)...	0° 27' to 1° 42'	0° 33' to 2° 03'
Maximum side-to-side variation	0° 45'	1° 0'
Toe-in (off-set coil springs - August 1978 on)	0.04 to 0.12 in (1.0 to 3.0 mm)	

Rear suspension (Popular and Popular Plus models)

Type	Three-leaf half elliptical springs with vertical telescopic dampers. Stabiliser bar fitted on 1300 models only

Wheels and tyres (Popular and Popular Plus models)
Wheels

Type	Pressed steel wheels with chrome hub caps (1100 models), styled wheels (1300 models)
Rim width	4.5 in (114.3 mm)
Diameter:	
1100 models (early)	12 inch
1300 models and later 1100 models	13 inch

Tyres

Size and type:	
1100 models (early)	6.00 x 12 in crossply tubeless 155 SR x 12 in radial ply (optional)
1300 models and later 1100 models	155 SR x 13 in steel braced radial ply tyres

Pressures - lbf/in^2 (kgf/cm^2)

Tyre size	Normally laden*		Fully laden**	
	Front	Rear	Front	Rear
6.00 x 12	22 (1.5)	27 (1.9)	24 (1.7)	30 (2.1)
155 SR x 12	22 (1.5)	27 (1.9)	24 (1.7)	36 (2.5)
155 SR x 13	22 (1.5)	24 (1.7)	24 (1.7)	36 (2.5)

Normally laden: vehicle loaded with up to 3 persons
**Fully laden: vehicle loaded with more than 3 persons*
Note: *At sustained speed of more than 80 mph (130 km/h), tyre pressures to be increased by 3 lbf/in^2 (0.2 kgf/cm^2)*

Bodywork and fittings
Body dimensions (Popular and Popular Plus models)

Overall length (with overriders)	4058 mm (159.8 in)
Overall length (without overriders)	3978 mm (156.6 in)
Overall width	1596 mm (62.8 in)
Overall height (unladen)	1398 mm (55.1 in)
Wheelbase	2407 mm (94.7 in)

Track

Front (12 in wheels)	1258 mm (49.5 in)
Front (13 in wheels)	1270 mm (50.0 in)
Rear (12 in wheels)	1284 mm (50.6 in)
Rear (13 in wheels)	1296 mm (51.0 in)

Kerb weight - kg (lb)

	Popular	Popular Plus
1.1 litre 2 door	814 (1795)	829 (1828)
1.3 litre 2 door	831 (1832)	838 (1848)
1.1 litre 4 door	—	854 (1883)
1.3 litre 4 door	—	863 (1903)

Note: *Add 8 kg (18 lb) for automatic transmission models*

3 Engine

Crankshaft front oil seal - removal and refitting

1 A revised procedure applies to the renewal of the crankshaft front oil seal, but it entails the use of an oil seal remover, adaptor, and installing ring, which should be obtained from a tool-hire agent. The new procedure eliminates the removal of the sump and timing cover, and can therefore be carried out with the engine 'in situ'.

2 Disconnect the battery negative terminal and bend the lead away from the battery.

3 Drain the cooling system and remove the radiator (Chapter 2).

4 Loosen the alternator mounting bolts and adjusting bolt, swivel the alternator towards the engine, and remove the fan belt.

5 Unbolt the fan and pulley from the water pump hub, and carefully place them to one side.

6 Remove the crankshaft pulley (see Chapter 1, Section 12, paragraphs 2 and 3).

7 Using the oil seal remover and adaptor, carefully extract the existing oil seal from the timing cover.

8 Clean the oil seal location with lint-free cloth, and then smear some fresh engine oil onto the sealing lip of the new oil seal.

9 Carefully place the seal over the crankshaft and into the front cover, then fit the installing ring, crankshaft pulley, and retaining bolt, tightening the bolt until the seal is fully entered.

10 Unscrew the retaining bolt, and remove the crankshaft pulley and installing ring, then refit the pulley and tighten the retaining bolt to a torque of 22 to 28 lbf ft (3.1 to 3.9 kgf m). Hold the crankshaft stationary using the same methods described in Chapter 1, Section 12.

11 Refit the fan and pulley to the water pump hub, and then locate the fanbelt into position and adjust it as described in Chapter 2.

12 Refill the cooling system (Chapter 2), and reconnect the battery negative terminal.

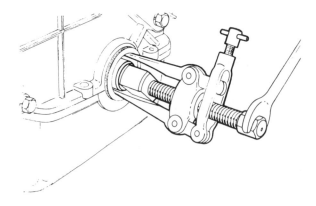

Fig. 13.1 Removing the crankshaft front oil seal with special tool (Sec 3)

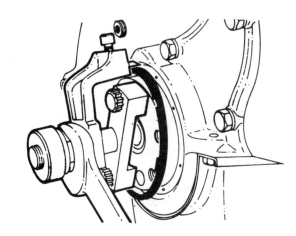

Fig. 13.2 Cutting the crankshaft rear oil seal abutment (Sec 3)

Crankshaft rear oil seal - removal and refitting

13 By using a new service tool, it is possible to renew the crankshaft rear oil seal without removing the oil seal carrier or the sump. The tool set comprises a cutter, seal remover, and seal installer and, if it can be obtained, a considerable saving can be made in time and cost.

14 With the engine removed (see Chapter 1) and the flywheel detached from the crankshaft, bolt the tool to the crankshaft.

15 Turn the cutter with an open-ended spanner, at the same time slowly advancing the knurled nut until the oil seal abutment has been removed.

16 Remove the cutting tool and fit the removal tool to the oil seal; by turning the centre bolt against the crankshaft, the oil seal can be extracted.

17 Clean the oil seal location with lint-free cloth and smear a little fresh engine oil onto the sealing lip of the new oil seal.

18 Place the oil seal into the carrier and drive it fully home using the special installing tool.

19 Wipe away any foreign material from the end of the crankshaft and refit the flywheel, tightening the retaining bolts to the specified torque settings.

20 Refit the engine (see Chapter 1).

21 By using this method to remove the crankshaft rear oil seal, the oil seal carrier centralising lugs are detached, and therefore, if the oil seal carrier is removed for any subsequent repairs, it will be necessary to use a further centralising tool to align it correctly, in relation to the crankshaft.

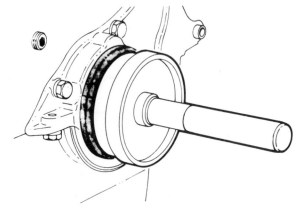

Fig. 13.3 Crankshaft rear oil seal installing tool (Sec 3)

4 Cooling system

Viscous-coupled fan — description

1 As from April 1979, all models are fitted with viscous-coupled fans. The unit operates in a similar manner to a torque converter in that the drive is transmitted through fluid under the influence of centrifugal force.

2 The unit also incorporates limited torque output which in effect limits the maximum speed, thereby reducing fan noise and excessive power absorption.

3 Since the unit is sealed, there are no repair or maintenance procedures and, if a fault develops, a replacement item should be obtained.

4 The removal and refitting procedures are similar to those for the conventional fan described in Chapter 2.

5 Fuel system and carburation

Motorcraft single venturi (1V), automatic choke carburettor — adjustment

1 A revised procedure has been introduced for adjusting the vacuum choke plate pull down on 1V automatic choke car-burettors. A preload tool weighing between 50 and 65 grams is required to make the adjustment and it is suggested that enquiries are made at the local Ford garage or automobile tool hire specialist. The adjustment is carried out with the engine running, and is therefore more accurate than the method des-cribed in Chapter 3, Section 19.

2 First remove the air cleaner (Chapter 3), and run the engine until it has reached the normal operating temperature.

3 Switch off the engine and position the fast idle cam so that the arrow is pointing towards the top of the fast idle lever.

4 Connect a tachometer to the engine and check that the fast idle speed is correct (see Specifications); adjust if necessary by bending the adjusting tag.

5 With the engine switched off, unscrew and remove the three retaining screws and withdraw the choke housing and bi-metal spring assembly, carefully placing it to one side.

6 The choke lever is now exposed and the preload tool can now be positioned on the lever as shown in Fig. 13.4.

7 Start the engine and make sure it is still at the normal operating temperature, and then move the throttle to the high cam position (Fig. 13.4). Note that this is not the 'fast idle' position referred to in paragraph 3.

8 The preload tool should now be floating, and the specified clearance between the choke plate and carburettor wall can be checked using the shank of a suitable twist drill. If adjustment is required, switch off the engine, and bend the pull down lever accordingly (see Fig. 13.4).

9 After checking the adjustment, refit the choke housing and bi-metal spring assembly, making sure that the alignment marks coincide and that the bi-metal spring is located in the centre slot on the choke operating link. Tighten the retaining screws evenly and refit the air cleaner.

Motorcraft 1V carburettor (automatic transmission models) — adjustment

10 A revised adjustment procedure has been introduced for Escort 1.3 litre automatic transmission models in order to eliminate engine stalling when changing from 'N' to 'D' during the engine warm-up period.

11 Remove the air cleaner (Chapter 3) and run the engine until it reaches the normal operating temperature.

12 Stop the engine, open the throttle, and turn the fast idle cam until the V-mark points towards the upper edge of the throttle lever, then release the throttle to retain it in this position.

13 Connect a tachometer to the engine, start the engine, and

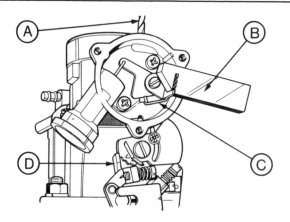

Fig. 13.4 Adjusting the vacuum choke plate pull-down (1V carburettors) (Sec 5)

A Twist drill	C Pull down lever
B Automatic-choke preload tool	D Throttle high cam setting

adjust the fast idle speed to 1900 $\pm$ 100 rpm by bending the throttle lever lug with a pair of pliers.

14 Switch off the engine and check the V-mark setting by first removing the choke housing and bi-metal spring assembly (three retaining screws).

15 Follow the instructions given in Chapter 3, Section 19, paragraphs 2 to 4 inclusive, but use a 3.5 mm diameter drill between the choke plate and air horn.

16 Re-adjust the vacuum choke plate pull down to 2.8 mm $\pm$ 0.25 mm (0.11 $\pm$ 0.01 in) using the method described in paragraphs 1 to 9 inclusive of this Section, but locate the bi-metal spring in the top slot of the choke operating link.

Note: The above procedure applies only to automatic trans-mission Escort 1.3 litre models fitted with carburettor 771F-9510-KCA; later models are fitted with an anti-stall device

Sonic Idle carburettors (1V) — description and adjustment

17 From May 1975, the Ford 'Bypass' (Sonic) Idle carburettor was progressively introduced on Escort models and, since their initial production in July of that year, all Escort Popular models were equipped with this carburettor. The carburettor idle system differs from the conventional type in that the majority of the idle air flow and all of the idle fuel flow passes through the bypass system. The remaining airflow flows past the carburettor butterfly which is held in a slightly open position.

18 During idle, with the butterfly almost closed, air is drawn into the bypass system (see Fig. 13.5). This air travels along the air distribution channel and mixes with the fuel entering via the mixture screw; the resulting mixture is drawn into the engine via the sonic discharge tube.

19 The Sonic Idle carburettor may be instantly recognised by the following:

a) Seven screws retaining the upper body, compared with six on previous units

b) The distributor advance/retard vacuum pick-up tube is increased in length from 14 mm (0.52 in) to 35 mm (1.37 in)

c) The idle mixture screw is repositioned to a point just above where the vacuum pick-up tube was previously situated (see Fig. 3.27, Chapter 3)

d) The vacuum pick-up tube is repositioned to a point just above where the idle mixture screw was previously situated

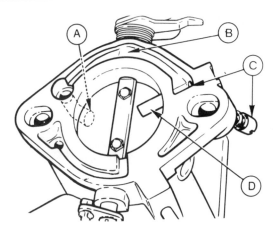

Fig. 13.5 Sonic Idle carburettor (Sec 5)

A   Air entry into bypass system
B   Air distribution channel
C   Mixture screw
D   Sonic discharge tube

20 Adjustment procedures for the Sonic Idle carburettor are as given in Chapter 3, Section 17 (except where a tamperproof carburettor is fitted), and all specification details are given in the Specifications section of this Supplement. It should be remembered that where a Sonic Idle carburettor is fitted, the following

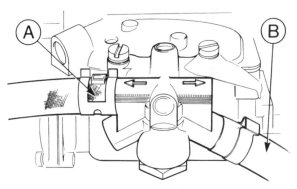

Fig. 13.6 Weber fuel return system (Sec 5)

A   Fuel return pipe   B   Fuel supply pipe

amendments will apply:

a) A revised inlet manifold (which may also be used with earlier single venturi carburettors). The carburettor flange gasket must be fitted with the tab towards the front of the engine
b) A revised initial advance ignition timing of 6° BTDC at 800 rpm (1.1 and 1.3 litre engines), and 10° BTDC at 800 rpm (1.6 litre engines)

Sonic Idle carburettors (2V) — description and adjustment
21 The Weber dual venturi carburettor described in Chapter 3

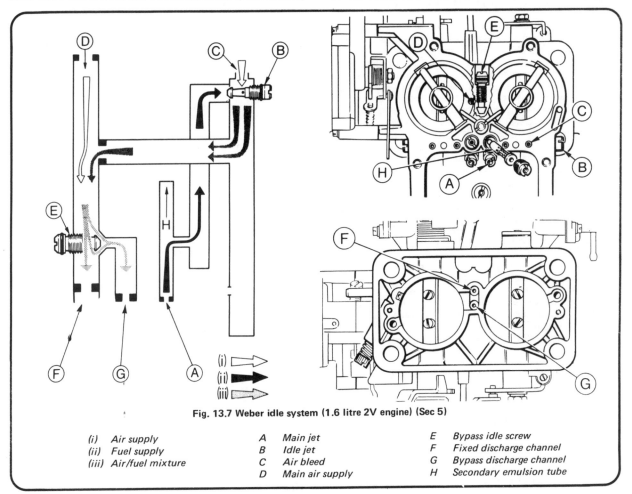

Fig. 13.7 Weber idle system (1.6 litre 2V engine) (Sec 5)

(i)	Air supply	A	Main jet	E	Bypass idle screw
(ii)	Fuel supply	B	Idle jet	F	Fixed discharge channel
(iii)	Air/fuel mixture	C	Air bleed	G	Bypass discharge channel
		D	Main air supply	H	Secondary emulsion tube

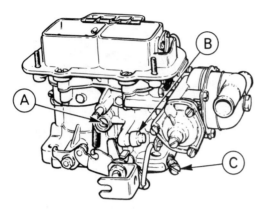

Fig. 13.8 Weber bypass idle carburettor (Sec 5)

A   *Bypass idle speed screw*
B   *Basic idle speed screw*
C   *Mixture screw*

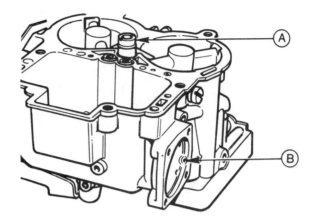

Fig. 13.9 Location of anti-stall device (carburettor dismantled)
(Sec 5)

A   *Discharge tube*   B   *Fuel entry*

was modified in May 1975 and progressively introduced on the appropriate Escort models. In addition to the bypass idle characteristic, the modified Weber 2V carburettor includes a fuel return system (Fig. 13.6), and on some models (mainly automatic transmission) an anti-stall device.

22 The fuel return system ensures that the temperature of fuel entering the float chamber is maintained at a constant level at all times, and this in turn keeps the quantity of fuel vapour from the float chamber to the engine constant. Previously, if the engine was left idling for long periods, the idle mixture became over-rich.

23 Refer to Fig. 13.7. and observe that, on the Weber bypass idle system, fuel is initially supplied via the float chamber to the secondary main jet (A). Fuel then travels up to the secondary idle jet (B) where air is introduced into the system through the drilling (C). The air/fuel mixture then passes through a restrictor and is atomised as it enters the main bypass air flow (D). The mixture then passes through the fixed discharge channel (F) and the bypass discharge channel (G), the latter being adjustable by the bypass idle screw (E), and thence to the engine.

24 Adjustment of the modified Weber 2V carburettor is similar to that described in Chapter 3, Section 28, but it should be remembered that the basic idle speed screw (Fig. 13.8) should not be adjusted during normal routine servicing; it should only require adjustment after a carburettor overhaul or if the correct idle speed is impossible to achieve using the bypass idle screw. It is also imperative that an exhaust gas analyser is used to make the adjustment to the mixture screw.

25 The anti-stall device fitted to some models consists of a housing, diaphragm and spring. Engine vacuum is applied by an external tube to one side of the diaphragm which is then pulled back against spring tension. This action draws fuel from the accelerator pump reservoir to the opposite side of the diaphragm. If the engine attempts to stall, there will be an initial drop in engine vacuum and, immediately this occurs, the diaphragm will be released and spring pressure will pump a quantity of fuel through the accelerator pump discharge tube, thus temporarily enriching the mixture and overcoming the stall.

26 Where an anti-stall device is fitted (mainly automatic transmission models) it is important to set the engine idle speed correctly; if it is too low, the anti-stall device will give an intermittent fuel delivery causing 'hunting'.

Tamperproof carburettors – description and adjustment

27 From May 1976, all carburettors will not only be of the Sonic Idle type, but will also be tamperproof in respect of the idle mixture adjustment. This is effected by a plastic plug being installed over the idle mixture adjustment screw, and has been

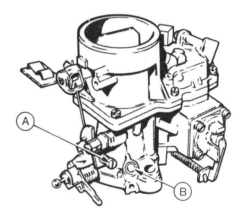

Fig. 13.10 Tamperproof carburettor (1V engines) (Sec 5)

A   *Idle speed screw*
B   *Plastic sealing plug over idle mixture screw*

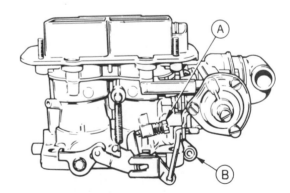

Fig. 13.11 Tamperproof carburettor (1.1 and 1.3 2V engines)
(Sec 5)

A   *Basic idle speed screw*
B   *White plastic plug fitted over mixture screw*

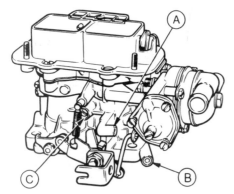

Fig. 13.12 Tamperproof carburettor (1.6 2V engines) (Sec 5)

A   Basic idle speed screw
B   Mixture screw
C   Bypass idle speed screw

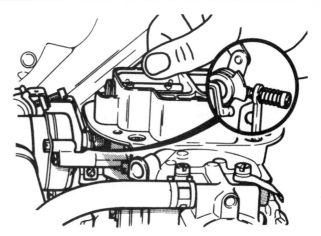

Fig. 13.13 Fast idle speed adjustment on the Weber (2V) carburettor automatic choke (Sec 5)

introduced to comply with new EEC regulations.

28 The carburettor body is slightly modified to accommodate the recessed idle mixture screw which is beneath a white plastic plug. The carburettor is so designed that after the initial running-in period of a new engine, the percentage of carbon monoxide (CO) in the exhaust gas will be in accordance with a predetermined requirement (this may mean that during running-in, the requirement may not be met). Therefore, in order to comply with the regulations, adjustment should only be made with an exhaust gas analyser coupled to the car exhaust system.

29 Should adjustment be necessary, the white plastic plug may be punctured in its centre using a small screwdriver, and then prised out. Where this adjustment has been found necessary, a blue replacement plug should be pressed in on completion.

30 It is not essential for satisfactory operation of the carburettor to have the plastic plug fitted after any adjustment, but future legislation may (officially) restrict the adjustment procedure and supply of replacement plastic plugs to authorised dealers. Where adjustment is carried out, the exhaust gas CO content at idle speed is given in the Specifications Section.

31 When using an exhaust gas analyser on tamperproof carburettors it is imperative to obtain the correct reading, due to the fine CO percentage limits imposed on them. The engine must be at its normal operating temperature and the CO meter and exhaust gas analyser must be connected to the engine in accordance with the manufacturers instructions.

32 Run the engine at 3000 rpm for approximately 30 seconds then allow it to idle. Then, as soon as the meters have stabilised, and within 10 to 30 seconds, record the CO percentage. If it takes longer than 30 seconds to make any adjustment, the engine should be run at 3000 rpm for 30 seconds again.

33 If it is found impossible to adjust the carburettor within the specification limits, the ignition timing, valve clearances, and general engine condition should be checked.

Weber (2V) carburettor automatic choke — fast idle adjustment

34 The fast idle adjustment procedure has been altered for 1600 cc models, and is now made with the choke in the 'high cam' position instead of in the 'phase point' position as previously.

35 Remove the air cleaner, and run the engine until it reaches its normal operating temperature.

36 Stop the engine and connect a tachometer.

37 Partially open the throttle, then fully close the choke plates and release the throttle. The fast idle adjusting screw should now be located on the high section of the fast idle cam (see Fig. 13.13).

38 Release the choke plates and check that they return to the fully open position. If not, the engine coolant may not have

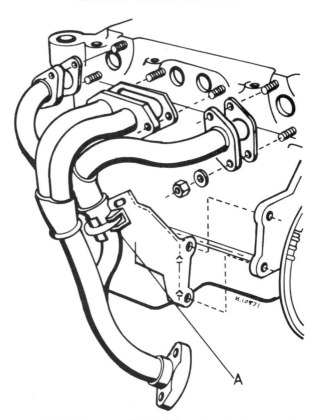

Fig. 13.14 Exhaust manifold for 2V engines, showing correct position of U-bolt (A) (Sec 5)

reached the normal temperature or alternatively the automatic choke may be faulty.

39 Without touching the throttle pedal, start the engine and check that the fast idle speed is as given in Specifications. If necessary, adjust the fast idle screw to give the correct speed.

40 Stop the engine, disconnect the tachometer, and refit the air cleaner.

Exhaust manifold (2V engines) — removal and refitting

41 Disconnect the front exhaust pipe from the manifold downpipe.

42 Unscrew the nuts and withdraw the U-bolt and clamp from the support bracket.

43 Unscrew and remove the retaining nuts and washers, and withdraw the manifold from the cylinder head. Remove the gaskets.
44 Clean the manifold and cylinder head mating faces, also the manifold downpipe-to-front exhaust pipe mating faces.
45 Locate the new gaskets over the studs on the cylinder head.
46 Refit the manifold, flat washers, and nuts, and tighten the nuts evenly to the specified torque.
47 Refit the U-bolt and clamp to the support bracket with the flat washers and nuts. Tighten the nuts to the specified torque. Note that only genuine parts should be used and the specified torques observed, otherwise the exhaust manifold may subsequently crack.
48 Reconnect the front exhaust pipe to the manifold downpipe.

6   Ignition system

Distributor – renewal
1 With the introduction of Sonic Idle and tamperproof carburettors in 1975, and subsequent economy improvements, detail changes were made to the distributors to provide better advance curves. Because there are a number of distributors incorporating different characteristics, it is important to obtain the correct replacement.
2 The distributors are colour-coded to assist in obtaining the correct unit; the replacement distributor must always bear the same colours as the original unit.

Spark plugs – modification
3 A revised spark plug is now fitted to 1.3 (2V) and 1.6 (2V) engines to give improved performance. The plug is the new version Motorcraft AGR 12 type and should not be confused with the earlier AGR 12 type which had the word 'Racing' on its insulator.

7   Clutch

Self-centering release bearing – description
1 As from October 1977 a self-centering release bearing is fitted, which gives improved operation to the original non-centering type. The bearings can be identified with reference to Fig. 13.15.
2 Wear in the non-centering type can give rise to jerky pedal action when disengaging the clutch, so it is recommended that the later type is fitted whenever work on the clutch or gearbox is undertaken.
3 Before fitting the release bearing, always lubricate the hub bore and release lever contact face with a molybdenum disulphide grease.

8   Manual gearbox and automatic transmision

Speedometer drivegear seal – description
1 Two alternative types of speedometer drivegear are fitted to models manufactured from July 1978 on; one is of steel, the other plastic. The accompanying seals for each type of drivegear are different, and it is important to fit the correct type, otherwise damage to the shaft, particularly the plastic type, may occur.

Gear lever – description and modification
2 As from August 1980 a modified gear lever (see Fig. 13.16) is fitted to all manual Escort models. The new type eliminates gear lever rattles and has in fact been used as a service modification since November 1978.

3 The modified gear lever can be identified by checking the metal cap('D' in Fig. 13.16) which does not have inward protruding tabs on the later type.
4 In the event of excessive rattling, the original gear lever can be modified as described in paragraphs 5 to 10, or alternatively a complete new gear lever may be fitted.
5 First remove the gear lever as described in Chapter 6.
6 Remove the existing bush and fit the new damping bush.
7 Move the selector rod to engage 3rd gear.

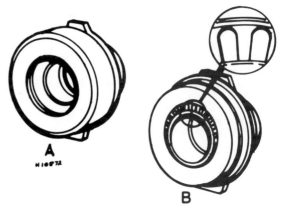

Fig. 13.15 Non self-centering (A), and self-centering (B) types of clutch release bearing (Sec 7)

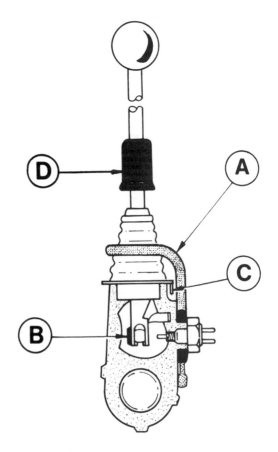

Fig. 13.16 Cross-section of modified gear lever (Sec 8)

A   Rubber strap   C   Tab washer
B   Damping brush   D   Metal cap

8 Lubricate the gear lever fork with molybdenum disulphide grease, then refit the gear lever and bend down the tab washer.
9 Locate the rubber strap over the gear lever then secure it beneath the reversing light switch.
10 If necessary, a double rubber gaiter may be fitted on the transmission tunnel.

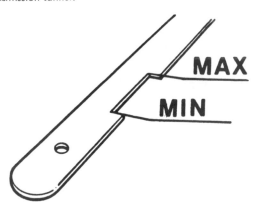

Fig. 13.17 Automatic transmission fluid level dipstick
(May 1979 on) (Sec 8)

Fig. 13.18 Splitting the axleshaft bearing retaining ring (Sec 10)

Fig. 13.19 Pressing off the axleshaft bearing (Sec 10)

Automatic transmission fluid level dipstick — description
11 As from May 1979 (build code WL) the automatic transmission fluid level has been raised and a new dipstick fitted (see Fig. 13.17). The hole in the dipstick is for production purposes only.
12 The fluid level checking method remains identical to that described in Chapter 6, Section 19.

9 Propeller shaft

General description
1 With the exception of 1.1 saloons (LC and HC) and economy saloons and vans (HC), all Escort models are now fitted with a two section propeller shaft. Removal and servicing instructions for both types are given in Chapter 7.

10 Rear Axle

Axleshafts (halfshafts) — removal
1 Refer to Chapter 8, Section 3, paragraph 3; if a slide hammer is not available, the halfshaft and bearing can be pressed out of the axle casing by screwing two suitable bolts into the backplate retaining screw holes from the rear of the backplate.
2 First turn the bearing retainer so that it blanks off the screw holes, then screw the bolts from the rear at diametrically opposite points, a few turns at a time, until the bearing is pushed out.

Rear hub bearing/oil seal — renewal
3 A special U-clamp is manufactured for this operation and, if one can be obtained, renewal of the hub bearing/oil seal is quite straightforward.
4 First, to remove the bearing, drill an 8 mm (0.3 in) diameter hole in the bearing retaining ring, being careful not to drill the axleshaft.
5 Support the ring on a vice, and split it across the drilled hole with a cold chisel.
6 Place the clamp in a vice and bolt the shaft to it as shown in Fig. 13.19. By turning the centre bolt anti-clockwise, the hub bearing will be pushed from its location.
7 Wipe clean the axleshaft, and place the new bearing into position as shown in Fig. 13.20, making sure that the closed end is facing the wheel studs. By screwing the clamp centre bolt clockwise, the bearing and retaining ring will be pushed into position; make sure both items are fully seated.

Fig. 13.20 Fitting the axleshaft bearing and retaining ring
(Sec 10)

8 The axleshaft is now ready to be refitted as described in Chapter 8, but first smear a little lithium-based grease to the outer bearing cup to assist its entry into the axle casing.

Differential carrier assembly (Timken) — oil leaks

9 Where there is indication of oil seepage from the studs connecting the differential carrier to the rear axle housing, the studs should be sealed by using a suitable sealing compound (ie., Ford specification GESM-4G4504-A).

10 First remove the appropriate nut and thoroughly clean the stud with petrol.

11 When dry, apply the sealer to the stud thread and tighten a new self-locking nut to the correct torque setting.

Pinion oil seal (Salisbury) — description

12 As from April 1978 (build code 8D24), a new type of pinion oil seal and pinion flange is fitted to Salisbury type rear axles. The earlier type has a 2.36 in (60 mm) diameter metal band partially covering the oil seal to prevent the ingress of dirt, whereas the later type has a 3.27 in (83 mm) diameter dirt slinger.

13 Each type of seal is matched to a different type flange, therefore it must be remembered that if one component is changed to a different type, the other component must also be changed.

11 Braking system

Rear brake shoe inspection aperture — description

1 As from August 1978 (build code UP), a brake shoe inspection aperture is incorporated in the rear brake backplate together with a blanking plug. The aperture is positioned over the fastest wearing section of the leading brake shoe on each rear brake.

2 The rear brake shoe linings should be checked every 6000 miles (9600 km) by jacking-up the rear of the car, supporting it on axle stands, and removing the blanking plugs. It is recommended that the drums are removed for cleaning every 12000 miles (19300 km).

Brake pad anti-squeak coating — description

3 Cars manufactured in late 1977 are fitted with disc brakes having a PVC coating on either the outer face of the brake pad backplate or on the pad shims. *When fitting brake pads, it is important to note that the anti-squeak coating must only be incorporated on one of the components, i.e. it is not permissible to have the coating on both the backplate and the shims.*

Teves (ATE) master cylinder — description

4 The Teves (ATE) master cylinder fitted to cars manufactured from November 1978 on incorporates two seals in the cylinder bore mouth instead of the single seal fitted on earlier types. The inner seal retains the brake fluid, and the outer seal maintains vacuum in the servo. The seals are separated by a spacer which is vented to atmosphere by a small drain hole.

5 During the operation of the master cylinder over an extended period, it is normal for a small accumulation of brake fluid to pass through the drain hole and stain the front face of the servo. This does not indicate a faulty master cylinder.

6 If, however, droplets of fluid are visible in the drain hole, the master cylinder should be removed and either overhauled or renewed.

Brake fluid level warning system — description

7 As from October 1978 (build code UR), all Saloon models are fitted with a brake fluid level warning indicator switch in the master cylinder reservoir cap. When the fluid drops to the predetermined minimum level in the reservoir, the switch contacts close and a warning light is illuminated on the instrument panel.

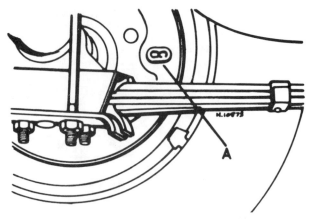

Fig. 13.21 Brake shoe inspection aperture location (A) (Sec 11)

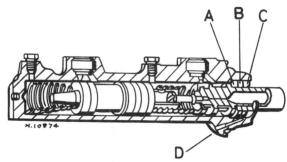

Fig. 13.22 Teves (ATE) brake master cylinder — cutaway view (Sec 11)

A Secondary seal   C Vacuum seal
B Spacer   D Drain hole

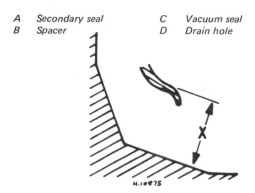

Fig. 13.23 Brake pedal free height checking dimension (X) (Sec 11)

8 A test switch is provided to check that the warning light is operating correctly.

Master cylinder (with level warning system) — removal and refitting

9 The procedure is identical to that described in Chapter 9, but it will be necessary to disconnect the plug on the reservoir cap on removal, and reconnect it on refitting. Test the operation of the level warning system by removing the filler cap with the ignition switched on.

Brake pedal free height — checking

10 Chock the front and rear wheels, and fully release the handbrake.

11 Measure the distance from the floor to the top of the pedal, using a pointed rod pressed through the carpet and sound deadener (see Fig. 13.23). Note that where a servo is fitted, the

engine should be idling during the check.

12 If the free height is not as specified, first check that the floor and brake pedal are not damaged or distorted. If still not correct, the pedal linkage or bushing may be worn, or the fault may lie in the master cylinder or servo unit (where fitted).

Handbrake — revised adjustment procedure

13 Follow the instructions given in Chapter 9, Section 19, paragraphs 1 to 5 inclusive, and then turn the adjusting nut to remove all slack from the mechanism; this is indicated by a *total* clearance of 4.0 to 5.0 mm (0.16 to 0.20 in) existing at the handbrake actuating lever abutment points ('C' Fig. 9.34). It is in order for a zero clearance to exist on one side and the maximum total clearance on the other side, as both will equalise when the handbrake is operated.

14 Fully apply the handbrake, then release it fully to settle the mechanism. Then check that the sum of the abutment clearances at each side totals between 3.0 and 4.5 mm (0.12 and 0.18 in); again it is in order for a zero clearance to exist on one side.

15 The handbrake cable should not be tightened outside the above limits otherwise the self-adjusting mechanism will not operate correctly; with this system it is in order for the handbrake lever to travel up to 10 notches before the rear brakes are fully applied.

12 Electrical system

General

1 Models produced between August and October 1977 (build codes TG to TY) may be fitted with Femsa or Nippondenso starter motors and/or Motorola alternators. The following paragraphs describe the additional procedures required for these components.

Alternator brushes (Motorola) — inspection, removal and refitting

2 Undo and remove the two screws and washers securing the regulator to the rear of the alternator. Detach the two regulator wires and lift off the regulator.

3 Undo and remove the two screws and washers that secure the brush box to the alternator and carefully turn the brush box outwards.

4 Check that the carbon brushes are able to slide smoothly in their guides without any sign of binding.

5 Measure the length of the brushes and if they have worn down to 0.2 in (5 mm) or less, they must be renewed.

6 Hold the brush wire with a pair of engineer's pliers which will act as a heat sink and unsolder it from the brush box. Lift away the two brushes.

7 Insert the new brushes and check to make sure that they are free to move in their guides. If they bind, lightly polish with a very fine file.

8 Solder the brush wire ends to the brush box, taking care that solder is allowed to pass to the stranded wire.

9 Whenever new brushes are fitted, new springs should be fitted.

10 Refitting the brush box is the reverse sequence to removal.

Starter motor (Nippondenso) — description

11 The Nippondenso starter motor is similar to the Bosch unit and therefore the information given in Chapter 10 will apply. However, there are a few differences which are given in the following paragraphs.

12 The armature shaft thrust arrangement is different as shown in Fig. 13.26.

13 The commutator should be undercut by the specified amount with reference to Fig. 13.27. Any chipping should be removed with fine sandpaper.

14 If worn, the bush in the commutator housing can be removed

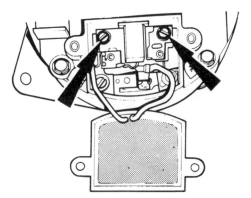

Fig. 13.24 Motorola alternator brush box screw location (arrowed) (Sec 12)

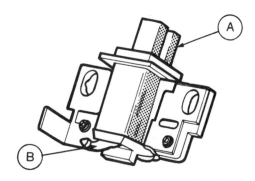

Fig. 13.25 Motorola alternator brush box (Sec 12)

A   Brushes   B   Brush box

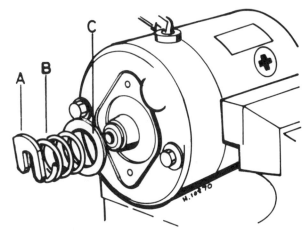

Fig. 13.26 Armature shaft thrust components on the Nippondenso starter motor (Sec 12)

A   C-washer   C   Rubber washer
B   Spring

with a suitable diameter drift, and the new bush pressed into position. The new bush must be immersed in clean engine oil for a minimum of 20 minutes before fitting.

15 If the bush in the drive end housing is worn, the complete housing must be renewed.

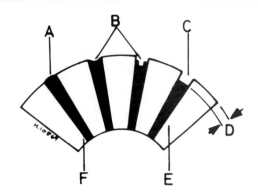

Fig. 13.27 Commutator undercutting diagram for the Nippondenso starter motor (Sec 12)

A   Protruding segment   D   Depth of undercut
B   Incorrect profile   E   Segment
C   Correct profile   F   Mica insulation

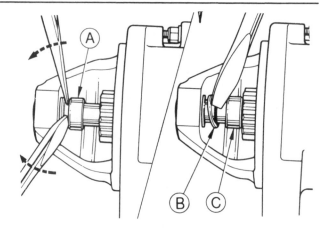

Fig. 13.28 Levering the collar (A) along the shaft to (C) to remove the circlip (B) (Sec 12)

Starter motor (Femsa) — dismantling and reassembly

16 Slacken the screw securing the brush cover band, and slide the band off the motor. Remove the rubber seal.
17 With a piece of wire bent into the shape of a hook, lift back each of the brush springs in turn and pull out the brushes.
18 Lever the thrust collar back along the armature shaft and prise the circlip from its groove (Fig. 13.28).
19 Remove the two nuts and washers that secure the commutator end housing and pull off the housing. Lift off the shims.

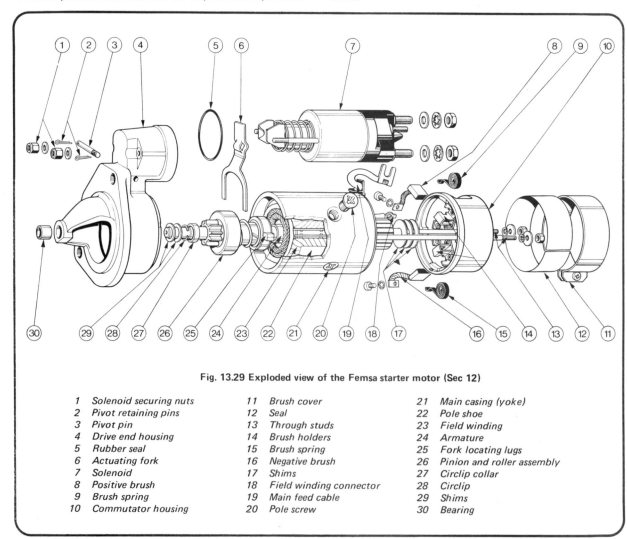

Fig. 13.29 Exploded view of the Femsa starter motor (Sec 12)

1	Solenoid securing nuts	11	Brush cover	21	Main casing (yoke)
2	Pivot retaining pins	12	Seal	22	Pole shoe
3	Pivot pin	13	Through studs	23	Field winding
4	Drive end housing	14	Brush holders	24	Armature
5	Rubber seal	15	Brush spring	25	Fork locating lugs
6	Actuating fork	16	Negative brush	26	Pinion and roller assembly
7	Solenoid	17	Shims	27	Circlip collar
8	Positive brush	18	Field winding connector	28	Circlip
9	Brush spring	19	Main feed cable	29	Shims
10	Commutator housing	20	Pole screw	30	Bearing

20 Slacken the lower terminal on the solenoid, and slide out the solenoid-to-motor cable.

21 The actuating arm pivot pin is splined at one end, and must be tapped out from the opposite end with a suitable drift, after removing the split pin.

22 Withdraw the armature assembly from the yoke, allowing the circlip, collar and shims to drop clear. Pull off the yoke.

23 Unclip the starter pinion from the actuating arm and remove the pinion and arm from the drive end housing.

24 Remove the two securing nuts and washers, and remove the solenoid and seal from the drive end housing.

25 If the brushes are worn to 0.47 in (12 mm) or less they should be renewed. Unscrew the two crosshead screws and refit the new brushes. Check for sticking brushes, and clean them if necessary with a petrol moistened cloth.

26 If cleaning the commutator with a petrol moistened cloth fails to remove the burnt areas and spots, wrap a piece of glass-paper around the commutator and rotate the armature.

27 If this fails to remove all the burnt areas, or if the commutator is very badly worn, mount the armature in a lathe. With the lathe turning at high speed, take a very fine cut off the commutator and finish the surface by polishing with glass-paper. **Do not undercut the insulators between the segments.**

28 With the starter motor dismantled, test the four field coils for an open circuit. Connect a 12 volt battery with a 12 volt bulb between the lead from the motor to the solenoid, and the brush connector. An open circuit is proved by the bulb not lighting.

29 If the bulb lights it does not necessarily mean that the field coils are in order, as there is the possibility that one of the coils is earthed to the starter yoke or pole shoes. To check this, remove the test lead from the brush connector and place it against a clean portion of the starter yoke. If the bulb lights, the field coils are earthing. Renewal of the field coils calls for the use of a wheel-operated screwdriver, a soldering iron, caulking and riveting operations, and is beyond the scope of the majority of owners. The starter yoke should be taken to a reputable electrical engineering works for new field coils to be fitted. Alternatively, purchase an exchange starter motor.

30 If the armature is damaged this will be evident on inspection. Look for signs of burning, discolouration and for conductors to have lifted away from the commutator.

31 If a bearing is worn so allowing excessive side-play of the armature shaft, the bearing bush must be renewed. To renew the drive end bracket bush, tap out the bush with a suitable diameter drift. To remove the commutator end housing bush, select a threaded tap of suitable diameter and screw it into the bush. Hold the tap in a vice and knock off the housing, using a block of wood to prevent damage to the housing.

32 Soak new bushes in engine oil for 20 minutes before fitting.

33 New bushes must be pressed into position using a small mandrel of the same diameter as the internal diameter of the bush with a shoulder on it. Place the bush on the mandrel and press into position using a bench vice.

34 Using a test lamp and battery test the continuity of the solenoid coils. Connect them between the 'STA' terminal and a good earth point on the solenoid body. If the lamp fails to light, renew the solenoid.

35 Check the operation of the drive clutch. It must provide instantaneous take up of the drive in one direction and rotate easily and smoothly in the opposite direction.

36 Make sure that the drive moves freely on the armature shaft splines without binding or sticking.

37 Reassembly is the reverse of this procedure. The following additional points should be noted:

a) *When fitting the solenoid, the small spade terminal should be to the right (Fig. 13.30).*

b) *Fit shims at the commutator end of the armature shaft to remove all endfloat with the end housing fitted.*

c) *Ensure that the rubber seal under the brush cover band is carefully positioned to prevent entry of water.*

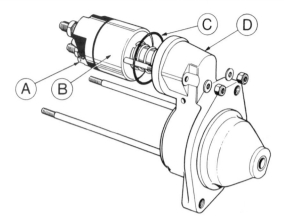

Fig. 13.30 Femsa starter motor end housing and solenoid (Sec 12)

A Terminal
B Solenoid

C O-ring
D End housing

Fig. 13.31 Reversing light switch location (arrowed) (Sec 12)

Reversing light switch — removal and refitting

38 Jack-up the front of the car and support it on axle stands.

39 Disconnect the battery earth lead.

40 Locate the switch on the gearbox extension housing and disconnect the wiring plug.

41 Unscrew and remove the switch.

42 Refitting is a reversal of removal, but make sure that the wire is well clear of the exhaust and the gearbox.

Ignition switch cylinder assembly — removal and refitting

43 Escort models manufactured since mid-1976 are fitted with a revised steering column lock assembly, and the switch cylinder and barrel can be withdrawn without the need to detach the complete switch.

44 First disconnect the battery negative lead.

45 Remove the steering column shroud as described in Chapter 10, Section 66, then insert the ignition key and turn it to the accessory position '1'.

46 Locate the small hole in the switch perimeter and insert a suitable small diameter tool to depress the lock spring, at the same time pulling the key and cylinder away from the housing. It may be necessary to turn the key slightly in both directions while removing the cylinder.

47 The cylinder can be removed from the barrel by first ensuring that the key is fully entered. Then carefully remove the retaining circlip and withdraw the key 5 mm (0.2 in); the barrel

can now be separated from the cylinder.

48 Reassembling and refitting the switch is a reversal of the removal procedure, but make sure that the barrel is refitted to the cylinder in its original position. Turn the key to the accessory position '1' in order to fit the retaining circlip. When the assembly is refitted, check its operation in all the positions before finally reconnecting the battery negative lead.

---

13 Suspension and steering

Stabilisers bars — general

1   As from February 1977, all Escort 1.1 litre saloons, in common with Van and Estate car models, do not have rear stabilisers bars fitted. In order to balance the complete suspension, the front stabiliser bar on these models is reduced from 22 to 20 mm diameter and it is therefore imperative that an identical bar is fitted as a replacement.

Stabiliser bar (rear) — removal and refitting

2   An alternative method of removing the rear stabiliser bar together with a revised dimension setting has been introduced.
3   First follow the instructions given in Chapter 11, Section 19, paragraph 1.
4   Using a suitable lever (see Fig. 13.34), pull the stabiliser bar slightly rearwards while the retaining clamps are unbolted from the axle casing; this will relieve any strain on the retaining bolts.
5   Detach the exhaust silencer hanger from the left-hand side mounting bolt extension, then unscrew and remove the stabiliser bar mounting bolts from the floor pan side members.
6   The stabiliser bar can now be removed from one side of the car.
7   Slacken the locknuts at the end of each bush housing, and unscrew the bushes from the bar followed by each locknut. Slide the rubber mounting bushes off the bar.
8   Refitting is a reversal of the removal procedure but, when positioning the end bush housings, make sure that the centre line of the bush is:

$$271.0 \, {}^{+\,2.0}_{-\,3.0} \, \text{mm} \, (10.67 \, {}^{+\,0.08}_{-\,0.12} \, \text{in})$$

from the centre line of the transverse section of the bar; the difference between each side dimension should not exceed 2.5 mm (0.10 in). Enter the left-hand side mounting bolt from outside and the right-hand side mounting bolt from the inside, and finally tighten all nuts and bolts to the specified torque with the weight of two people (or equivalent) on the rear suspension; this will be indicated by the rear spring eye centres and the centre of the axle tube being in line (see Fig. 11.48).

Stabiliser bar end bushes — renewal

9   When renewing the stabiliser bar end bushes follow the instructions given in Chapter 11, Section 20 but make sure that the recesses are positioned as shown in Fig. 13.35.

Adjustable shock absorbers and cartridge inserts — general

10 In addition to the normal shock absorbers and McPherson strut cartridge insert replacement parts, Ford have introduced adjustable units which are marketed under the Motorcraft Auto-flex Super label. These units, when removed from the car, can be adjusted by fully retracting the upper piston onto the lower cylinder assembly so that an internal key is engaged, and then turning the piston end half a turn at a time. This action compresses an internal spring and also progressively covers by-pass orifices, and the damping effect will therefore be increased.
11 The removal and refitting procedure for shock absorbers is identical to that given in Chapter 11, but with the cartridge insert the amount of shock absorbers fluid is reduced from 326 cc to 50 cc.

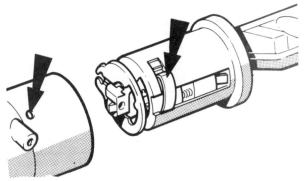

Fig. 13.32 Location of the ignition switch cylinder retaining spring (Sec 12)

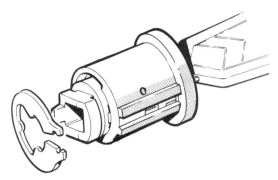

Fig. 13.33 Fitting the ignition switch barrel retaining circlip (Sec 12)

Fig. 13.34 Removing the stabiliser bar clamp (Sec 13)

12 Once removed, the unit can be adjusted by first collapsing the upper piston and turning it anti-clockwise until the adjusting nut engages into the base unit. At this stage, the position of the piston assembly in relation to the base assembly should be marked, using chalk or a fibre tip pen.
13 Check whether the unit has already been adjusted by turning the piston assembly anti-clockwise until it stops; the total adjustment range is between four and five half turns. Now, from the original position, turn the piston assembly two half turns clockwise, and the unit will now have an additional damping effect.
14 Disengage the adjusting nut by pulling the upper piston assembly out of the base assembly by about ½ inch.
15 Once disengaged, the piston can be turned freely without affecting the adjustment, and the unit can then be reassembled and refitted as necessary.

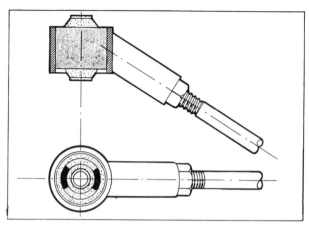

Fig. 13.35 Correct position of rear stabiliser bar end bush
(Sec 13)

Fig. 13.37 Cutaway view of the steering wheel collapsible can
(Sec 13)

A Collapsible can   B Column tube

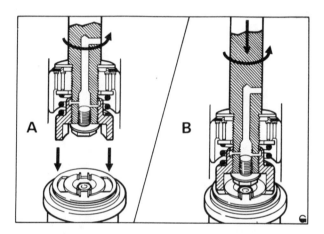

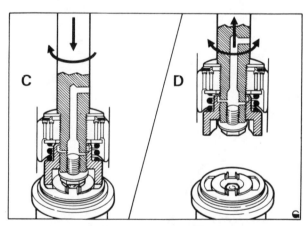

Fig. 13.36 Adjusting procedure for adjustable shock absorbers
and cartridge inserts (Sec 13)

16 Where shock absorber units are fitted at the same time to each side of the car, it is important that both units are adjusted by the same amounts, otherwise the handling of the car will be adversely affected.

Wheel alignment — general

17 1978 on models are fitted with a front suspension incorporating off-set coil springs. The wheel alignment data for these models is revised and is given in Specifications.

Steering wheel collapsible can — precautions

18 The steering wheel incorporates a collapsible can as shown in Fig. 13.37 which progressively collapses under excessive pressure as may occur during a front end impact.

19 If the collapsible can is damaged or distorted, it will not function correctly in an emergency; therefore, it is particularly important to check the can after impact. Where damage or distortion is found, the steering wheel must be renewed.

20 If the can has been partially collapsed or stretched, it is not permissible to return it to its original position

---

14 Bodywork and fittings

General description

1 In addition to the L, GL, Sport and Ghia versions referred to in Chapter 12, there are now Popular and Popular Plus versions, and Linnet, Harrier and Goldcrest special editions. On the Popular and Popular Plus versions the front seats are not adjustable for rake although they are for position.

2 The Popular Plus version is available in either two or four door options and has carpets and full width parcel tray, together with fabric trim and extra sound insulation. The Linnet, Harrier and Goldcrest have a higher trim level than the Popular Plus and Sport.

Heater unit — general

3 Escort models manufactured from late 1975 onwards are fitted with a modified heater unit which is supplied in both standard and heavy duty options. Although the unit is similar in design to the heater described in Chapter 12, there are a few fundamental differences which are outlined in the following paragraphs.

Heater unit — removal and refitting

4 Follow the instructions given in Chapter 12, Section 32, but, where fitted, remove the centre console first, as described in Section 39, and also remove the glove compartment.

5 Refitting is a reversal of the removal procedure but set the heater controls as shown in Fig. 13.43 before connecting the control cables to the heater unit; the valves should be in the end position.

Heater unit — dismantling and reassembling

6 With the heater removed from the car, carefully pull off the foam ring, disconnect the plug and withdraw the supply cables from the bracket mountings.

7 From within the motor housing, remove the two retaining clamps using a pair of circlip pliers.

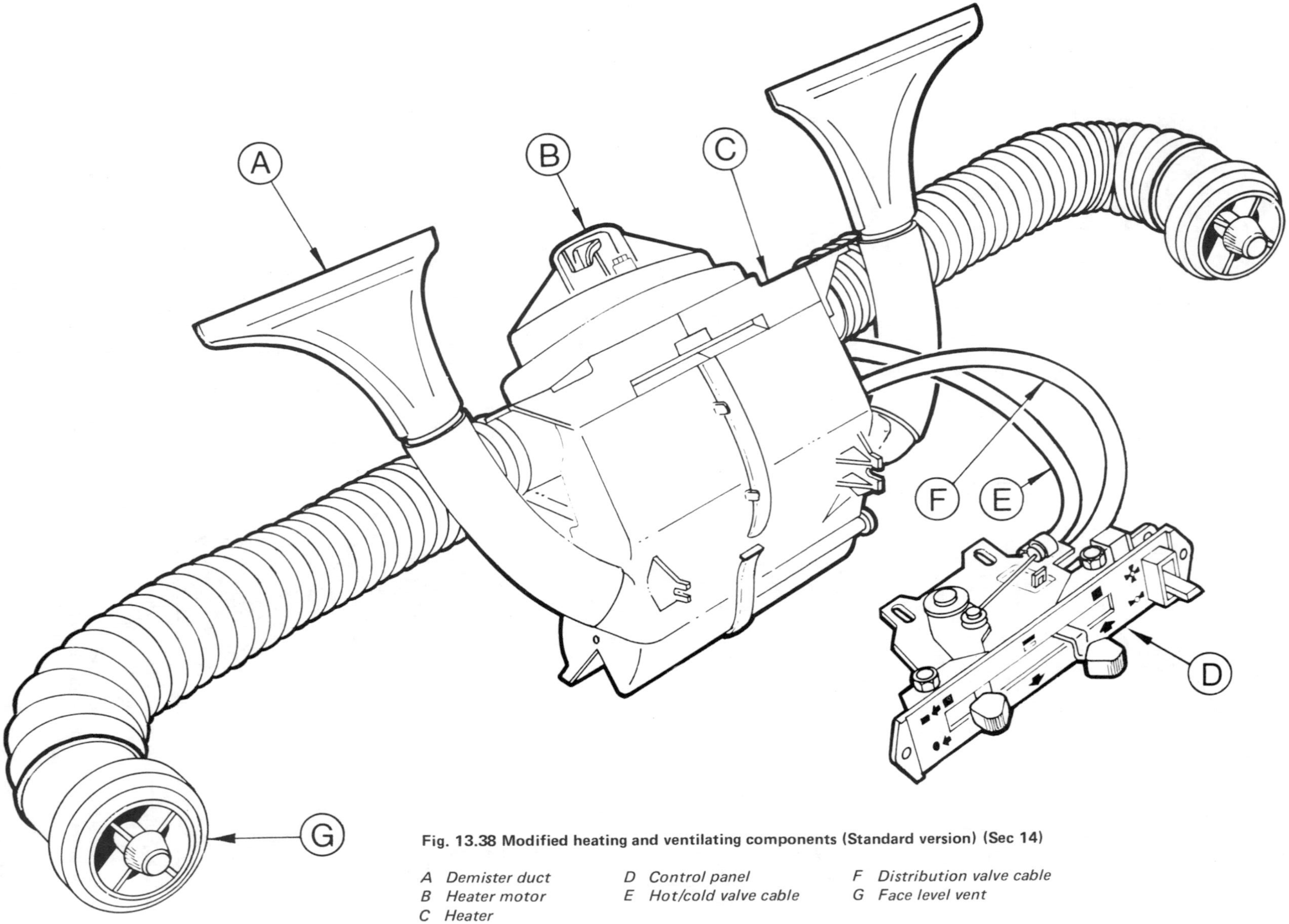

Fig. 13.38 Modified heating and ventilating components (Standard version) (Sec 14)

A Demister duct
B Heater motor
C Heater
D Control panel
E Hot/cold valve cable
F Distribution valve cable
G Face level vent

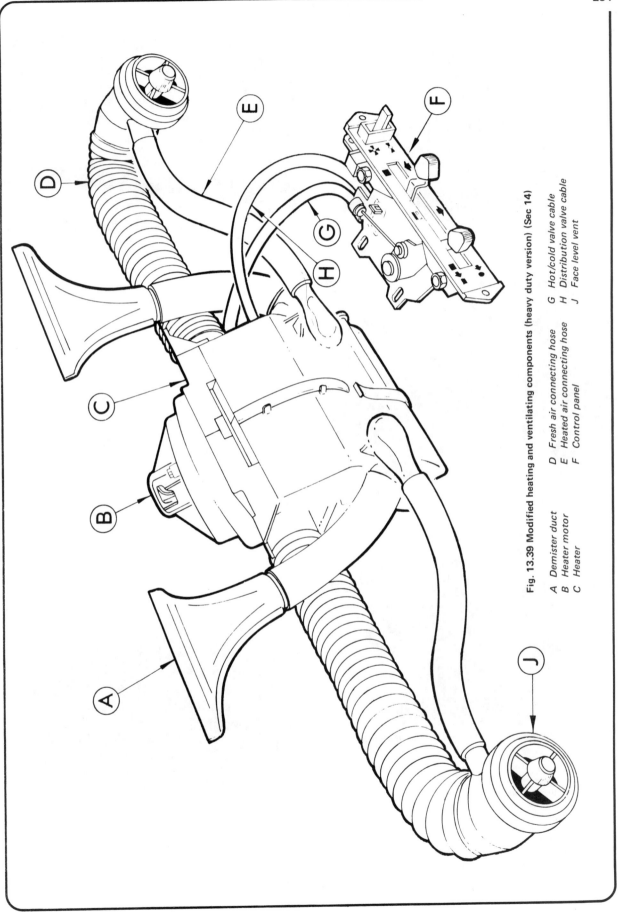

Fig. 13.39 Modified heating and ventilating components (heavy duty version) (Sec 14)

A Demister duct
B Heater motor
C Heater
D Fresh air connecting hose
E Heated air connecting hose
F Control panel
G Hot/cold valve cable
H Distribution valve cable
J Face level vent

Fig. 13.40 Modified heater unit assembly (Sec 14)

Fig. 13.41 Cable clamp locations (arrowed) on modified heater
(Sec 14)

Fig. 13.42 Location of heater-to-cowl retaining bolts
(modified heater) (Sec 14)

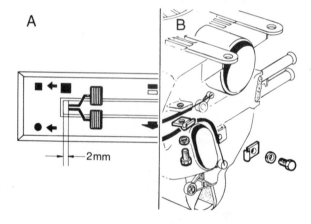

Fig. 13.43 Fitting the heater control cables (modified heater)
(Sec 14)

A   Position of control panel levers
B   Temperature and distribution valves in their end position

Fig. 13.44 Separating the heater housing halves (modified
heater) (Sec 14)

Fig. 13.45 Removing the heater resistance plug (modified
heater) (Sec 14)

8   The two halves of the heater housing can now be separated by depressing the lugs and prising the assembly apart.
9   Carefully remove the heater motor blower and withdraw the resistance plug from the casing.
10 Slide the centre housing partition panel away and then carefully withdraw the heater radiator matrix.
11 Reassembly is a reversal of the dismantling procedure but make sure that the blower motor is correctly fitted to the locating lug and that the regulating flaps are free to move. After the first dismantling, it is advisable to secure the two halves together with additional spring clamps.

Heater controls — removal and refitting
12 The modified control panel is similar to the original design

Fig. 13.46 Removing the partition panel (modified heater) (Sec 14)

Fig. 13.47 Refitting the blower motor (modified heater) (Sec 14)

Fig. 13.48 Correct location of heater motor supply leads (modified heater) (Sec 14)

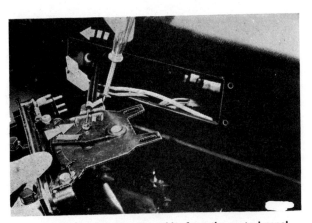

Fig. 13.49 Disconnecting the cables from the control panel (modified heater) (Sec 14)

Fig. 13.50 Refitting the cable clip to the control panel, showing lever adjustment clearance (modified heater) (Sec 14)

except that the control cables are fitted to the right-hand side.

13 Follow the instructions given in Chapter 12, Section 35 but, where fitted, the centre console should first be removed; on GL and Ghia models it will also be necessary to remove the instrument cluster bezel by extracting the six screws located behind the instrument panel.

14 Refitting is a reversal of the removal procedure but refer to paragraph 5 of this Section before connecting the control cables.

Face level vent — removal and refitting

15 When removing the face level vent from a heavy duty heater installation, it will be necessary to disconnect both air supply hoses (see Fig. 13.39).

Window regulator knob — renewal

16 As from September 1977 a new design window regulator knob is fitted to comply with EEC legislation. If the knob breaks as a result of accidental impact, it can be renewed by following the procedure given in paragraphs 17 to 20.

17 Remove the regulator handle as described in Chapter 12.

18 Using a screwdriver, rotate the remaining plastic retainer 1/8th turn anti-clockwise and remove it from under the handle.

19 Press out the plastic retainer and cap from the knob using a suitable drift with the knob located over a tube of internal diameter 1.125 in (28 mm). Do not prise the cap from the front of the knob.

20 Assemble the knob in reverse order, but note that the diameter of the retainer ('X' in Fig. 13.51) was increased in late 1978. It is in order to fit the larger diameter retainer to cars manufactured before 1978 but not vice versa.

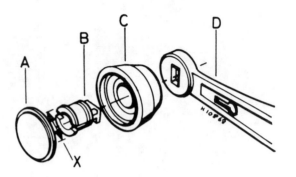

Fig. 13.51 Exploded view of modified window regulator handle (Sec 14)

A Cap
B Retainer

C Knob
D Arm

General repair procedures

Whenever servicing, repair or overhaul work is carried out on the car or its components, it is necessary to observe the following procedures and instructions. This will assist in carrying out the operation efficiently and to a professional standard of workmanship.

Joint mating faces and gaskets

Where a gasket is used between the mating faces of two components, ensure that it is renewed on reassembly, and fit it dry unless otherwise stated in the repair procedure. Make sure that the mating faces are clean and dry with all traces of old gasket removed. When cleaning a joint face, use a tool which is not likely to score or damage the face, and remove any burrs or nicks with an oilstone or fine file.

Make sure that tapped holes are cleaned with a pipe cleaner, and keep them free of jointing compound if this is being used unless specifically instructed otherwise.

Ensure that all orifices, channels or pipes are clear and blow through them, preferably using compressed air.

Oil seals

Whenever an oil seal is removed from its working location, either individually or as part of an assembly, it should be renewed.

The very fine sealing lip of the seal is easily damaged and will not seal if the surface it contacts is not completely clean and free from scratches, nicks or grooves. If the original sealing surface of the component cannot be restored, the component should be renewed.

Protect the lips of the seal from any surface which may damage them in the course of fitting. Use tape or a conical sleeve where possible. Lubricate the seal lips with oil before fitting and, on dual lipped seals, fill the space between the lips with grease.

Unless otherwise stated, oil seals must be fitted with their sealing lips toward the lubricant to be sealed.

Use a tubular drift or block of wood of the appropriate size to install the seal and, if the seal housing is shouldered, drive the seal down to the shoulder. If the seal housing is unshouldered, the seal should be fitted with its face flush with the housing top face.

Screw threads and fastenings

Always ensure that a blind tapped hole is completely free from oil, grease, water or other fluid before installing the bolt or stud. Failure to do this could cause the housing to crack due to the hydraulic action of the bolt or stud as it is screwed in.

When tightening a castellated nut to accept a split pin, tighten the nut to the specified torque, where applicable, and then tighten further to the next split pin hole. Never slacken the nut to align a split pin hole unless stated in the repair procedure.

When checking or retightening a nut or bolt to a specified torque setting, slacken the nut or bolt by a quarter of a turn, and then retighten to the specified setting.

Locknuts, locktabs and washers

Any fastening which will rotate against a component or housing in the course of tightening should always have a washer between it and the relevant component or housing.

Spring or split washers should always be renewed when they are used to lock a critical component such as a big-end bearing retaining nut or bolt.

Locktabs which are folded over to retain a nut or bolt should always be renewed.

Self-locking nuts can be reused in non-critical areas, providing resistance can be felt when the locking portion passes over the bolt or stud thread.

Split pins must always be replaced with new ones of the correct size for the hole.

Special tools

Some repair procedures in this manual entail the use of special tools such as a press, two or three-legged pullers, spring compressors etc. Wherever possible, suitable readily available alternatives to the manufacturer's special tools are described, and are shown in use. In some instances, where no alternative is possible, it has been necessary to resort to the use of a manufacturer's tool and this has been done for reasons of safety as well as the efficient completion of the repair operation. Unless you are highly skilled and have a thorough understanding of the procedure described, never attempt to bypass the use of any special tool when the procedure described specifies its use. Not only is there a very great risk of personal injury, but expensive damage could be caused to the components involved.

Conversion factors

Length (distance)

Inches (in)	X 25.4	= Millimetres (mm)	X 0.0394	= Inches (in)
Feet (ft)	X 0.305	= Metres (m)	X 3.281	= Feet (ft)
Miles	X 1.609	= Kilometres (km)	X 0.621	= Miles

Volume (capacity)

Cubic inches (cu in; in^3)	X 16.387	= Cubic centimetres (cc; cm^3)	X 0.061	= Cubic inches (cu in; in^3)
Imperial pints (Imp pt)	X 0.568	= Litres (l)	X 1.76	= Imperial pints (Imp pt)
Imperial quarts (Imp qt)	X 1.137	= Litres (l)	X 0.88	= Imperial quarts (Imp qt)
Imperial quarts (Imp qt)	X 1.201	= US quarts (US qt)	X 0.833	= Imperial quarts (Imp qt)
US quarts (US qt)	X 0.946	= Litres (l)	X 1.057	= US quarts (US qt)
Imperial gallons (Imp gal)	X 4.546	= Litres (l)	X 0.22	= Imperial gallons (Imp gal)
Imperial gallons (Imp gal)	X 1.201	= US gallons (US gal)	X 0.833	= Imperial gallons (Imp gal)
US gallons (US gal)	X 3.785	= Litres (l)	X 0.264	= US gallons (US gal)

Mass (weight)

Ounces (oz)	X 28.35	= Grams (g)	X 0.035	= Ounces (oz)
Pounds (lb)	X 0.454	= Kilograms (kg)	X 2.205	= Pounds (lb)

Force

Ounces-force (ozf; oz)	X 0.278	= Newtons (N)	X 3.6	= Ounces-force (ozf; oz)
Pounds-force (lbf; lb)	X 4.448	= Newtons (N)	X 0.225	= Pounds-force (lbf; lb)
Newtons (N)	X 0.1	= Kilograms-force (kgf; kg)	X 9.81	= Newtons (N)

Pressure

Pounds-force per square inch (psi; lbf/in^2; lb/in^2)	X 0.070	= Kilograms-force per square centimetre (kgf/cm^2; kg/cm^2)	X 14.223	= Pounds-force per square inch (psi; lbf/in^2; lb/in^2)
Pounds-force per square inch (psi; lbf/in^2; lb/in^2)	X 0.068	= Atmospheres (atm)	X 14.696	= Pounds-force per square inch (psi; lbf/in^2; lb/in^2)
Pounds-force per square inch (psi; lbf/in^2; lb/in^2)	X 0.069	= Bars	X 14.5	= Pounds-force per square inch (psi; lbf/in^2; lb/in^2)
Pounds-force per square inch (psi; lbf/in^2; lb/in^2)	X 6.895	= Kilopascals (kPa)	X 0.145	= Pounds-force per square inch (psi; lbf/in^2; lb/in^2)
Kilopascals (kPa)	X 0.01	= Kilograms-force per square centimetre (kgf/cm^2; kg/cm^2)	X 98.1	= Kilopascals (kPa)

Torque (moment of force)

Pounds-force inches (lbf in; lb in)	X 1.152	= Kilograms-force centimetre (kgf cm; kg cm)	X 0.868	= Pounds-force inches (lbf in; lb in)
Pounds-force inches (lbf in; lb in)	X 0.113	= Newton metres (Nm)	X 8.85	= Pounds-force inches (lbf in; lb in)
Pounds-force inches (lbf in; lb in)	X 0.083	= Pounds-force feet (lbf ft; lb ft)	X 12	= Pounds-force inches (lbf in; lb in)
Pounds-force feet (lbf ft; lb ft)	X 0.138	= Kilograms-force metres (kgf m; kg m)	X 7.233	= Pounds-force feet (lbf ft; lb ft)
Pounds-force feet (lbf ft; lb ft)	X 1.356	= Newton metres (Nm)	X 0.738	= Pounds-force feet (lbf ft; lb ft)
Newton metres (Nm)	X 0.102	= Kilograms-force metres (kgf m; kg m)	X 9.804	= Newton metres (Nm)

Power

Horsepower (hp)	X 745.7	= Watts (W)	X 0.0013	= Horsepower (hp)

Velocity (speed)

Miles per hour (miles/hr; mph)	X 1.609	= Kilometres per hour (km/hr; kph)	X 0.621	= Miles per hour (miles/hr; mph)

*Fuel consumption**

Miles per gallon, Imperial (mpg)	X 0.354	= Kilometres per litre (km/l)	X 2.825	= Miles per gallon, Imperial (mpg)
Miles per gallon, US (mpg)	X 0.425	= Kilometres per litre (km/l)	X 2.352	= Miles per gallon, US (mpg)

Temperature

Degrees Fahrenheit = (°C x 1.8) + 32

Degrees Celsius (Degrees Centigrade; °C) = (°F - 32) x 0.56

**It is common practice to convert from miles per gallon (mpg) to litres/100 kilometres (l/100km), where mpg (Imperial) x l/100 km = 282 and mpg (US) x l/100 km = 235*

Safety first!

Professional motor mechanics are trained in safe working procedures. However enthusiastic you may be about getting on with the job in hand, do take the time to ensure that your safety is not put at risk. A moment's lack of attention can result in an accident, as can failure to observe certain elementary precautions.

There will always be new ways of having accidents, and the following points do not pretend to be a comprehensive list of all dangers; they are intended rather to make you aware of the risks and to encourage a safety-conscious approach to all work you carry out on your vehicle.

Essential DOs and DONTs

DON'T rely on a single jack when working underneath the vehicle. Always use reliable additional means of support, such as axle stands, securely placed under a part of the vehicle that you know will not give way.

DON'T attempt to loosen or tighten high-torque nuts (e.g. wheel hub nuts) while the vehicle is on a jack; it may be pulled off.

DON'T start the engine without first ascertaining that the transmission is in neutral (or 'Park' where applicable) and the parking brake applied.

DON'T suddenly remove the filler cap from a hot cooling system — cover it with a cloth and release the pressure gradually first, or you may get scalded by escaping coolant.

DON'T attempt to drain oil until you are sure it has cooled sufficiently to avoid scalding you.

DON'T grasp any part of the engine, exhaust or catalytic converter without first ascertaining that it is sufficiently cool to avoid burning you.

DON'T syphon toxic liquids such as fuel, brake fluid or anti-freeze by mouth, or allow them to remain on your skin.

DON'T inhale brake lining dust — it is injurious to health.

DON'T allow any spilt oil or grease to remain on the floor — wipe it up straight away, before someone slips on it.

DON'T use ill-fitting spanners or other tools which may slip and cause injury.

DON'T attempt to lift a heavy component which may be beyond your capability — get assistance.

DON'T rush to finish a job, or take unverified short cuts.

DON'T allow children or animals in or around an unattended vehicle.

DO wear protection when using power tools such as drill, sander, bench grinder etc, and when working under the vehicle.

DO use a barrier cream on your hands prior to undertaking dirty jobs — it will protect your skin from infection as well as making the dirt easier to remove afterwards; but make sure your hands aren't left slippery.

DO keep loose clothing (cuffs, tie etc) and long hair well out of the way of moving mechanical parts.

DO remove rings, wristwatch etc, before working on the vehicle — especially the electrical system.

DO ensure that any lifting tackle used has a safe working load rating adequate for the job.

DO keep your work area tidy — it is only too easy to fall over articles left lying around.

DO get someone to check periodically that all is well, when working alone on the vehicle.

DO carry out work in a logical sequence and check that everything is correctly assembled and tightened afterwards.

DO remember that your vehicle's safety affects that of yourself and others. If in doubt on any point, get specialist advice.

IF, in spite of following these precautions, you are unfortunate enough to injure yourself, seek medical attention as soon as possible.

Fire

Remember at all times that petrol (gasoline) is highly flammable. Never smoke, or have any kind of naked flame around, when working on the vehicle. But the risk does not end there — a spark caused by an electrical short-circuit, by two metal surfaces contacting each other, or even by static electricity built up in your body under certain conditions, can ignite petrol vapour, which in a confined space is highly explosive.

Always disconnect the battery earth (ground) terminal before working on any part of the fuel system, and never risk spilling fuel on to a hot engine or exhaust.

It is recommended that a fire extinguisher of a type suitable for fuel and electrical fires is kept handy in the garage or workplace at all times. Never try to extinguish a fuel or electrical fire with water.

Fumes

Certain fumes are highly toxic and can quickly cause unconsciousness and even death if inhaled to any extent. Petrol (gasoline) vapour comes into this category, as do the vapours from certain solvents such as trichloroethylene. Any draining or pouring of such volatile fluids should be done in a well ventilated area.

When using cleaning fluids and solvents, read the instructions carefully. Never use materials from unmarked containers — they may give off poisonous vapours.

Never run the engine of a motor vehicle in an enclosed space such as a garage. Exhaust fumes contain carbon monoxide which is extremely poisonous; if you need to run the engine, always do so in the open air or at least have the rear of the vehicle outside the workplace.

If you are fortunate enough to have the use of an inspection pit, never drain or pour petrol, and never run the engine, while the vehicle is standing over it; the fumes, being heavier than air, will concentrate in the pit with possible lethal results.

The battery

Never cause a spark, or allow a naked light, near the vehicle's battery. It will normally be giving off a certain amount of hydrogen gas, which is highly explosive.

Always disconnect the battery earth (ground) terminal before working on the fuel or electrical systems.

If possible, loosen the filler plugs or cover when charging the battery from an external source. Do not charge at an excessive rate or the battery may burst.

Take care when topping up and when carrying the battery. The acid electrolyte, even when diluted, is very corrosive and should not be allowed to contact the eyes or skin.

If you ever need to prepare electrolyte yourself, always add the acid slowly to the water, and never the other way round. Protect against splashes by wearing rubber gloves and goggles.

When jump starting a car using a booster battery, for negative earth (ground) vehicles, connect the jump leads in the following sequence: First connect one jump lead between the positive (+) terminals of the two batteries. Then connect the other jump lead first to the negative (−) terminal of the booster battery, and then to a good earthing (ground) point on the vehicle to be started, at least 18 in (45 cm) from the battery if possible. Ensure that hands and jump leads are clear of any moving parts, and that the two vehicles do not touch. Disconnect the leads in the reverse order.

Mains electricity

When using an electric power tool, inspection light etc which works from the mains, always ensure that the appliance is correctly connected to its plug and that, where necessary, it is properly earthed (grounded). Do not use such appliances in damp conditions and, again, beware of creating a spark or applying excessive heat in the vicinity of fuel or fuel vapour.

Ignition HT voltage

A severe electric shock can result from touching certain parts of the ignition system, such as the HT leads, when the engine is running or being cranked, particularly if components are damp or the insulation is defective. Where an electronic ignition system is fitted, the HT voltage is much higher and could prove fatal.

Index